The GIANT Encyclopedia of
Preschool Activities
for Four-Year-Olds

Dedication

This book is dedicated to all the wonderful, curious, and enthusiastic four-year-olds and wonderful, curious, and enthusiastic adults who teach them

The
GIANT
Encyclopedia of
Preschool Activities
for
Four-Year-Olds

*Edited by Kathy Charner
and Maureen Murphy*

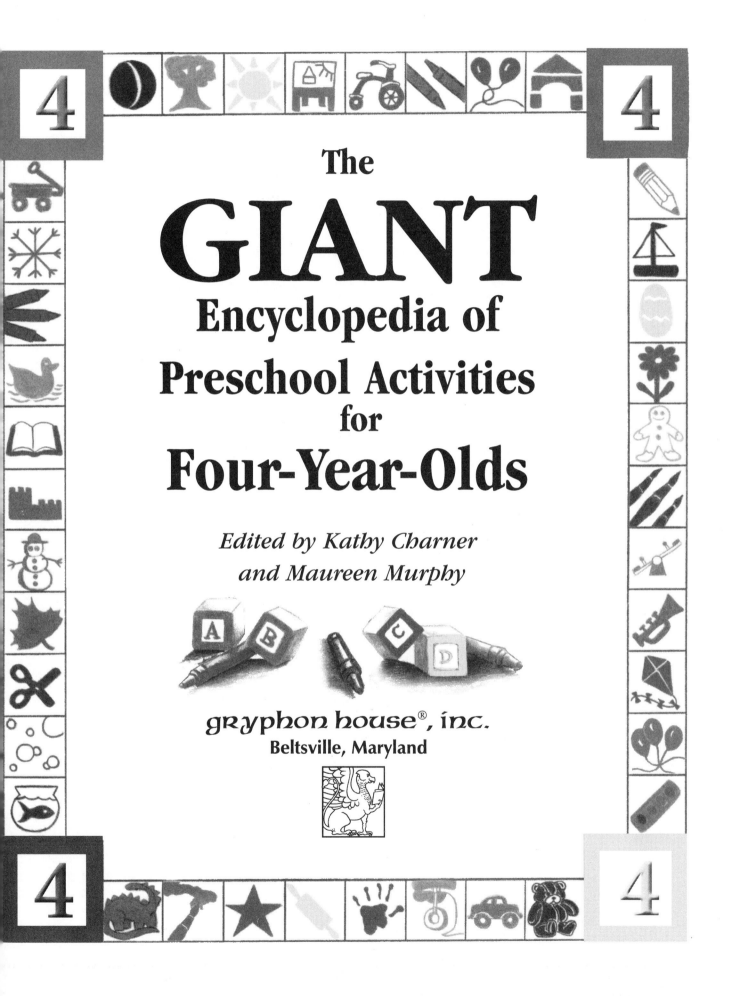

gryphon house®, inc.
Beltsville, Maryland

Disclaimer

The publisher and the authors cannot be held responsible for injury, mishap, or damages incurred during the use of or because of the activities in this book. The authors recommend appropriate and reasonable supervision at all times based on the age and capability of each child.

Bulk purchase

Gryphon House books are available at special discount when purchased in bulk for special premiums and sales promotions as well as for fund-raising use. Special editions or book excerpts also can be created to specification. For details, contact the Director of Marketing at the address below.

Copyright

Illustrations: K. Whelan Dery
Cover art: Beverly Hightshoe

Library of Congress Cataloging-in-Publication Data

The giant encyclopedia of preschool activities for four-year-olds / Kathy Charner, editor ; illustrations, K. Whelan Dery.
     p. cm.
Rev. ed. of: It's great to be four. c2001.
  ISBN 0-87659-238-8
  1. Education, Preschool--Activity programs. 2. Creative activities and seat work. I. Charner, Kathy. II. It's great to be four.
  LB1140.35.C7418 2004
  372.5--dc22
                                                                      2003019452

Table of Contents

Blocks

Books

Fingerplays, Songs & Poems

Games

General Tips

Gross Motor

Language

Literacy

Math

The GIANT Encyclopedia of Preschool Activities for Four-Year-Olds

Morning Greeting

Music & Movement

Outdoor Play

Rest or Nap Time

Sand & Water

Science & Nature

Snack & Cooking

Social Development

Transitions

Monthly Planning

Introduction

Four-year-old children are energetic, inquisitive, enthusiastic and filled with wonder about the world around them. They arrive in our classrooms eager to learn about almost any topic imaginable. For them, every activity is an opportunity for learning.

Their insatiable curiosity rewards teachers' efforts at planning and presenting activities. Fours tend to idolize their teachers, and that adulation offers more rewards than a paycheck.

Working with four-year-olds also has its challenges. Because they are interested in everything, it's difficult for fours to focus their attention on one thing for a long period of time. Teachers accommodate this by presenting information in several different ways over a period of time. For example, to learn about dental care, children might use toothbrushes to brush surface stains off of ceramic tile. They might also sing a brush-my-teeth song, visit a dentist's office, and compare the way the surface of their teeth feels after eating apples and after eating marsh-mallows.

These unique youngsters have enormous energy; they don't enjoy sitting for long periods of time. Wise teachers plan and present activities that can be done while children move around, stand at tables, recline on the floor, or climb on play-ground equipment.

Because these children are rapidly learning language, teachers include many communication activities that encourage youngsters' love of experimenting with language and trying out new words and phrases. They expose the children to letters, numbers, and written language, but they put the emphasis on experienc-ing these things, not on memorizing or mastery.

When involving four-year-olds in activities, keep in mind the following sugges-tions:

■ Children explore with all of their senses. Be certain that all items you present are non-toxic, that they present no choking hazard, and that they are too large to put in ears and noses.

■ Children are daring. Their lack of experience can result in poor judgment. Plan ahead for safety. If children will be jumping or climbing, be certain the surface below is cushioned.

■ Because their motor skills aren't yet refined, fours are accident-prone. Cover surfaces to prevent damage from spills, nicks, and stray crayon marks.

■ Neckties, scarves, belts, and pocketbook straps become hazardous when children wrap them around their necks. Cut these and put Velcro fasteners on each cut end. Show children how to un-fasten these closures, and supervise while they practice this skill, before you put the items where children can play with them.

■ Some four-year-old children are shy. Invite, but never insist that a child participate in an activity. Many young children learn as much from observing their friends' experiences as they do from participating. When the shy child feels safe and secure in a non-threatening environment, he or she will begin to join in. Be patient.

■ Fours like to feel big and important. Let them help you prepare for activities.

■ Support four-year-olds' love of language. Don't just allow talking; value it. Cheer with them when they invent new words and when they discover rhyming sounds. Sing with them to experience the rhythm of language. Read with them to instill the love of the written word.

■ Encourage their inventive and creative abilities. Let them experiment with other ways of doing the activities you present. Be willing to learn from them.

■ Four-year-olds want to be just like their elders. Be sure you are setting an example for what you want them to be.

This book is a result of a contest we conducted asking teachers to send us their great activities for four-year-olds. We selected the very best entries, and the result is this book of more than 600 activities. The contributing teachers have successfully used these activities with the children they teach. We trust that you and your children will benefit from the years of experience reflected in these pages.

How to Use This Book

Each activity in this book contains some or all of the following sections:

Materials needed

Each activity includes a list of readily available materials. Investigate all possible sources of free materials in your community, including donations from paper stores, framing shops, woodworking shops, lumberyards, and, of course, parents.

What to do

The directions are presented in a step-by-step format. Patterns and illustrations are included where necessary.

More to do

Additional ideas for extending the activity are included in this section. Many activities include suggestions for integrating the activity into other areas of the curriculum such as math, dramatic play, circle time, blocks, language, snack, and cooking.

Related books

Under this heading are titles and authors of popular children's books that can be used to support the activity.

Related songs and poems

Familiar songs related to the original activity and original songs and poems written by teachers are in this section.

Indexes

This book has three indexes. The first is an index of the materials used in the activities, the second is an index of the books referenced in the activities, and the third is an alphabetical index of the activities by title.

The GIANT Encyclopedia of Preschool Activities for Four-Year-Olds

Handprints on Glass

Materials

Washable tempera paint
Markers

What to do

1. Paint one hand of each child and encourage him to make a handprint on the classroom window.
2. Write the child's name under his handprint for a "clearly" wonderful window display!

❧ Charlene Woodham Peace, Semmes, AL

Art Appreciation

Materials

Art books
Paint, paintbrushes, paper

What to do

1. Look for books that contain art by the "masters" at garage sales, bargain bookstores, and thrift stores.
2. Put these books in your classroom library, Art Area, and Dramatic Play Area.
3. When the children look at these books, they will develop an awareness of color and style and an appreciation of fine art.
4. From time to time, point out various artwork in the books and provide materials so the children can produce paintings "in that style." Put out bright colors for creating "modern" art or provide thin brushes for creating small details.

Related books

The Art Lesson by Tomie dePaola
No Good in Art by Miriam Cohen

❧ Barbara F. Backer, Charleston, SC

Chalk Recipe

Materials

1 tablespoon (15 g) powdered tempera paint, various colors
2 tablespoons (30 ml) water
Paper cups
Tongue depressor or Popsicle stick
2 tablespoons (30 g) plaster of Paris

What to do

1. Help the children mix tempera paint and water in a paper cup. Stir the mixture with a tongue depressor until smooth.
2. Add plaster of Paris and continue stirring until smooth. (If necessary, add additional plaster of Paris until the solution is creamy.)
3. Leave the tongue depressor in the cup to use as a handle.
4. Allow it to dry overnight, or until it is very hard (about six hours).
5. Peel off the paper cup. Use the chalk!

More to do

Encourage the children to practice writing their names, letters, and numbers with the homemade chalk.

❖ Kaethe Lewandowski, Centreville, VA

Michelangelo Drawing

Materials

Long sheet of paper
Scissors
Tape
Table
Crayons

What to do

1. This activity will improve children's language, social, cognitive, creative, and motor skills.

2. Help children cut out sheets of paper to fit the underside of a table in the classroom.

3. Tape the paper to the underside of a table. Place a container of crayons under the table.

4. Encourage the children to lie on their backs to draw their creations.

More to do

More Art: Discuss Michelangelo and what he created (and how). Show the children photographs of his work. Discuss the children's drawings in the same way you discussed Michelangelo's work. Continue to introduce simple works of art into your program on a regular basis.

Field Trips: Take a trip to an art gallery or museum.

Language: Ask open-ended questions about the children's art.

❖ Terri Herson, Gonic, NH

String Swing

Materials

Scissors
Twine or yarn
Washable markers
Large white paper

What to do

1. Help the children cut yarn or twine into 5" to 6" (12 to 15 cm) pieces.

2. Help the children tie a piece of twine or yarn to the non-ink end of each marker.

3. Encourage the children to hold the piece of twine and dangle the marker so that the point touches a piece of paper.

4. The children can gently swing the markers in circles, back and forth, or other movements to form a variety of interesting patterns and color schemes.

More to do

Use kaleidoscopes to extend this discussion of color and patterns.

Related book

My Crayons Talk by Patricia Hubbard

❧ Charlene Woodham Peace, Semmes, AL

Color Days

Materials

Art materials that focus on one color

What to do

1. Focus on one color.
2. On a particular day, week, or period of time, use materials that are one color. For example, put one color of paint at the easel, decorate the room with one color of crepe paper and balloons, and put out one color of clay or playdough.
3. Send a note home to parents ahead of time to explain what you are doing and to ask that each child wear a certain color on a specified day.
4. Serve a snack that is the same color as the rest of the materials.
5. At the end of the week (or time period), have a rainbow-colored parade with color banners (see page 87).

❧ Lisa M. Chichester, Parkersburg, WV

Magic Color Tricks

Materials

Red, yellow, and blue fingerpaint
Teaspoon
Fingerpaint paper
Smocks and covered table

What to do

1. Ask the children to select one color of fingerpaint—red, yellow, or blue.
2. Place a teaspoon of the chosen color in the center of a piece of paper.
3. Encourage the child to spread the color over the entire paper.
4. Ask him to choose a second color.
5. As he spreads the second color over the first color, ask him what he sees happening to the paper.
6. If desired, children may try a third color. Again, ask them to describe the results.

More to do

Extend the activity by making color "equations" using both an appropriate color marker and the word.

RED + YELLOW = ORANGE

BLUE + YELLOW = GREEN

The children can be color "magicians" by taking colored cellophane paddles (made or purchased) and layering them on top of each other.

Related books

The Color Kittens by Margaret Wise Brown

Little Blue and Little Yellow by Leo Lionni

Chant

Chant the following.

RED, YELLOW, AND BLUE

RED, YELLOW, AND BLUE

The colors do tricks

When we know how to mix

Our RED, YELLOW, AND BLUE

Iris Rothstein, New Hyde Park, NY

Favorite Shades

Materials

Blue, green, or purple tempera paint

3 clear containers

White and black tempera paint

Paint stirrers

Paint color sample cards in various colors and shades

Assorted collage objects (see list) in the basic colors (red, orange, yellow, green, blue, purple) as well as pink and white

10 shoeboxes

White glue or stapler

Construction paper in the 10 colors

What to do

1. Have a discussion with the children about their favorite colors.
2. Choose one color and look for it around the room. Note how every item is the stated color, but not all are exactly the same. Discuss shades of color.
3. Pour one color of paint (green, blue, or purple) into three clear containers.
4. Mix white tempera paint into one container and black tempera paint into another one. Leave the third container the same.
5. Compare the three different shades of the same color.
6. Look at paint sample cards that show dark and light shades of different colors.
7. Sort collage objects (see list) by color. Place objects of each color into ten separate shoeboxes.
8. Ask each child to select his favorite color.
9. Encourage the children to create a collage. Each child will glue or staple items from the box containing items of his chosen color onto a piece of construction paper of the same color.

Assorted collage items
beads
bottle caps
colored foil
colored noodles
cotton balls
crepe paper
fabric scraps
foam pieces

> pipe cleaners
> ribbon
> tissue paper

More to do

More Art: Put one color of paint at each easel, along with white and black paint for mixing. Encourage the children to mix colors on a piece of paper by finger-painting or watch them blend where two colors meet on wet paper. Use an eyedropper to drop colored water onto a coffee filter to mix colors.

Related books

Brown Bear, Brown Bear, What Do You See? by Bill Martin, Jr.
The Colors by Monique Felix
Colors Around Us by Shelly Rotner and Anne Woodhull
Little Blue and Little Yellow by Leo Lionni
My Many Colored Days by Dr. Seuss
White Rabbit's Color Book by Alan Baker

❖ Sandra Gratias, Perkasie, PA

Clothespin Art

Materials

Scissors
String or yarn
Spring-type clothespins
Paint
Meat tray
Paper

What to do

1. Cut short lengths of string or yarn.
2. Give each child a clothespin and a piece of string. He will use the clothespins to hold the string.
3. Pour paint into one or more clean meat trays.
4. Encourage the children to pull the strings through the paint, and then across a piece of paper.

More to do

Encourage children to collect items with which to paint (for example, empty thread spools, plastic bottle caps, cookie cutters, and sponges cut into shapes). On a nice day, give the children a bag and take them on a hike to collect items with which to paint (for example, stones, twigs, and leaves). Press these items into the paint, then onto paper.

❦ Constance Heagerty, Westbourough, MA

Silly String Art

Materials

Newspaper or sheets
Paint smocks or shirts
Construction paper
Tracing patterns
Scissors
Tempera paint in a variety of colors
Paint pans
12" (30 cm) pieces of string or yarn

What to do

1. Explain to the children that this activity focuses on the holiday or unit that you have been discussing in class, as well as their creativity. (Use tracing patterns that relate to the theme or celebration.)
2. Cover the workstation with newspaper or sheets. Help the children put on paint smocks or shirts.
3. Distribute construction paper and a pattern for each child to trace. If you have been discussing circus or zoo animals, for example, use elephant patterns.
4. Help each child trace the pattern onto the construction paper and cut it out. (If necessary, precut the patterns so that all of the children will be successful with this activity.)
5. Pour tempera paint into paint pans.
6. Demonstrate how to hold one end of a piece of string while dipping the rest of it into the paint.
7. Next, take the string and splat, whip, or twirl it onto the construction paper cutout. Tell the children they can make a design that relates to the theme or

just have fun. This is a chance for them to demonstrate their creativity as well as work on their fine motor skills.

8. When the children are finished painting, set the projects aside to dry. Then, encourage the children to discuss the different designs and why they chose them.

More to do

A simpler version of this activity is to create Silly String Art on a plain sheet of paper.

Language: Ask the children to examine the other children's work and then create a story about what they "see" in the design of the paint. Some children will get very creative with this part of the project.

Math: Encourage the children to count how many drops, twirls, or lines of paint are on each project. Then, ask them to make number comparisons between the different pieces of artwork to see who used the most lines, and so on.

Related books

Cat's Cradle: A Book of String Figures by Anne A. Johnson
String Games by Michelle Foerder

❖ Mike Krestar, White Oak, PA

Feather Duster Painting

Materials

Paint
Liquid soap
Pie tins
Feather duster
Paper

What to do

1. Pour paint and liquid soap into a pie tin.
2. Encourage the children to dip a feather duster into the paint and use it to paint on a piece of paper. (Use one tin and one feather duster for each color of paint.)
3. Layering the colors produces a nice effect.

More to do

This painting technique is great for large objects, such as boxes, and backgrounds for murals.

❧ Sandra Nagel, White Lake, MI

Easy Easel Painting

Materials

Large, inexpensive plastic tablecloth
Easels
Masking tape
Newspaper
Empty, clean yogurt cups with lids
Scissors
Short-handled paintbrushes
Tempera paint
Liquid starch
Smocks or old, extra-large T-shirts
Cup hooks
Large, primary pencils
String cut into 2′ (60 cm) lengths, one for each easel
3″ (7 cm) large paper clips, 2 for each easel
Easel paper

What to do

1. Put a plastic tablecloth on the floor underneath the easels. Tape newspaper to the easels for easy cleanup.
2. In the lid of each yogurt cup, cut a hole large enough to fit a short-handled paintbrush. (If the brushes have long handles, cut them to about 8″ (20 cm) long. This is much easier for children to handle.)
3. Pour tempera paint into each yogurt cup until it is half full. Add a tablespoon of starch. (Starch makes the paint easier to wash out of clothing.)
4. Paint each brush handle the color of the paint in which you are going to put it.
5. Put the lids on the cups and put one brush through the lid hole of each color.
6. Help the children put on smocks or old T-shirts.
7. Screw a cup hook into the side of the easel leg.

8. Tie a pencil on one end of a string. Tie the other end to the cup hook.

9. Attach two large paper clips to the top of the easel, one on each side.

10. Encourage the children to use the clips to attach paper to the easel and the pencil to write their names.

11. The color-coded paintbrush tips make it easy to put the brush back into the correct cup.

❧ Barbara Saul, Eureka, CA

Paint Scraping

Materials

Newspaper
Tape
Tempera paints in various colors
Small paper cups
Paintbrushes
Scraping objects (see list)
Painting shirts
White drawing paper

What to do

1. Cover tables with newspaper and tape it down. Also, cover a portion of the floor with newspaper.

2. Fill small paper cups half full with tempera paint. Put a paintbrush in each cup.

3. Place the cups of paint in the center of each table. Put at least one cup of each color on every table. Scatter the scraping objects (see list) around the tables.

4. Help the children put on their paint shirts.

5. Ask them to paint over an entire sheet of paper in any design. (Remind them to put the brush back in its designated color.)

6. Before their paintings dry, demonstrate how to use the scraping objects to embellish their paintings with texture. Show them how to scrape the paint while it is still wet to create stripes, textures, and swirls.

7. Encourage the children to experiment using this technique. For example, driving small vehicles over wet paint makes tire prints, and pressing small animals

into it leaves tracks. They may want to bring objects from home or try objects using in the classroom.

Scraping objects
clear kitchen wrap (wadded up)
combs
hairbrushes
plastic knives and forks
Popsicle sticks
small toy cars
straws
string
toothbrushes
toy animals

Related books

A Button for Corduroy by Don Freeman
Corduroy by Don Freeman
When reading these stories with the children, emphasize Don Freeman's technique, which is similar to this activity.

❖ Barbara Saul, Eureka, CA

Painting with Vinegar

Materials

Newspaper
Smocks
Vinegar
Bowl
Tissue paper (cut up)
White paper
Paintbrush

What to do

1. Cover the table with newspaper and help children put on smocks.
2. Pour vinegar into a bowl. Encourage the children to explore the properties of vinegar by letting them smell it.
3. Demonstrate how to place a piece of tissue paper on a sheet of white paper and hold it in place. Use a paintbrush to spread vinegar over the tissue paper.
4. Tell the children, "Vinegar is an ingredient that you can use in the kitchen. We are creating art with it."
5. Help the children lift the tissue paper off the white paper.

❖ Cristy Bawol, Utica, MI

Self Portrait

Materials

Mirror
Washable paints
Brushes
Paper

What to do

1. Ask the child to stand or sit in front of a mirror and paint his reflection directly on the mirror. Stand next to him to hold the paint and help if needed. (Provide colors that are appropriate for skin, hair, and eye coloring.)
2. When the child has finished painting his face, place a piece of paper over the wet paint and gently press.
3. Remove the paper and let it dry.
4. Clean the mirror for the next child.

Related book

All About Me by Catherine Bruzzone and Lone Morton

❖ Phyllis Esch, Export, PA

Golden Fall Fingerpainting

Materials

Paint smocks
Newspaper
Fingerpaint paper
Red and yellow fingerpaint
Gold paint
Paper plates or Styrofoam trays
Sponges, cut in different leaf shapes

What to do

1. Help the children put on paint smocks.
2. Cover the work surface with newspaper and put fingerpaint paper on top of the newspaper.
3. Give the children a choice of colors: red, yellow, or orange. (Make orange paint by blending red and yellow.)
4. Encourage the children to cover the entire paper with color. Show them how to use their whole hands rather than their fingertips.
5. When they are finished, help them wash their hands.
6. Let the paintings dry overnight. If necessary, weight the dry paintings to flatten and uncurl the edges.
7. The following day, help the children put on their smocks again. Give each child his dry fingerpainting.
8. Pour gold paint onto paper plates or trays.
9. Show children how to dip a leaf-shaped sponge into the paint, wipe off the excess, and make prints on top of their fingerpaintings.
10. When the sponge prints are dry, display them to catch the sunlight.

More to do

More Art: Using double-sided tape, affix leaves to tables and make leaf rubbings with unwrapped crayons.
Math: Cut out leaves of varying types and sort into categories.
Science: Collect leaves and discuss shapes, colors, and sizes.

Related books

Red Leaf, Yellow Leaf by Lois Ehlert
Squirrels by Brian Wildsmith
Why Do Leaves Change Color? by Betsy Maestro

❦ Susan O. Hill, Lakeland, FL

Textured Finger Paint

Materials

Smocks
Tape
Bubble wrap
Fingerpaint
Construction paper

What to do

1. Help the children put on smocks.
2. Tape sheets of bubble wrap to a table.
3. Place a dab of fingerpaint on the bubble wrap.
4. Encourage them to rub the paint around the bubble wrap.
5. When they are finished, capture their picture by pressing a sheet of construction paper onto the bubble wrap. Lift carefully.

❦ Teresa J. Nos, Baltimore, MD

Punch Pictures

Materials

Pencils (semi-sharpened to a dull tip)
Paper
Tape
Large needlepoint screens (available in craft stores—use wide-point squares)

What to do

1. Help each child write his or her name on a sheet of paper.
2. Tape the edges of the paper to a needlepoint screen, folding the tape over the edges.
3. Encourage the child to punch designs through the screen and paper using a semi-sharpened pencil.
4. When the child is finished, remove the screen from the paper and fold the tape over the edges of the paper.
5. Reuse the needlepoint screen as often as desired.

NEEDLEPOINT SCREEN

MEG

(SCREEN GOES UNDER THE PAPER

MEG

PENCIL

❧ Dani Rosensteel, Payson, AZ

Punchilism

Materials

Hole punches in a variety of shapes
Paper in a variety of colors
Small bowls
Glue

What to do

1. Using a variety of hole punches and paper, ask the children to punch out holes.
2. Encourage the children to sort the shapes by color or shape and place them into small bowls.
3. The children can glue the holes to a piece of paper to create pictures.

More to do

Make cards for special occasions. For example, use heart punches for Valentine's Day, tree punches for Christmas, and so on. Fold a piece of paper in half and encourage children to decorate the front of it using the holes. As children dictate sentiments, write them on the inside of the card.

Related book

The Valentine Bears by Eve Bunting

Ann Gudowski, Johnstown, PA

Puzzling Art

Materials

Cardboard puzzle pieces
Paint
Paintbrushes
Newspaper
Glue
Paper

What to do

1. Collect cardboard puzzle pieces from puzzles that are missing pieces.
2. Put the pieces in the art center along with paint and brushes.
3. Encourage the children to paint the puzzle pieces.
4. Place puzzle pieces on a piece of newspaper to dry.
5. When the puzzle pieces are dry, encourage the children to create works of art by gluing the pieces together and onto a piece of paper.

More to do

Fine Motor: Ask the children to trace the puzzle pieces to help improve their fine motor skills.

Literacy: Choose pairs of puzzle pieces that fit together. Write an upper-case letter on one puzzle piece and its matching lower-case letter on the other piece to create a letter matching game.

Math: Use the painted puzzle pieces for a sorting activity. After the children sort the pieces by color, use the pieces for a counting activity. Count each group of color and record the numbers on a simple graph.

Related books

Jigsaw Puzzles: Animal by Jane Burton
Seasons Puzzles by Carolyn Mitchell

❖ Ann Gudowski, Johnstown, PA

Watercolor Art Book

Materials

Hole punch
9" x 12" (22 cm x 30 cm) white paper
9" x 12" (22 cm x 30 cm) colored paper
Smocks
Watercolor paints and brushes
Cups of water
Pen
2 pieces of yarn, each about 6" (15 cm) long

What to do

1. Help the children punch two holes into one side of each piece of white paper, making sure to line up the holes. Explain that these will be the inside pages of a book.
2. Punch two holes on one side of each piece of colored paper, making sure the holes line up with the white paper. Explain that these will be the cover of the book.
3. Help the children put on smocks.
4. Give each child a piece of white paper, watercolor paints, a brush, and a cup half filled with water. Ask each child to create one page for a book. Encourage the children to paint whatever is in their imagination.
5. When the children finish their pictures, ask each child to dictate a couple of sentences about his picture. Use a pen to write his description at the bottom of the paper.
6. Allow the paintings to dry.
7. Ask each child to put his page in the book. Help him put one piece of yarn through the top hole and one through the bottom hole.
8. Put a piece of colored paper on the front and one on the back to make a cover.

9. When finished, show the pictures to the children and read the words about each one. Keep the book on the book-shelf.

More to do

Make a book that focuses on a theme, such as "In the Summer Time," "Our Trip to..." or "We are Happy (Sad, Excited)."

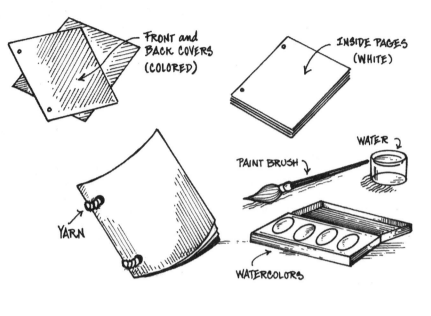

FRONT and BACK COVERS (COLORED)

INSIDE PAGES (WHITE)

WATER

PAINT BRUSH

YARN

WATERCOLORS

❦ Tracey Neumarke, Chicago, IL

Clean Mud

Materials

3 rolls of toilet tissue
Large container
Water (warm works best)
⅓ cup (80 m) Borax
1 bar of Ivory soap (or 1 cup of Ivory flakes if you can find them)
Grater
Airtight container

What to do

1. With the children, unroll three rolls of toilet tissue.
2. Tear the toilet tissue into small pieces and put it into a large container.
3. Grate Ivory soap into the container.
4. Add water and Borax (to soften the mixture) to the tissue.
5. Mix together until it has the consistency of cooked oatmeal.
6. Encourage the children to experiment with the texture and properties of this mixture.

7. This enjoyable mixture will keep for up to a week in an airtight container.

❧ Teresa Ball, San Jose, CA

Playdough Pizza

Materials

Homemade playdough, any recipe (no added color)
Red paint
Glue
Scissors
White yarn
Construction paper, in brown, green, and beige

What to do

1. Help children "knead" playdough to form a flat pizza dough shape.
2. Mix red paint with glue.
3. Ask children to spoon the red paint mixture onto the "crust" for sauce.
4. Pre-cut or help children cut yarn into small pieces to resemble shredded cheese. Add it to the pizza.
5. Pre-cut or help children cut out other toppings, such as green peppers, mushrooms, and pepperoni to add to the pizza.

More to do

Dramatic Play: Set up a pizza parlor in the classroom. Provide aprons, pizza pans, spatulas, fake pizza, and other props.
Snack: Make individual pizzas using English muffins as the base.

Related book

Pizza Party by Grace MacCarone

 Sandra Suffoletto Ryan, Buffalo, NY

Candy Canes

Materials

Soda clay (recipe follows)
Wire ornament hangers
Wax paper
Red tempera or acrylic paint
Watercolor brushes

What to do

1. With the children, make balls of clay (see recipe below) about the size of a walnut. Form "snakes" out of the balls.
2. Bend the snakes into cane shapes.
3. Press ornament hangers into the curved ends of the canes.
4. Place them on a piece of wax paper to dry (about a day or two).
5. Paint red stripes on the shapes to make candy canes.

Soda Clay
1 box baking soda
1 cup (125 g) cornstarch
Pan
Mixing spoon
1 ¼ cups (300 ml) cold water
Stove or hot plate
Plate
Cloth
Container with lid

Mix together baking soda and cornstarch in a pan. Add water. Stir over moderate heat until the mixture thickens and resembles mashed potatoes. Scrape it onto a plate and cover it with a damp cloth. When it is cool enough to handle, knead until smooth. Store clay in a tightly covered container.

♣ Mary Jo Shannon, Roanoke, VA

Soda Clay Christmas Ornaments

Materials

16 oz (450 g) baking soda
Cornstarch
Measuring cups
Pot
Stirring spoon
Cold water
Oven or hot plate
Plate
Damp cloth
Covered container
Rolling pin or any smooth cylinder
Christmas cookie cutters (simple shapes such as stars, bells, or trees)
Plastic straws (cut into thirds)
White paper
Tempera paints and brushes
Clear polyurethane, optional (adult only)
Yarn or ribbon

What to do

1. Make Soda Clay. Mix 16 oz (450 g) of baking soda and 1 cup (125 g) of cornstarch in a pot. Add 1¼ cup (300 ml) of cold water. Stir over moderate heat until the mixture thickens and resembles mashed potatoes. Scrape it onto a plate and cover with a damp cloth. When it is cool enough to handle, knead until smooth. Store it in a tightly covered container.

2. Give each child a piece of clay (about the size of an egg), a rolling pin, a cookie cutter, and a section of plastic straw.

3. Help the children roll the clay until it is about ¼" (6 mm) thick.

4. Encourage them to cut out a shape with the cookie cutter.

5. Show the children how to cut a hole into the top of the shape using the straw.

6. Place each shape on a piece of white paper and write the child's name on the paper. (At this stage, all stars look alike!)

7. Allow the shapes to dry thoroughly, at least overnight.

8. Encourage the children to paint their dried ornaments. If desired, spray the

finished ornaments with clear polyurethane (adult only) to make them shine like ceramic.

9. Attach a ribbon or piece of yarn to make a hanger.

More to do

Language: Use the following words as you work with the clay: *knead, smooth, soft, white, cold, wet, thick, thin, roll, cylinder, round, even, large, small, and hole.*

Science: Describe the difference between wet clay and the dry ornament. How did the clay change in appearance? In the way it feels? Why do you think this happened?

❧ Mary Jo Shannon, Roanoke, VA

Race Car Printing

Materials

Newspaper
Paint
Shallow pans
Paint smocks
White paper
Small racecars (one for each child)

What to do

1. Cover a table with newspaper.
2. Pour paint into shallow pans (at least two of each color) and place them on the table.
3. Help the children put on smocks.
4. Give each child a piece of white paper and a toy car. Ask them to roll the wheels of the car through a pan of paint.
5. Encourage the children to roll their cars across their paper to make tracks.

More to do

Ask the children to think of other objects they could use to make tracks. Try making tracks with those objects and then compare the different types of tracks.

❧ Darleen A. Schaible, Stroudsburg, PA

Press Prints

Materials

Fingerpaints in a variety of colors
Large, smooth art or mess trays
12" x 18" (30 cm x 45 cm) construction paper

What to do

1. Put out several colors of fingerpaint and give each child an art tray.
2. Encourage the child to create a design.
3. When he is finished, help him carefully place a large piece of paper over the painted area of the tray.
4. Gently press the paper down onto the paint so that it absorbs as much paint as possible.
5. Slowly lift the paper. The painting on the tray transfers to the paper.
6. Hang it to dry and mount it for display.

More to do

Instead of fingerpaint, use tempera paint. Then, encourage children to make a design in the paint using different objects, such as a potato masher, comb, or bubble wrap. Press a piece of paper onto the paint as above.

Related books

Mouse Paint by Ellen Stoll Walsh
Paddington's Colors by Michael Bond

🍀 Tina Woehler, Oak Point, TX

Foam Tray Printing

Materials

Foam meat trays
Scissors
Kindergarten pencil with blunt point
Tempera paint

Shallow container
Wide, plastic foam brushes (1-wide are great)
Drawing paper

What to do

1. Help the children cut a foam meat tray into a square. This will be the printing plate.
2. Encourage the children to use a pencil to draw designs or words onto the tray.
3. Pour thick, liquid tempera paint into a shallow container.
4. Ask the children to use a wide, plastic foam brush to spread a thin layer of paint across the design. Try not to get paint into the grooves.
5. Help the children place a piece of drawing paper over the printing plate, and ask them to firmly press over the design.
6. Carefully peel the paper from the plate and allow the print to dry.

More to do

More Art: Cut and fold paper into cards to make Christmas cards or cards for other special occasions. Make appropriate designs on the printing plates (meat trays). Wash the plate and reuse it with a different color. Try using other colors of paper for variety.
Science: Discuss mirror images. Use mirrors and observe the image as printed words are reflected in it.

❧ Mary Jo Shannon, Roanoke, VA

Ants and Spiders

Materials

Inkpads
Paper
Markers or crayons

What to do

1. Help the children press their thumbs onto an inkpad, and then onto a piece of paper.
2. Encourage the children to draw insects by drawing six or eight legs on their thumbprint.

3. Encourage them to be creative. For example, they can draw parallel lines to make tunnels and put their ants inside them. Or, when making spiders, they can add a web or two.

4. This can also be a great counting activity by counting the legs on the spiders or ants.

More to do

Take a "bug walk" and encourage children to look for bugs. When you get back to the classroom, draw pictures of the bugs.

❖ Phyllis Esch, Export, PA

Elbow Printing

Materials

Newspaper
Masking tape
Washable tempera paint
Disposable paint trays
Paint smocks
Large white paper, at least 11" x 17" (27 cm x 42 cm)

What to do

1. Cover the work surface with newspaper and secure it with masking tape.
2. Pour a small amount of tempera paint into a shallow paint tray. Prepare several different colors of paint.
3. Help the children put on smocks.
4. Encourage children to dip their elbows into the paint and "stamp" it on a piece of paper.
5. Experiment with a variety of colors and patterns. (This activity is for the brave at heart! It is messy, but worth the effort. It is interesting to observe the children as they explore varying amounts of pressure, different colors, and so on.)

More to do

Four-year-olds have a developing awareness of their bodies. The elbow can be an interesting part of this art/science lesson on the various body parts. Play "Simon Says" or "Twister" for active learning!

Related book

From Head to Toe by Eric Carle

Song

"Hokey Pokey" ("You put your right elbow in... you put your right elbow out...")

🍀 Charlene Peace, Semmes, AL

Handprint Flowers

Materials

Tape
Mural paper
Long wall
Tempera paint
Pie tins
Green markers

What to do

1. Tape mural paper to a long wall.
2. Pour flower-colored paint into pie tins.
3. Ask each child to dip his hand into the paint and make a print on the mural.
4. Help the children wash their hands.
5. Give them green markers to draw stems and leaves on their print.
6. Write the child's name underneath his flower print.

🍀 Lisa M. Chichester, Parkersburg, WV

Riding the Bus

Materials

Yellow construction paper
Scissors
Empty spools of thread
Black paint

What to do

1. Help the children cut yellow paper into the shape of a bus.
2. Help the children to dip empty spools into black paint.
3. Encourage the children to paint "wheels" all over the bus using the spools.

More to do

Dramatic Play: Set up chairs to resemble bus seating with a driver seat in front. Place a small bucket on the floor next to the driver seat. Ask one child to be the bus driver. Give each child (except the driver) a block to use as a token. While "riding on the bus," sing "Wheels On the Bus," changing the destination to where ever the children want to go.

❧ Diane K. Weiss, Fairfax, VA

Bubble Art

Materials

White paper or construction paper
Scissors
Water
Dish soap
Shallow pan
Food coloring
Straws

What to do

1. If desired, cut a piece of paper into the shape of a butterfly or flower.
2. Mix water and dish soap in a shallow pan to make soapy water. Add food coloring to it.

3. Help the children use straws to blow into the water to create bubbles.

4. Place construction paper or the paper shapes on top of the bubbles, making them pop. This will leave colored rings on the paper pattern.

More to do

Put bubbles without food coloring in the sensory table.

❧ Sandy L. Scott, Vancouver, WA

"Swimmy" Fish

Materials

Swimmy by Leo Lionni
Scissors
Sponges
Blue construction paper
Orange and black paint
Shallow containers

What to do

1. Read the book *Swimmy* to the class.
2. Help the children cut sponges to make simple, small fish shapes.
3. Pre-cut or ask the children to cut a piece of blue paper into a large fish shape.
4. Pour orange paint into a shallow container.
5. Encourage the children to dip the sponge shapes into the paint and press them all over the large blue fish, filling it in.
6. Pour black paint into a shallow container. Encourage children to dip a fish-shaped sponge into it to make a "Swimmy" eye.

More to do

Math: Count how many little fish it takes to fill a large fish.
More Math: Sort big and little fish.
Snack: Serve tuna fish on crackers.

❧ Sandra Suffoletto Ryan, Buffalo, NY

Texture Stamps

Materials

Corrugated cardboard
Scissors
Glue
Items with different textures (see list)
Hot glue gun
Large corks
Paint
Shallow containers
Paper

What to do

1. Help the children cut a piece of cardboard into 3″ x 3″ (7 cm x 7 cm) squares.
2. Give each child a square. Encourage the children to glue a different textured item (see list) to one side of their cardboard.
3. When the glue is dry, use a hot glue gun to attach a cork to the empty side of the cardboard (adult only). A texture stamp!
4. Pour paint into shallow containers.
5. Using the cork as a grip, the children can dip each texture stamp into paint and press it onto paper to create a texture print.

Textured items
burlap
coarse paper
cotton balls
crumbled paper
dried glue
fur
leaves
sand
straw
tiny shells
wood chips

More to do

Ask the children what other items they would like to use for a texture print and make a stamp for them to use.

Related book

Is It Rough? Is It Smooth? Is It Shiny? by Tana Hoban

❀ Ann Gudowski, Johnstown, PA

Springtime Art

Materials

Tempera paint in spring colors
Small cookie sheets
Strawberry baskets
Large sheets of white paper
Flower pictures and glue or flower stickers

What to do

1. Pour each color of pastel paint onto a separate cookie sheet.
2. Encourage the children to place the bottom of a berry basket into the paint.
3. Ask them to gently move it around in the paint to coat it.
4. Encourage the children to place the paint-coated berry basket on a large piece of white paper, making any design. (The children may use all five colors or just one.)
5. The children may want to glue flower pictures or stickers on the finished pictures.
6. Allow the pictures to dry before displaying them.

More to do

Language: Ask the children if they can think of words that rhyme with "spring."
Create a poem or story with the words they say. For example:

Can a bright blue bird
*With a bright blue **wing***
Fly in the spring,
Taking winter away

To play for some other day?
*Can you hear the newly bloomed bluebells **ring**?*
When they pop up from their garden beds
On the first day of spring?
*Can you hear the rain **sing**,*
*And when it hits the window still makes a **ping**?*
Standing in the rain
*Can you feel it **sting**?*
*And the rain won't let you **swing**.*
It's too wet right now,
But that's okay
'Cause it's just spring anyhow.

❧ Penni Smith, Riverside, CA

Yarn Mosaic

Materials

Assorted scraps of yarns in different textures, colors, widths, and lengths
Scissors
Paper plates
Markers
Glue in squeeze bottles

What to do

1. Help the children cut scraps of yarn into small manageable pieces, about 2" to 4" (5 to 10 cm).
2. Help each child write his name on the back of a paper plate.
3. Ask them to turn their plates over. Encourage them to use glue to make designs. (Remind children to use glue dots and lines rather than glue lakes and puddles.)
4. Encourage the children to place yarn scraps onto the wet glue.
5. Allow the plates to dry.

More to do

Add hanging cords and decorate a tree with the hanging plates.

❧ Dani Rosensteel, Payson, AZ

The Power of Pumpkins

Materials

Scissors
Orange construction paper
Black construction paper
Glue
Green construction paper
Green yarn
Stapler

What to do

1. Help the children cut out a large oval shape from orange paper.
2. Using black construction paper, help the children cut out shapes, such as triangles, circles, squares, and rectangles. (Make sure the shapes are small enough to fit on the orange oval.)
3. Ask the children to identify the shapes.
4. Encourage the children to design a pumpkin face using the black shapes. When they are satisfied with their arrangement of shapes, help them glue the pieces in place.
5. Cut out a rectangle from green construction paper. Glue it to the top of the pumpkin face to make a stem.
6. Hang green yarn across a window, wall, or counter. Staple each pumpkin to the yarn to create a pumpkin patch.

More to do

Games: Play "Pin the Nose on the Pumpkin." Draw two shapes for eyes on a large pumpkin. Cut out a triangle shape from felt or construction paper and insert a thumbtack or a loop of tape in its upper corner. Cover the child's eyes with a bandana or scarf. Carefully place the triangle with the tack in his hand. Position the child about 5' (1.5 m) from the pumpkin. Encourage the child to try and pin the nose on the pumpkin.
Snack: Soak pumpkin seeds in salt water overnight. Spread out the seeds on a cookie sheet and sprinkle lightly with salt. Bake the seeds in an oven on low heat (about 200°) for about two hours, stirring every thirty minutes. Allow them to cool. They are ready to eat!

Related book

The Biggest Pumpkin Ever by Steven Kroll

❖ Jeannie Gunderson, Casper, WY

Rainbows of Our Own

Materials

Magazine pictures (from home)
Zipper closure plastic bags
A Rainbow of My Own by Don Freeman or *The Tiny Seed* by Eric Carle
Pencils
Light blue construction paper
Paste
Cotton balls

What to do

1. Ask parents to cut out pictures in magazines that contain large areas of a single color, such as grass, bricks, or background colors. Ask them to place the pictures in a zipper closure plastic bag so their child can bring them to school.
2. Read *A Rainbow of My Own* or *The Tiny Seed* to the children.
3. Help the children draw rainbows on light blue construction paper. Emphasize that they should draw the arc of the rainbow from one side of the page to the other.
4. With the children, tear the magazine pictures into many small pieces.
5. Show the children how to fill in each stripe of the rainbow by pasting the torn paper to it. Use one color for each stripe.
6. If desired, they can paste green or brown paper underneath the rainbow to make a land formation.
7. Encourage the children to paste cotton balls at each end of the rainbow to make clouds.
8. Explain to the children that their pictures have texture. Have a short discussion about texture.
9. Put the leftover paper into the Art Center for the children to explore.

A R T

More to do

More Art: Show children the illustrations in Eric Carle's books. Point out that they made their textured pictures the very same way he makes his pictures.
Science: Bring in a hanging crystal and demonstrate how it makes rainbows.
Sensory: Ask each child to find something in the room that is textured. Ask them to describe the object: Is it smooth, furry, soft, etc.?

Song

"Somewhere Over the Rainbow"

❧ Barbara Saul, Eureka, CA

Shape and Color Collage

Materials

Roll of clear adhesive paper
Scissors
Tape
Glitter or colored sand in shaker bottles and small confetti

What to do

1. Help the children cut adhesive paper into 12" (30 cm) squares to make a small collage or 18" (45 cm) squares for a large collage.
2. Tape the square of adhesive paper to a flat surface (paper backing side up).
3. Peel the paper backing off the adhesive paper.
4. Help the children cut out freeform shapes from the piece of paper backing.
5. Ask the children to stick their shapes to the adhesive paper to cover certain areas.
6. Encourage the children to sprinkle glitter, colored sand, or confetti over the exposed areas of the adhesive paper. (Sweep up the excess and pour it into its container.)
7. The children can remove some of the freeform shapes and use a different media (glitter, colored sand, or confetti) to cover that area. (Again, sweep up the excess and put it back into its container.)
8. Encourage the children to repeat step 7 until they have removed all the freeform shapes from the adhesive and covered all the areas with glitter, colored sand, or confetti.

9. Cover the collage with another piece of adhesive paper (the same size). Press together firmly and add a border of clear tape to keep the two pieces together, if necessary.
10. Hang and display each creation.

More to do

Make your own colored sand by putting ½ cup (125 g) of clean, sterilized play sand in a zipper closure plastic bag. Add a few drops of food coloring and a few drops of rubbing alcohol. (The alcohol helps the food coloring adhere to the sand.) Close the bag and ask the children to shake it vigorously to distribute the food coloring. Make several colors. In place of confetti, the children can use safety scissors to cut bright magazine pictures into very small pieces.

Related books

Chuck Murphy's Color Surprises by Chuck Murphy
The Color Box by Dayle Ann Dodds
Freight Train by Donald Crews

❖ Virginia Jean Herrod, Columbia, SC

My Home

Materials

Drawing of the rooms of a home on a 11" x 14" (27 cm x 35 cm) sheet of paper
Magazines
Scissors
Glue

What to do

1. Talk about the children's homes. Discuss what belongs in each room of a home.
2. Divide the children into groups of three or four.
3. Give each group a large drawing of the inside view of a house.
4. Ask the children to look through magazines and cut out pictures of things that belong in the different rooms of a house. For example, for a bedroom, they might look for pictures of a bed, toy chest, and a chest of drawers.
5. Encourage them to glue these pictures onto their house pictures.

More to do

Blocks: Encourage the children to build block homes.
Dramatic Play: Set up the housekeeping corner as a different room each day.
Sand Table: Encourage the children to create homes in the sand.

Related book

McDuff Comes Home by Rosemary Wells

♣ Suzanne Maxymuk, Cherry Hill, NJ

Seashore Pictures

Materials

Glue
Paintbrush, medium size
Poster board or tag board
Sand
Seashells, various types
Small stones
Aluminum foil
Blue marker
Plastic wrap
Tape

What to do

1. Help the children brush a thin layer of glue on the bottom third of a piece of poster board.
2. Encourage them to sprinkle sand onto the glue.
3. Next, the children can dip shells into glue and attach them to the paper on top of sand.
4. Repeat the process using rocks.
5. Ask the children to crumple pieces of foil, uncrumble it, and glue it flat onto the remaining paper above the sand. This will be the water.
6. Color the foil with a blue marker.
7. Put plastic wrap over the blue-colored foil to give the effect of water. Wrap it around the edges of the paper and glue or tape the edges down.

More to do

Language: Ask the children to dictate an original story to go with their beach picture. Write it down for them.

Math: With the children, count the number of shells and rocks they used on their picture.

Science: The children can look at various books about shells and identify the shells in the classroom.

Related books

A Beach Day by Douglas Florian
Exploring the Seashore by William H. Amos
The Seashore Book by Charlotte Zolotow
Those Summers by Aliki

❖ Mary Rozum Anderson, Vermillion, SD

City/Country

Materials

Masking tape
Corrugated cardboard, approximately 3' x 3' (1 m x 1 m) (use a cut-up carton)
Paint and brushes
Small and medium-sized boxes in various shapes
Construction paper scraps
Scissors
Glue
Small shoebox
Wood scraps, preferably small cubes/rectangles about 1" – 2" (2 - 5 cm)
Sandpaper
Thumbtacks

What to do

1. With the children, divide a piece of cardboard in half using masking tape.
2. Paint one side gray (this will be the city) and the other green (this will be the country).

3. To make houses (for the country) and skyscrapers, apartments, and stores (for the city), encourage children to paint small and medium boxes in a variety of colors.

4. Help the children cut construction paper scraps into window and door shapes and glue them to the houses and buildings.

5. Encourage a child to paint a small shoebox red to make a barn.

6. Tape a domed piece of construction paper to the barn to make a roof. Again, the child can use paper scraps to make doors and windows. Or, if desired, help him cut doors into the box so that they open.

7. Sand wood scraps and encourage children to paint them to look like cars or train cars.

8. Help them use thumbtacks or scrap paper to make wheels. (Supervise the use of thumbtacks.)

9. With the children, assemble a city by placing the buildings, cars, trains, and stores crowded together on the gray area of the board. Explain to children how cities are built.

10. Encourage the children to place the barn, smaller houses, and paper trees on the green area of the board to make a country area.

11. If desired, glue some of the buildings to the cardboard.

12. The two sides should look very different. As you work with the children, explain the differences between the two areas. Talk about the importance of keeping some green areas, trees, and space. Many books are available that do a splendid job of illustrating city life and country life.

More to do

You can incorporate or add various areas to the basic City/Country board. For example, make airplanes out of small travel-size toothpaste boxes and add construction paper "wings." Set up an airport near the city. Another example is to paint a corner of the board blue and set up a "water" area. Make boats out of walnut shell halves. Add people and animals to the board.

Related books

City Mouse/Country Mouse by many authors
The Little House by Virginia Lee Burton

❧ Maxine DellaFave, Raleigh, NC

Crazy Socks

Materials

Pair of socks for each child
Pompoms, fabric scraps, and rickrack
Hot glue gun (adult only)
Paint pens

What to do

1. Ask each child to bring in a pair of socks from home.
2. Encourage the children to choose pompoms, fabric scraps, and other materials to put on their socks.
3. Using a hot glue gun set on a low temperature, attach the items onto the children's socks (adult only).
4. Encourage the children to use paint pens to decorate the socks. They can create dots, squiggly lines, or other designs on the sock.
5. If desired, help each child write his name on the crazy socks using the paint pens.
6. Allow the socks to dry for about five hours. Then, wear them with pride!

❖ Lisa M. Chichester, Parkersburg, WV

Tie Dye Color Socks

Materials

Pair of white socks
Fabric dye, such as Rit, in a variety of colors
Shallow pans
Rubber bands

What to do

1. Ask each child to bring a pair of white socks from home.
2. Pour different colors of dye into shallow pans.
3. Show the children how to use rubber bands to tie their socks and how to dye their socks.

❖ Lisa Chichester, Parkersburg, WV

Classroom T-shirts

Materials

White T-shirts, one for each child
Fabric paint
Fabric markers

What to do

1. At the end of the year, give each child a white T-shirt.
2. Help each child dip his hand into fabric paint and make handprints all over the front of his T-shirt.
3. The children can also use fabric markers to make pictures or sign the back of their shirts. This activity makes a great memory!

❧ Lisa M. Chichester, Parkersburg, WV

Bleached T-Shirts

Materials

Leaves, rocks, and twigs
Solid color T-shirts
Bleach (adult only)
Spray bottle

What to do

1. Do this activity outdoors.
2. With the children, collect a variety of leaves, twigs, and rocks.
3. Give each child a T-shirt and ask him to lay it flat on the ground.
4. Encourage the children to spread the leaves, twigs, and rocks on their shirts.
5. Spray the shirts with bleach (adult only). Before doing this, make sure the children are not nearby.
6. The shirts will change colors in a couple minutes, so quickly rinse them in water to stop the bleach from eating through them.
7. The rocks, twigs, and leaves will leave a design on the shirt.

More to do

Make a collage with collected materials.

❖ Sandy L. Scott, Vancouver, WA

First Day of School Craft Ideas

Materials

8½" x 11" (21 cm x 27 cm) construction paper, various colors
Markers or crayons
Decorations, such as stickers or glitter
Laminate or clear contact paper

What to do

1. Each child will use a piece of construction paper to create his own place mat.
2. Help the children trace their hands on the construction paper.
3. The children can color or use decorations to decorate their place mats.
4. If desired, write their names in block style on the place mats.
5. To make the place mats more durable, laminate or cover them in clear contact paper.
6. Use the place mats for eating snacks.

❖ Deborah R. Gallagher, Bridgeport, CT

Doily Painting

Materials

Doilies (9" (22 cm) works well)
Scissors
Paper
Paint
Sponge paintbrushes

What to do

1. Help the children gently fold a small stack of doilies in half without making a crease on the fold.
2. Cut out a heart from the center of the folded doilies. Separate the doilies.
3. Help the children place one doily on a piece of paper
4. Encourage them to paint all over and around the doily with a sponge paintbrush. Then, gently lift up the doily.
5. This makes a great Valentine!

❧ Catherine Shogren, Eagan, MN

Gift from Our Heart

Materials

Construction paper, red and other colors
Scissors
Markers
Pencil
Glue
String or pipe cleaner

What to do

1. Help the children cut out a large heart, approximately 8" x 8" (20 cm x 20 cm), from red construction paper.
2. Using other colors of construction paper, help them cut out small heart shapes, about 2" x 2" (5 cm x 5 cm).
3. Give each child a small heart shape and markers.
4. Explain to them that the hearts will be a farewell gift for a child who is leaving the class.
5. After the child draws a design on his heart, ask him what he wants to tell the child who is leaving. Write his message on the heart with a pencil.
6. Glue all the small hearts onto the big heart.
7. Cut a small hole in the top of the heart and attach a string or pipe cleaner to hang it.
8. Give the heart to the child who is leaving as a farewell gift from his classmates.

❧ DooHyun Shin, Lakewood, WA

Mother's Day Card

Materials

Pastel construction paper
Markers, crayons, stickers, and stamps
Scissors
Tea bags

What to do

1. Help children fold pastel construction paper in half.
2. Draw the outline of a cup and saucer on the folded construction paper.
3. Help the children cut out the cup and saucer so that the fold is the top of the cup.
4. Encourage them to decorate the cup using markers, stickers, stamps, or crayons.
5. Inside the card, tape a tea bag and the following verse:

   I love you, Mom
   For all you are,
   You take good care of me.
   You're sweet. You're nice.
   You're cuddly too.
   You're just my cup of tea.

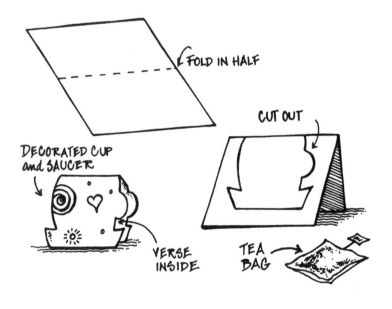

♣ Teresa J. Nos, Baltimore, MD

Pizza Chef

Materials

Construction paper in a variety of colors
Scissors
Glue

What to do

1. Discuss the five food groups and talk about healthy foods with the children.
2. Explain to the children that they are going to create a paper pizza.
3. Help each child cut out a large brown circle (to make a "crust"), and then a slightly smaller red one (to make "sauce").
4. Ask the children to create "toppings" for their pizza by cutting out vegetable, meat, and cheese shapes from colored paper.
5. Glue the pieces together to form pizzas.

More to do

Cooking: Make English muffin pizzas.
Field Trips: Visit a pizza parlor.

Related books

Little Red Hen: Makes a Pizza by Philemon Sturges
Pete's Pizza by William Steig

❖ Suzanne Maxymuk, Cherry Hill, NJ

Decorative Window Scenes

Materials

Washable tempera paint
Paintbrushes
Heavy clear laminate
Permanent marker
Scissors
Spray adhesive (adult only)
Stencil sponges
Acrylic paints, if desired

What to do

1. Help the children decorate the windows in the room using washable tempera paint and paintbrushes.
2. There are many themes you can use. For example, during the winter, children can create a window snow scene, painting snowmen, sleds, children in snow-suits, snow angels, snow forts, and snowballs. Create a winter scene that is typical for your area. (Children love the blizzard look.)
3. Other themes include the ocean, dinosaurs, bugs, and other creepy crawlers.
4. If you have something special in mind, make your own stencils. Using heavy clear laminate (leftover from other laminated items), trace patterns for each season, celebration, theme, or event.
5. Cut the heavy clear laminate into different stencils.
6. Spray adhesive (adult only) on the back of the stencil, put it on the window, and help the children paint. Place and replace the stencil on the window as often as desired.
7. Encourage the children to experiment using a small foam stencil sponge in a dabbing motion.
8. If desired, use acrylic paints to make the scene last all year. You can easily remove the paint with window cleaner.

❧ Debbie Barbuch, Sheboygan, WI

Spring Bulletin Boards

Materials

It Looked Like Spilt Milk by Charles G. Shaw
Light blue bulletin board paper
White paint
Bulletin board, covered in white

What to do

1. Read *It Looked Like Spilt Milk* to the children.
2. Tear or cut the lower edge of a piece of light blue bulletin board paper into a shape that resembles the sky (What you are cutting or tearing is the horizon line.) Spread it over the length of the art table.
3. Invite one child at a time to paint a "cloud." Discuss what the children are painting.

4. Hang the "sky" at top of the bulletin board.

More to do

Start this bulletin board at the beginning of a spring unit. Post the words "March Winds Blow" below the sky. The following week, encourage the children to paint flowers, cut them out, and "plant" them along the bottom of the board. Add a grass border and the words "FLOWERS GROW."

Marybeth A. Hurd, Flower Mound, TX

Moles on the Move

Materials

Mole's Hill: A Woodland Tale by Lois Ehlert
Green tempera paint
Paintbrushes
White drawing paper
Construction paper, various colors
Scissors
Glue
Stamp pads
Stamps of woodland animals, such as a bear, skunk, squirrel, rabbit, owl, porcupine, and raccoon

What to do

1. Read the story *Mole's Hill: A Woodland Tale* to the class.
2. With the children, paint green hills on a piece of paper.
3. When the paint is dry, help the children cut out flowers from different colored construction paper.
4. Using green paper, help them cut out stems and leaves (one set for each flower).
5. Encourage the children to glue the stems, leaves, and flowers all over the hill.
6. Help the children cut out a brown oval or circle and glue it near the bottom side of hill. This will be the mole hole.

7. Encourage the children to press animal stamps onto a stamp pad and stamp them all over the paper above the hill.

PAPER FLOWERS

GREEN HILL

OVAL GLUED DOWN

STAMPS

More to do

Dramatic Play: Put tables together to make tunnels. Cover them with sheets, leaving both ends open. Encourage the children to play in the tunnels and pretend to be woodland animals.

Song

Moles on the Move (Tune: "Frère Jacques")
> Crawling, crawling,
> Crawling, crawling,
> What do I hear?
> What do I hear?
>
> Little feet are moving,
> Little feet are moving
> Where will they go?
> Where will they go?

Look in the tunnel,
Look in the tunnel,
See those eyes!
See those eyes!

Little moles are digging,
Little moles are digging,
What a surprise!
What a surprise!

❖ Diane Weiss, Fairfax, VA

Island Adventure

Materials

Pictures of islands
Blue poster board or matte board
Brown and green modeling clay
Cotton balls
Glue
Construction paper, optional

What to do

1. Show the children pictures of islands and explain that islands are land areas that are completely surrounded by water.
2. Give each child a piece of blue poster board or matte board and a small piece of brown modeling clay.
3. Show them how to smear bits of clay on the center of the poster board. Explain that the blue at the bottom of their boards will represent the sea and the blue at the top will represent the sky. Encourage them to spread and smear the clay to represent the size and shape of the island they are forming.
4. Continue adding smears of clay until the island takes shape. Remind children to keep blue "water" all around their islands, and to avoid extending the clay to the edges of the paper.
5. Encourage the children to add plants and bushes to their islands using very small bits of green clay. Show them how to smear the green into the brown to simulate foliage.
6. Stretch a cotton ball until the cotton is extremely thin, resembling wispy

clouds. With small dabs of glue, attach the clouds in the island sky.

7. If desired, add other features to the island, such as people, sea animals, or boats using construction paper.

More to do

Dramatic Play: Place masking tape on the rug to create an island in the classroom.

Math: Sort various pictures of land scenes into two categories: islands and non-islands.

More Math: Tape an island to a rug and use a yardstick to measure it. Then measure it with a meter stick.

Music: Sing "Down by the Bay."

Science: Provide objects for a sink-and-float activity. Encourage the children to make predictions before dropping an object into the water.

Water Play: Provide containers, funnels, sifters, and water wheels in the sand and water table.

❖ Susan O. Hill, Lakeland, FL

Stars and Planets

Materials

Smocks
Fingerpaint paper
Ballpoint pen
Water
Blue and red fingerpaint
Spoon
Silver glitter in a shaker
Pictures or photographs of planets and moons
Scissors
Construction paper
Glue

What to do

1. Help the children put on paint smocks.
2. Give each child a piece of fingerpaint paper. Write each child's name on the

non-slick side of it using a ballpoint pen.

3. To anchor the paper, wet the table. Place the paper on the table, slick side up.

4. On each child's paper, place a spoonful of blue paint on one half and a dab of red on the other half.

5. Ask the children to put one hand into each color and spread the colors separately on the paper.

6. When they have spread each color smoothly and thoroughly, encourage the children to blend them together. Encourage them to swirl the paint, keeping some of the blue areas unmixed, all the way to the edges of the paper.

7. When they have finished painting, ask them to shake silver glitter on the wet paint to make stars in the sky.

8. Allow the paintings to dry overnight. The next day, weight the dry paintings with several heavy objects to flatten the curled edges.

9. Show the children a variety of pictures and photos of the planets. Invite them to create their own set of planets and moons by cutting out circles from the construction paper. Provide help and patterns if necessary.

10. Give each child his own fingerpainted sky scene. After the children experiment moving their planets around the sky, show them how to glue the celestial bodies in place.

11. Allow the pictures to dry before displaying them.

More to do

Math: Count the planets in our solar system. Make planet cutouts, number them, and order them by distance from the sun, then by size.

Science: Put out a large globe and encourage the children to explore their own planet.

Related books

My Picture Book of the Planets by Nancy Krulik
The Planets by Gail Gibbons

Song

Sing the following to the tune of the ABC song.

> *Mercury, Venus, Earth, and Mars;*
> *All these planets, so many stars.*
> *Jupiter, Saturn, Uranus, too;*
> *Neptune and Pluto, then we're through;*
> *Shining brightly oh, so high!*
> *All the planets in the sky.*

 Susan Hill, Lakeland, FL

Fingerplay Glove

Materials

Gloves
Pompoms, yarn, moveable eyes
Glue
Velcro stick-on squares

What to do

1. Ask each child to bring a clean glove from home. (Cotton gardening gloves work well.)
2. Supply each child with pompoms (one for each finger of the glove), yarn, moveable eyes, and other materials.
3. Encourage the children to create pompom "people" by using glue to attach materials to the pompom, such as yarn (for hair) and tiny moveable eyes. Add other materials, if desired.
4. Put Velcro stick-on squares on the backs of the pompom characters and on the fingers of the gloves. This will allow the children to change the characters from season to season.
5. Create characters to go with any fingerplay you desire. For example, glue green felt leaves and a black felt jack-o-lantern to orange pompoms for the fingerplay "Five Little Jack-O-Lanterns."

❧ Lisa M. Chichester, Parkersburg, WV

Carp Windsocks

Materials

Paper
Scissors
Markers
Glue or stapler
Paper punch
Notebook paper hole reinforcers or tape
String or yarn, cut into 18" (45 cm) pieces

What to do

1. Using the illustrations as guides, cut out or help the children cut out carp shapes from paper. (Each child will need two carp shapes.)
2. Encourage the children to use markers to decorate the carp shapes.
3. To reinforce the paper, fold the top/mouth area of the carp shapes.
4. Help the children glue or staple the sides of the two carp pieces together. (If you use glue, allow it to dry.)
5. Punch three holes, somewhat evenly spaced, on the folded mouth opening (adult only). Use notebook paper hole reinforcers or tape to reinforce the holes.
6. Tie one string in each hole. Bring the three strings together and tie them together. Make a loop to hang the carp.

Related books

A Carp for Kimiko by Virginia L. Kroll
Char Siu Bao Boy by Sandra S. Yamate
Dragon Kite of the Autumn Moon by Valerie Reddix

Sandra Nagel, White Lake, MI

MAKE 2 COPIES

ATTACH TO AN 8 X 12 PAPER OR CUT AS ONE ON LARGER PAPER

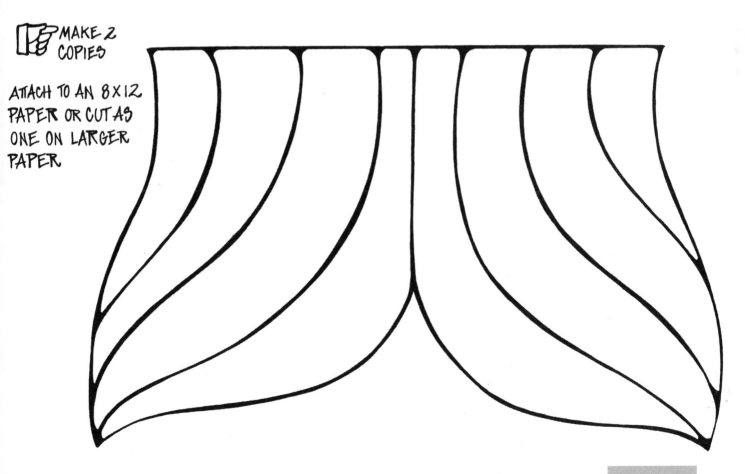

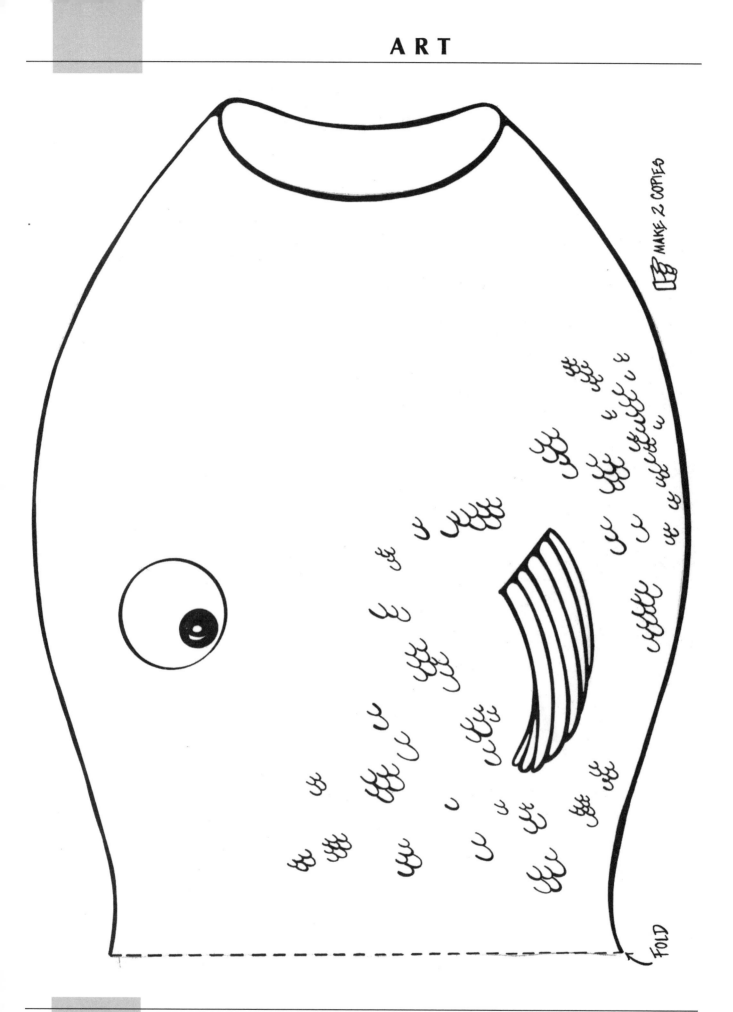

MAKE 2 COPIES

FOLD

Frog Puppet

Materials

Construction paper, in green, black, white, and red
Scissors
Glue
Paper plates
Stapler
Green paint
Paintbrushes

What to do

1. Encourage children to do this activity independently, but offer help to those who need it.
2. Using green, white, and black construction paper, make eyes. Glue the various parts of the eye together.
3. Cut out a tongue from red construction paper.
4. Cut one paper plate in half.
5. Staple the edges of the plates together.
6. Paint the paper plates green.
7. When the paint dries, glue on the eyes and tongue. (It's fun to glue a plastic or paper fly on the tip of the tongue.)
8. Show the children how to place their hands in the plates to make the mouth open and close.

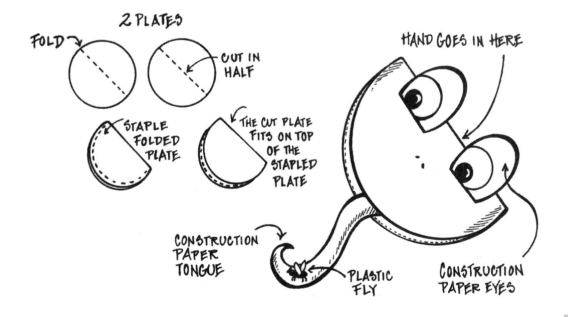

2 PLATES
FOLD
CUT IN HALF
STAPLE FOLDED PLATE
THE CUT PLATE FITS ON TOP OF THE STAPLED PLATE
HAND GOES IN HERE
CONSTRUCTION PAPER TONGUE
PLASTIC FLY
CONSTRUCTION PAPER EYES

More to do

Make other animals with paper plates.

Related books

The Frog Who Wanted to Be a Singer by Linda Goss
Frogs by Gail Gibbons

Songs or Poems

Grump Went the Little Green Frog

Grump went the little green frog one day.
Grump went the little green frog.
Grump went the little green frog one day.
And the frog went grump, grump, grump.

Five Little Speckled Frogs

Five Little Speckled Frogs
Sat on a great big log,
Eating some most delicious bugs.
Yum, yum.
One dove into the pool
Where it was nice and cool.
Now there are four green speckled frogs
Gulp, gulp.

(Repeat with four, then three, two, one, zero frogs.)

Sandra Nagel, White Lake, MI

Rainbow Fish

Materials

Newspaper
Scissors
Paper plates
Stapler
Blue and green paint
Shallow trays

Paintbrushes
Glitter or decorative snow
Wiggly eyes

What to do

1. Cover painting surfaces with newspaper.
2. Help the children cut out a large "V" from the side of a paper plate. (This space will become the fish's mouth.)
3. Help the children staple the "V" shape (point side in) to the opposite side of same paper plate. (This will become the fish's tail.)
4. If desired, using the illustration of the "Rainbow Fish," cut out a dorsal fin (top) and pectoral fin (long, thin triangle) from the extra paper plates. Staple the dorsal fin along the top of the fish shape and the pectoral fin (point up) just below the fish's mid-point, with the edge overhanging the fish about ½" to 1" (1 cm to 2 cm). (See illustration.)
5. Pour blue and green paint into shallow pans. Encourage the children to paint the fish.
6. While the paint is still wet, they can sprinkle glitter or decorative snow on the fish to achieve the sparkly look of the "Rainbow Fish."
7. As a finishing touch, help them glue on a large wiggly eye.

More to do

Bulletin Board: Use blue fadeless paper as a background. Twist green tissue paper to make seaweed. Ask children to make additional sea creatures to add to the underwater scene.

Related books

The Rainbow Fish and the Big Blue Whale and other "Rainbow Fish" books by Marcus Pfister

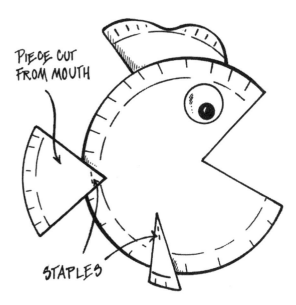

❀ Deborah R. Gallagher, Bridgeport, CT

Thimble People

Materials

Thimbles
Glue
Decorating materials, such as moveable eyes, pompoms, and scraps of fabric

What to do

1. Give each child a thimble.
2. Encourage him to glue decorating materials to the thimble to make "people." For example, glue movable eyes, a tiny pompom nose, and scrap material as clothes or scarves to the thimble.

❧ Lisa M. Chichester, Parkersburg, WV

Spool People

Materials

Empty spools
Decorations, such as moveable eyes, pompoms, pipe cleaners, and yarn
Glue

What to do

1. Put out the empty spools and decorating materials.
2. Encourage the children to decorate the empty spools to make imaginative creations! For example, make spool people by attaching moveable eyes, a pompom nose, a pipe cleaner for arms, and yarn for legs and hair.

❧ Lisa M. Chichester, Parkersburg, WV

Hair Claw/Clip Monsters

Materials

Hair clips
Tempera paint and paintbrushes
Feathers and items to make eyes and noses
Glue

What to do

1. Purchase (or ask parents to purchase) a hair clip for each child in the class.
2. Show the children how the clip looks like a monster with teeth when they open it.
3. Make monster faces on the clips. Encourage the children to paint their hair clips, glue on goo eyes and other items to make facial features, and glue on feathers to make hair.
4. Children can wear them in their hair or clip them to their backpacks for a fun monster friend!

FEATHERS

BLACK TEMPERA PAINT

RED TEMPERA PAINT

WHITE TEMPERA PAINT

WIGGLY EYES

❖ Lisa M. Chichester, Parkersburg, WV

Block Heads

Materials

Small pieces of 2″ x 4″ (5 cm x 10 cm) wood
Markers
Glue
Decorating items such as pipe cleaners, buttons, pompoms, and yarn

What to do

1. Place wood pieces, markers, glue, and decorating items on the art table.
2. Encourage the children to decorate the wood to make creative people.
3. After the glue dries, place the creations on display.
4. The children may also want to name their creations or tell a story about them. Write down their names and stories to display with the creations.

More to do

Children can create larger Block Heads using various blocks of wood or cardboard tubes.

❧ Melissa Browning, Milwaukee, WI

Paper Creature

Materials

Newspaper
Masking tape
Paint
Paintbrushes

What to do

1. For this activity, it will be helpful for children to work with a partner, especially when it is time to attach body parts.
2. With the children, crumple newspaper to make one body part of a "creature." (For example, to make a "turtle creature," crumple a large ball of newspaper to make the body, attach a smaller ball for the head, and four more balls of

newspaper for the feet. Add a tail, if desired.)

3. Encourage the children to attach this shape to another crumpled shape with tape. Repeat the process until they finish making a creature.

4. Paint the creatures and allow time for drying.

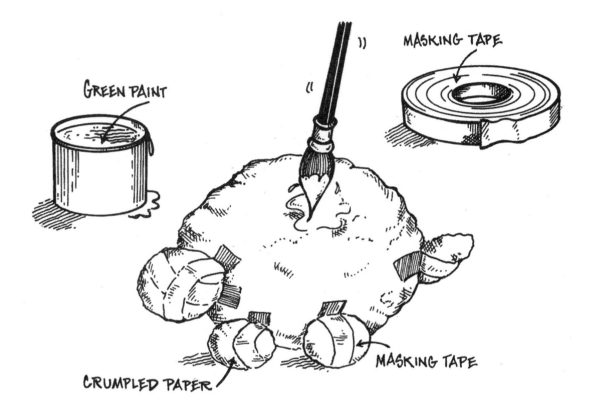

GREEN PAINT

MASKING TAPE

CRUMPLED PAPER

MASKING TAPE

More to do

Field Trips: Visit a local natural history museum.

Literacy: Write or dictate a "write-up" of each creature for museum visitors (see below).

Science: Create a "creature museum." Discover the living habits (nesting, eating, sleeping, location, and so on) of existing creatures. Or make up new creatures.

❖ Lauren Brickner-McDonald, Mountain Lakes, NJ

Apple People

Materials

Apples
Popsicle sticks
Glue
Scrap material
Pompoms, moveable eyes, yarn

What to do

1. Give each child an apple to eat. Ask them to nibble carefully around the core, but keep the core in one piece.
2. Save the cores.
3. Put a Popsicle stick into the bottom of each apple core.
4. Encourage the children to make "apple people." They can form a dress by gluing a piece of scrap material around the stick.
5. Ask the children to glue yarn to the "head" to make hair and add moveable eyes and pompom noses.
6. Allow the apple puppet to dry up. The dried puppet will keep for a while.

♣ Lisa M. Chichester, Parkersburg, WV

Did You Ever See a Jabberwocky?

Materials

"The Jabberwocky" by Lewis Carroll
Medium and small Styrofoam balls (some cut in half)
Assorted colors and lengths of pipe cleaners, Popsicle sticks, and plastic straws
Feathers, beads, colored toothpicks, and thin colored foam shapes

What to do

1. Read the poem "The Jabberwocky" by Lewis Carroll to the children.
2. Discuss with the children what a Jabberwocky might be and what it might

look like.

3. Read the poem again to the children.

4. Encourage the children to use the various materials to create their own Jabberwocky. Use Styrofoam balls to make heads and bodies and attach the pieces together using Popsicle sticks and pipe cleaners. Decorate the creature using foam shapes, paper pieces, feathers, and so on. Stick them directly into the Styrofoam or use toothpicks to attach them.

Related books

Animals, Animals by Eric Carle
A Jar of Tiny Stars: Poems by NCTE Award Winning Poets by Bernice E. Cullinan
Where the Sidewalk Ends by Shel Silverstein

❧ Sandra Gratias, Perkasie, PA

Picture Frames

Materials

Take-out containers from restaurants
Scissors
Art paper
Markers
Glue
Modeling dough or other building materials

What to do

1. Cut take-out boxes along their hinges, separating the tops from the bottoms. Use the halves that are not divided into compartments as picture frames.

2. Pre-cut art paper so that it will fit into the "frames."

3. Give each child a piece of art paper and markers. Encourage the children to draw designs on the paper.

4. Help each child glue his artwork onto the flat surface and the sides of a tray. The box will form a frame.

5. Use the divided compartment halves to display small, three-dimensional items that the children make with modeling dough or other building materials.

❧ Barbara F. Backer, Charleston, SC

Popsicle Stick Frames

Materials

Markers
Popsicle sticks
Glue

What to do

1. Help each child write his name on a Popsicle stick.
2. Give the children more Popsicle sticks. Help each child glue four sticks together (including the one with his name on it) to make a frame.
3. Allow the frames to dry.
4. Encourage the children to color their frames with markers.
5. Help them glue a photograph or one of their drawings to the backs of the frames.
6. Allow the glue to dry. Trim the edges, if necessary.

❧ Dani Rosensteel, Payson, AZ

Colored Stone Picture Frames

Materials

Popsicle sticks
Glue
Craft stones
Cardboard
Scissors

What to do

1. Give each child four Popsicle sticks.
2. Encourage the children to glue colored craft stones onto one side of each Popsicle stick.

3. Help them glue together the four Popsicle sticks to form a picture frame.

4. Cut cardboard into squares (to fit the Popsicle sticks).

5. Help each child glue a piece of cardboard to the back of his sticks. Make sure to leave an open space in front to put a picture.

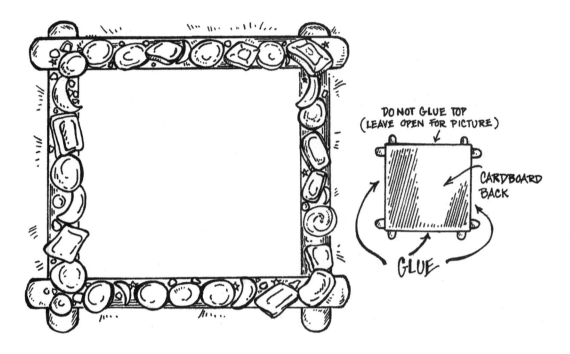

DO NOT GLUE TOP
(LEAVE OPEN FOR PICTURE)

CARDBOARD
BACK

GLUE

❀ Lisa M. Chichester, Parkersburg, WV

Seashell Frame

Materials

Photograph of each child

Newspaper

Smocks

Cardboard or heavy poster board

Scissors

White glue

Small shells

Sand

Bowl

Teaspoon

Hot glue gun (adult only)

Paper clips

What to do

1. Ask children to bring in photographs of themselves. Or, use a Polaroid camera and take pictures of them during school activities.
2. Cover a table with newspaper. Help the children put on smocks.
3. Cut a piece of cardboard into 6" x 8" (15 cm x 20 cm) rectangles.
4. Give each child a cardboard rectangle and ask him to glue his photograph in the center. If necessary, trim the picture to fit.
5. Put small shells on the table so the children can select which ones they want to use. (If necessary, limit the amount of shells to eight to ten per child).
6. Help one child pour ½ cup (125 g) sand into a bowl.
7. Ask another child to stir the sand as you pour glue into it. (The mixture should be moist enough so that it falls off the spoon but is not runny.)
8. With the children, spoon the sand mixture onto the cardboard rectangles, framing their pictures.
9. Encourage them to press their shells into the sand mixture on their frames.
10. Allow the frames to dry for at least three days.
11. Use a hot glue gun to attach a paper clip on the back of the frame for the hook (adult only).
12. Help the children write their names, the year, and name of their school on the back.

More to do

Games: Play "Hide the Shells." Ask the children to hide their eyes while you hide the shells. Then the children go find them. (Remember to set some ground rules before starting the game.)
Math: Count the leftover shells or sort them by shape, color, or size.

❧ Darleen A. Schaible, Stroudsburg, PA

Spool Necklace

Materials

Empty spools
Scissors
Yarn
Tape

What to do

1. Give each child at least four empty spools.
2. Help the children cut yarn into manageable lengths, no longer than 3' (1 m).
3. Encourage them to wrap the lengths of yarn around each spool. (Tape ends down.)
4. The children can then take one of the 3' (1 m) lengths of yarn and string the spools on it to make a necklace.
5. Or, use it as a gift for kitty!

❖ Lisa M. Chichester, Parkersburg, WV

Peng-eei

Materials

Stiff paper (cut from a cereal box)
Markers
Scissors
Hole punch
Sparkles, pompoms, and glue, optional
Round Popsicle sticks or drinking straws

What to do

1. With the children, draw a circle (or a triangle or square if desired) on a piece of stiff paper.
2. Help the children cut out the circle. (If the box is too hard to cut with children's scissors, cut it out for them.)
3. Help the children write their names on their circle.
4. Punch a hole in the middle of the circle.
5. Encourage the children to decorate their circles with markers. If desired, provide sparkles, pompoms, and glue.
6. Put a round Popsicle stick or drinking straw through the hole.
7. Peng-eei is a traditional play in Korea. The word "peng" means spinning. The children can twist the Popsicle stick and let the Peng-eei spin on the table or the floor.

More to do

Math: Make a graph so children can compare and visualize the different shapes.

Science: Encourage children to make different shaped peng-eeis, such as triangles and squares. They can compare the shapes of the peng-eei and see how long each shape spins. They also can color the surface of the peng-eei and see the color combination when it spins (yellow + blue = green).

❧ DooHyun Shin, Lakewood, WA

DECORATED WITH MARKERS

STRAW

SPARKLES

CIRCLE OF STIFF PAPER

Color Banners

Materials

Felt
Paint pens
Dowel rods
Glue

What to do

1. Give each child a piece of felt.
2. Put out only one color of paint pens to focus on one color. If desired, write the name of that color on the felt.
3. Encourage the children to decorate the felt using the paint pen.
4. Use glue to attach the felt to a dowel rod. Hang it in the classroom until it is time to focus on another color.

🍀 Lisa M. Chichester, Parkersburg, WV

Spaghetti and Meatball Plate

Materials

Scissors
White or off-white yarn
Glue
Paper plates
Large brown pompoms
Red paint

What to do

1. Help the children cut white yarn into 12″ (30 cm) lengths.
2. Encourage the children to put glue on a paper plate and add a pile of yarn to look like spaghetti.
3. Glue one or two pompoms onto the plate for meatballs.

4. Drizzle red paint over the top to look like sauce (Hint: Mix some glue into the paint for extra hold.)

More to do

Games: Play the "Spaghetti Maze Game." String long lengths of yarn around the room, under tables, around chairs, and over low shelves. Attach an end to a pompom "meatball." Encourage the children to wind the yarn around the pompom as they follow the "spaghetti" maze to the end.

Related books

Cloudy with a Chance of Meatballs by Judi Barrett
More Spaghetti, I Say by Rita Golden Gelman
Spaghetti and Meatballs for All by Marilyn Burns
Strega Nona by Tomie dePaola

❧ Sandra Suffoletto Ryan, Buffalo, NY

Clowning Around

Materials

Plain-colored party hats
Permanent marker (adult only)
Glue
Shallow plastic plates
Cotton swabs
Pompom balls, in a variety of sizes

What to do

1. Ask the children to choose a party hat.
2. Write the child's name on the inside of his hat with a permanent marker.
3. Squirt glue into shallow plastic plates. Place several cotton swabs onto the plates.
4. Put pompoms on other plates.
5. Help the children put glue on their hats in several spots using the cotton swabs. Then, encourage them to attach the pompoms to the hat.
6. Place the hat on its side to dry for several hours.
7. With the children, wear the hats to enhance a circus parade event, for dress up, or for a birthday party.

More to do

More Art: Make animal masks using paper plates, tempera paint, crayons or markers, glue, yarn, tissue paper, craft foam, and a hole puncher. Cut out two holes for eyes. Punch a hole on either side of the paper plate and thread two pieces of yarn through it. Decide what animal mask to create and decorate the animal's face on the plate. Tie the yarn around the head to attach the mask.

Blocks: Add circus animals and a circus train to the Block Center.

Dramatic Play: Add Halloween masks and costumes or dress-up clothes to the Dramatic Play Area and pretend to be at a circus.

More Dramatic Play: Create a clown center by placing washable face paints on a table or make-up dresser complete with mirrors and diaper wipes. Take pictures of the clowns.

Music: Play circus music while the children play in the centers.

Related books

Carnival by M.C. Helldorfer
Spot Goes to the Circus by Eric Hill

❖ Tina R. Woehler, Oak Point, TX

Easter Bonnets

Materials

Hole punch
Paper plates
Colored tissue paper
Glue sticks or paste
Ribbons or yarn

What to do

1. Punch a hole into each side of a paper plate.
2. Encourage the children to scrunch pieces of tissue paper to resemble flowers.
3. Help them glue the tissue paper to the bottoms of the plates using glue sticks or paste.
4. Run a ribbon or piece of yarn through one hole, over the tissue flowers, and through the other hole.
5. Tie the ribbons to secure the hat on a happy little child.

More to do

When all the hats are complete, have a parade.

 Mary Jo Shannon, Roanoke, VA

Name Hats

Materials

White baseball hat (paint stores sell inexpensive paint hats)
Permanent fabric markers
Fake pearls, scrap materials, pompoms
Glue

What to do

1. Give each child a white hat.
2. Encourage each child to decorate his hat with fabric markers.
3. Help each child write his name on the front of the hat using a fabric marker.
4. If desired, glue fake pearls, scrap fabrics, and pompoms to finish the funky hat!

 Lisa Chichester, Parkersburg, WV

Paper Plate Baskets

Materials

Inexpensive, white paper plates
Crayons
Water
Dishpan
Soda can
Rubber band
Hole punch
Colored pipe cleaners
Easter grass or raffia

What to do

1. With the children, color a paper plate with designs and patterns (for example, stripes, dots, rainbows, or flowers) using lots of different colors.
2. Ask them to turn the plate over and color the other side the same way.
3. Pour water into a dishpan. Put each plate into the water for about 30 seconds, until it is soft enough to mold easily.
4. Help the child form the plate over a soda can, applying equal pressure over it.
5. Place a rubber band around the plate to hold it to the can.
6. Encourage the child to flare out the edges of the plate.
7. Let it dry for several hours or overnight.
8. Help the child remove the paper plate from the can. The plate will be stiff and will hold its shape.
9. Punch two holes opposite each other on the flared edges of the plate.
10. Attach a pipe cleaner in the holes to make a handle.
11. Encourage the children to put Easter grass or raffia into their baskets and fill with whatever they want.

More to do

For Mother's Day, fill the basket with candy hugs, kisses, and a tea bag for "Five Minutes' Peace." For Easter, fill the basket with Easter candy.

Related book

Five Minutes' Peace by Jill Murphy

❖ Bettejane Grey, Woodbridge, VA

Make Boats

Materials

Collage materials (see list)
Clear plastic or Styrofoam salad bar container
Stapler, tape, glue, and rubber bands
Scissors
Yarn or string
Tub of water, water table, child's wading pool, or real pond or lake

What to do

1. Spread out collage materials for boat building.
2. Ask children to select a base for their boat (plastic or Styrofoam container).
3. Encourage the children to attach collage materials to their bases using tape, glue, rubber bands, or a stapler. Be careful not to load up one side of the container, or the boat might tip over and sink!
4. Help the child poke a hole near the top edge of the container and insert a long piece of yarn or string. Tie it gently so the container does not tear. Add extra tape or staples to make it strong. The children will pull the string to propel their boats through the water.
5. When the boats are complete, float them in water. Carefully supervise the children around water. Remember to have fun—it's okay to get wet!

Collage materials
aluminum foil
buttons
paper and fabric scraps
plastic flowers
pompoms
ribbon
stickers
string

More to do

Literacy: Read *The Story of Ping* by Marjorie Flack. Place a little toy duck in the homemade boat and play out the story of the little duck named Ping.

More Literacy: Read *Little Toot and the Lighthouse* by Linda Gramatky-Smith, and play out the story of Little Toot with the homemade boat. Add a block of wood for the lighthouse. Flash the lights to simulate lightening, and bang on pie-pans to make thunder.

Science and Math: Add balls of clay, one at a time, to a floating empty plastic container. How many balls of clay does it take to sink the boat? This allows exploration in the areas of displacement as well as balance, weight, and flotation.

More Science and Math: Fill a dish tub with water. Assemble items that float and items that sink. Explore to see which ones float and which ones sink. Place heavy and light items into the boat and see what happens. Which ones allow the boat to continue floating and which ones cause it to sink?

Social Studies: Tell the children about the traditional festival called Loy Krathong, which is when the people of Thailand celebrate water and its bounty. It takes place just before harvest time in mid-November on a night with a full moon. Children make a wish and float their lighted boat at night. Encourage children to decorate their boats with additional items, such as nuts, pennies, and candles and put on your own festival.

Related books

Boats, Boats, Boats (My First Reader) by Joanna Ruane
Global Art: Activities, Projects, and Inventions From Around the World by
   MaryAnn F. Kohl and Jean Potter

❧ MaryAnn F. Kohl, Bellingham, WA

Moose Hangings

Materials

Felt or burlap
Scissors
Needle and thread or glue
Dowel rods
Paintbrush
Brown, yellow, red, and black paint
Shallow pans
Permanent marker or fabric paint pen
String

What to do

1. Help the children cut felt or burlap into pieces approximately 12" x 14" (30 cm x 35 cm).
2. Sew or glue the top of the felt piece to make a sleeve for a dowel rod.
3. Cut the dowel rod so that it is approximately 13" (32 cm) long.
4. Paint the child's foot with brown paint and help him make a footprint in the middle of the felt piece. Be sure to leave space for two handprints.
5. Paint the child's hand with yellow paint. Ask him to rub his hands together, then help him place his hands above his footprint to make antlers.
6. When the hand and footprints are dry, add eyes and a nose. Pour red paint into a pan and black paint in another pan. Help the child place his thumb in the red paint and press it onto the footprint to make a nose. After he wipes off his thumb, he will press it into the black paint to make eyes.

7. Help the child's print his name and date using a permanent marker or fabric paint pen.

8. Put the dowel through the sleeve.

9. Tie a string to both ends of the dowel rod to make a wall hanging.

10. These make great holiday gifts.

STRING

FELT WITH A SLEEVE FOR THE DOWEL

BROWN and YELLOW PAINT

FELT

HENRY 5-30-02

NAME and DATE

PAN WITH RED and BLACK PAINT

More to do

Vary the shape of the felt or burlap. Make a deer, reindeer, or Rudolph the red-nosed reindeer instead of a moose. Use paper instead of material. Punch holes and pull string through to make a hanger. Cut the edges with pinking shears.

Related books

1,2,3, Moose: A Pacific Northwest Counting Book by Andrea Helman
Big Jim and the White-Legged Moose by Jim Arnosky
Happy Moose, Grumpy Moose by John Clementson
Morris Goes to School by Bernard Wiseman
One Moose, Twenty Mice by Clare Beaton

Sandra Nagel, White Lake, MI

Treasure Bucket

Materials

Scissors
Empty, well washed gallon bleach bottles
Hole punch
Permanent marker
Watercolor markers
Plastic clothesline, 12" (30 cm) for each bucket

What to do

1. Cut off the top of a bleach bottle to make a bucket shape (adult only).
2. Use a hole punch to make a hole on each side of the bucket. Make sure to place them exactly opposite of each other so the bucket will be balanced.
3. Attach the clothesline to the two holes to make a handle.
4. Write the child's name on the bucket with a permanent marker (adult only).
5. Encourage the children to use watercolor markers to decorate the buckets.
6. Use the buckets in the Block Center, outside, in the sand table, and wherever they are needed.

More to do

Games: Line up several buckets and encourage the children to try to toss beanbags into them.
Language and Math: Collect objects and put them into the buckets. Ask children to describe the items. With the children, count the objects. Arrange them in order of size from smallest to largest.
Math: In the sandbox, count how many measuring cups are needed to fill a bucket.

❧ Mary Jo Shannon, Roanoke, VA

Seashore Sand Globe

Materials

Small baby food jars
Blue spray paint (adult only)
The Seashore Book by Charlotte Zolotow
Assorted small shells, and a larger shell for each child
Dry sand
Hot glue gun (adult only)

What to do

1. Prior to this activity, paint the lids of baby food jars with blue spray paint (adult only).
2. Read *The Seashore Book* by Charlotte Zolotow with the class. Discuss what items are found on the beach and ask children about their own beach experiences.
3. Give each child a jar and a painted lid.
4. Put out an assortment of shells. Ask the children to choose shells and put them into their Seashore Sand Globe.
5. Help the children pour ¼ cup (60 g) dry sand into their jars on top of the shells.
6. Put a small amount of hot glue around the inside edge of the jar lid (adult only). Screw the lid on the jar and turn the jar upside down so the Sand Globe is resting upside down. The lid becomes the base of the Sand Globe.

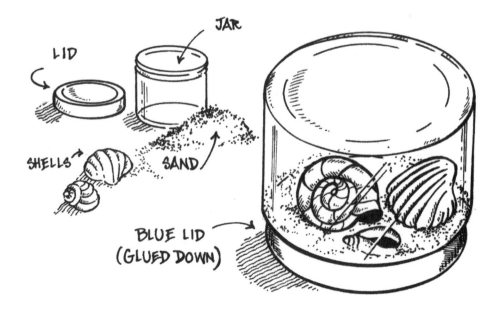

More to do

Math: Children can use small seashells to learn numbers by putting them in groups of one through ten.

Related books

Exploring the Seashore by William H. Amos
Harry by the Sea by Gene Zion
Those Summers by Aliki

❖ Mary Rozum Anderson, Vermillion, SD

Hemlock Cone Candle Rings

Materials

Brown paper bags
Scissors
White glue
Cones from a hemlock tree (they look like tiny pinecones)
Candles, optional

What to do

1. Help children cut out 2" (5 cm) circles from brown paper bags.
2. Cut out the center of the circle, leaving a rim about ½" (1 cm) wide. Give each child two of these.
3. Encourage the child to spread white glue on the rim and place cones into the glue.
4. Allow it to dry completely.
5. A pair of these rings makes a great gift. (Put candles in the middle of the rim, if desired.)

More to do

Language: Talk about the concepts of a pair or a circle.
Math: Count the cones in the ring.
Science: Explain that cones are seed holders. (If you have fresh cones, you may be able to tap them and see seeds fall out.) Tell the children how squirrels and birds eat the seeds and that some seeds start new trees. Experiment with planting some of the seeds.

❖ Mary Jo Shannon, Roanoke, VA

Birdseed Strings

Materials

Round cereal, such as Cheerios
String cut into 18" (45 cm) lengths
Plastic craft needles
Wax paper
Plastic spoon
Peanut butter
Soap and water
Birdseed
Zipper closure plastic bag

What to do

1. Tie a piece of round cereal to one end of each string and put the needle on the other end of the string.
2. Give each child a string and plastic needle.
3. Ask the children to fill the string with more cereal. When they have finished, help them tie a piece of cereal to the other end of the string.
4. Place each string of cereal on a piece of wax paper.
5. Spoon a blob of peanut butter onto each piece of wax paper.
6. Encourage the children to smear peanut butter all over the cereal, coating it with a thick layer.
7. Help the children wash their hands.
8. Put birdseed in a zipper closure plastic bag. Place the peanut butter-coated cereal strings into the bag, zip it shut, and shake to coat the cereal with birdseed.
9. Hang the strings on a tree outside to feed the birds. Or, send them home with children so they can feed the birds at their homes.

Related book

Annie and the Wild Animals by Jan Brett

❖ Vickie DiSanto, Mt. Pleasant Mills, PA

Earth Formations

Materials

Large sheets of sturdy paper
Paintbrushes and paint
Construction paper of various colors
Glue
String
Scissors

What to do

1. Begin this activity by discussing earth formations, especially mountains, hills, plains, deserts, rivers, lakes, and oceans.

2. Help the children make paper formations of each of these earth formations. Make them large enough to wear or hold. For example:
   - Mountains: Make large pointed hats to fit over the head and shoulders. Cut openings for the eyes. Paint these silver and gray.
   - Hills: Construct these the same way as the mountains, only smaller and rounder. Paint them green.
   - Plains: Make trees and houses from construction paper. Place them on a large, flat piece of brown paper.
   - Deserts: Construct sand dunes and cacti on a large, flat piece of yellow or gold paper.
   - Rivers: Use a long, blue strip of paper. (Three children will need to hold it.)
   - Lakes: Make a large, round blue surface on a large piece of paper.
   - Oceans: Use a huge, flat deep blue piece of paper to make an ocean. Several children will need to hold it.

3. Produce a little drama in which the children will say who they are. For example:
   - Mountain: I am a mountain, very tall. I reach very high, far above all.
   - Hill: I am a hill: bumpy, round, and green. I am covered with trees and bushes.
   - Plain: I am a plain: land flat and good. You might build your house here.

♣ Lucy Fuchs, Brandon, FL

Art for All Ages Art Festival

Materials

Artwork created by children, collected throughout the year
Paper
Markers
Nametags

What to do

1. Throughout the year, collect a variety of the children's artwork, including drawings, paintings, collages, and clay work. Collect at least five examples from each child. If desired, frame the paintings and drawings (but it is not necessary).

2. Choose a date to have your "First Annual Art for All Ages Art Festival." With the children, design and send out a flyer to parents announcing this event. Explain that each child will be represented as a local artist. (An example: "You are cordially invited to our First Annual Art of All Ages Festival! Local artists from [class name] will be prominently featured! Be sure to make plans to attend.") Include the date, time, and location on the flyer.

3. Give parents plenty of notice so they can make arrangements to attend. If possible, make it an all-day event so it will be easier for parents to attend. In addition, send home a reminder a couple of days before the festival.

4. Design an "About the Artist" card for each featured artwork. Include:
   - Title of Piece
   - Name of Artist
   - Current Date
   - A short blurb about the artist. For example, "When Malcolm is not dabbling in watercolors, he likes to play in the Block Area." (Interview the children to find out these facts. Be creative, have fun! The more you make this sound like a "real" artist's biography, the more fun it is.)

5. Provide a healthy snack to serve at the festival. Ask parents to volunteer to do this, or take a day and prepare something with the children. Make your snack a work of art in itself. (See "More to do" for ideas)

6. With the children, create nametags to wear at the party.

7. Designate a specific amount of wall space for each child. Post his "About the Artist" card in this space and arrange the art around it. Use the tops of bookshelves for artwork you cannot hang. If you run out of space, spill over into the hallway or common area. (Remember where you put each child's work.)

8. Greet parents as they arrive. Use your best manners—the children will follow

your lead. Introduce the child as you would any important artist, and let the child lead the parents on a tour of his artwork. Encourage parents to take their time to look at other children's work. Go around with them and comment on the child's use of color and positive and negative spaces. The children will benefit from hearing positive things about their work.

9. After the festival, send artwork home with the parents.

More to do

Snack: Cube Stackers—Stir 1½ cups (360 ml) boiling apple juice into one package of gelatin. Stir until gelatin is completely dissolved. Spray an 8" (20 cm) square baking pan with non-stick coating or wipe it with cooking oil. Pour the gelatin into the pan. Refrigerate at least three hours (or overnight). Cut the gelatin into cubes and put them on a plate. Serve them with a bowl of fruit (such as berries, bananas, apples slices), and you have the ingredients for constructing interesting sculptures and freeform art before eating them. Make several colors of cubes to enhance the fun! (Depending on your class size, you may need to double or triple this recipe.)

More Snack: Fun Color Parfait—Prepare gelatin according to the package directions (make two contrasting colors). Pour each color into separate 9" x 9" (22 cm x 22 cm) pans and refrigerate at least four hours (or overnight). Cut each pan of gelatin into ½" (1 cm) cubes. Layer alternating flavors and whipped topping in dessert glasses to create a Fun Color Parfait. (Serves 8.)

Related books

1 to 10 and Back Again: A Getty Museum Counting Book
100 Artists Who Shaped World History by Barbara Krystal
Alligator Ice Cream by Cherene Raphael
Andy's Wild Animal Adventure by Gerda Marie Scheidl
April Wilson's Magpie Magic by April Wilson
The Boy Who Loved to Draw by Barbara Brenner
Drawing Lessons from a Bear by David McPhail

❦ Virginia Jean Herrod, Columbia, SC

First Day of School Castle

Materials

Blocks
Laundry basket
Camera
Film

What to do

1. On the first day of school before the children arrive, start building a castle with blocks.
2. Place the remaining blocks in a small laundry basket next to the castle you have started.
3. As each child arrives, ask her to grab a handful of blocks from the basket and add them to the structure.
4. After every child has arrived and added blocks to the Welcome to School Castle, ask them to stand in front of it. Use the camera to snap a memorable picture!

❖ Lisa M. Chichester, Parkersburg, WV

Blocks

Materials

Blocks
Block props and accessories

What to do

1. It is fun to add different props to the Block Center once in awhile. It encourages the children to use their imagination and extends their creative play.
2. Add a box of puppets but don't tell the children what to do with them. Children will often make stages, caves, beds, or houses for the puppets. This encourages a lot of social interaction and language experiences among the children.
3. Other things you can add to the Block Center are several small blankets or

one large sheet or blanket, a basket of play food, dress-up clothes, plastic animals, or cars and trucks. Rotating materials in and out of different centers allows children to stretch their imagination.

More to do

Change the toys and props at the sand and water tables, too. Or instead of always having cookie cutters at the playdough table, add pegs, scissors, craft stickers, or small plastic animals.

✤ Audrey F. Kanoff, Allentown, PA

Milk Carton Blocks

Materials

½ pint (240 ml) milk cartons
Packaging tape
Contact paper

What to do

1. Save small milk cartons.
2. Rinse them out well and allow them to dry overnight.
3. Fold over the top of the milk carton and secure it with packaging tape to form a "block."
4. Cover them with different colors of contact paper to make inexpensive, colorful building blocks.

Note: Milk carton blocks are very light and are, therefore, safe.

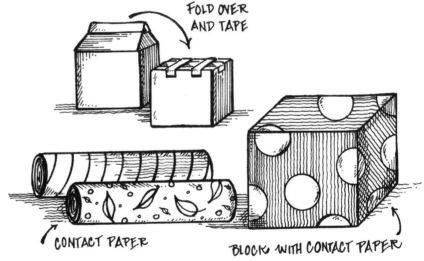

FOLD OVER AND TAPE

CONTACT PAPER

BLOCK WITH CONTACT PAPER

✤ Charlene Woodham Peace, Semmes, AL

Structures

Materials

Blocks
Camera
Film

What to do

1. Encourage the children to build block structures in the Block Center.
2. Take a picture of each child with her own structure.
3. Attach the pictures to a wall or bulletin board in the Block Center.
4. Encourage parents to look at the photographs on Back to School night.

Related book

Click! A Book about Cameras and Taking Pictures by Gail Gibbons

❖ Elizabeth Thomas, Hobart, IN

Block Center Hall of Fame

Materials

Blocks
Camera and film
Paper and pen
Glue or tape
Construction paper
Marker

What to do

1. When the children (alone or in groups) are in the Block Center making buildings, take a picture of them and ask them to describe their creations.
2. Write down who is in the picture and their exact descriptions.
3. When the pictures are developed, tape or glue the photo on a piece of construction paper. Write the child's name and her description of her creation underneath the picture.

4. Hang the pictures in the Block Center under the heading "Block Center Hall of Fame." This is a great way to encourage language development because the children can see how their spoken words are written. Children love to see their pictures hanging in the classroom, too.

More to do

At the end of the year, give the pictures to the children to bring home. Parents love to see pictures of their children, especially when they are creative and humorous.

❧ Gail Morris, Kemah, TX

Follow the Velcro Road

Materials

Construction paper
Markers or tempera paint and brushes
Laminate or clear contact paper
Glue or tape
Craft sticks
Clay
Sewable Velcro strips
Toy vehicle set
Small people set

What to do

1. With the children, make road signs using construction paper and markers or tempera paint.
2. Laminate the signs or cover them with clear contact paper for durability.
3. Glue or tape the signs to craft sticks.
4. Help the children roll clay into several balls with flattened bottoms. Then, place the bottoms of the craft sticks into the clay balls.
5. Allow the clay to dry, until hardened.
6. Separate the soft Velcro pieces from the rough pieces.
7. Using the rough-sided Velcro, place a strip onto the carpet to form a road. If desired, cut the Velcro to make shorter roads or curves in the road.
8. Place toy cars, people, and signs on the carpet for roadway fun!

More to do

Dramatic Play: Make a bus, train, or airplane using a refrigerator box. Place the box on its side. Using a knife, cut out several windows along the sides of the box and a driver's windshield in front. Cut out the bottom of the box for exit and entrance purposes. If desired, ask the children to paint the box. Place chairs inside for children to sit on during their travels.

More Dramatic Play: Create a travel center in the Dramatic Play Area. Put old tickets from previous travels, suitcases, old charge cards, play money, old uniforms (train conductor, pilot, and so on), hats, trays, pretend food, cups, magazines, pillows, and blankets. Display promotional posters of airlines, train stations, and other travel-related destinations or methods of travel.

Field Trips: Take a walk with the children and look at the types of signs along the road. When you return to the classroom, make road signs and display them around the room.

Social Studies: Invite a transportation worker to visit the classroom or take a tour of an airplane, taxi, bus, or train. Take plenty of photos for future reference.

Related books

Flying by Donald Crews
Freight Train by Donald Crews
The Little Engine That Could by Watty Piper
School Bus by Donald Drews
Wheels on the Bus by Paul O. Zelinsky

❖ Tina R. Woehler, Oak Point, TX

Where Do You Live?

Materials

Empty cereal boxes, one for each child
Glue
Tape
Crayons/markers
Black and white construction paper rectangles and squares
Scissors
Brown construction paper

What to do

1. Before beginning this project, open cereal boxes at their seams and turn them inside out, with the plain side facing out. Re-glue the seams and, if necessary, tape the sides. Allow them to dry.

2. Have a discussion with the children about the different types of homes in which people live, such as apartments, houses, trailers, and boats. Explain that they will each make a home that looks like their own home.

3. Give a box to each child.

4. Ask the children what color the outside of their homes are and encourage them to lightly color their box that color. They may choose to color just the front of the box or all four sides.

5. If the child lives in an apartment, she may want to decorate it vertically. If she lives in a house, she may want to decorate it horizontally. If she lives in a trailer, she can add wheels to it.

6. Children may choose to draw windows and doors or glue cutout rectangles and squares on the box. Encourage the children to draw other additions on the house, too.

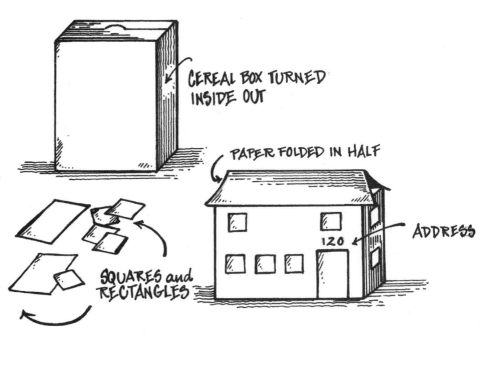

CEREAL BOX TURNED INSIDE OUT

PAPER FOLDED IN HALF

ADDRESS

SQUARES and RECTANGLES

120

7. Fold a piece of brown construction paper in half vertically to form a roof. Cut it, if necessary, and help the child glue it in place.

8. Help children write the numbers of their address over their front doors.

Related book

A House Is a House for Me by Mary Ann Hoberman

♣ Constance Heagerty, Westborough, MA

Our Town in the Block Area

Materials

Camera and film, or existing pictures of your town
Clear contact paper, tape, or glue
Blocks

What to do

1. Take photos of various buildings, structures, or landmarks in your town, depending on your focus. For example, take pictures of a hospital, grocery store, bank, post office, police station, famous statues, and fountains. If desired, use existing pictures of your town.
2. Using clear contact paper, attach the photos to standard 3" x 4" (7 cm x 10 cm) wooden building blocks. (Tape or glue also works, but contact paper protects the photos better.) This is a great way to make use of old blocks.
3. Put the blocks in the Block Area so children can use them to make a town. Encourage them to construct roads and drive cars around the "buildings."

More to do

More Blocks: Create clay people and workers to use with the blocks.
Home Connection: Ask parents to provide a photo of their house. Make a block for each child's house. If you run out of blocks, use small boxes or small milk cartons. Practice the names of roads and addresses with each child.
Social Studies: Visit or videotape the town and the insides of some buildings to show the children what happens in their town each day.

Related books

Curious George Goes to the Hospital by Margaret Rey
Mommies at Work by Eve Merriam

Song

"We All Live Together" by Greg & Steve

❖ Shirley Salach, Northwood, NH

Building a Community

Materials

Blocks in various shapes, sizes, and materials
Vehicles
Stand-up fingers
Art supplies (such as scissors, Popsicle sticks, tape, paper, markers, pencils, dough
to help the Popsicle sticks stand up)
Polaroid camera and film

What to do

1. When the children are learning about their neighborhood and community, make a neighborhood community in the Block Corner. As a group, decide what your community will have and what buildings to include.
2. Make a list of the things the community will have. Help the children decide who will be in charge of building different parts of the community.
3. Post the list in the Block Corner.
4. This project will continue throughout the week. If the classroom is too small to leave the project intact, take a picture of each day's accomplishments before the children take them apart and put them away.

More to do

Encourage children to draw simple maps of their community.

Related book

Me on the Map by Joan Sweeny

❖ Ann Gudowski, Johnstown, PA

Blueprints for Block Area

Materials

Blocks
White paper
Marker
Building blueprint (optional)

What to do

1. Trace blocks onto white paper to create a pattern for children to duplicate.
2. Encourage the children to begin duplicating the block structure on TOP of the paper, then duplicate it NEXT TO or IN FRONT OF the paper.
3. After the children have practiced copying the block patterns, explain to them that real builders have to follow blueprints. Emphasize the complicated features of a real blueprint that only plumbers, electricians, carpenters, and other workers understand. If desired, show them a real building blueprint.
4. Trace blocks to make your own blueprint of a structure that the children will build. Hang it in the Block Area and challenge children to construct a building by following the block blueprint.
5. If children master this challenge, make blueprints that are smaller than actual size to increase the difficulty level.
6. Challenge them to create their own blueprints for peers to build.

More to do

Math: Photocopy various classroom materials. Encourage children to duplicate the photocopied sheet by arranging the actual materials on a blank sheet of paper.

More Math: Add parquetry designs and blocks to the Block Center.

Related books

Beaver the Carpenter by Lars Klinting
Building a House by Byron Barton
Housebuilding for Children by Les Walker
My Apron: A Story from My Childhood by Eric Carle

 Shirley R. Salach, Northwood, NH

Maps

Materials

Real maps that have been laminated
Tape
Toy cars and traffic signs
Blocks
Globe

Various classroom maps, such as fire exit or nap map
Pencils
Paper
Cardboard boxes
Scissors
Toy construction vehicles
Construction hats, optional

What to do

1. Before children arrive, tape a laminated map to the floor in the Block Center. When the children ask what it is, explain that it is a map that tells you where to go in a city. Point out all the different things on the map.

2. Encourage the children to play with the map by placing blocks, toy cars and traffic signs on it.

3. At Circle Time, show the children a globe and other maps, such as the fire exit map and the nap map that the substitute uses. Explain that maps provide directions so that people can find things.

4. With the children, make a map of the classroom.

5. Put paper and pencils in the Block Center and encourage children to make signs and draw maps after they build a block city.

6. The next day, help the children cut out the corners of boxes to make mountains. Help them make rivers or lakes using construction paper.

7. On another day, add toy construction vehicles because roads are often under construction. If desired, put construction hats in the center for them to wear.

More to do

Bury "treasure" outside on the playground. Make a treasure map of the playground and encourage the children to use it to find the buried treasure.

✤ Holly Dzierzanowski, Austin, TX

The Book House

Materials

Scissors
Large cardboard box
Paint and markers
Cloth scraps
Pillows, rug, or stuffed toys

What to do

1. Cut out a door and windows from a large cardboard box.
2. Encourage the children to decorate the Book House using paint and markers. For example, they can draw flowers, grass, and shrubs near the bottom of the house. They can also draw shutters around the windows.
3. Use cloth scraps to make curtains for the windows.
4. Ask the children to help fill the house with pillows, an old rug, or stuffed toys.
5. Make the rule: "No one enters the Book House unless they are going to look at books." Place the house near the book corner and watch the children flock to it to read!

❧ Lisa M. Chichester, Parkersburg, WV

Book Club

Materials

Carpet squares
Books

What to do

1. This activity is intended to promote reading and sharing books at home with parents and then sharing the books with the class.
2. Send home a sheet like the one on the next page so parents can list the books they read to their children.
3. Set aside time once a week to have a Book Club.
4. Each week, ask the children to bring in a book from home with a certain theme.

5. Before the Book Club meets, place carpet squares on the floor for the children to sit on.
6. When children arrive on the designated day, divide them into pairs to read or look at their books with a "book buddy."
7. Plan an art project and a snack that relates to the theme.
8. At the end of each Book Club, read one of the books to the children. Discuss the theme as well as the author and illustrator.

Book_____ Author_____

Book_____ Author_____

Book_____ Author_____

Book_____ Author_____

Book_____ Author_____

❧ Lisa M. Chichester, Parkersburg, WV

Book Worm

Materials

Scissors
Construction paper
Markers
Tape
Variety of age-appropriate books

What to do

1. In advance, cut out 25 circles, about 3" (7 cm) in diameter, from construction paper. (You will probably need more as the book worm grows!)
2. Draw a face on one of the circles and tape it to a wall in the classroom. Explain that each time you or a helper reads a book to one or more children in the class, the worm will grow another segment (circle) to its "body."
3. Each time you or a helper reads a book to the children, write the title of the

book on a circle and add it to the end of the worm.

4. If desired, color-code the circles to show whether you read a book to the whole class or to an individual. For example, write the titles of all the books you read during Circle Time on green circles. Assign other colors to each child and add a circle of that color when you or a helper reads a book to him during Center Time.

5. Continue to watch the bookworm grow over a period of several weeks. It will begin to creep all around the room! The children will be amazed to see how many books they have read.

More to do

Home Connection: Encourage parents to start their own Book Worm at home with their child. If desired, send home some pre-cut circles to motivate them to read to their children.

Math: Count the circles on the Book Worm each day. For example, how many more circles are there than yesterday? How many more circles do we need to reach 20? Are there more blue circles or more circles of other colors? (Be careful not to compare one child to another.)

❧ Suzanne Pearson, Winchester, VA

Books in Bloom

Materials

Old book jackets
Scissors
Construction paper
Markers and other art materials
Laminate or clear contact paper
Glue or tape
2 or 3 dowel rods, in various lengths between 36" to 48" (90 cm to 120 cm)
Contact cement
Large flowerpot

What to do

1. Cut out two to three flowers, approximately 14" to 16" (35 cm to 40 cm) in diameter, from old book jackets.
2. With the children, use construction paper, markers, and other art materials to decorate the flowers.
3. Laminate the flowers or cover them with clear contact paper.
4. Glue or tape each flower to a dowel rod.
5. Using contact cement, attach the dowels at varying heights to the back of a large flowerpot.
6. Fill the pot with a variety of good books to make a "book choice" center.
7. On the front of the pot write, "Books in Bloom."

Related books

Mouse TV by Matt Novak
Planting a Rainbow by Lois Ehlert

❧ Charlene Woodham Peace, Semmes, AL

Crown Your Door With Books

Materials

Yardstick
Newspaper
Pencil
Scissors
Tape
Poster board
Washable colored markers

What to do

1. Use a yardstick to measure across the top of the outside hall door and about a foot down either side.
2. Write down the measurements. Use double sheets of old newspaper to make a pattern to create a "door crown." This crown will go from the left side of the door's frame, across the top, and down the right side. (Think of it as a hood for the door.)
3. The exact size of the crown will depend on the area available around the door's sides and top. Adjust the newspaper pattern until it fits perfectly around the door. Tape the pattern together.
4. Using the pattern, cut out a crown from poster board. If desired, make extra crowns and save them for future use, or keep the newspaper pattern.
5. Ask the children to remember some of their favorite book characters. To refresh their memories, show them numerous books you've read together.
6. Encourage each child to draw a different book character on the door crown using washable colored markers.
7. Write each character's name and the classroom artist's name beneath the drawing.
8. Books are truly the crowning glory to your room. What a great way to show others that your class loves books!

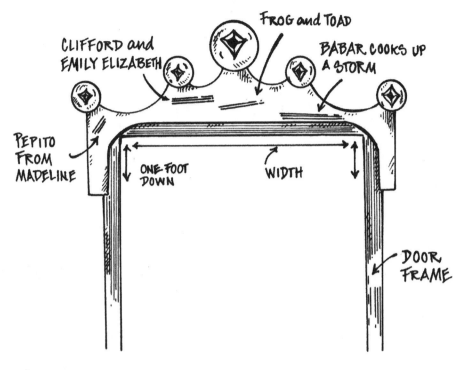

More to do

Dedicate a door crown to a particular author or holiday and add characters accordingly.

❀ Nancy Dentler, Mobile, AL

Door Decor

Materials

Scissors
White drawing paper
Construction paper
Glue
Crayons

What to do

1. Tell the children that the people and animals in books are called characters. Book characters are our friends because we enjoy reading stories! Explain that when we have family and friends who we love, we often enjoy looking at pictures of them.

2. Explain to the children that they will make pictures of their story friends to decorate the outside of the classroom door.
3. Cut white drawing paper into 4″ (10 cm) squares and construction paper into 5″ (12 cm) squares.
4. Help each child glue a square of drawing paper on top of a square of construction paper. The larger construction paper square forms a "frame."
5. Brainstorm a list of favorite book characters. You may want to prepare a list ahead of time to prompt children if they need more suggestions. (Make sure to write down many more characters than there are children in the class.)
6. Ask each child to select a book character and draw it on a paper square. If possible, have sample books available so children can look at their characters before or as they are drawing. Encourage them to draw the character anyway they choose, and tell them it is wonderful to be creative and original.
7. Help the artists sign their pictures. Add the character's name and the book title(s) in which the character appears.
8. Display the characters on the outside of the classroom door or on a bulletin board with the caption: "Book Characters We Love!"

❧ Nancy Dentler, Mobile, AL

Reading Button Hugger

Materials

White paper
Pencil
Fine-tip black marker
Crayons
Scissors
Tape

What to do

1. Draw a circle about the size of your palm on a piece of paper. Add a rounded tab at the top of the circle about the size of your index finger from the first knuckle up.
2. Trace over the circle and tab with a black marker. Inside the circle (at the top) write, "Today we read" and leave the bottom two thirds of the circle blank.
3. Draw an "X" near the top of the tab.

child's name. Make a journal for yourself, too!

6. After you read and discuss a new book with the children, give each of them his Book Lover's Journal.

7. Tell them that a journal is a book we make by drawing and writing our own thoughts. Explain that they will have their own journals to write and draw their thoughts about the books they read.

8. Show the children your journal and your response to the book you just read to the class. For example, make a simple drawing and add a sentence or two about the book.

9. Encourage the children to draw and write their responses. Add words or sentences that they dictate to you.

10. Date each journal entry to show growth over time. This is wonderful to show to families at Open House!

❧ Nancy Dentler, Mobil, AL

Character Cup

Materials

Clear, plastic beverage cups
White paper
Scissors
Crayons
Fine-tipped black marker

What to do

1. Ask the children what they like to drink when they are thirsty. Tell them some of the beverages you like to drink.

2. Explain to the children that they are going to use their imaginations. Ask each child to think of a favorite book character and invent a drink that the character would enjoy. Some examples might be carrot juice for Peter Rabbit, a cup of milk for the Three Little Kittens, and a vanilla milkshake with honey for Pooh Bear.

3. Cut white paper into strips that fit inside the cups to simulate beverages.

4. Give each child a cup and paper insert.

5. Encourage the children to color their insert the appropriate color: orange for carrot juice, yellow for apple juice, and so on.

6. Then, ask each child to dictate a sentence about the beverage as you write it on the insert. For example, "Pooh Bear would like a vanilla milkshake with honey," or "Peter Rabbit would love sweet carrot juice!"
7. Write the child's name on the bottom of the cup using a black marker.
8. Display the character cups next to the books with the same characters.

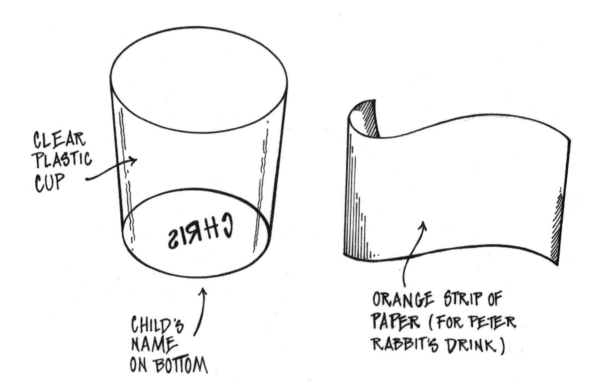

CLEAR PLASTIC CUP

CHILD'S NAME ON BOTTOM

ORANGE STRIP OF PAPER (FOR PETER RABBIT'S DRINK)

❧ Nancy Dentler, Mobile, AL

Make a Book

Materials

White paper, any size
Hole punch
Tape
Yarn

What to do

1. Stack four pieces of white paper together.
2. Fold the stack of paper in half.
3. Punch holes ¼" (6 m) apart along the fold.
4. Wrap a piece of tape around one end of a piece of yarn. (This will act like a needle).
5. Help the children "sew" through the holes from top to bottom.
6. Encourage the children to draw in their books.

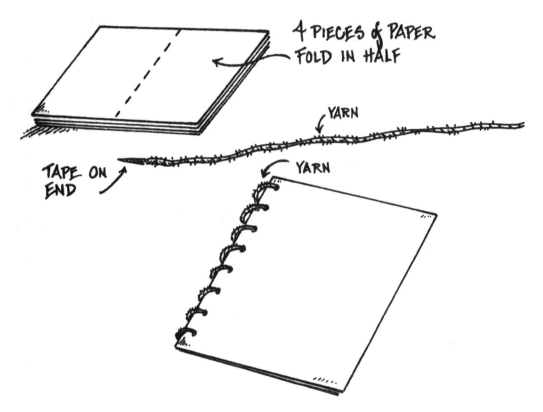

Song

As the children sew, sing:
Go in and out the window
Go in and out the window,
Go in and out the window,
As we have done before.

Susan Rubinoff, Wakefield, RI

Field Trip Book

Materials

Camera and film
Glue
Poster board, cut to book size
Markers
Laminate or clear contact paper
Hole punch
Metal rings or yarn

What to do

1. Bring a camera on your next field trip and take pictures of the children.
2. Glue the photos onto pages of poster board. Ask the children to dictate simple captions and write them under the pictures.
3. Laminate the pages or cover them with clear contact paper.
4. Punch holes along the sides of the pages and attach them together using yarn or metal rings.
5. Place the books on a shelf or let each child take the book home to share with his family.

❖ Cindy Winther, Oxford, MI

I Can Write My Own Book

Materials

Old magazines
Scissors
Typewriter, optional
White paper
Markers
Glue
Construction paper or cardboard
Hole punch and yarn or stapler

What to do

1. Cut out pictures from old magazines, such as children playing, animals, and outdoor scenes.
2. Ask each child to choose a magazine picture. Then, ask him to dictate a short story about the picture he has chosen.
3. After you write or type the child's story, read it back to him to make sure it is accurate.
4. Encourage the children to draw a picture of their short story using paper and markers.
5. Fold a piece of construction paper or cardboard in half to make a book cover. Help the children glue their pictures on the front of their book covers.
6. Ask the children to place their story inside the book cover. Staple it together, or punch holes along the side and tie it together with yarn.

❦ Lisa M. Chichester, Parkersburg, WV

A Book of My Own

Materials

Colored construction paper
Scissors
File folders, one for each child
Camera and film
Old magazines and catalogues
Glue
Markers, crayons, or paint
Clear contact paper
Hole punch
Metal rings or yarn

What to do

1. This activity will take a period of time to complete.
2. Ask each child to choose four pieces of colored construction paper.
3. Cut the paper into 8" (20 cm) squares and place them in the child's folder.
4. Have fun taking pictures of the children. Take pictures of each child at different times during the day, including outside play. If possible, get double prints. Place photos in the appropriate child's folder for later use.

5. At a later time, go through the photos in the folders and cut out the particular child with a friend or two. Discard the background. You may be able to cut out more than one pair of children from a photo. Place the photos back in the appropriate files.

6. Give the children magazines and catalogues and help them cut out pictures of favorite toys, animals, things they would like to learn more about, and any other pictures that they like. Place them in each child's folder for later use.

7. When it is time for children to create their own books, give them their paper squares.

8. On three of the squares, number the pages one to five, using both sides of the paper.

9. Next, give each child his magazine pictures. Encourage the children to glue the pictures onto the pages. For example, they can glue pictures of their favorite toys on page one, favorite animals on page two, things they want to learn about on page three, and their favorite things on pages four and five.

10. Encourage the children to dictate a sentence or two about each page in their book. Write it under the pictures.

11. Invite the children to make a clever cover using the fourth square of construction paper. (Sponge painting might be fun.)

12. When each child is finished decorating his cover, glue a close-up photo of the child on it. Title the book using the child's name (for example, "Susan's Book").

13. Cover all the pages with contact paper and trim to fit.

14. Punch holes along the side of the book and fasten with rings or yarn.

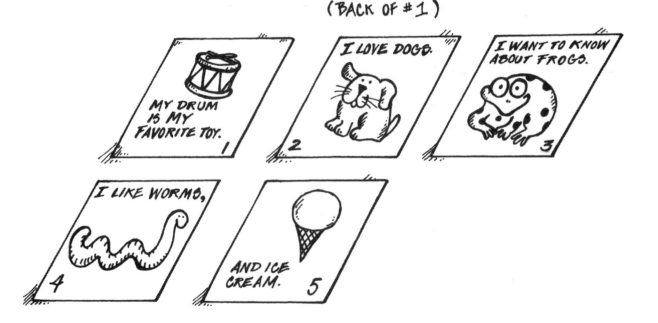

More to do

Invite them to "read" their books to you and to their parents. Explain to them that they made a book just like the ones you read to them!

❖ Barbara Fischer, San Carlos, CA

Food Riddle Book

Materials

Envelopes
3" x 5" (7 cm x 12 cm) index cards
Crayons, markers, or colored pencils
Laminate or clear contact paper
Hole punch
Metal rings

What to do

1. (This is one of my favorite activities I do with my class.) For one month, discuss "Food" as a theme.
2. At the end of the month, discuss what a riddle is and do a few together. Encourage the children to make up their own food riddles.
3. Ask the children to pick a food and state three things that describe it without telling what it is.
4. On an envelope approximately 6" x 4" (15 cm x 10 cm), write the child's riddle at the top. For example, the envelope would look like this:

My Food Riddle

I am juicy.
I am red.
I have skin on me.
What am I?

By_____(child writes his own name)

5. Ask the child to draw a picture of his food on a plain index card. Write "I am a(n) (name the food)" and place it inside the envelope.
6. Laminate the envelopes or cover them with clear contact paper.

7. Punch a hole in a corner of the envelope and attach a metal ring through it. Combine the class riddle envelopes to make a food riddle book.

8. Read the book to the class. The children will have a great time guessing the food riddles.

9. Encourage the children to take turns taking the book home to share with their families.

❧ Debbie Barbuch, Sheboygan, WI

Books, Books, and More Books

Materials

Tape player
Tapes
Books
Zipper closure plastic bag or stickers

What to do

1. One of the best ways to introduce children to books and reading is to play stories on tape.

2. Instead of spending a lot of money and worrying about whether the tapes get damaged, make your own tapes. Or, send home a blank tape and a book so parents can make tapes. The children will love hearing their favorite stories read by you or their parents. Homemade tapes are a fast and inexpensive way to create a whole reading library!

3. To make sure the tape and book stay together, put the tape in a zipper closure bag and staple the bag to the book.

4. Or, put matching stickers on the book and its corresponding tape. If the tape and book get separated, the children can easily match them.

❧ Sandra Hutchins Lucas, Cox's Creek, KY

If I Could Be the Teacher

Materials

Tape recorder and blank tapes
White paper
Markers
Laminating paper or clear contact paper
Black marker
Hole punch
Yarn or brads

What to do

1. Tell the children that they are going to write a story called "If I Could Be the Teacher."
2. Ask each child the question separately and use a tape recorder to record what he says.
3. Write the child's story on a piece of white paper.
4. Give the child his story and ask him to illustrate it.
5. After the children have finished, laminate the pages or cover them with contact paper.
6. Make a cover and on the front write, "If I Could Be the Teacher." Put all of the pages inside the cover, punch holes along the side, and use yarn or brads to attach it together.
7. Read the book to the class.
8. Put the tape into the Listening Center and the book in the Book Center. The children will enjoy reading it all year.

More to do

Make a book for Mother's Day or Father's Day. Change the title to: "If I Was the Mother" or "If I Was the Father."
Dramatic Play: Set up a "school" in the Dramatic Play Center and encourage the children to pretend to be the teacher. The dolls and stuffed animals can be children.

❧ Holly Dzierzanowski, Austin, TX

Gingerbread House

Materials

"Hansel and Gretel" sticker book, optional
Felt
Glue
Pictures of candy canes, gumdrops, and other candy
Flannel board

What to do

1. Purchase a "Hansel and Gretel" sticker book that has a gingerbread house ready to decorate or make a house using felt.
2. Glue felt to the backs of the pictures of candy and to the gingerbread house (unless it is already made of felt).
3. Place the felt gingerbread house and felt-backed candy pieces in the Book Center. Encourage the children to construct their own gingerbread house on the flannel board.

More to do

Read the story "Hansel and Gretel" to the children.

Related book

The Cookie House by Margaret Hillert

❧ Jackie Wright, Enid, OK

Our Space Diary

Materials

White construction paper, one piece for each child
Crayons or markers
Three hole punch
Three ring binder

What to do

1. Read the books listed below or other books about space travel with the children. Have a discussion about what they might see if they were in a space ship in outer space.
2. Give each child a piece of white construction paper. Encourage the children to use markers or crayons to draw what they think they would see from their space ship windows.
3. Ask each child to dictate what he "sees" and write it at the bottom of the page for him.
4. Punch holes into all of the drawings and put them into a binder.
5. The children can look at the book as often as desired and talk about what they can see in outer space.

Related books

I Want to Be an Astronaut by Byron Barton
Papa, Please Get the Moon for Me by Eric Carle
Twinkle, Twinkle, Little Star by Iza Trapani
Zoom Zoom Zoom I'm Off to the Moon by Dan Yaccarino

♣ Diane Weiss, Fairfax, VA

The Mitten Story Puppets

Materials

The Mitten by Alvin Tresselt
Paper plates
Markers or crayons
Collage wool, pompoms, googly eyes, and other collage materials
Glue
Large craft sticks

What to do

1. Read the story *The Mitten* by Alvin Tresselt to the children, preferably more than one time.
2. In the Art Center, give the children paper plates to use to create animals from the mitten story. Encourage the children to draw faces and/or use collage materials to create their own versions of the animals.
3. The children can glue large craft sticks to the plates to make stick puppets.

More to do

Encourage the children to use their puppets to act out the story. Use a sheet or blanket as a mitten.

✤ Deborah Hannes Litfin, Forest Hills, NY

Where Is the Gingerbread Boy?

Materials

Gingerbread cake mix
Ingredients to add to cake mix (see back of cake mix box)
Large bowl
Mixing spoon
Gingerbread Boy spring form pan
Oven

What to do

1. Pour the gingerbread cake mix in a large bowl. Mix in all the necessary ingredients. Make sure that each child gets a turn to stir.
2. Pour the batter into a Gingerbread Boy spring form pan.
3. Place the pan into an oven and bake it according to the directions on the box (adult only).
4. When the cake is done, ask the children to gather around the oven. Take the cake from the oven and run away with it (adult only). The children will follow you shortly after.
5. Hide the gingerbread boy cake somewhere in the classroom. As soon as a child finds it, it is snack time!

Related book

The Gingerbread Boy by Kathy Wilburn

✤ Ingelore Mix, Gainesville, VA

Play Bat

Materials

Stellaluna by Janelle Cannon

What to do

1. Read *Stellaluna*.
2. Have the children tell you things that the bats did in the story. (Flying at night, eating fruit, hang upside down, etc.)
3. Write their answers on the board and if possible draw a simple picture so they can "read" the picture.
4. Create hand and body motions for each suggestion they give you and then sing the following song using those motions.

Related book

Bat Jamboree by Kathi Appelt

Song

Did You Ever See a Fruit Bat? (Tune: "Did You Ever See a Lassie?")
Did you ever see a fruit bat, a fruit bat, a fruit bat,
Did you ever see a fruit bat...sleep in a cave?
(Put two hands together and lay head down on them)
Did you ever see a fruit bat... eating some fruit
(pretend that you are biting an apple)
Did you ever see a fruit bat... flying at night
(flap your arms like you are flying)

🍀 Vicki Whitehead, Fort Worth, TX

Sunflower House

Materials

Sunflower House by Eve Bunting
Large appliance box
Craft knife (adult only)

Yellow and green paint
Glue or tape
Large paintbrushes
Construction paper or green tissue, optional
Blue paper
White cotton or batting
Pictures of sunflowers

What to do

1. Read the book *Sunflower House* to the children.
2. Cut a door into a large appliance box using a craft knife (adult only). Cut out circles to make windows.
3. Encourage the children to paint the house with yellow and green paint. (It looks best if you paint the top section yellow and the lower section green.)
4. If desired, cut out petals, stems, and leaves from construction paper or green tissue paper and glue them around the windows.
5. Help the children glue or tape white cotton or batting onto blue paper.
6. Take the top off the box and tape the blue paper over the opening so that when the children look up, they see the "sky."
7. Children can decorate the outside and inside of the box with pictures of sunflowers.

More to do

Art: This is a good project for painting with feather dusters.
Science: Bring in sunflowers for the children to look at and touch. Grow sunflowers.
Snack: Serve real sunflower seeds, and possibly other seeds, such as baked pumpkin seeds.

Related books

Missing Sunflowers by Maggie Stern
Sunflower by Miela Ford
The Sunflower by Marliese Dieckmann

Song

"You Are My Sunshine"

♣ Sandra Nagel, White Lake, MI

Book Character's Shopping List

Materials

Several books about one character, such as *Arthur, Clifford,* or *Madeline*
Large white paper or poster board
Thin, black marker
Colored pencils or washable markers

What to do

1. Read several books featuring the same character to the children.

2. Show the children a copy of your weekly shopping list. Read a few of the items on the list, including both food and non-food items. Explain why people make shopping lists. Ask them if their families use a shopping list, and ask them to name some items that might be on a shopping list.

3. Explain that they are going to use their imaginations to create a shopping list for the book character.

4. On the top of a piece of large paper or poster board write, "Shopping List for _____" and fill in the character's name.

5. As a group, brainstorm items that might be on that character's shopping list. Write the items on the paper, leaving plenty of room between each item. For example, items on a list for the caterpillar in *The Very Hungry Caterpillar* by Eric Carle might be sunglasses, an apple, two pears, three plums, four strawberries, five oranges, chocolate cake, an ice cream cone, a pickle, Swiss cheese, salami, a lollipop, cherry pie, a sausage, a cupcake, watermelon, green leaves, and some flowers.

6. Encourage the children to draw pictures next to the items listed on the chart. Display the chart next to the character's books.

❖ Nancy Dentler, Mobile, AL

Guessing Our Book Guest

Materials

Bag or box
Index cards
Index card file box
Laminate or clear contact paper

What to do

1. Select a second book in a series that you have already read to the children. For example, if they are familiar with *Clifford, the Big Red Dog* by Norman Bridwell, select a new book in that series.

2. Put the new book into a bag or box. Explain to the children that there is a surprise book inside of it.

3. Give the children clues or hints about the book. Encourage them to guess the identity of the book or main character after they hear the clues. For example:
   - Clue #1: This book is about an animal.
   - Clue #2: This book is about a dog.
   - Clue #3: Norman Bridwell wrote this book.
   - Clue #4: This dog's best friend is Emily Elizabeth.
   - Clue #5: This dog is not small.
   - Clue #6: This dog is red.
   - Answer: This dog is Clifford the Big Red Dog.

4. After the children guess the identity of the character, read and discuss the new book.

5. Over time, prepare a collection of Guess Our Book Guest cards and book sets. Write the clues on an index card, laminate them, and store them in an index card file box. You'll always be ready for an imaginative story time with favorite book guests.

More to do

Decorate a gift bag or box to reflect the season of the year or to provide a hint about the book's character. It's fun to use different gift boxes and bags to keep the children's interest high.

Nancy Dentler, Mobile, AL

Mirror, Mirror, Who Do I See?

Materials

Hand-held mirror (preferably unbreakable)
Pictures of favorite book characters that you've read about in class
Tape

What to do

1. Explain to the class that when someone looks in a mirror, he can see what he looks like on the outside. Tell them that this is a *reflection*.
2. Show each child his reflection in the mirror, and let him see your reflection.
3. Explain that the class has many favorite characters from the books you've read together. Tape a picture of one of these characters on the mirror without showing it to the children.
4. Encourage the children to guess the character's identity by asking questions about the character.
5. The first time you do this activity, model some questions the children might ask. For example, is this character a person, an animal, or a thing? Is it a boy, a girl, a man, or a woman? What color hair does it have? Is it tall or short? What does it like to do?
6. If the children are stumped, give them some guided suggestions.
7. When they guess the character (or if they are unable to figure it out), turn the mirror around and show them the picture of the book character.
8. This activity is a great way to encourage children to think about descriptions of book characters and to remember favorite friends from books. Be sure to have a number of pictures of book characters available because the children will want to participate in this activity frequently!

❖ Nancy Dentler, Mobile, AL

My Favorite Illustration Bookmarks

Materials

Children's books
Scissors
Colored paper
Thin black marker
Colored pencils
Laminate or clear contact paper

What to do

1. Select one of your favorite children's books that you have previously read to them. Explain that pictures in books are also called *illustrations*. Mark some of your favorite pictures with a bookmark and show them to the children.
2. Tell the children what bookmarks are—they mark a place in a book. Explain that they can use bookmarks to mark where their favorite illustrations are in a book.
3. Cut out bookmarks from construction paper and write "My Favorite Illustrations" near the top with a black marker.
4. Give each child a bookmark and encourage him to decorate it. They can draw favorite book characters, or any other picture that is meaningful to them.
5. On the back of each bookmark, write the child's name.
6. Laminate the bookmark or cover it with clear contact paper for durability.
7. Model and practice using the "favorite illustration" bookmarks in class. As a class, share your favorite pictures in books using the bookmarks.
8. Explain to the parents (in person or in your class newsletter) how children can use the "favorite illustration" bookmark. Encourage them to read together at home using this new tool!

❧ Nancy Dentler, Mobile, AL

Super Sock Day

Materials

Teacher's socks, purchased or decorated to relate to a book
White paper
Pencil
Thin black marker
Scissors
Colored pencils or washable markers

What to do

1. Buy socks related to a book's theme. If you can't purchase them, make your own illustrated socks using plain white socks and fabric paints.

2. Draw a large sock outline on a piece of white paper. Outline the shape using a thin black marker. Along the base write, "A sock for _____." Photocopy this template so you have enough to give one sock shape to each child.

3. Wear your theme socks on the day you read the related book. Explain how your socks are linked to the book you've read.

4. Encourage the children to use their imaginations to draw picture socks that a certain character might like to wear. For example, if you make socks for a bear, draw pictures of honey, a cave, fish, or the forest. A sock for a dog character might include a bone, leash, water bowl, or a cat to chase! If necessary, show the children an example of a completed character sock.

5. Encourage the children to illustrate their character's sock. Write down the name of each character on the sock.

6. Ask the children to share their character socks with the other children. They can tell the name of their character and why they drew the pictures on the sock. ("I made a sock for

SOCK OUTLINE

A SOCK FOR KEISHA

HALLOWEEN THEME

A SOCK FOR SAM

PET THEME

Harry, the Dirty Dog. I drew a bone because dogs like bones. I drew a leash so Harry could go for a walk.")

7. Display the character socks so everyone can enjoy them!

❖ Nancy Dentler, Mobile, AL

Silly Stuff

Materials

(See books listed in activity)

What to do

1. By the time children are four-and-a-half-years old, they become "Silly Willies." They are developing a sense of humor and seem to enjoy the feeling of laughter. Their laughter can be contagious. Once they begin laughing, it may not matter what is said—everything is funny!

2. They enjoy rhymes, nonsense, and outrageous things. "Silly" books that four-year-olds love include:
   - *Down By the Bay,* a traditional song illustrated by Nadine Bernard Westcott
   - *Get Out of Bed!* and *50 Below Zero* by Robert Munsch

3. Children also enjoy the rhyming and word play of Dr. Seuss.

More to do

Language: Encourage the children to verbalize parts of the story with you. Children pick up on the repetitive parts of stories.

More Language: To extend an activity, ask the children to develop their own story following the pattern of the story they just read. Beware: They may be outrageous and very, very silly!

Music and Movement: Play music to go with the activity.

❖ Sandra Nagel, White Lake, MI

Story Time Snack

Materials

Lunch kit with special book snack inside

What to do

1. Plan a special story-time snack to match some of your favorite books. (Check to see if any of the children have food allergies and plan accordingly.)
2. With the children, brainstorm what kinds of snacks your favorite book characters might enjoy. For example, Pooh Bear would love honey graham crackers; the little boy in *The Carrot Seed* would like slivers of baby carrots and dip; and Madeline would adore a thin slice of French bread and butter. You will think of many delicious story time snacks!
3. Help the children wash their hands before story time.
4. Introduce, read, and discuss a wonderful book.
5. Explain that you will now enjoy a snack that the book's character would love.
6. Happy reading and happy snacking!

❖ Nancy Dentler, Mobile, AL

Catch the Tale: If You Give a Mouse a Cookie

Materials

If You Give a Mouse a Cookie by Laura Joffe Numeroff
Poster board
Colored markers

What to do

1. Show the children the cover of *If You Give a Mouse a Cookie*. Ask them if they can guess what the story is about (a mouse and a cookie).
2. Read the title, author, and illustrator of the book, pointing out each word with your finger.

3. Read the first page of the book. Ask the children to guess what might happen next. After they guess, continue reading the story.
4. Discuss the story when you finish the book.
5. Make a graphic organizer showing the events of the story. Ahead of time, prepare a blank organizer. On a piece of poster board, draw arrows in a circle shape and leave space between them to write events in the story.
6. At the top of the circle draw the boy, the mouse, and a cookie.
7. Fill in the pictures as you interact with your class. For example, draw an arrow pointing down to a glass of milk. Then, draw an arrow pointing down to a straw. Next, draw an arrow pointing down to a napkin.
8. Continue this way through the story, adding arrows and events in a big circle.
9. With these pictures to help them, the children can re-tell the story in their own words.

More to do

Snack: Serve a mouse-size book snack! If children are not allergic, give them a mini chocolate chip cookie (about the size of your thumbnail) and a tiny cup of milk. If desired, make slice and bake chocolate chip cookies, or bake them from scratch if your appetites are not mouse-size!

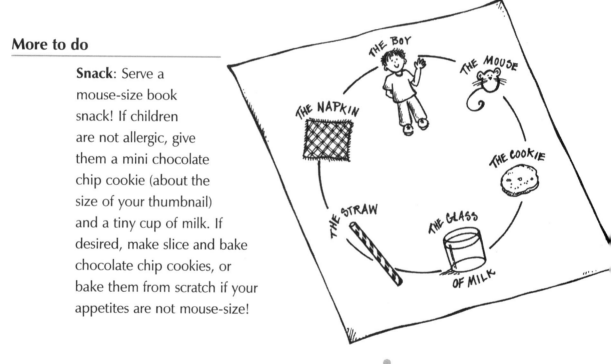

✤ Nancy Dentler, Mobile, AL

Eating Good Books

Materials

Bread machine and ingredients
The Giant Jam Sandwich by John Vernon Lord
Large loaves of French bread
Jam
Butter
Butter knives

What to do

1. With the children, mix together ingredients to make bread and bake it in a bread machine.
2. As the bread is baking, read *The Giant Jam Sandwich* to the children. The aroma of the bread will provide a nice touch as you read.
3. When the bread is done, cut it into individual slices. Serve it at snack time or send the slices home.
4. Cut a thin loaf of French bread lengthwise (adult only). Make a sandwich.
5. Encourage the children to spread jam on one side and butter on the other side. Add golden raisins to represent wasps.

More to do

Music and Movement: Staple together small squares of red (jam), yellow (butter), and tan (bread) paper to make pretend sandwiches. Place them on the floor. Play music and the children can pretend to be bees and "buzz" around the room. When the music stops, the children land on a sandwich and stay there. When the music starts again, they buzz again. Make sure that every child always has a paper sandwich to land on. Or, play it like musical chairs and take away one paper sandwich each time the music stops.

Social Studies: Send an invitation to a neighborhood bakery, asking a baker to come visit the class. Our invitation resulted in a baker (in full outfit), different grains for the children to handle, soft dough to touch, sifted flour to feel, and tiny loaves of bread to smell. The baker spoke with the children and gave each child a full-size loaf of bread to take home to their family. (When I received a confirmation from the baker, I suggested that he bring his business cards to attach to each child's school bag.) Later, help the children write and send thank-you notes.

❧ Diane L. Shatto, Kansas City, MO

Everyone Loves Birthday Presents!

Materials

Birthday Presents by Cynthia Rylant
Poster board
Marker
Crayons
Paper
Scissors
Glue

What to do

1. Ask the children what they remember about one of their birthdays.
2. Tell them that you are going to read them a book called Birthday Presents. In this book, parents describe the day their child was born, and all her birthdays up until she is five years old.
3. Show the children the cover of the book, pointing out the title, author, and illustrator. Before you read the book, ask them if they can tell from the pictures how the girl felt on her birthdays. Was she happy?
4. Read and discuss the book with the children.
5. On a piece of poster board, make a chart with five columns. Label the columns ages one through five. Leave enough room to glue small pictures to the chart.
6. Divide the class into five small groups. Explain that each group will draw small pictures representing gifts appropriate for a certain age. One group will draw presents for one-year-olds, another group for two-year-olds, and so on.
7. Brainstorm with each group some of the presents they might draw.
8. Cut out the pictures and glue them in the appropriate age column.
9. Write the name of the item beside each thing (rattle, ball, book). Title the chart "Birthday Presents."

❦ Nancy Dentler, Mobile, AL

Five Little Ducks

Materials

Five Little Ducks, any version
5 small rubber ducks
1 large rubber duck
1 blue plastic placemat

What to do

1. Read Five Little Ducks to the children.
2. Read the book again, but this time sing the words as you show the pictures.
3. Place rubber ducks on a blue plastic placemat.
4. Ask one child to act out the song using the rubber ducks.
5. Encourage the child to take one duck away each time the song tells him to.
6. Repeat the activity so every child has a chance to act out the song.

Related books

All My Little Ducklings by Monica Wellington
Come Along, Daisy! by Jane Simmons
Daisy and the Egg by Jane Simmons
A Duck So Small by Elisabeth Holstein
Have You Seen My Duckling? by Nancy Tafuri
Just You and Me by Sam McBratney

✤ Quazonia J. Quarles, Newark, DE

Gingerbread Boy

Materials

Books about the Gingerbread Boy
Outline of a gingerbread person
Mirror
Markers in basic colors and skin tones
Glue
Beads or buttons

Scraps of ribbon and yarn
Glitter
Large cookie jar shape

What to do

1. With the children, look at and discuss the "Gingerbread People" in various Gingerbread books.
2. Give each child a gingerbread person outline.
3. Ask each child to look in a mirror and identify his hair color, eye color, and facial parts.
4. Encourage the children to decorate their gingerbread outlines to reflect themselves. Encourage them to color their outlines using markers that match their skin tone, hair, and eyes.
5. They can also glue on beads or buttons to make eyes and yarn to make hair.
6. Encourage the children to decorate the body in their favorite colors. If desired, they can sprinkle glitter on the body too. Some children like to print the initial of their first name on the body.
7. After the gingerbread people are dry, glue them to a large cookie jar shape.
8. Hang the cookie jar on a wall or bulletin board. Encourage the children to compare and contrast their gingerbread people.

More to do

Language: Encourage the children to verbalize what they are doing as they create their gingerbread people. They can also make up stories about their gingerbread person.
Snack: Make gingerbread cookies or sugar cookies in people shapes. Let the children decorate them and share them with each other.

Related books

Gingerbread Baby by Jan Brett
The Gingerbread Boy by Paul Galdone
The Gingerbread Man by Jim Aylesworth

Sandra Nagel, White Lake, MI

Goodnight Moon

Materials

Goodnight Moon by Margaret Wise Brown
Black construction paper
Yellow construction paper
Glue
Silver glitter, optional

What to do

1. Read Goodnight Moon to the children.
2. Tell the children that they are going to make a moon picture.
3. Demonstrate how to tear a large circle from a piece of yellow paper and paste it to a piece of black paper.
4. Help the children make torn-paper moons and glue them to black paper.
5. Encourage the children to use their scraps to make stars and glue them in their night sky.
6. If desired, they can apply glue and glitter to their nighttime scenes.

More to do

Language: Ask the children to take turns telling each other what is in their rooms.

More Language: Read this poem to the children:

I see the moon.
The moon sees me.
The moon sees the one I long to see.
So good for the moon.
And good for me.
And good for the one I long to see.

Related book

Papa, Please Get the Moon for Me by Eric Carle

Barbara Saul, Eureka, CA

Hats Off for Books

Materials

Bag
Assorted hats
Ho for a Hat! by William Smith

What to do

1. Bring in several different hats from your home, such as a baseball cap, hard-hat, party hat, or summer straw hat. Put them into a bag.
2. Before the children arrive, put on one of the hats. Without mentioning what you are doing, change into different hats throughout the day. These hat tricks will grab the children's attention!
3. When you gather the children for story time, ask if they have noticed anything different about you that day. They will undoubtedly point out your varied headgear!
4. Explain that people wear different hats for different reasons. Ask the children to name different hats and why they are worn.
5. Show them the book *Ho for a Hat!* Tell them that this book celebrates the fun of wearing hats! Point out the author and illustrator, and the twenty different hats pictured on the cover.
6. Ask the children to help you read the book out loud. Explain that "Ho for a hat!" means "Hurray for hats!" or "Hats are great!" or "I love hats!" Explain that when you point to this sentence, they should all say "Ho for a hat!" together. Practice several times.
7. Read *Ho for a Hat!* with enthusiasm, remembering to pause to cue your audience for their response.

More to do

Dramatic Play: Place different hats in the dress-up center. The children can pretend to have various careers and cultures as they wear the different hats.
Language: Make a special bulletin board display of the children's artwork. Ask them to draw a picture of their face and top it with a fantastic original hat. Encourage them to dictate a sentence to you explaining what they do in their hats.

❦ Nancy Dentler, Mobile, AL

Let Me Hear You Whistle

Materials

Whistle for Willie by Ezra Jack Keats

What to do

1. Begin story time by whistling for a dog and looking around. Ask the children if they know what you are doing. Can they guess that you are calling a dog?
2. Explain that in the book you will be reading, young Peter wants to learn how to whistle so he can call for his dog Willie.
3. Show the children the cover of the book. Read the title, the author, and the illustrator.
4. Ask the children if they can tell what breed of dog Willie is from the cover illustration (dachshund).
5. Read the book with enthusiasm. Remember to whistle when Peter whistles in the book.

More to do

Gross Motor: With the children, draw your way from the outside school door to the gym, lunchroom, or playground along the sidewalk using colored chalk.

Music: Practice whistling (or trying to whistle) together as a class. Explain that it takes a lot of practice, but that they will all be able to whistle someday.

More Music: Find an adult or two who are skilled whistlers. Have them perform a whistling concert in your class. They could perform well-known songs such as "Twinkle, Twinkle Little Star" and "Mary Had a Little Lamb." Ask the adults to explain how they have used whistling, such as to call a dog, to find a friend in a crowd, or just when they're happy.

Outdoors: Draw an interesting path on a sidewalk or outside walkway the same way Peter did.

❖ Nancy Dentler, Mobile, AL

When I Was Young

Materials

When I Was Young in the Mountains by Cynthia Rylant
Tape recorder and blank tapes
Construction paper
Markers, colored pencils, or crayons
Hole punch
Yarn

What to do

1. Read When I Was Young in the Mountains to the children.
2. Encourage the children to tell stories about when they were younger. Use a tape recorder to capture their thoughts.
3. Give the children construction paper, markers, crayons, and colored pencils and ask them to make an illustration for their own story.
4. Ask the children if they know any stories about when their parents were young. Again, use a tape recorder to capture their thoughts.
5. Recruit parents to tell their own childhood stories. Send a note home to parents explaining about the book you read. Ask them to write a short story about a childhood memory of their own and send it in with their child. Make sure they write their name and the location of their story.
6. Read the stories to the children.
7. Give the children construction paper, colored pencils, markers, and crayons. Encourage them to design an illustration to go with their own parent's story.
8. With the children, design a cover and stack the pages together into a book. Put each child's story on the page preceding his parent's story.
9. Punch holes into one side and thread yarn through to bind the book.
10. Enjoy reading your book!

More to do

Invite the parents to visit the classroom and read the book together with their child.

🍀 Virginia Jean Herrod, Columbia, SC

Little Lumpty's Lesson

Materials

"Humpty Dumpty" rhyme (in an illustrated Mother Goose book)
Large baking pan with sides
Raw egg
Little Lumpty by Miko Imai

What to do

1. Read "Humpty Dumpty" to the children and show them his picture.
2. Discuss the story. Ask the children what kind of creature Humpty Dumpty is. If they guess that he is an egg, ask them what happens to an egg if it falls. Discuss what happens, and proceed with the next step. If they cannot guess what he is, give them a clue.
3. Place a baking pan on the floor. Hold an egg high above the pan.
4. Ask the children to count backwards with you from five to zero. When you get to zero, drop the egg into the pan. Discuss the results. Ask them if there is a way to put the egg back together again.
5. Read *Little Lumpty* to the children.
6. Discuss the story, and ask what lesson Little Lumpty learned.

More to do

Art: Measure across the top edge of your bulletin board to find out its length. Starting at the upper left corner, measure across one third of the length and make a small mark. From the bottom left corner, draw a line up to meet the mark, creating a triangle. Cut out a triangular piece of blue bulletin board paper to fit it into the space. This will be the sky. Cover the remainder of the bulletin board with green paper, for the earth. Measure the edge where the sky meets the earth. Cut a piece of white or red bulletin board paper this length and 6" wide. Decorate this paper to look like a wall. (Adjust these measurements to be in proportion with your board.) Place the wall along the sky/earth line. Provide the children with a variety of papers, scissors, markers and glue sticks. Give the children 3" squares of construction paper and 3" x 4" rectangles of construction paper and have them add roofs, windows, and doors to create the houses of the town of Dumpty. Have the children use the art supplies to make the egg people who live in Dumpty. Let the children glue their houses and egg people to the bulletin board. Have one child make a Lumpty egg and glue him atop the wall. Let the children continue to add items to the town over the next few days. Encourage their creativity.

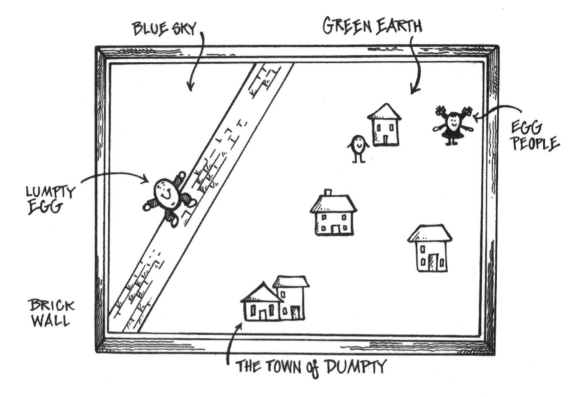

BLUE SKY

GREEN EARTH

EGG PEOPLE

LUMPTY EGG

BRICK WALL

THE TOWN of DUMPTY

Language: Write the words to the "Egg Song" (see below) on a chart. Point to the words as you and the children sing the song. Sing the song several times each day for a week. Leave the chart where the children can use it independently and soon they will be "reading" the chart and singing the words.

Math: Cut out nine 4" x 8" (10 cm x 20 cm) rectangles from poster board. With a marker, decorate each rectangle to look like a wall. Using the numbers 0 - 8, write one number on each "wall." Cut out 36 egg shapes from 2 ½" x 1 ¾" (6 cm x 4 cm) poster board. To play the game, ask a child to spread out the walls and count the correct number of eggs to put onto each wall. Store all the game pieces in a large, plastic zipper big.

Snack/Math: For this activity, you will need scrambled eggs, hard-cooked eggs cut into slices, paper plates, plastic forks or spoons, and paper egg shapes—one for each child. Write each child's name on one paper egg shape. Create a chart with the heading, "I Like My Eggs." Divide the chart in half vertically below the heading. Label one side "Scrambled" and the other side "Hard-Cooked." At snack time, serve each child a tablespoon of scrambled egg and a slice of hard-boiled egg. (Provide water, juice, or milk for a drink.) After the children have finished their snacks, ask each child to glue his paper egg on the chart in the column that shows which kind of egg he liked best. Which kind of egg has the most? Which kind has the least?

Song

Egg Song (Tune: "On Top of Old Smokey")
I like my egg scrambled.
I like my egg fried,
Or cooked in the shell with
The yellow inside.

For meals or for snacks now
You'll hear me beg,
"Oh, Mama, please give me a tasty egg."

❖ Barbara Backer, Charleston, SC

Living Long Ago

Materials

Ox-Cart Man by Donald Hall
Small samples of foods mentioned in the story: potato, apple, maple sugar, and
   wintergreen peppermint candy

What to do

1. Ask the children how people took things from one town to another before
   there were cars, trucks, or airplanes.
2. Tell them that one way people moved things long ago was to put items in a
   cart and use an ox to pull it.
3. Show them the cover of *Ox-Cart Man*. Ask them if they can find an ox, a cart,
   and the ox-cart man.
4. Read the title of the book, the author, and illustrator. Explain that the book
   explains how people lived and worked long ago in our country.
5. Read the book and discuss it with the children.
6. Encourage the children to taste some foods mentioned in the book. Omit
   certain foods if any of the children are allergic to it. Offer small samples of the
   following foods for the children to taste: baked potato, apple slices, maple
   sugar candy, and wintergreen peppermint candy.
7. Show the children a two-pound (2 kg) bag of something. Explain that the two-
   pounds of wintergreen peppermint candy that the ox-cart man bought had to
   last the family for a whole year! Candy was a rare treat.

❖ Nancy Dentler, Mobile, AL

Michael, Michael, What Do You See?

Materials

Brown Bear, Brown Bear, What Do You See? by Bill Martin, Jr.
White drawing paper
Crayons, felt pens, pencil, glue

What to do

1. Interactively read the book to the children. For example, before turning to the next page, ask them to predict what will happen next. Encourage them to join you in saying the repeated rhymes.
2. Ask the children to quietly look at things around the room. Or, take the children outside for this part of the activity. If you have magnifying glasses or different colored lenses, encourage them to look through these.
3. Allow time for the children to talk about the things they saw.
4. At the top of white drawing paper, write:

   _____, _____What do you see?
   I see a _____looking at me!
   Photocopy the page so you have enough for each child.
5. Pass out the paper and ask the children to draw a picture of what they saw. As they are drawing, circulate through the group. On each child's paper, fill in his name two times on the first two lines. Ask them what they saw and write it on the third line.

More to do

The next day, reread the book followed by the children's pages. Bind the pages together and make a book that the children can take turns bringing home. Or, display the pages on a bulletin board.

Follow the same procedure using the book Polar Bear, Polar Bear, What Do You Hear? by Bill Martin, Jr. This time ask the children to listen quietly and illustrate what they heard.

❧ Barbara Saul, Eureka, CA

Rabbits in the Wild vs. Rabbits for Pets

Materials

Are You Asleep, Rabbit? by Alison Campbell and Julia Barton
Home for a Bunny by Margaret Wise Brown
White paper
Pen or pencil

What to do

1. Read both books to the children.
2. Draw a line down the middle of a sheet of white paper.
3. On one side write, "The Same," and on the other side write, "Different."
4. Ask the children if the rabbits lived in the same place or in different places. Did they look the same or different? Continue looking at the similarities and differences between the rabbits.
5. Encourage children to create their own comparing and contrasting questions.
6. Record their observations on the chart.

More to do

As a follow-up, make a second chart. Draw a line down the middle of a piece of paper. On one side write, "Pet" and on the other side write, "Wild." Ask questions such as where do pets sleep? Where do wild rabbits sleep?

✿ Constance Heagerty, Westborough, MA

Trains Are Terrific!

Materials

Freight Train by Donald Crews
Empty boxes (cartons that held reams of paper are perfect)
Large white paper
Glue or tape

Crayons or washable markers

Hole punch

Scissors

Sturdy yarn or string

What to do

1. Ask the children if they have ever seen a train. Did the train have many cars attached to it?
2. Explain that trains that carry people are called passenger trains. Trains that carry things are called freight trains.
3. Show the children the book you are going to read. Tell them that the pictures in the book are so wonderful that it won a Caldecott Honor Award for the illustrations.
4. Read and discuss the book with the children.
5. Make your own freight train with the children.
6. Before this activity, cover boxes (without tops) with white paper.
7. Divide the children into small groups and assign each group a train car to make. If you follow the book's examples, make a red caboose, an orange tank car, a yellow hopper car, a green cattle car, a blue gondola car, a purple boxcar, a

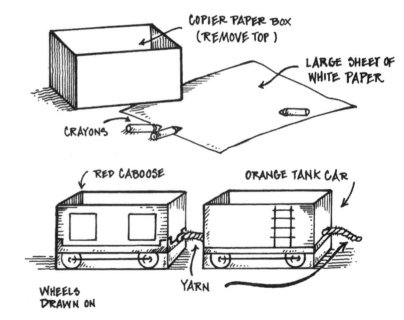

black tender, and a black steam engine. Encourage the children to color their train cars the appropriate color and add additional details.
8. Punch holes in the front and back of the boxes and string sturdy lengths of yarn through the holes to join them.
9. Take the freight train on a trip around the room!

❖ Nancy Dentler, Mobile, AL

We Spy

Materials

I Spy books by Jean Marzollo and Walter Wick
Miscellaneous materials from home or classroom
Blocks, shelves, and various fabrics, optional
Camera and film

What to do

1. If available, show the children an I Spy book.
2. Invite the children to bring in an assortment of small items from home so that they can make a classroom "We Spy" book. (It is helpful to provide parents with a list of suggested items.)
3. Encourage the children to sort all of the contributed items. Help them decide which categories to use for different pages of their "We Spy" book, such as vehicles, ocean creatures, animals, and so on.
4. Encourage the children to arrange or display items in any fashion. Blocks or shelves make great displays for the items, and various types of fabrics, quilts, or blankets make great backdrops, but these are not essential. To eliminate crowding and confusion, you may want to assign two or three children for each page.
5. When children have finished organizing items for a specific page, photograph their display.
6. Allow children to create displays for as many pages as time, film, or funds allow! Keep in mind that arranging and photographing items takes much longer than you may anticipate. You may want to allow an entire week to complete this project.
7. Get the film developed. If funds allow, make enlarged color copies for your book.
8. Ask children to examine the pages and tell you a few things that they spy. Keep a list of the items they spy and their page numbers. Make sure you have one or two entries for each child.
9. Print the text for each page.
10. For the cover, you may want to select some illustrations from the children, or make some type of group creation.

More to do

Parents may wish to purchase their own copy of the "We Spy" book. If so, invite them to a "book signing" in your classroom.

Shirley R. Salach, Northwood, NH

What Can You Hear at the Zoo?

Materials

Polar Bear, Polar Bear, What Do You Hear? by Bill Martin, Jr.

What to do

1. Ask the children if they have ever been to a zoo. Explain that there are many different animals at the zoo that make different sounds.
2. Show the children the cover of the book, and read the title, author, and illustrator. Ask the children if they can guess some other zoo animals that might be mentioned in the book.
3. As you read each page, encourage the children to make the animal noises with you. They can roar like a lion, snort like a hippo, hiss like a boa constrictor, and so on.
4. At the end of the story, the zookeeper hears ten animals in the book. Assign animal roles to the children, and ask them to make their individual sounds all at the same time. No wonder the zookeeper heard them all!

More to do

Art: Paint large sheets of paper in animal colors, such as black and white for a zebra, yellow and brown for a tiger, and pink and white for a flamingo. After the pages dry, cut them into animal shapes. Glue the shapes to a large sheet of paper and add details to the animal collage using crayons or markers.

Listening Center: Animal sounds can come alive in your listening center! Ask each child to select a favorite animal. Encourage them to practice the sound their animal makes. Then, record each child making his animal sound. Ask children to make the sound, pause, and say, "This is (child's name) and I like (name the animal)." Children can listen to the tape and guess the animal during each pause.

Science: Decorate a shoebox to look like a zoo cage. Draw zoo animal pictures on index cards and place them inside the box. One at a time, children will pick a card and make the sound of that animal. Other children will guess the name of the animal they heard.

❦ Nancy Dentler, Mobile, AL

Rise and Shine

Materials

None needed

What to do

1. Sing the following song to the tune of "Jimmy Crack Corn."
2. Sing it at the beginning of Circle Time. Sing a different child's name with each line and ask the child stand when her name is sung.

    The sun is up. It's time to shine.
    The sun is up. It's time to shine.
    The sun is up. It's time to shine.
    We'll do our best today.

    (Child's name) is here – rise and shine!
    (Child's name) is here – rise and shine!
    (Child's name) is here – rise and shine!
    We'll do our best today.

❧ Dotti Enderle, Richmond, TX

Go-Togethers

Materials

Variety of objects to classify, such as a comb/brush, toothbrush/toothpaste, washcloth/soap, coat/hat, hammer/nail, paper/pencil, fork/spoon, key/lock, shoe/sock, shirt/shorts, shovel/pail, and salt/pepper shakers
Suitcase

What to do

1. Place all or some of the objects (see Materials list) in a suitcase.
2. Choose one of the objects during group time. Show it to the children, identify it, and discuss what it is.
3. Encourage the children to guess what item might be in the suitcase that would "go with" the selected item.

More to do

Place the suitcase in a learning center. During center time, encourage the children to match the objects by themselves or in pairs.

❖ Barbara L. Lindsay, Mason City, IA

Seasonal Dress-Up

Materials

Clothes and accessories representing every season, such as sandals, mittens, hats, T-shits, coats, sweaters, umbrellas, and shorts
Large suitcase or trunk
4 clotheslines
Clothespins
Paper and markers
Books about the seasons

What to do

1. Put clothes and accessories that represent every season into a large suitcase or trunk.
2. Hang four clotheslines around the room (one for each season). Clip clothespins on all of them.
3. Make four signs showing a season onto each one. Hang one sign on each clothesline.
4. With the children, read a couple of books about the different seasons.
5. Discuss the importance of choosing the right clothes for the weather during the various seasons.
6. Ask the children to choose an item from the trunk or suitcase, one at a time. Each child will decide which season the article of clothing would be worn by someone.
7. If the children agree, ask the child to hang the article of clothing on the appropriate clothesline.

More to do

Ask the children to choose a particular kind of weather. Then, encourage them to rummage through the suitcase and decide which clothes they would need for that weather. Ask a child to put on various clothes and the other children can guess which season and what type of weather she is dressed for.

♣ Vicki Whitehead, Fort Worth, TX

Circle Time Rhyme

Materials

None needed

What to do

1. To begin Circle Time or Story Time, recite this rhyme to draw the children's attention:

   Touch your shoulder, touch your chin.
   Now it's time to begin.
   Touch your elbow where it bends.
   No more talking to our friends.
   Touch your belly, touch you knees.
   Now it's time to LISTEN PLEASE.

♣ Christine Maiorano, Duxbury, MA

Nursery Rhyme Theater

Materials

Dress-up clothes
Nursery rhyme props, such as a bowl and spoon, a plastic spider (or one made from construction paper), a chair, and anything else that belongs

What to do

1. Familiarize the children with nursery rhymes by reading or reciting them during Circle Time.
2. Encourage the children to act out the nursery rhymes. For each nursery rhyme, assign each child a part for each character in the rhyme. Also, assign a

narrator to recite the rhyme.

3. Some examples are:

Little Miss Muffet

Parts: Miss Muffet, spider, narrator

Props: Dress-up clothes, bowl and spoon, chair, spider

Humpty Dumpty

Parts: Humpty Dumpty, King's horses, King's men, narrator

Props: hat (for Humpty), chair (for the wall)

Little Bo Peep

Parts: Bo Peep, sheep, narrator

Props: Dress-up clothes

Hickory, Dickory, Dock

Parts: mouse, clock (someone making the sound of a clock), narrator

Props: chair (for the mouse to "run" up, stand, and then jump down)

More to do

Home Connection: Videotape the children acting out the nursery rhymes. Show the video to the children so they can see their performance. Put on a show for parents on a special day.

Literacy: Ask the children to draw their favorite nursery rhymes using markers or crayons. Put all of the drawings together and make a class book of nursery rhymes.

Suzanne Pearson, Winchester, VA

Mother Goose in a Bag

Materials

6 to 8 white or brown lunch bags

Small plastic or fabric trinkets for each bag (The trinkets should be representative of a familiar nursery rhyme. For example, use a small dish and spoon to represent "Hey Diddle Diddle," a pair of child's mittens for "Three Little Kittens," and a small black sheep for "Baa, Baa Black Sheep.")

What to do

1. Put one trinket into each of the lunch bags and fold them closed.
2. At Circle Time, gather six to eight children and give each one a bag.
3. Encourage the children to open their bags, one at a time, and identify the trinket inside.
4. Ask the children which nursery rhyme they think the trinket represents.
5. After they guess the nursery rhyme, recite it together.
6. Continue the activity until all of the children have had a turn.

More to do

More Circle Time: For a real treat, ask an adult to dress up as Mother Goose and visit the classroom to do this activity. Or, dress up yourself!

Dramatic Play: Encourage the children to act out a favorite nursery rhyme using the props.

Related book

The New Adventures of Mother Goose by Bruce Lansky

❧ Virginia Jean Herrod, Columbia, SC

Sit-a-Pons

Materials

Poster board
Stickers, markers, paint, glue, and glitter
Laminate or clear contact paper

What to do

1. Cut poster board into 12" (30 cm) diameter circles. Make one for each child.
2. Help each child print her name in the center of her circle.
3. Encourage the children to decorate their circles with a variety of items.
4. Laminate the circles or cover them with clear contact paper. (See illustration on the next page.)
5. Use these "Sit-a-Pons" at Circle Time, so each child will have her own place.

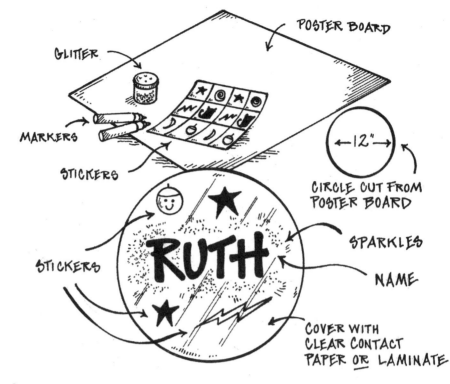

More to do

Games: Turn the circles over on the floor and play "Musical Shapes." Use different colors of poster board to play color games.

Literacy: Use the circles to practice name recognition.

🍀 Cindy Winther, Oxford, MI

Sticker Circle Time

Materials

Stickers

What to do

1. Each month, use different seasonal stickers to make Circle Time more fun! Use these stickers as markers for each child's personal space in the circle. For example, in October, use Halloween stickers; in November, use Thanksgiving stickers; and so on. Place the stickers in a horseshoe formation where the children will sit each day.

🍀 Lisa M. Chichester, Parkersburg, WV

Blanket Day

Materials

Blankets from home
Book about blankets
Paper and pen

What to do

1. Send a note home with the children explaining that they will be allowed to bring their favorite blanket to school the next day. Ask the parents to write a short note about the child's blanket (such as who made it or who gave it to the child). Bring in a few extra blankets for children who forget to bring their own.

2. Encourage the children to spread out their blankets on the floor and lie on them at Circle Time.

3. As the children lie on their blankets, read them a book about blankets. Good choices are *Owen* by Kevin Henkes, *On Mother's Lap* by Ann Herbert Scott, or *Ira Sleeps Over* by Bernard Waber.

4. Encourage the children to share their blankets. If they brought a note from their parents, read it aloud to the class.

5. Use the blankets to practice concepts:
   - Put the blanket *under* you.
   - Put the blanket *over* you.
   - Get *on top of* the blanket.
   - Put the blanket *beside* you.
   - Get *under* the blanket.

6. Make a floor graph. On each piece of paper, write a descriptive word for the children's blankets, such as *red*, *blue*, *quilt*, and so on. Read the words out loud and with the children, talk about the different kinds of blankets. Place the labels on the floor and ask the children to put their blankets in the appropriate categories. Discuss which group has more, less, or is equal.

7. Teach the children this poem:
   I have a special blanket,
   At night it's on my bed,
   And when I lay me down to sleep,
   It's where I put my head.

More to do

Literacy: Ask the children to dictate stories about their blankets. After you write down their words, they can illustrate them. Make a class book with their stories. Encourage the children to take turns bringing the book home to share with their families.

More Literacy: Ask the children to respond to the following statements. Write down their responses and make a sensory booklet for each child.

My blanket feels like _____

My blanket looks like _____

My blanket smells like _____

Self-concept: Take photographs of the children with their blankets and hang the photos on the bulletin board.

❧ Barbara Saul, Eureka, CA

The Gift of Reading

Materials

Books
Wrapping paper
Tape
Scissors
Bows or ribbons

What to do

1. Wrap a book that you are going to introduce to the children in bright wrapping paper. Decorate it with bows or ribbons.
2. Place this "gift" in the Circle Time area to build the children's excitement.
3. Ask a child to unwrap the gift. Then, share the book with the children at Circle Time and add it to the Book Center.
4. Give your class the "gift of reading" regularly!

❧ Charlene Woodham Peace, Semmes, AL

Music Menu

Materials

Construction paper
Scissors
Markers
Photo album (inexpensive type
with magnetic pages)

What to do

1. This activity reinforces pre-read-
ing skills as the children see the
picture symbols associated with
songs.
2. Create cutouts for each song, poem, and fingerplay that you
use during Circle Time. Use markers to decorate them.
3. Write the title of the appropriate song, poem, or fingerplay on each cutout.
For example, write "Old MacDonald" on a cow.
4. Label the pages in a photo album with the titles.
5. Place the cutouts on the appropriate pages in the photo album.
6. Encourage the children to use this "Music Menu" to select favorite songs, fingerplays, and poems.

❖ Charlene Woodham Peace, Semmes, AL

Bring a Sound to School

Materials

None needed

What to do

1. Send a note home asking parents to do the following:
   - Before your child leaves for school, turn off the radio and/or television.
   - Be very quiet and still and listen to a sound (such as a bird singing, a
     baby crying, a dog barking, or a refrigerator humming).

■ On a piece of paper, write the sound your child heard and have her bring it to class.

2. With the children, discuss the sounds during Circle Time. Were the sounds loud? Were they scary? Who or what makes sounds like that?

More to do

Bring a tape recorder on a field trip or picnic to record sounds.

❖ Ingelore Mix, Gainesville, VA

Circle Time

Materials

None needed

What to do

1. Provide opportunities for movement when singing songs at Circle Time.
2. For example, if you sing a song about weather every day, start adding body movements to go with the rhythm. For example, encourage the children to stamp their feet, pat their shoulders, jump up and down, and so on as you sing the song.

More to do

Encourage the children to come up with new ways to move their bodies as they sing a song. Ask them, "What shall we do with our bodies when we sing?" or "How can we move our bodies when we sing?"

❖ Sandra Suffoletto Ryan, Buffalo, NY

Name That Sound

Materials

Tape player and tapes
Pictures or small objects

What to do

1. Make a tape recording of noises with one theme. For example, make separate tapes of sounds made by zoo animals, farm animals, transportation sounds, sounds heard around the house, and outside noises.
2. At Circle Time, play a tape and encourage the children to identify the sounds. The children will love listening to see if they can guess the sounds.
3. If desired, show them pictures or small objects of the sounds on the tape. Give one to each child and when a child hears her sound, she stands up and shows her object. The child can also make the sound she hears.
4. The children can also act like the object or animal on the tape.
5. Be prepared for a lot of laughter!

More to do

Art: Put old magazines in the Art Center. Encourage the children to look for pictures of things they have heard and cut them out. Help them make a book of sounds.
Literacy: After listening to the tape, put it in the Library Area so the children can listen to it by themselves.

Related book

The Listening Walk by Paul Showers

❖ Sandra Hutchins Lucas, Cox's Creek, KY

Group Time

Materials

None needed

What to do

1. At Group Time sing:

Look around the room with me,
Look around the room with me,
Look around the room with me,
I see something _____ (round, blue, wooden, and so on)

❧ Marilyn Harding, Grimes, IA

Mirror, Mirror in My Hand

Materials

Small hand or purse mirrors, one for each child

What to do

1. Give one mirror to each child.
2. Ask the children to look in the mirror and make silly faces.
3. Ask the children to describe what they did to make their silly face. For example, did they stick out their tongues, puff out their cheeks, or wrinkle their noses?
4. Encourage the children to do the following things:
   ◼ Look in the mirror and describe the color of your eyes.
   ◼ How many eyes do you have? What color are they?
   ◼ Can you wrinkle your nose? Purse your lips? Make a big grin? Look happy? Look sad?
   ◼ Smile. How many teeth can you see?
   ◼ Stick out your tongue. Wiggle it.
   ◼ What color is your hair? Is it long or short?
5. Ask a child to give the commands to the rest of the children while you observe to see who may have difficulty following directions.

Related book

From Head to Toe by Eric Carle

❧ Margie Kranyik, Hyde Park, MA

Destinations

Materials

Magazines or newspapers that have pictures of cars
Glue
3" x 5" (7 cm x 12 cm) index cards
Laminate or clear contact paper
Shoebox

What to do

1. Cut out pictures of cars from magazines or newspaper classified sections.
2. Glue the pictures onto index cards.
3. Cover the cards with clear contact paper or laminate them.
4. Place the cards in a shoebox.
5. At Circle Time, ask each child to draw one out. Take turns asking each child, "Where are you going in your car?" The child will then hold up her picture and tell the class where she is going in her "car."
6. Most children will describe familiar locations. Encourage them to dream up fantasy places as well.

More to do

Cut out pictures of other forms of transportation such as a bus, train, truck, horse, and so on. Ask the children to describe where they might be going if they were driving one of these.

Related books

ABCDrive by Naomi Howland
Albert Goes to Town by Jennifer Jordan
Miss Spider's New Car by David Kirk
Richard Scarry's Cars and Trucks and Things That Go by Richard Scarry

❖ Dotti Enderle, Richmond, TX

Mystery Box

Materials

Small box that can be held in the hands and will stay closed
Item to put in the box

What to do

1. At Circle Time, use the Mystery Box to introduce a concept or topic.
2. Put something inside the box to pique the children's curiosity. For example, when introducing the topic of birds, place a feather inside the box.
3. Ask each child to hold the box. (No peeking!)
4. Encourage all the children to guess what is in the box before you open it.

More to do

Use the box to introduce a book at story time or a new material for art.

❖ Sharon Dempsey, May's Landing, NJ

The "Me Bag"

Materials

Paint and brushes, markers, and decorative items
Pillowcase, canvas bag with handles, or small duffle bag

What to do

1. With the children, paint or decorate a pillowcase, canvas bag, or small duffle bag to make a class "Me Bag."
2. Write the following instructions on the bag:
   ■ This is our class "Me Bag."
   ■ When it comes home, fill it with _____ items (choose a number)
   ■ Bring the bag back to class the next day.
3. Give the "Me Bag" to a child to bring home. (Make sure every child has a turn.) The child (with the parent's help) will choose items, put them in the bag, and bring it to class the next day.
4. When the child brings in the bag, tuck it away so the other children are not

tempted to peek into it.

5. At Circle Time, encourage the child to show and talk about her items with the rest of the children. Pack the child's items into her backpack or a grocery bag for her to take back home at the end of the day.

More to do

To extend this activity, model how to give clues. Put an item into the "Me Bag" and provide clues before showing it to the children. Encourage them to try and guess what the article is. Eventually the children will be able to do this by themselves.

♣ Terri L. Pentz, Melbourne Beach, FL

Bag a Beast

Materials

Large, cloth drawstring bag
Plastic or fabric toy animals (such as a horse, cow, cat, pig, tiger, and lion)

What to do

1. Place toy animals in a drawstring bag.
2. Teach the children the following familiar song:

   ### A-Hunting We Will Go
   A-hunting we will go.
   A-hunting we will go.
   Hi ho the derry oh,
   A-hunting we will go.

3. Now, change a couple lines of the song:
   A-hunting we will go.
   A-hunting we will go.
   We'll catch a (animal name)
   And (rhyming action),
   And then we'll let it go.

4. Ask a child to pull out a toy animal from the bag and identify it. Encourage the children to come up with a word that rhymes with that animal.
5. With the children, sing the song and insert the name of the animal in the third line and the rhyming word in the fourth line. (You can change the fourth line

according to the chosen animal and to make the rhyme make sense.) For example:

> *A-hunting we will go.*
> *A-hunting we will go.*
> *We'll catch a cat,*
> *And give it a rat,*
> *And then we'll let it go.*

> *A-hunting we will go.*
> *A-hunting we will go.*
> *We'll catch a horse,*
> *And hug it, of course,*
> *And then we'll let it go.*

6. Continue until all the children have had a turn choosing an animal.

More to do

Art: Make binoculars by taping together two toilet paper rolls and adding a string. Paint or decorate them with markers and stickers. Avoid using glitter as the binoculars will be close to the children's eyes.

Dramatic Play: Place the toy animals in the Dramatic Play Center to stimulate more play.

Science: Put real binoculars in the Discovery Center. Explain how binoculars help hunters see things in the distance. Encourage the children to use the binoculars outdoors. Ask them to describe and draw a picture of what they see.

Related books

Animal Fact/Animal Fable by Seymour Simon
Every Living Thing by James Herriot
Johnny Lion's Book by Edith Thacher Hurd

❦ Virginia Jean Herrod and Nina Smith, Columbia, SC

Question Day

Materials

Sentence strips
Pocket chart
YES and NO cards
Index cards
Markers

What to do

1. This is a daily graphing activity to do during Circle Time.
2. To prepare for this activity, write a question on a sentence strip. For example, to relate to a theme such as Transportation, ask, "Have you ever flown in an airplane?", connect to the daily routine, "Did you bring your lunch from home today?" or relate to a child, "Do you have a pet?" Use pictures or graphics to help the children "read" the questions.
3. Attach the sentence strip to the top of the pocket chart.
4. Place YES and NO cards below the sentence strip to form what will become two columns.
5. Write each child's name on index cards and put them on a table or chalkboard ledge. (See the illustration on the next page.)
6. As each child enters the classroom, ask her to locate her name card, read the question, and place her card in the appropriate column.
7. At Circle Time, discuss the graph. Begin by asking, "Who can read today's question?" Encourage the children to share their observations, such as "more people said NO" or "only two people said YES."
8. Then, guide the discussion to touch on a few concepts, such as counting, more and less, identifying/reading each other's names, rhymes ("Who sees a name that rhymes with MOO?"), syllabication ("Who sees a name with two claps?"), first and last letters, positional words, and ordinal numbers. The list is almost endless!

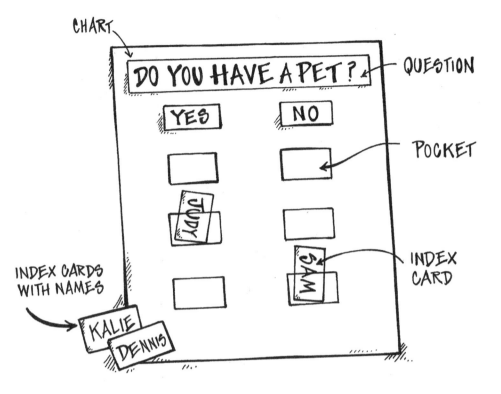

More to do

Write a question on the sentence strip that requires three or four columns, such as "Which do you like best: APPLES, APPLE JUICE, or APPLESAUCE?" Extend the activity to literature by asking, "Which story (or character) did you like best?" (This activity is so well loved by the children that if I do not have time to put up a question, they ask for one! Sometimes they even suggest their own questions.)

❧ Ruth Cohenson, Pleasantville, NJ

Weather Reporter

Materials

Basket
Weather-appropriate clothing, such as a raincoat, gloves, sunglasses, and scarves

What to do

1. Put different weather-appropriate clothing in a basket.
2. Each day during Circle Time, select a child to be the weather reporter.

3. Ask the child to pick out the appropriate clothing for the weather from the basket and put it on.

4. The rest of the children sing, "What is the weather, weather, weather? What is the weather report today?" (Tune: "Mamma's Little Baby Loves Shortening Bread")

5. The weather reporter describes the weather. For example, if it is a rainy day, she will say, "Today we are seeing some clouds outside. I think we will need our rain coats and umbrellas." Then the class will sing, "Sara says it's rainy, rainy, rainy. Sara says the weather is rainy today."

6. Pick one child each day until every one has a turn.

❧ Lisa M. Chichester, Parkersburg, WV

Shape Person

Materials

Construction paper
Scissors
Bag or box
Tape
White poster board
Marker
Blindfold, optional
Paste, optional

What to do

1. Cut out circles, squares, triangles, rectangles, and ovals in various sizes from construction paper.

2. Put the shapes into a bag or box.

3. Tape white poster board to a wall and draw the outline of a person on it.

4. At Circle Time, ask each child to reach into the bag and pick a shape. Before the child pulls it out of the bag, ask her to guess what it is by touch. If desired, use a blindfold to ensure the child does not see the shape.

5. After she guesses what the shape is, ask her to remove it from the bag and tape or paste it onto the outline of the shape person.

6. Continue adding other shapes to fill in the shape person.

More to do

When a child pulls out a shape from the bag, encourage the children to suggest things that have that shape. For a circle, the chicken might say plate, steering wheel, bicycle wheel, and so on.

❧ Melissa Markham, Huddleston, VA

Take a Walk

Materials

None needed

What to do

1. Circle Time can be more than just sitting in the classroom. If you can, take the children on seasonal walks to observe changes in flowers, trees, and the weather.
2. Go through a downtown area to observe community helpers.
3. Stop at the library and check out books for the classroom library.
4. When you come back to Circle Time, list the things that the children found interesting on a piece of poster board. Hang the poster with the children's observations in the classroom for all to see.

Song

We Are Going for a Walk Today (Tune: "Mary Had a Little Lamb")
We are going for a walk today,
Walk today, walk today.
We are going for a walk today.
I wonder who we'll see.

❧ Sue Myhre, Bremerton, WA

Nature

Materials

Naturalist from a state office
Posters
Pamphlets and books (from teacher or naturalist)
Hides and skeletons, optional

What to do

1. Ask a naturalist to come in and talk to the children about animals, flowers, and so on and how to care for them.
2. If possible, the naturalist can show the children animal hides and/or animal skeletons alongside a picture of the animal. The naturalist can describe each animal's special characteristics, where it lives, and other interesting information.
3. Encourage the children to ask as many questions as desired.
4. Then give the pamphlets and books about snakes, turtles, flowers, and other outdoor things to the children.

❧ Marilyn Harding, Grimes, IA

Nutrition/Good Health

Materials

Nutritionist or dietitian
Food posters, including one showing Food Pyramid
Food cards
Ingredients to make popcorn, sandwiches, or cereal cookies

What to do

1. Invite a nutritionist or dietitian to visit the classroom.
2. At Circle Time, the nutritionist can talk to the children about healthy foods and why it is important to eat them.
3. Show the children various food posters, such as the Food Pyramid.

4. Make or purchase food cards. Hold them up, one at a time, and ask if it is a healthy food, or one that should be eaten in moderation.

5. Make popcorn, sandwiches with a healthy filling, or cereal cookies.

❧ Marilyn Harding, Grimes, IA

What Do Parents Do All Day?

Materials

Parents
Various job-related props, pictures, and activities

What to do

1. Invite parents to come in and talk about their jobs for ten minutes. Reassure them that teachers will be there to help and that you can meet with them beforehand if they need help planning.
2. Suggest the use of props, pictures, and hand-on activities. Assure them that any job is interesting to four-year-olds!
3. Examples of props and activities parents can use are:
   - Bank employee – bring logo giveaways and a money chart from the bank
   - Community band member – bring uniform and instrument; lead a class parade
   - Real estate agent – bring copies of pictures of houses to color
   - Deli worker – bring rubber gloves, cardboard squares, white plastic wrap, and tape so children can wrap their own "cheese"
   - Medical technician – bring a microscope and germ slides
   - Factory worker – bring products in various stages of completion
   - Accountant – bring adding machines

More to do

Art: Make art projects using real occupational tools such as tweezers, eyedroppers, or potter's tools.
Dramatic Play: Set up stations in the classroom for children to act out jobs. For example, set up a doctor or veterinarian office in the Housekeeping Center and a post office in the Writing Center. Encourage the children to play "beauty salon" with dolls or practice carpentry at the workbench. Put artist's tools in the Art Center.
Games: Play a memory take-away game using occupational tools.
Language: Help the children decorate and sign thank-you cards.
Manipulatives: Put puzzles and books about jobs and tools on the shelves.

Related book

Newton, Nell, and Barney: Someday I Want to Be... by Virginia Esquinaldo

❖ Sandra Gratias, Perkasie, PA

Dino Footwear

Materials

Socks
Felt
Scissors
Fabric glue

What to do

1. Ask the children to bring in a pair of socks from home.
2. Cut out "toenails" from colored felt.
3. Help the children glue the toenails onto their socks.
4. Encourage the children to wear their socks over their shoes for a dino stomping parade!

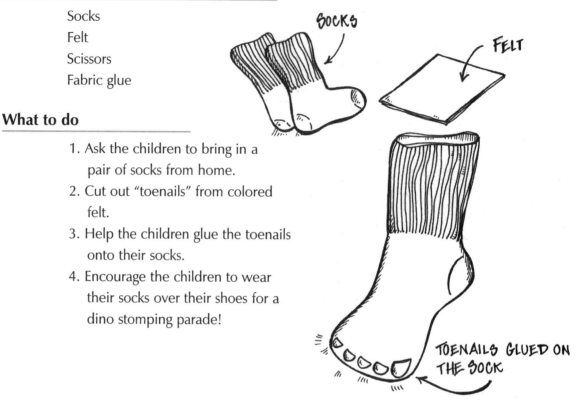

SOCKS

FELT

TOENAILS GLUED ON THE SOCK

❀ Lisa M. Chichester, Parkersburg, WV

Dramatic Play

Materials

Rocking boat
3 chairs and 3 dishes (large, medium, and small)
Large paper
Small stool
Bowl and spoon
Blocks

What to do

1. Encourage the children to use various props to act out favorite stories. For example:
   - Three Billy Goats: Turn over a rocking boat to make a bridge. Children act like goats as they go over it, one by one. One child will be the troll.
   - Three Bears: Use three chairs, three dishes, and large paper to make beds.
   - Little Miss Muffet: Say the poem and act it out using a small stool, bowl, and spoon.
   - Humpty Dumpty: Use blocks to build a low wall and act out the story.

❖ Marilyn Harding, Grimes, IA

Babies' Nappies (Diapers)

Materials

Table or blanket
Baby dolls
Paper towels
Scissors
Small ruler
Tape on a dispenser

What to do

1. Set up a diapering area for baby dolls in the Dramatic Play Center. Make a changing table using a table or blanket.
2. Discuss how part of taking care of babies is making sure they are wearing a "clean" diaper.
3. Show the children how to cut or tear a paper towel into wide strips to use as a diaper. If they want to be sure of the size (or if you want to incorporate measuring), use a ruler to measure the baby's "bottom" and cut a strip to fit.
4. When the child's baby doll is "wet," he can bring it to the changing station and change the diaper using a paper towel and tape.
5. Children have a wonderful time with this very simple activity. They love to pretend the baby has a soiled diaper so they can make a new one for their doll. Although this activity does not require a lot of paper (a couple of sheets go a long way), encourage them not to waste paper (trees).

More to do

Extend this activity to make bandages. Set up a doctor or vet office and encourage children to tear paper towels to make bandages. Children can bring their injured pets (stuffed/plush pets) to the vet's office and bandage the pet's paw or tail.

❧ Maxine Della Fave, Raleigh, NC

Kitchen

Materials

Kitchen items

What to do

1. Place various kitchen items in the Dramatic Play Area. (Ask the children to keep the kitchen items in this area.)
2. Encourage the children to take turns playing different roles, such as chef, dish washer, and so on. No more than four children should be in the area at a time.
3. While the children are playing with the kitchen items, introduce them to different kitchen terms and language. For example:

You are using the _____.

You are wearing a _____.

What do think a chef would do if _____.

Where are you working as a chef?

You are looking at the _____.

It is important for chefs to wash their hands before preparing food.

Germs can be spread through food if your hands are not washed correctly.

Cooking is preparing food for eating.

A cooking utensil is a tool used in a kitchen to prepare food.

A chef is a person who prepares food for eating.

❧ Cristy Bawol, Utica, MI

Shoe Store

Materials

Variety of old shoes, such as slippers, scuba shoes, boots, baby shoes, high heels, men's dress shoes, ballet shoes, and soccer shoes
Empty shoeboxes
Shoe polish
Socks
Cash register
Pretend money
Shopping bags
Poster with different foot sizes
Paper and pencils

What to do

1. Use all of the materials listed above to set up a "shoe store" in the Dramatic Play Center. Encourage the children to buy and sell shoes.
2. Make a poster with different size feet so the children can measure their feet over and over again.
3. The children can use paper and pencils to make signs for the shop.

More to do

Art: Make prints using shoes that have unusual prints on the bottom.
Language: Introduce the children to the word *pair*.
Math: Trace the children's feet onto a piece of paper and cut them out. Help the children use the feet shapes to measure how many feet it takes to go across the room.

✤ Holly Dzierzanowski, Austin, TX

Let's Be Clowns

Materials

Pictures of clowns
Dress-up clothing, such as shirts, skirts, aprons, ties, hats, purses, and wigs
Face makeup
Camera and film

What to do

1. With the children, talk about clowns. Show them pictures of clowns too.
2. Put dress-up clothing in the Dramatic Play Area and encourage the children to dress up like clowns.
3. Paint the faces of those who are willing.
4. Encourage the children to act like clowns.
5. Take pictures of the clowns. After you get the photos developed, give them to the children to keep.

More to do

Games: Encourage the clowns to crawl on the floor carrying a stuffed animal on their backs. See who can keep the animal from falling off.

Gross Motor: Make a line on the floor using masking tape. Encourage the clown to walk on the "balance beam," trying not to fall off.

More Gross Motor: An adult can hold a plastic hoop to the side in the air and the clowns can toss stuffed animals through it.

♣ Diane Weiss, Fairfax, VA

Farmers' Market

Materials

Plastic bins, baskets, or boxes
Harvest vegetables
Cash register
Puppet theater
Bingo chips
Bags

What to do

1. Set up a Farmers' Market in the Dramatic Play Center.
2. Label plastic bins or boxes and fill them with various vegetables from the garden, such as apples, potatoes, onions, carrots, and peppers.
3. Make a farmers' stand by setting up a cash register in a puppet theater.
4. Some children will work for the farmer and some will be shoppers. Give children bingo chips and bags to go shopping at the market. Encourage them to fill their bags, go to the cash register, and count how many items are in their bags. They can "pay" the farmer one chip for each item.

5. The children who work for the farmer can sort and return the food to their appropriate bins. Rotate roles so each child gets a turn being the farmer.

🍀 Christine Maiorano, Duxbury, MA

Fasching Fun!

Materials

Construction paper
Scissors
Glue
Decorations, such as glitter and feathers
Popsicle sticks
Confetti

What to do

1. Fasching is a German holiday that celebrates the coming of spring and the end of winter. Traditionally, the village people have a parade and dress up in wild outfits to scare away the evil spirits of winter and welcome the good spirits of spring.
2. Have your own Fasching parade! Cut out masks from construction paper using the pattern on the next page.
3. Encourage the children to decorate their masks with feathers, glitter, and other materials.
4. Glue the mask to a Popsicle stick to make a handle.
5. Celebrate with confetti and a special snack.

🍀 Lisa M. Chichester, Parkersburg, WV

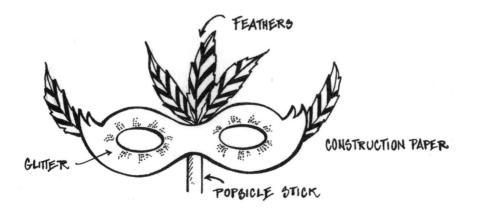

FEATHERS

GLITTER

CONSTRUCTION PAPER

POPSICLE STICK

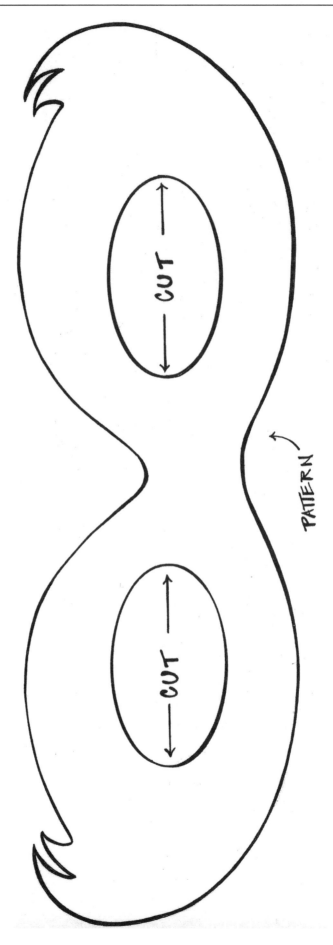

CUT

PATTERN

CUT

Boat

Materials

Large appliance box, such as a refrigerator box
Utility knife (adult only)
Tempera paints and brushes
Glue
Scissors
Large blue paper
Duct tape
Long stick, such as a broomstick
Chairs

What to do

1. Place a refrigerator box on its back.
2. Use a utility knife to cut an opening in the middle of the box to place chairs (adult only).
3. Cut out two pie shapes from the front of the box on the floor base (see illustration on the next page).
4. Ask the children to paint the outside of the box.
5. Help the children cut out wave shapes from large blue paper and glue them around the base of the boat.
6. Use duct tape to attach a long stick to the back of the boat. Cut out a large triangle from large paper and tape it to the top of the stick to make a sail.
7. Place chairs inside the boat and go sailing!

More to do

Use the boat for a variety of themes, such as vehicles, the ocean, fish, boats, the rain forest, or a jungle. Hang pictures and posters of famous artwork with boats. Add fishing poles, toy walkie–talkies, binoculars, camera, goggles, diving masks, and flippers to the boat play.

Related books

I Love Boats by Flora McDonnell
Mouse's Tale by Pamela Johnson
My Blue Boat by Chris L Demarest

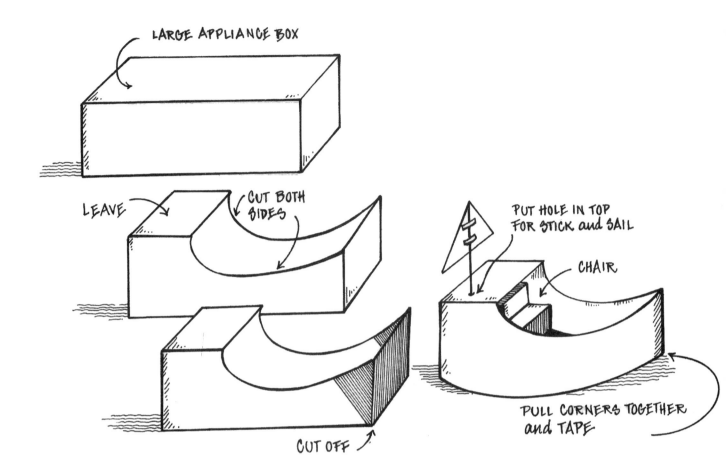

Songs

A Diver Went to the Sea

(Tune: "Row, Row, Row Your Boat")

A diver went to the sea, sea, sea.
To see what he could see, see, see.
But all that he could see, see, see.
Was ME in the deep blue sea, sea, sea.

Add other items to the song, such as ocean animals (octopus, seahorse, whale) or silly things (boot, tire, swing, balloon).

❧ Sandra Nagel, White Lake, MI

Going on a Train Ride

Materials

Book about riding on a train
Large cardboard boxes (big enough for a child to sit in)
Construction paper
Scissors
Glue
Markers
Maps, atlas, or Amtrak travel planner
Suitcases and large canvas bags
Train props, such as an engineer's hat, stop watch, and a whistle
Hole punch

What to do

1. Read a story to the children about riding on a train. Good choices are *The Polar Express* by Chris Van Allsburg or a *Thomas the Train Book*.
2. Explain to the children that they are going to make their own trains, plan a trip to anywhere, pack their bags, make their tickets, and go!
3. Give each child a cardboard box. Encourage the children to design their own railroad car using the materials listed above.
4. Encourage the children to work together to plan where to go using maps, an atlas, or an Amtrak travel planner.
5. Ask the children to pack some items (real or imagined) to take on the trip. Remind them to think about what they will need when they get there (for example, sunglasses and sun screen if they go to Florida). Discuss things to do when they get there.
6. The children can take turns being the train engineer and conductor. The engineer wears an engineer's hat (this can be made out of paper) and rides in the front box. The conductor can look at a watch, blow a whistle when it is time to go, collect tickets, and use a hole punch to punch each ticket.

More to do

Read the children a book about the circus. Make the train a circus train that carries animals. Instead of going on a "train" ride, go on a "plane" or "boat" ride.

❧ Kathleen Wallace, Columbia, MO

Jeep

Materials

Large appliance box, such as a refrigerator box
Utility knife (adult only)
Scissors
Tempera paints and brushes
Paper plates
Glue or tape
Chairs
Hole punch
Long shoestring

What to do

1. Place a refrigerator box on its back.
2. Use a utility knife to cut an opening in the middle of the box to place chairs (adult only).
3. Save the part you cut out of the box. Cut out a circle from this piece of cardboard to make a steering wheel.
4. Encourage the children to paint the outside of the box.
5. Help the children glue paper plates onto the box to make lights and wheels.
6. Place chairs inside the box opening for seats.
7. Punch two holes into the steering wheel circle. Tie it to the Jeep using string. (See illustration on the next page.)

More to do

Use the Jeep to go on a safari, as part of a jungle or vehicle unit. Encourage the children to use toy walkie-talkies, binoculars, and cameras with their Jeep play.

Related book

Sheep in a Jeep by Nancy Shaw

❖ Sandra Nagel, White Lake, MI

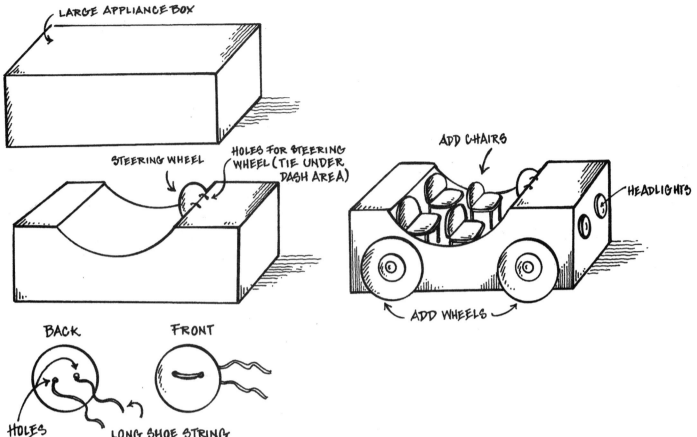

LARGE APPLIANCE BOX

STEERING WHEEL

HOLES FOR STEERING WHEEL (TIE UNDER DASH AREA)

ADD CHAIRS

HEADLIGHTS

ADD WHEELS

BACK

FRONT

HOLES

LONG SHOE STRING

Lemonade Stand

Materials

Lemons and limes

Sharp knife (adult only)

Paper and pen

Hand-held juicer

Rebus lemonade recipe cards

Pitcher and mixing spoon

3 cups (720 ml) lemon or lime juice

2 cups (500 g) sugar

4 cups (960 ml) water

2 cups ice

½ cup (120 ml) cranberry juice

Cups

Large appliance box

Paint and brushes, construction paper, string, and tape

Cash box and play coins

What to do

1. Introduce the children to lemons and limes. Encourage each child to see, touch, and smell them. Slice a few (adult only) so the children can taste them.
2. As the children explore the limes and lemons, ask them to describe the fruits. Write down what they say and post the list.
3. Ask the children to guess what might happen if you push the lemon or lime on the juicer. Encourage some of the children to try it.
4. Present the group with the rebus recipe card and make pink lemonade.
5. Mix lemon or lime juice, sugar, water, ice, and cranberry juice in a pitcher. Pour the lemonade into cups so the children can taste it.
6. Suggest that the children make more lemonade and pretend to sell it at a lemonade stand.
7. Encourage the children to decorate a large appliance box using paint and construction paper. While some children are working on the stand, others can squeeze lemons to make juice.
8. When the children finish making the stand and lemonade, add a cash box and play money so they can sell the lemonade.

More to do

Make rebus recipe cards for other foods that children can make and sell with the lemonade. Good examples are peanut butter and jelly sandwiches or cookies.

❖ Ann Gudowski, Johnstown, PA

Pet Shop

Materials

Pet store props, such as pet cages, stuffed or plastic animals, fishnets, pet store advertisements, leashes, pet bowls, pet brushes, and aquarium materials

Plastic fish

Bucket or large container

Scoop

Zipper closure plastic bags

Cash register and play money

Markers and paper

Books on how to take care of pets

What to do

1. Put pet store props (see materials) in the Dramatic Play Center to make a pet store.
2. Put plastic fish in a bucket or large container of water. Encourage the children to scoop fish into zipper closure plastic bags. This is a great math activity (for example, ask children to scoop two red fish and one blue fish).
3. The children can purchase fish, pets, and supplies at the cash register.
4. Encourage the children to use markers and paper to make money, checks, or signs for the animal's cages. Four-year-olds have wonderful creativity, and they will help you think of all kinds of things to do with the pet store!

More to do

Blocks: Put some plastic pets in the Block Center and see if the children can build homes for them.
Field Trip: Take a field trip to a local pet store. When you come back to class, ask the children if they have new ideas for things to add to their pet store.
Science: Put pet food samples in the Science Center and encourage children to figure out which pet eats which food.
Social Studies: Invite a veterinarian to visit the class and talk about how to take care of pets.

Related book

I'm Going to Be a Vet by Edith Kunhardt

Song

"How Much Is that Doggie in the Window?"

❧ Holly Dzierzanowski, Austin, TX

Tykesville Post Office

Materials

Empty liquor carton that has bottle dividers
Sheets of play stamps
Play money and toy cash register
Tall, thin box with removable top
Utility knife (adult only)

Marker
Paper and pencils
Envelopes
Canvas bag with straps
Stamp pad and stamp

What to do

1. Set up a post office in the Dramatic Play Center. Place an empty liquor carton with dividers on its side, stamps, play money, a cash register, and a stamp pad and stamp on a low table.
2. Label the cubbies inside the box with the children's names.
3. Make a mailbox by cutting a slot into the center of the lid on a tall, thin box.
4. Encourage the children to draw pictures or dictate letters to their friends. The children can put their letters into envelopes (these can be recycled from junk mail), seal them closed, and print their friend's names on them.
5. The children can take their letters to the "post office" to buy stamps and put their letters into the "mailbox."
6. The child who is the mail carrier can empty the mailbox and put the letters into a canvas bag.
7. Postal workers can cancel the stamps on the letters using a stamp, and then sort them into the cubbies.
8. The mail carrier can deliver the mail to the recipients.
9. Make sure the all the children get a turn playing different roles.

More to do

Art: Encourage the children to design their own stamps using sheets of paper divided into a grid.
Field Trip: Visit a post office. Mail real Valentines or Mother's or Father's Day cards.
Social Studies: Invite a postal worker (perhaps a parent) to visit the classroom.

Related book

The Post Office Book by Gail Gibbons

❧ Sandra Gratias, Perkasie, PA

The Garden Shop

Materials

Flower Garden by Eve Bunting

Gardening props, such as plastic flowerpots, gardening gloves, watering can, and spray bottle

Water table or large low rectangular plastic containers filled with soil

Small broom and dustpan

Small cups and marker

Soil

Fast growing seeds, such as grass or beans

What to do

1. Read the book *Flower Garden* with the children.
2. Take a field trip to a garden shop. Discuss with the children what sorts of things happen at a garden shop and how plants grow.
3. Place gardening props in the Dramatic Play Center and encourage the children to begin to explore the world of gardening. Place a small broom and dustpan in the area as well and encourage the children to sweep up after themselves.
4. Tell the children that they will plant their own plants and will be responsible for watering them.
5. Provide each child with a small cup. Help each child write his name on his cup.
6. Ask the children what they need to grow a plant. Provide the items that they name. Hopefully, they have learned from their field trip, the book, and group discussions that they need soil, water, seeds, and sun.

More to do

If the grounds of your facility allow for one, have the children (and some parent volunteers) plant a garden outside. Discuss with the children what they need to do to help the garden grow. With the children's help, make a job chart and assign the children small daily gardening jobs. You may want to consider the following jobs: weed police and watering patrol.

Related books

Planting a Rainbow by Lois Ehlert
The Reason for a Flower by Ruth Heller
Seeds (Seasons) by Gail Saunders-Smith

❉ Ann Gudowski, Johnstown, PA

Talent Show

Materials

Rope or sturdy string
King–size sheet
Chairs
Play money and tickets (made or bought on a roll)
Popcorn and punch
Record or tape player
Records or tapes
Costumes, optional
Tinker toys

What to do

1. Using rope or string, hang a king-size sheet to make a stage curtain in an appropriate spot in the classroom. Place chairs in front of the curtain for the audience to sit.
2. With the children, assign roles. Who will be performers, who will sell tickets, and who will sell popcorn and drinks?
3. If there are children who wish to sing their favorite songs, use records or tapes as an accompaniment.
4. Allow plenty of rehearsal time. If desired, children can wear costumes.
5. The Talent Show may consist of children singing songs, telling simple jokes and riddles, doing fingerplays, acting out a fairy tale, or playing a musical instrument. Use tinker toys to make pretend microphones.

More to do

Home Connection: Videotape this activity to show at Open House. The parents and relatives will enjoy seeing their little stars perform.

Penni Smith, Riverside, CA

Surf's Up

Materials

Pictures or items about the ocean from home

Books about the ocean

Beach materials, such as snorkel set (mask and fins), sunglasses, sand shovels and buckets, beach umbrella, beach balls, sun visors, water can and water, folding chairs, shells, starfish, sand dollars, and plastic ocean animals

Small plastic pool filled with sand

Large sheet or piece of plastic

What to do

1. Send a letter home informing parents that the children will be learning about the ocean.
2. Ask parents to send in pictures (photographs or magazine) or beach items for their child to show and share with the rest of the children.
3. When the children bring in their items from home, encourage them to share them with the class.
4. Read books about the ocean with the children. Have a discussion about the ocean.
5. Provide beach materials (see above) and a plastic pool with sand (put a sheet or plastic underneath) and encourage the children to explore, pretend, and create as they learn about the ocean.

More to do

Art: Provide children with glue, colored sand, small shells, and paper to make beach collages.

Music: Play island music and whale sounds during free play.

Water Play: Fill a water table with water, boats, and plastic ocean animals.

Related books

Commotion in the Ocean by Gils Andreae

The Magic School Bus on the Ocean Floor by Joanna Cole

The Ocean Alphabet Book by Jerry Pallotta

Out of the Ocean by Debra Frasier

See What's in the Sea by Jean Pidgeon

Swimmy by Leo Lionni

❖ Anne Gudowski, Johnstown, PA

Smile, You're on Camera

Materials

Old photographs and negatives
Empty film canisters
Slide projector and screen
Spotlight
Chairs
Old cameras
Disposable cameras
Proofs of professional photos
Make-up light

What to do

1. Invite a photographer to visit the classroom or take the children to an actual studio. (Self-employed photographers may have a dark room for the children to see.) This is a great topic to cover during or after the children have had school photographs taken.

2. In advance, ask parents or film processing businesses for old photos, empty film canisters, and old negatives.

3. Set up a photography area in the Dramatic Play Center. Set up a slide projector screen, a small spotlight, a few chairs, and other desired props. The children may wish to photograph themselves together or individually. They may use the disposable cameras or just pretend to take photos with empty cameras.

4. Use old proofs of professional photos and a make-up light so the children can view and "choose" their photos.

More to do

Art: Help the children cut old photos and glue them onto paper to create a collage. If desired, make a cardboard cutout of a specific object and ask the children to glue their photos onto it. Use the photos to make a mural as well.
Bulletin Board: Take a photograph of each child in the class. Using white poster board and an exacto knife, cut out a 5" x 7" (12 cm x 17 cm) frame for each child and a 4" x 6" (10 cm x 15 cm) insert. Pour different colored paints into empty film canisters and encourage the children to paint their frames. After the paint has dried, tape the prints to the frames. Create a bulletin board with all the photos.

Related books

Click: A Book About Cameras and Taking Pictures by Gail Gibbons
Finder's Keepers for Franklin by Paulette Bourgeois
My First Camera Book by Anne Kostick

❖ Tina R. Woehler, Oak Point, TX

A-Camping We Will Go

Materials

We Were Tired of Living in a House by Liesel Moak Skorpen
Camping props, such as flat sheets, rope, rectangular blocks for a fire ring, empty
paper towel rolls for fire wood, sticks, cotton balls for marshmallows, campfire
cooking utensils, flashlight, canteen, and sleeping bags

What to do

1. Read *We Were Tired of Living in a House* to the children.
2. Place camping props in the Dramatic Play Area and encourage the children to
explore, create, and pretend.

More to do

Literacy: Ask the children to dictate campfire stories. Write them down and read
them back to the children.
Music: Play campfire songs during free play. Provide a guitar, bongo drums,
individual harmonicas (found at party supply stores), and other instruments for
the campers to make music.
Science: Supply earthworms, frogs, and insects for the curious campers to
explore.

Related books

The Grouchy Ladybug by Eric Carle
Just Me and My Dad by Mercer Mayer
The Lonely Firefly by Eric Carle
The Very Hungry Caterpillar by Eric Carle
Where the River Begins by Thomas Locker

❖ Ann Gudowski, Johnstown, PA

Pounding Toy

Materials

Piece of foam, about 1" (2 cm) thick
Golf tees or short large-headed nails
Small hammers or mallets

What to do

1. Encourage the children to hammer golf tees or nails into pieces of foam. (If they don't pound in the tees or nails completely, they can take them out and hammer them in again).
2. Use pieces of foam that are used for packages during shipping. Replace them when needed without cost.

More to do

Introduce this activity before or after a carpenter comes in and shows his or her tools and how they are used.

♣ Marilyn Harding, Grimes, IN

Dropping Berries

Materials

Jars with assorted sized mouths and height
Seeds
Paper and pencil, optional

What to do

1. The goal of this activity is to help children learn to coordinate their wrist, hand, finger, finger-thumb, and eye-hand movements by dropping seeds into the jars.
2. Encourage the children to stand as close to the jars as they desire. Ask them to try and drop seeds into each jar at least twice.
3. Help the children determine the easiest way to drop the seeds successfully into the different jars. Ask them which jar is the easiest and which is the hardest.

4. Record the results, if desired

5. The children are demonstrating their increasing awareness of and ability to evaluate their accomplishments, as well as to set new standards and goals.

❧ Hilary Lisa Lehman McKee, East Lansing, MI

Pop and Squeeze

Materials

Scissors
Bubble wrap

What to do

1. Cut out squares of bubble wrap.
2. Encourage the children to squeeze and pop the bubbles. (They can hold the bubble wrap and squeeze it, or put it on table and push it.)

❧ Marilyn Harding, Grimes, IA

Clipping Clothespins

Materials

Plastic bowl (large, empty margarine containers work well)
Colored plastic clothespins

What to do

1. Place a few clothespins in a bowl. (Increase the number of clothespins as the children's skill develops.)
2. Demonstrate grasping the clothespin with the thumb and two fingers, squeezing to open the clothespin.
3. Place the clothespin on the rim of the bowl, demonstrating how to release your grasp to close the clothespin.
4. Repeat step two, removing the clothespin and placing it in the bowl.
5. Invite the child to clip the clothespins to the bowl, then remove them.

More to do

Games: Play a relay game with clothespins. Divide the children into two teams and give each child a clothespin. Children will grasp a paper cup with the clothespin, race to the goal line, return, and transfer the cup to the next child in line.

Language: Sort the clothespins by color and learn the color names.

Math: Count the clothespins. Group them by color, leaving space between the colors. How many are there of each color? Which color has the most? The least?

❦ Mary Jo Shannon, Roanoke, VA

Color Sorter

Materials

Assorted colored beads
Bowl or other container
Thread box with multiple compartments

What to do

1. Place assorted beads into a bowl or other container.
2. Encourage the child to sort the beads by color using the compartments in a thread box.

More to do

To increase fine motor dexterity and develop the pincher grasp, ask the child to use plastic tweezers to pick up and sort the beads.

Math: Ask the child to put one bead into the first compartment, two beads into the second compartment, three beads into the third compartment, and so on.

❦ Laura Gremett, Sunnyvale, CA

Sorting Buttons

Materials

Muffin tin
Buttons in a variety of colors

What to do

1. Place buttons in the top left cup of a muffin tin. The number of colors and size of buttons you use depends on the child's attention span and manual dexterity. Larger buttons are easier to handle, while small buttons are more challenging. Make sure to use a different number of buttons for each color, such as three reds, two whites, and one blue. To teach the concept of *equal*, use the same amount of two colors of buttons.

2. Encourage the child to work from left to right, placing a different color into each cup. Encourage the child to find others that match.

3. Keep the activity interesting by changing the items to be sorted. For example, use seashells, beads, fabric swatches, or cloth with different textures.

More to do

Art: Use buttons with other materials to create a collage.

Games: Play the game, "Button, Button, Who Has the Button?" Ask the children to sit in a circle. One child is IT and leaves the group. The rest of the children hold out their hands in a "prayer" position. Hold your hands in the same position, but place a button between your palms. Move from child to child, sliding your hands through the children's hands. Release the button to one child (who tries to avoid showing surprise). When you have visited all the children, they say, "Button, button, who has the button?" IT returns and tries to guess who has the button. If IT does not guess after three tries, the person who has the button reveals it and becomes the new IT.

Language: Add to the children's vocabulary by discussing colors and names and the concepts of *more*, *less*, *few*, *total*, and *equal*.

Math: Count the button in each cup. Which color has the most buttons? Which has fewest? Are there more blue than red? How many buttons in all?

♣ Mary Jo Shannon, Roanoke, VA

Rose Necklace

Materials

Heavy thread
Needle
Dried rose buds, available in various stores
Beads, optional

What to do

1. Thread the needles.
2. Help the children thread rosebuds onto the string. (How much help children will need depends on the children's ability.) Ten to twenty look and smell beautiful.
3. If desired, thread beads onto either end of the roses.
4. Knot the ends of the necklace together, and it is ready to wear!

More to do

Use thin wire and "sew" the rosebuds onto the wire. Shape the wire into a heart and tie the two ends together with a piece of ribbon.

❧ Susan Rubinoff, Wakefield, RI

Rustic Frame

Materials

Scissors
Leather thong or yarn
Sticks, approximately 6" (15 cm) long and ½" (1 cm) in diameter
Clear contact paper
Photo of child
Hole punch
Yarn
Plastic lacing needles

What to do

1. Before starting this activity, cut leather thong or yarn into 6" (15 cm) pieces.
2. Help each child arrange sticks into a square shape as an adult holds the sticks steady.
3. Encourage the child to take a piece of leather or yarn and tie the sticks together in one corner of the frame (a simple knot will hold), then repeat on the other three corners. Set the frame aside.
4. Cut clear contact paper so that it is 1" (2 cm) wider than the photo.
5. Peel the backing from the contact paper, revealing the sticky side.
6. Help the child place her photo face down in the center of the contact paper. Make sure there is a margin at least ½" (1 cm) around the photo.
7. Place a second piece of contact paper over the back of the photo. Encourage the child to smooth out any bubbles.
8. Trim the raw edges of the contact paper, making sure to leave a ½" (1 cm) margin around the photo.
9. Punch holes around the edges of the photo.
10. Thread a needle with yarn. Help the child "sew" around the photo and the frame, connecting the photo to the frame.

❧ Dani Rosensteel, Payson, AZ

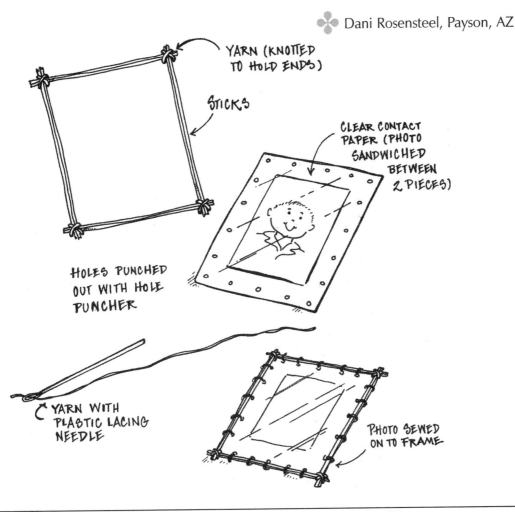

YARN (KNOTTED TO HOLD ENDS)

STICKS

CLEAR CONTACT PAPER (PHOTO SANDWICHED BETWEEN 2 PIECES)

HOLES PUNCHED OUT WITH HOLE PUNCHER

YARN WITH PLASTIC LACING NEEDLE

PHOTO SEWED ON TO FRAME

The Nuts and Bolts of It

Materials

4 sets each of small, medium, and large nuts and bolts
3 pieces of 2" x 4" (5 cm x 10 cm) wood, each 16" (40 cm) long
Super glue
Ruler

What to do

1. Glue the top of a large bolt 2" (5 cm) from the end of one of the 2" x 4" boards.
2. Glue three more large bolts to the board, at 4" (10 cm) intervals.
3. Repeat this procedure on another 2" x 4" board, using four medium-size bolts.
4. On the last 2" x 4" board, repeat the process again using four small bolts.
5. Allow the boards to dry.
6. Provide a board and the correct size and number of nuts to a child. Consider the child's fine motor abilities when choosing a board for her to use—the larger the bolt, the easier it is for a child to manipulate.
7. Show the child how to manipulate the nut and bolt together and encourage her to practice her fine motor skills.

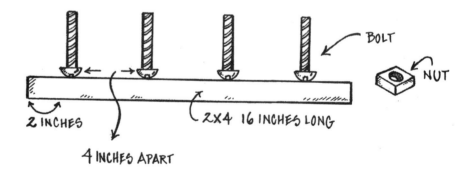

More to do

Make a board with assorted bolt sizes. This will challenge children to problem solve as they locate and match the correct nut and bolt combinations.

🍀 Ann Gudowski, Johnstown, PA

Tong-Pong

Materials

Water table or large tub
Water
Ping-Pong balls
Kitchen tongs
Permanent marker (adult only)
Foam egg carton

What to do

1. Fill the water table or a large tub with water. Drop Ping-Pong balls into it.
2. Encourage the children to use kitchen tongs to catch the floating Ping-Pong balls.
3. Use this activity to teach numerals, letters, or shapes as well. For example, write the numbers 0-12 on the Ping-Pong balls using a permanent marker. Then, label an egg carton with the same numbers.
4. As the children catch the balls, encourage them to drop each ball into the carton cup that matches the number on their ball.
5. Another example is to use letters instead of numbers. Label the balls and egg carton cups with various matching letters.
6. Encourage the children to spell names and simple words with the balls.
7. Display short words and pictures to promote the literacy component of this activity.

More to do

Try burying the Ping-Pong balls in Styrofoam peanuts.

Bev Schumacher, Dayton, OH

Musical Boxes

Materials

Heavy cardboard or wooden boxes, without lids
Rubber bands in a variety of thicknesses

What to do

1. Put the cardboard boxes on the worktable along with many rubber bands.
2. The children can stand or sit around the table.
3. Demonstrate how to select a box and place two or more rubber bands around the open box, either lengthwise or width-wise.
4. Encourage the children to practice plucking or strumming their box.

More to do

Circle Time: The children may play their instruments while singing songs.
Science: Leave the boxes and rubber bands on a science table for a day or two so the children can experiment with the materials.

❖ Elaine C. Commins, Athens, GA

Tools for Precutting

Materials

Small objects, such as blocks, Styrofoam packing pieces, buttons, or beads
Bowls or containers
Tongs
Tweezers
Tempera paint
Cotton balls
Paper
Tray
Colored water
Bulb baster
Eyedroppers

What to do

All of the following activities use the squeeze/release motion that scissors require.

Tong Transfer

1. Fill a bowl with several objects and place it on a table.
2. Provide one empty container for each type of object.
3. Encourage the children to use tongs to pick up the objects and sort them into the empty bowls.
4. Repeat the activity using smaller objects and tweezers.

Cotton Ball Painting

1. Pour tempera paint into bowls.
2. Encourage the children to use tweezers to pick up a cotton ball. The child can dip it into paint and use it as a brush to paint on a piece of paper.
3. Give the child a new cotton ball when it gets too soggy or if she wants to change colors.
4. Discard used cotton balls or stick them to the picture for an interesting effect.

Bulb Blaster Water Transfer

1. Place a bowl of colored water on the left side of a tray.
2. Place an empty bowl on the right side of the tray.
3. Encourage the children to use a bulb baster to transfer water from the bowl on the left to the bowl on the right.
4. Do the same activity using smaller bowls and eyedroppers.

❧ Sandra Gratias, Perkasie, PA

Cutting Up

Materials

Child-sized, various toothed craft scissors
Craft items, such as different types of paper, craft foam, and ribbon
Construction paper
Glue sticks

What to do

1. Ask the children to choose a pair of scissors and a craft item.
2. Encourage the children to cut their craft items into strips or bits.
3. Ask the children to glue the cuttings onto construction paper to form their own creation or collage.

More to do

Place the cuttings onto clear contact paper instead of gluing them to construction paper to create a sun catcher. Cover the back of it with another piece of clear contact paper. Punch a hole at the top of the paper and lace a piece of yarn through it. Knot it and hang it near a window to enjoy.

❧ Tina Woehler, Oak Point, TX

The Cutting Box

Materials

Box
Markers or paint and brushes
Paper
Tape
Envelopes
Different materials for cutting, such as magazines, catalogs, wallpaper, newspaper, construction paper, tissue paper, and store advertisements
Children's scissors
String, optional
Paper and glue sticks

What to do

1. Choose a box that is low to the ground, so that the children will be able to sit around it and reach into it. Make sure it is shallow enough so that the children can see what is inside.
2. Encourage the children to decorate the box using markers or paint. Write "Cutting Box" on the side.
3. Make a paper "pouch" and tape it outside the box. Place a stack of envelopes inside the pouch. (The children will use the envelopes to store their cuttings.)
4. Place the cutting materials inside the box, along with children's scissors. If desired, attach a string to the box to hang the scissors.
5. Bring out the box once a week or as needed. (For example, I noticed a huge improvement in the children's cutting skills after they were given the chance to practice at their own pace and in a casual environment.)
6. Add fun scissors, such as those with zigzag and curved edges to add new interest to the center. Rotate the supplies to make it interesting for the chil-

dren who do not like to cut or who lack confidence in their cutting skills.

7. Add paper and glue sticks occasionally and encourage the children to glue their cutouts to the paper.

More to do

Change the items in the Cutting Box to reflect the classroom themes. For example:

■ Ask the children to cut out specific items from magazines that match the specific theme. For example: jobs, transportation, flowers and plants, letters, animals or pets, and so on.

■ Make a clothesline. Ask the children to cut out clothes for a specific season and use clothespins to hang them on the special clothesline. Discuss why we wear different clothes at different times of year.

■ Divide a piece of large poster board into different sections, such as the food groups, different colors, or different shapes. Hang the poster board on a wall. Ask the children to cut out items for each section and glue them in the appropriate area.

■ If the children are learning about the food groups, give each child a paper plate. Ask the children to cut out foods that make a balanced meal and glue them to the plate.

❧ Gail Morris, Kemah, TX

Face Puzzles

Materials

Close-up photo of each child's face
Copy machine
8 ½" x 11" (21 cm x 27 cm) pieces of tag board
Glue
Variety of wrapping paper (ask each parent to send in a sheet)
Lamination machine, optional
Scissors
Zipper closure plastic bags

What to do

1. Use a copier to enlarge each child's photo to fit onto an 8 ½" x 11" (21 cm x 27 cm) piece of tag board.
2. Carefully glue the enlarged photo onto the tag board.
3. Allow the glue to dry.
4. Cut out an 8 ½" x 11" (21 cm x 27 cm) piece of wrapping paper. Glue it onto the back of the tag board. Make sure to use different wrapping paper for each face.
5. If desired, laminate the pictures.
6. Help the children cut the pictures into eight to ten pieces.
7. Put the pieces into a zipper closure bag and zip it closed. Label the bag with a small photo of the child's face, her name, and a small piece of the wrapping paper that is on the back of the puzzle.
8. Encourage the children to choose a puzzle and put it together. When they finish, they can take it apart, put it into the correct bag, and pick another one. (Some children may need help putting the correct pictures into the bags and zipping them shut.)
9. Put the puzzles in a learning center and encourage the children to have fun with them.

More to do

Ask the children to draw a picture. Show them how to make it into a puzzle, using the same technique as above.

Games: Play a game by taking a puzzle out of a bag and giving the pieces to the children. Ask them to put it together and figure out who it is!

Home Connection: On Parents Night, encourage the parents to exchange the bags and try to put the puzzles together.

❧ Barbara Saul, Eureka, CA

Making Puzzles

Materials

Scissors
Magazine pictures, old photos, or panels from empty toy or food boxes
Construction paper or light oak tag and glue, optional
Large zipper closure plastic bags

What to do

1. Cut out pictures from magazines, old photos, or panels from empty toy containers or cardboard food boxes (cereal boxes work well). You may want to glue the magazine pictures onto construction paper or light oak tag.
2. Encourage the children to examine the pictures.
3. Ask the children to choose a picture to make their own puzzles.
4. Encourage the children to randomly cut up their pictures.
5. Ask the children to reassemble their puzzles, picture side up.
6. Then, ask the children to turn their puzzles over and reassemble them without using a picture to guide them.
7. If time allows, encourage the children to exchange bags and try other puzzles.

❦ Constance Heagerty, Westborough, MA

Personal Puzzles

Materials

Copy machine
Photo of each child's face (school photos are good)
Card stock paper or paper, poster board, and rubber cement
Scissors

What to do

1. Use a copier to enlarge each child's photo to fit onto an 8 ½" x 11" (21 cm x 27 cm) piece of card stock paper. Copy the enlarged photo onto card stock paper. (If you don't have access to card stock paper, make copies of the pictures on regular paper and then mount them on poster board using rubber cement.)
2. Give the children their own pictures and explain to them that they are going to make their own puzzles.
3. Provide specific suggestions for the two initial cuts so that the children have distinct visual clues for matching up the puzzle pieces.
4. Help the children with the cutting for this activity.
5. Ask the children to cut horizontally through the eyes and then put the pieces back together.
6. Ask the children to make the next cut from the bottom of the picture and go through the mouth and nose. Shuffle the pieces and ask the child to assemble them.

7. Next, the children can make two vertical cuts out of the top puzzle piece (hair and forehead). Shuffle the pieces and ask the child to assemble them.
8. Ask the children to make a diagonal cut across one of the large pieces that contains half of the nose and mouth. Shuffle them and ask the child to assemble the pieces.
9. Cut the remaining large piece into two pieces, separating the nose and the mouth. Shuffle the pieces and ask the child to reassemble them.

More to do

Ask the children to draw pictures on card stock paper. Cut the pictures into puzzle pieces. Save the puzzle pieces for another day and make additional cuts depending on the ability level of the children. Cut up free posters provided by book clubs and use them as basic floor puzzles to connect an activity to a special book or author.

❧ Mary Volkman, Ottawa, IL

Learning to Print Names

Materials

Markers
Heavier weight paper or white cardboard (3" x 12"-15" (7 cm x 30-37 cm)
Clear contact paper
Paper towel or cloth

What to do

1. Using markers, print the child's name on a piece of white cardboard.
2. Cover the cardboard with clear contact paper.
3. Encourage the child to trace over the top of the letters using a washable marker.
4. Wash off the tracings with a damp paper towel or cloth.
5. Repeat the activity using the entire alphabet and numbers.

More to do

Cleanup: Make a game out of clean-up time. Play short segments of music and encourage the children to clean up while the music is on. When the music stops, the children act like statues until the music resumes. (The children in my class enjoy this so much, they often ask to clean up so they can play the clean-up game!)

✤ Phyllis Esch, Export, PA

Quick Sticks

Materials

8" x 10" (20 cm x 25 cm) piece of card stock paper
Scissors
16 stickers (or clip art) of things that are quick, such as crickets, cheetahs, planes, shooting stars, and so on
Clear contact paper

What to do

1. Cut a piece of 8" x 10" piece of card stock paper into four 10" (22 cm) strips.
2. Place four stickers onto each strip of card stock paper, top to bottom. Place the stickers so that the objects become progressively quicker, with the fastest one at the bottom of the strip.
3. Cover the strips with clear contact paper for greater durability.
4. Hold a "Quick Stick" about 6" (15 cm) above the child's (sideways) cupped hand. (Hold the Quick Stick so that the quickest thing on it, such as the shooting star in the four things mentioned in the materials, is closest to the child's hand.)
5. Drop the stick and the child catches it by closing her thumb and fingers.
6. Tell the child that she is "quick as a…" Fill in the blank with whatever sticker she is touching.
7. Children love to do this over and over and their reflexes will continue to improve.

More to do

This is a good opportunity to talk about the concept of gravity.
Blocks: Make ramps in the Block Area or on the playground. Roll a variety of objects down the ramps. Encourage the children to experiment using different angles and lengths of their ramps. They can make predictions, problem solve, and design.

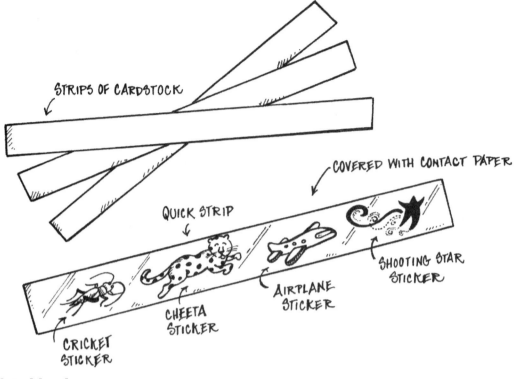

STRIPS OF CARDSTOCK

COVERED WITH CONTACT PAPER

QUICK STRIP

SHOOTING STAR STICKER

AIRPLANE STICKER

CHEETA STICKER

CRICKET STICKER

Related book

Quick as a Cricket by Audrey Wood

Song

The Quick Stick Song (Tune: "Are You Sleeping?")
Are you ready? Are you ready?
Here it comes; here it comes.
Catch that "Quick Stick"; catch that "Quick Stick."
How fast were you? How fast were you?

❧ Donna Borges, Crescent City, CA

Popsicle Stick Puppets

Materials

Laminate or clear contact paper
Pictures related to the theme
Scissors
Strapping tape
Popsicle sticks or craft sticks
Song sheets
Plastic bag

What to do

1. Laminate pictures related to the theme or cover them with clear contact paper.
2. Cut out the pictures and tape them to Popsicle or craft sticks.
3. Store the stick puppets in a plastic bag with the appropriate song sheets.

More to do

Use the stick puppets during Circle Time.

❧ Marybeth A. Hurd, Flower Mound, TX

Metamorphosis Glove Puppet

Materials

Pictures depicting the different life stages of a butterfly
Glue
Tag board
Scissors
Clear contact paper or laminate
Velcro
Work gloves

What to do

1. Find pictures that depict the different life stages of a butterfly: egg, caterpillar, chrysalis, and butterfly.
2. Glue the pictures to a piece of tag board and cut them out.
3. Cover the shapes with clear contact paper or laminate them.
4. Attach Velcro to the fingertips of a work glove and the backs of the pictures.
5. Use the glove to tell stories or fingerplays about a butterfly.

More to do

Raise a caterpillar in the classroom. Make a class book describing the children's observations.

Related books

A Butterfly Is Born by Melvin Berger
The Very Hungry Caterpillar by Eric Carle

❧ Jackie Wright, Enid, OK

Picture Songbook

Materials

Old magazines
Glue
Paper
Laminate, clear contact paper, or clear plastic sleeve
Hole punch
1" (2 cm) three-ring binder

What to do

1. Sing a song with the children that they already know. Then, look through old magazines with the children to find a picture that reminds everyone of the song. For instance, select a picture of a big red barn or farm scene for "Old MacDonald Had a Farm."
2. Glue the picture on a piece of paper and write the name of the song below it.
3. Cover it with clear contact paper, laminate it, or put it into a plastic sleeve.
4. Punch three holes along the side and put it in a three-ring binder.

5. Whenever the children learn a new song that they enjoy singing, find a picture of it and add it to the book.

6. Put the book at the music table or on a shelf where the children can reach it. At music time, the children can take turns looking in the book and selecting songs to sing.

More to do

This activity also works well for fingerplays, poems, and short repetitive stories.

❖ Kathleen Wallace, Columbia, MO

I Look in the Mirror

Materials

None needed

What to do

1. Sing the following song to the tune of "I'm a Little Teapot."

    I Look in the Mirror (adapted by Deborah R. Gallagher)

    I look in the mirror
    And who is that I see?
    A very special person
    Who looks a lot like me.
    Eyes so bright and shiny,
    A smile that's pearly white.
    It's great to be me,
    What a lovely sight!

❖ Deborah R. Gallagher, Bridgeport, CT

I'm Dressed Warmly

Materials

None needed

What to do

1. Sing the following song to the tune of "Twinkle, Twinkle Little Star."

   I'm Dressed Warmly

   When the winter's cold has come,
   Dress up warmly everyone.
   Put on your coat and zip it up;
   Scarf and mittens, hat on top.
   Winter's cold won't bother me,
   I'm dressed warmly as can be!

   ❖ Deborah R. Gallagher, Bridgeport, CT

Scissor Cutting

Materials

None needed

What to do

1. Sing the following song to the tune of "Open, Shut Them."

   Scissor Cutting

   Open, shut them, open, shut them
   Give a little snip.
   Open, shut them, open, shut them
   Make another clip.

Cut along the dotted lines
To cut out your design.
Use the scissors carefully,
And you'll do just fine.

Open, shut them, open, shut them
Give a little snip.
Open, shut them, open, shut them
Make another clip.

❦ Deborah R. Gallagher, Bridgeport, CT

I Love You

Materials

Poster paper
Marker

What to do

1. Write the following song on a piece of poster paper.
2. Sing the song to the tune of "London Bridge."
   I Love You
   I L-O-V-E Y-O-U
   Y-O-U Y-O-U
   I L-O-V-E Y-O-U
   I love you.

3. This song teaches children how to spell "I Love You." The capital letters signify that you sing the letters, not the whole word. Use this song around Mother's Day and Father's Day to help the children make a card.

❦ Bettejane Grey, Woodbridge VA

Mom and Dad

Materials

Poster paper
Markers

What to do

1. Write the following song on a piece of poster paper.
2. Sing the song to the tune of "Twinkle, Twinkle Little Star."

   Mom and Dad
   M-O-M that spells Mom.
   D-A-D that spells Dad.
   Write a note to Mom and Dad.
   They will be so very glad.
   M-O-M that spells Mom.
   D-A-D that spells Dad.

3. Use this song to teach the children how to spell Mom and Dad. Capital letters signify that you sing the letters, not the whole word.
4. Sing this song around Mother's Day and Father's Day to help children learn to write to their parents.

✤ Bettejane Grey, Woodbridge, VA

Grandma's Letter

Materials

None needed

What to do

1. Sing the following song to the tune of "I'm a Little Teapot."

   I sealed it and stamped it
   And put it in the box.
   I hope that Grandma
   Loves her note a lot.

Then she'll call me up to thank me so.
"Got your letter, I wanted you to know!"

❖ Deborah R. Gallagher, Bridgeport, CT

Please and Thank You

Materials

Poster paper
Markers

What to do

1. Write the following song on a piece of poster paper (without the italics).
2. Sing the song to the tune of "Frère Jacques." Emphasize the words in boldface type (not including the title).

    Please and Thank You
    Please and Thank You,
    Please and Thank You,
    That's polite.
    That's polite.
    *Saying **please** is what you **should** do.*
    ***Thank you**, you should say too.*
    You are right.
    That's polite.

3. Sing this song throughout the year to remind children about using good manners.

❖ Bettejane Gray, Woodbridge, VA

Who Can Use Their Inside Voice?

Materials

None needed

What to do

1. This is a great song to sing with the children to remind them they are becoming too noisy. Sing it to the tune of "Mary Had a Little Lamb."
   Who can use their inside voice, inside voice, inside voice?
   Who can use their inside voice? Show me quietly.

❖ Lisa M. Chichester, Parkersburg, WV

I Went to the Dentist

Materials

What to do

1. Sing the following song to the tune of "The Wheels on the Bus."
   I Went to the Dentist
   I went to the dentist the other day,
   The other day, the other day.
   I went to the dentist the other day.
   "Hmmmm," he said, "Let's see."

   The dental hygienist cleaned my teeth,
   Cleaned my teeth, cleaned my teeth.
   The dental hygienist cleaned my teeth,
   "Oh," she said, "That's good."

   Then she flossed between my teeth,
   Between my teeth, between my teeth.

Then she flossed between my teeth,
"Oh," she said, "That's good."

They took x-rays of my teeth,
Of my teeth, of my teeth.
They took x-rays of my teeth,
"Oh," she said, "That's good."

Then the dentist checked my teeth,
Checked my teeth, checked my teeth.
Then the dentist checked my teeth,
"Oh," he said, "That's good."

He said to me, "You don't have cavities.
You don't have cavities, you don't have cavities."
He said to me, "You don't have cavities."
"Aah," I said, "That's good!"

❧ Deborah R. Gallagher, Bridgeport, CT

The Vet

Materials

None needed

What to do

1. Sing the following song to the tune of "Here We Go 'Round the Mulberry Bush."

The Vet

I took my pet to the vet,
To the vet, to the vet.
I took my pet to the vet
"Ah," he said. "Let's see."

He checked my pet from head to tail,
Head to tail, head to tail.

He checked my pet from head to tail
To see if he was healthy.

He gave my pet a vac-cin-a-tion,
Vaccination, vaccination.
He gave my pet a vac-cin-a-tion
Just—like—me!

❧ Deborah R. Gallagher, Bridgeport, CT

Call for Help

Materials

None Needed

What to do

1. Sing the following song to the tune of "Here We Go 'Round the Mulberry Bush."

   ### Call for Help
   This is the way we call for help—
   Dial 9-1-1, dial 9-1-1.
   This is the way we call for help—
   Dial 9-1-1 for help.

   The paramedic checks us out,
   Checks us out, checks us out.
   The paramedic checks us out
   And helps us to get better.

   They take us to the hospital,
   The hospital, the hospital.
   They take us to the hospital
   In the ambulance.

The doctors and nurses help make us well,
Make us well, make us well.
The doctors and nurses help make us well
So we can go home.

❧ Deborah R. Gallagher, Bridgeport, CT

The Train

Materials

None needed

What to do

1. Sing the following song to the tune of "I'm a Little Teapot."
   The Train *(adapted by Deborah R. Gallagher)*
   I go on a train
   That runs on the track.
   It takes me to my Grandmother's
   And it comes right back.
   Riding on a train
   Is fun, you can see.
   Next time won't you come along with me?

❧ Deborah R. Gallagher, Bridgeport, CT

Senses

Materials

None needed

What to do

1. This is a great song to help children learn about senses and how they function.
2. Sing the following song to the tune of "The Farmer in the Dell."

You see with your eyes.
You see with your eyes.
Hi-ho, the derry-o
You see with your eyes.

3. Repeat the verse using each of the senses:

You hear with your ears.
You smell with your nose.
You taste with your mouth.
You feel with your skin (or fingers).

🍀 Phyllis Esch, Export, PA

My Round Ball

Materials

None needed

What to do

1. Sing the following song to the tune of "B-I-N-G-O."
   My Round Ball
   I have a ball
   It's shape is round.
   I like to bounce it up and down.
   Bounce, bounce, bounce my ball. (Sing three times)
   I like to bounce my ball.

🍀 Deborah R. Gallagher, Bridgeport, CT

A Triangle

Materials

None Needed

What to do

1. Sing the following song to the tune of "Have You Ever Seen a Lassie?"
2. Encourage the children to do the actions with you.

A Triangle

Have you ever seen a triangle?
A triangle, a triangle?
Have you ever seen a triangle?
It looks just like this. (make shape w/ fingers)
It has three sides. (hold up 3 fingers)
That look just like this. (make shape w/ fingers)
Have you ever seen a triangle?
It looks just like this. (make shape w/ fingers)

❖ Deborah R. Gallagher, Bridgeport, CT

Opposites Song

Materials

None needed

What to do

1. Sing the following song to the tune of "Twinkle, Twinkle Little Star."

Opposites Song

Over, under, up and down.
Gather together and circle 'round.
Open, shut, push and pull.
In and out, empty, full.
Opposites are fun, you will see.
Come along and sing with me.

❖ Deborah R. Gallagher, Bridgeport, CT

Fall Is Here

Materials

None needed

What to do

1. Sing the following song to the tune of "Row, Row, Row Your Boat."

    Fall Is Here

    Fall, fall, fall is here
    Let's all have some fun.
    Leaves are falling everywhere
    Bright colors, everyone.

    Fall, fall, fall is here
    Rake the leaves up high.
    Gather leaves both far and near
    Let's all give it a try.

    ❖ Deborah R. Gallagher, Bridgeport, CT

Butter Song

Materials

None needed

What to do

1. Sing the following song to the tune of "The Farmer in the Dell."

    Butter Song

    We're going to make some butter
    We're going to make some butter
    Hi, ho the derry-o
    We're going to make some butter.

Pour cream in a jar
Pour cream in a jar
Hi, ho the derry-o
We're going to make some butter.

Shake it up and down
Shake it up and down
Hi, ho the derry-o
We have made some butter!

❖ Deborah R. Gallagher, Bridgeport, CT

This Friend of Mine

Materials

None needed

What to do

1. This song will develop children's self-identity, as well as their language, social, and emotional skills.
2. Sing the following song to the tune of "The Muffin Man."
   Oh, do you know this friend of mine, friend of mine, friend of mine?
   Oh, do you know this friend of mine?
   His name is_____.

3. This is a great transition song to sing as children go to and from group time.

More to do

Coordinate sign language with the words.

❖ Terri Hersom, Gonic, NH

I'm a Little Pizza

Materials

Poster paper
Marker

What to do

1. Write the words of the following song on a piece of poster paper.
2. Sing the following song to the tune of "I'm a Little Teapot."

I'm a little pizza,
Kids love me,
With extra cheese and pepperoni.
I'm made of crust and tomato paste
And lots of yummy things
For you to taste!

More to do

Literacy: Ask the children to name their favorite pizza toppings and list them on a piece of poster paper next to their names.

Snack: Following up with a homemade pizza party would be lots of fun!

More Snack: Group pizza toppings according to food groups and ask the children to decide if their pizza creation makes a balanced meal. Ask them what they would need to eat with their pizza to make it a balanced meal. Fruit anyone?

♣ Angela Williamson La Fon, Banner Elk, NC

Spanish Greeting and Farewell Songs

Materials

None needed

What to do

1. Explain to the children that some people speak different languages and introduce the following Spanish songs to them.
2. Sing both of the songs to the tune of "Frere Jacques."

    ### Greeting
    Buenos dias. (Good morning)
    Buenos dias.
    Como estas? (How are you?)
    Como estas?

    Buenos dias, niños.
    Buenos dias, niños.
    Como estas?
    Como estas?

    ### Farewell
    Adios, adios. (Goodbye, goodbye)
    Adios, amigos. (Goodbye, friends)
    Adios, amigos.

    Hasta la mañana. (See you tomorrow)
    Hasta la mañana.
    Adios, adios.

Related books

Teach Me Spanish by Judy Mahoney and Mary Cronan
Teach Me More Spanish by Judy Mahoney and Mary Cronan

❧ Nancy DeSteno, Andover, MN

Sign the Alphabet Song

Materials

Chart of the American Sign Language Alphabet

What to do

1. Discuss with the children that another way of talking is by using our hands. Explain that they can say the ABCs using their hands and fingers.
2. Show the children the first letters of their names in sign language. This is to help them make the connection between letters and the signing of letters.
3. Sing the Alphabet Song, signing the letters as you sing.
4. Repeat the song and ask the children to watch for their letters as you sign.
5. Encourage the children to use their fingers and hands to make the letters with you. Show them how to place their fingers and hands for the different letters.
6. Display the chart so the children can look at it and explore making the signs.

More to do

Encourage the children to practice signing their names and other words.

Related book

Words in Our Hands by Ada B. Litchfield

❖ Sandra Nagel, White Lake, MI

Susie's Selling Lollipops

Materials

Construction paper, in a variety of colors
Scissors
Stapler
Popsicle sticks

What to do

1. Cut out circles from construction paper.
2. Help the children staple the circles to Popsicle sticks.

3. Give all of the sticks to one child to hold and help him spread them out like a fan.
4. Sing the following song to the tune of "The Muffin Man."

Oh, Susie's selling lollipops, lollipops, lollipops,
Susie's selling lollipops, which color do you want?

5. Each child names a color and selects it.
6. After the children name and select all the colors, ask another child to be the seller.

More to do

Explain to the children what a lollipop is—they may not be familiar with the name. Try naming flavors that the colors represent, such as cherry, orange, grape, and so on.

❖ Mary Jo Shannon, Roanoke, VA

I'm a Little Turtle

Materials

Green construction paper
Scissors
Crayons or markers
Glue
Popsicle sticks
Poster paper

What to do

1. Help the children cut out turtle patterns from green paper (see illustration). If desired, use white paper and color it green.
2. Encourage the children to decorate and individualize their turtles using crayons or markers.
3. Glue Popsicle sticks onto both of the two pieces of the turtle.
4. Insert the movable head into the neck of the turtle's body.
5. Write the following song on a piece of poster paper.
6. Sing the following song to the tune of "I'm a Little Teapot." Encourage the children to move the turtles' heads in and out as they sing.

I'm a Little Turtle

I'm a little turtle.
I live in a shell.
It is my house
And it protects me well.
When I sense danger I duck right in
And when it's safe I pop out again.

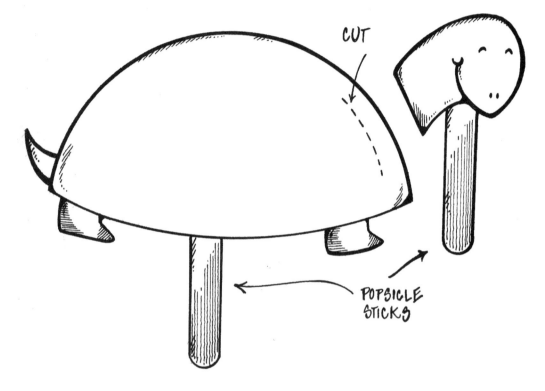

CUT

POPSICLE STICKS

More to do

Encourage the children to name their turtles. Ask them to share why they chose that name.

✿ Angela Williamson La Fon, Banner Elk, NC

Going on a Picnic

Materials

Pictures of items mentioned in the song, such as a picnic basket, watermelon, lemonade, sandwiches, and cookies
Felt
Glue
Tape of the song "Going on a Picnic"
Cassette player

What to do

1. Obtain pictures of the items mentioned in the song "Going on a Picnic." Glue felt to the backs of them.
2. Play a recording of the song and sing along as you place the mentioned items on the flannel board.
3. Encourage the children to manipulate the items and listen to the song during their free choice time.

More to do

Encourage the children to make up new verses to the song and draw their own pictures for the items they add.

Related books

One Hundred Hungry Ants by Elinor J. Pinczes
Sam's Snack by David Pelham

❧ Jackie Wright, Enid, OK

Old MacDonald's Farm Play

Materials

Pictures of farm animals
Paper plates
Craft supplies, such as construction paper, yarn, string, glitter, felt, cloth scraps, feathers, and pompoms
Scissors
Glue
Large tongue depressors

What to do

1. Sing "Old MacDonald Had a Farm" with the children.
2. Show the children pictures of the various animals in the song.
3. Explain to the children that they will be presenting a play about the song.
4. Ask each child to choose which animal he wants to be. Make sure that each animal is represented at least once.
5. Give each child a paper plate. Encourage the children to use the craft supplies to create their animal masks.
6. When the children are finished, help them glue tongue depressors to the masks to make a handle.
7. Practice singing the song with the children. As each animal is mentioned, the child with that animal mask will stand up.
8. Present the play to other classes.

More to do

Encourage the children to come up with other exciting places that Old MacDonald would like, such as Old MacDonald had a zoo, lake, train, playground, or pool. Help the children write their own lyrics and make a book.

Related book

Spot Goes to the Farm by Eric Hill

Songs or Poems

"Baa Baa Black Sheep"
"Farmer in the Dell"
"Little Boy Blue"
"Mary Had a Little Lamb"

Vicki Whitehead, Fort Worth, TX

Five Little Ducks
Storytelling Collars

Materials

White felt, 1 yard (1 m)
Scissors
Feathers
Glue
"Five Little Ducks" story

What to do

1. Fold the piece of felt lengthwise to allow a double fold of fabric about 12" (30 cm) wide.
2. On the folded edge of the felt, trace a large "U" shape. Make it large enough so that when it is cut out, it will create a hole that will fit over a child's head.
3. Trace a second "U" shape about 6" (15 cm) below the first "U" to create the bottom edge of the collar.
3. Glue several feathers to the front of each of the six collars to create story characters for retelling "Five Little Ducks."

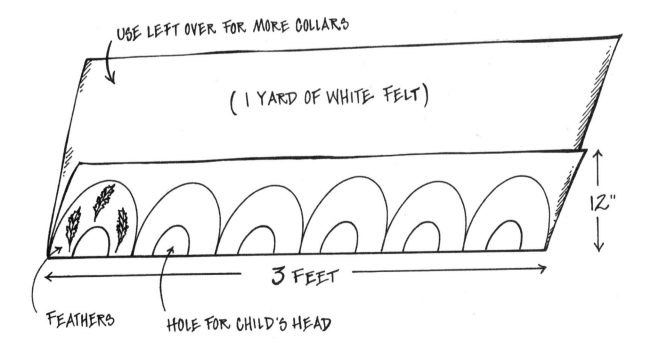

USE LEFT OVER FOR MORE COLLARS

(I YARD OF WHITE FELT)

12"

3 FEET

FEATHERS   HOLE FOR CHILD'S HEAD

4. Six children wear the storytelling collars and role play the song as the other children sing the song.

5. Create other storytelling collars for retelling books and fingerplays. Use any felt or fabric pieces to create the characters. Decorate as needed.

Songs

Fingerplay: (traditional)
Five little ducks went out one day
Over the hills and far away
Mother Duck said, "Quack, quack, quack, quack."
But only four little ducks came swimming back.

(Continue until no ducks come back)

Sad Mother Duck went out one day
Over the hills and far away
Mother Duck said, "Quack, quack, quack, quack."
And the five little ducks came swimming back.

❧ Ann Wenger, Harrisonburg, VA

Stamped Booklets

Materials

Paper
Pen, typewriter, or computer
Copier
Stapler
Rubber stamps and inkpad
Crayons

What to do

1. Teach the children a counting song or fingerplay, such as "Five Little Ducks," "Five Little Monkeys," "One Elephant Went Out to Play," "Ten in the Bed," and so on.

2. Type or print each line of the song or fingerplay on a separate piece of paper. Make copies of each page for each child.

3. Make a booklet for each child by stapling together the pages.
4. Give each child a booklet and a rubber stamp of the animal in the song. Encourage them to make one stamp on the first page, two on the second page, and so on.
5. Encourage the children to use crayons to draw pictures in their books.
6. Sing the song with the children as they follow along in their booklets.
7. Encourage the children to take their books home to teach their families the songs.

More to do

Instead of using stamp pads, encourage the children to draw directly on the rubber stamps using markers. Encourage the children to make stick puppets by cutting out paper animal shapes and gluing Popsicle sticks to them. With the children, make up other versions of the song by substituting other animals. The children can make a class stamp book of the new version.

Dramatic Play: Encourage the children to act out the song by moving like the animals mentioned. Substitute other animals, if desired.

Related books

Five Little Ducks by Raffi
Five Little Monkeys Jumping on the Bed by Eileen Christelow
Five Little Monkeys Sitting in a Tree by Eileen Christelow

❧ Laura Durbrow, Lake Oswego, OR

Five Speckled Frogs

Materials

5 plastic speckled frogs (found at novelty stores)
Medium-size piece of wood
Blue plastic placemat

What to do

1. Place the piece of wood on the blue placemat. Put the five speckled frogs on top of the wood.
2. Begin singing the song (see below) with the children. When you get to the part that says, "One jumped into the pool where it was nice and cool," place one frog on the blue placemat.

3. Continue singing the song. When you get to the part that says, "Now there are four speckled frogs," count how many frogs are left on the piece of wood.

4. Repeat the song until all of the frogs are in the "pond."

More to do

Fine Motor: Teach the children the finger movements of "Five Little Speckled Frogs."

Five little speckled frogs (Show five fingers.)
Sitting on a speckled log, (Use the forearm of your left arm to be the log. Rest your right hand on the log.)
Eating some moist delicious bugs. (Make an eating motion with your hands.)
Yum! Yum! (Rub your tummy in a circular motion.)
One jumped into the pool, (Make a diving motion with your right hand.)
Where it was nice and cool. (Pretend to swim.)
Now there are four speckled frogs. (Show four fingers.)
Ribbit! Ribbit! (Make a ribbit motion by your bending fingers.)

Gross Motor: Show the children how to play leap frog. Provide plenty of space and encourage the children to leap over each other.

Music and Movement: Pretend the carpet area is a pond. Collect green swatches of carpet for lily pads. Play music and encourage the children to hop from swatch to swatch. Play a version of "Musical Chairs": Remove a "lily pad" and when the music stops, the children must find a lily pad.

Related books

The Big Wide-Mouthed Frog by Ana Martin Larranaga
Froggy Learns to Swim by Jonathan London
Frogs by Gail Gibbons
Jump, Frog, Jump! by Robert Kalan
Red-Eyed Tree Frog by Joy Cowley
Tale of a Tadpole by Barbara Ann Porter

❧ Quazonia J. Quarles, Newark, DE

Five Little Pumpkins

Materials

Orange and brown felt
Scissors
Flannel board
Recording of "Five Little Pumpkins"
Tape player

What to do

1. Cut out five pumpkins from orange felt and a fence and gate from brown felt.
2. Put the pumpkins, fence, gate, and flannel board in the Listening Center along with a recording of the song "Five Little Pumpkins." Encourage the children to use them at free choice time.
3. Encourage the children to manipulate the desired number of pumpkins on the flannel board as the song progresses.

More to do

Place a copy of the book *Five Little Pumpkins* illustrated by Iris Van Rynbach in the Listening Center, too.

Related book

The Perky Little Pumpkin by Margaret Friskey

❖ Jackie Wright, Enid, OK

Five Little Ducks

Materials

Yellow felt
Scissors
Flannel board
Recording of "Five Little Ducks"
Tape player

What to do

1. Cut out five ducks from yellow felt.
2. Put the ducks, a flannel board, and a recording of the song "Five Little Ducks" in the Listening Center. Encourage the children to use them at free choice time.
3. Encourage the children to manipulate the desired number of ducks on the flannel board as the song progresses.

More to do

Place the book *Five Little Ducks* by Raffi (illustrated by Jose Aruego and Ariane Dewey) in the Listening Center, too.

Related book

In the Rain with Baby Duck by Amy Hest

❖ Jackie Wright, Enid, OK

Five Yummy Fruits

Materials

Five fruit felt shapes and a felt board or five plastic fruits in a bowl

What to do

1. Place five felt fruit shapes on a felt board. Ask five children to remove one fruit after each verse, as you sing the song.
2. Or, place plastic fruits in a bowl and ask five children to remove one fruit after each verse, as suggested by the song.
3. Sing the following song to the tune of "Row, Row, Row Your Boat."

   Five Yummy Fruits
   Five yummy fruits sit in the bowl,
   We bought them at the store.
   My dad chose one and ate it, CRUNCH!
   Then there were four.

Four yummy fruits left in the bowl,
Some grew upon a tree.
My mom chose one and ate it, CRUNCH!
Then there were three.

Three yummy fruits left in the bowl,
Fresh as the morning dew.
My sis chose one and ate it, CRUNCH!
Then there were two.

Two yummy fruits left in the bowl,
Ripened by the sun.
Brother chose one and ate it, CRUNCH!
Then there was one.

One yummy fruit left in the bowl,
I'm running out of time.
I really don't mind sharing, CRUNCH!
But this one is mine!

More to do

Snack: Make fruit salad for snack or lunch.

Related books

The Giving Tree by Shel Silverstein
The Story of Johnny Appleseed by Aliki
Strawberry by Jennifer Coldrey

♣ Kathryn Sheehan, Cape Elizabeth, ME

Five Apples

Materials

None needed

What to do

1. Hold up five fingers and encourage the children to say the following poem with you. (Put down one finger after each verse.)

   Five little apples hanging on a tree,
   The juiciest apples you ever did see.
   The wind came past and gave an angry frown
   And one little apple came tumbling down.

2. Repeat the verse, inserting the numbers four, three, two, and one.

   Four little apples hanging on a tree…

❖ Sandy L. Scott, Vancouver, WA

Five Little Cars

Materials

None needed

What to do

1. Hold up five fingers. Encourage the children to do the following fingerplay with you.

   Five Little Cars

   Five little cars driving down the street.
   The first one said, "Stop when a red light you meet."
   The second one said, "When it's green, you can go."
   The third one said, "And yellow means slow."
   The fourth one said, "We must always follow the rules."
   The fifth one said, "So don't be a fool!"
   Five little cars were driving down the street,
   And no accidents did they meet.

❖ Deborah R. Gallagher, Bridgeport, CT

Five Buzzing Bees

Materials

None needed

What to do

1. Hold up five fingers. Encourage the children to do the following fingerplay with you.

    Five Buzzing Bees
    Five buzzing bees
    Buzzing in the breeze.
    One flew through an open door
    And now there are four.

    Four buzzing bees
    Buzzing in the breeze.
    One chased me around a tree
    And now there are three.

    Three buzzing bees
    Buzzing in the breeze.
    One got stuck in some glue
    And now there are two.

    Two buzzing bees
    Buzzing in the breeze.
    One flew off to have some fun
    And now there is one.

    One buzzing bee
    Buzzing in the breeze.
    He flew off toward the sun
    And now—there is—none!

    ❧ Deborah R. Gallagher, Bridgeport, CT

Five Little Letters

Materials

None needed

What to do

1. Hold up five fingers. Encourage the children to do the following fingerplay with you.

   ### Five Little Letters

   Five little letters came in the mail one day.
   "We can't wait to be read!" they seemed to say.
   Mommy came along and picked up the first.
   "I'll read it later," she said and put it in her purse.
   Daddy came along and said "This is for me!"
   I looked them over and now there are three.
   My brother came along and picked up his letter.
   "Grandma says she's feeling much better!"
   My sister came along taking the fourth,
   "My friend wants me to visit her up north!"
   I don't know who the last one is for
   I hope it's for me, that's for sure!

   ❧ Deborah R. Gallagher, Bridgeport, CT

Six Little Snowflakes

Materials

None needed

What to do

1. Hold up six fingers. Encourage the children to do the following fingerplay with you. Fold down one finger at a time with each verse.

   ### Six Little Snowflakes

   Six little snowflakes falling in a row,
   One floated down and said, "Oh oh."

Five little snowflakes falling from the sky,
One blew away and said, "Oh my."

Four little snowflakes all colored white,
One melted fast—oh, what a sight!

Three little snowflakes floating through the air
One blew that-a-way and left two—that's a pair!

Two little snowflakes softly falling down,
One landed on a snowman that was standing on the ground.

One little snowflake, the last of a great snowfall
But don't worry, he'll soon land with others,
And make a great snowball!

More to do

Use six pre-cut flannel board snowflakes. During each verse of the poem, take away one snowflake. Ask six children to stand up and pretend to be snowflakes. One child sits down as each snowflake disappears.

❖ Sue Myhre, Bremerton, WA

Two Big Dinosaurs

Materials

None needed

What to do

1. Fingerplays and songs are excellent for circle time but are also wonderful for transition times and as a spur of the moment time filler. Many children have favorites and can recite them by heart. As children grow and reach the ages of four and five, their imaginative and creative skills emerge. It's a perfect time to explore the creation of new and original fingerplays and songs.
2. The following fingerplay is a favorite one.

Two Little Blackbirds

Two little blackbirds sitting on a hill, (hold up both thumbs)
One named Jack and the other named Jill. (Bend one thumb then the other)
Fly away, Jack. Fly away, Jill. (Hide thumbs behind back)
Come back, Jack. Come back, Jill. (Hold up both thumbs in front again)

3. Try this fingerplay several times with the children. Then ask them:
   - What kind of animal do you like? (dogs, dinosaurs, lizards, and so on)
   - What do they look like? (furry, big, green, and so on)
   - Where do they live? (backyard, swamp, jungle, and so on)
   - How do they move? (run, stomp, crawl, and so on)
4. Modify the fingerplay, adding some of the children's names for extra special fun. Change the actions to suit the animal. You may wish to write the fingerplay on a large piece of paper and use the rebus method of pictures and words combined.

Two Big Dinosaurs

Two big dinosaurs sitting in the swamp, (hold up both fists)
One named Kolby, the other named Isaac. (Bend one fist then the other)
Stomp away, Kolby. Stomp away, Isaac. (Hide fist behind back)
Come back, Kolby. Come back, Isaac. (Hold up both fists in front again)

5. Try the fingerplay several times and ask each child to make suggestions for animals, movements, and habits. The children will enjoy hearing their names in this playful little rhyme.
6. Other songs and fingerplays that are easily modified include "The Bear Went Over the Mountain," "Five Little Monkeys," "Where Is Thumbkin," and "Found a Peanut." Modifying a song or a fingerplay is a perfect way to add to themes, but most important, it makes what seems old new again.

More to do

Sing songs that children can make up their own verses to, such as "Down by the Bay," "My Mama Don't Wear No Socks," or "She'll Be Coming 'Round the Mountain."

Literacy: Make a list of words to describe things.

More Literacy: Encourage the children to dictate or tape record their own stories.

Related books

Down by the Bay by Raffi
Little Rabbit Foo Foo by Michael Rosen

❖ Mark Crouse, Port Williams, Nova Scotia, Canada

Drum Beat

Materials

Drumsticks or wooden spoons, optional
Piano or keyboard, if available

What to do

1. Divide the children into two groups.
2. The first group of children will sing (in an even beat):
   Omph — pah – pah
   Omph — pah – pah
   The children will repeat this phrase until the end of the song when they will yell, "Bubblegum!" On the "Omph," the children bend their knees, and on the "pah," they stand straight again.
3. While the first group of children is singing the above phrase, the second group will sing:
   This is the beat of the drum,
   Sometimes this may sound quite glum.
   Maybe you wish we could hum
   That this is the beat of the drum.
   I'd rather be chewing (both groups of children yell) BUBBLEGUM!
4. If desired, give the children sticks or wooden spoons to tap out the beat. If the children use sticks or spoon, ask them to sit on the floor.
5. If you have a piano or keyboard, play notes and encourage the children to sing along. (For example: C G G, C G G, C G G, and so on.)

More to do

Encourage the children to take turns keeping the beat to the song on any musical instrument (for example, a triangle, finger cymbals, and so on).

❖ Marianne Birge, Medina, OH

Yodelay Hee Hoo

Materials

None needed

What to do

1. Say or chant the following silly rhyme with the children.
   Would it be funny if cats meowed, "Yodelay - hee - hoo?"
   Would it be silly if dogs barked, "Yodelay - hee - hoo?"
   Wouldn't it be crazy if we sang, "Yodelay - hee - hoo?"

More to do

Encourage the children to answer "Yodelay - hee - hoo!" instead of "Yes" to a question.

❖ Marianne Birge, Medina, OH

Singing a Rainbow

Materials

Popsicle sticks
Crepe paper (red, yellow, orange, pink, purple, green, and blue)
Tape or glue

What to do

1. Attach a different color of crepe paper to each Popsicle stick using tape or glue.
2. Give each child a Popsicle stick and crepe paper.
3. Teach the children the words to the rainbow poem:
   Red and yellow and orange and pink
   Purple and green and blue,
   I can sing a rainbow, sing a rainbow, with my friends like you.
4. The children will wave their colors each time it is mentioned in the poem.

❖ Lisa M. Chichester, Parkersburg, PA

Little Leaves

Materials

None needed

What to do

1. Before reciting the following rhyme, ask the children to stand up and put their hands over their heads. Encourage the children to move according to the song's directions.

   Little leaves are falling down (start moving hands down)
   Red and yellow, orange and brown, (start moving body down)
   Twirling, whirling without sound (still moving closer to the ground)
   Falling gently to the ground.

More to do

Give the children paper leaves to hold.

❖ Sandy L. Scott, Vancouver, WA

Sun Safe

Materials

None needed

What to do

1. Teach the children the following poem.

   A floppy, yellow sunbonnet
   With a lot of pretty flowers on it.
   Jenny puts the bonnet on
   To shade her from the summer sun.

   Ooey gooey sunscreen
   For feet and face and in-between.
   Steven rubs the sunscreen in,
   So the sun won't burn his skin.

More to do

Ask the children if they can think of other ways to protect their skin from the sun's rays (for example, a shade tree, an umbrella, or sunglasses).

❧ Dotti Enderle, Richmond, TX

My Gloves

Materials

Gloves

What to do

1. Say the following rhyme with the children and do the actions.
   These are my gloves. (Point to gloves.)
   Can you see? (Ask everyone.)
   Look what I do. Isn't it clever of me? (Put gloves on.)
   Each finger goes in its own house. (Show children how it's done.)
   And there they stay warm and still like a mouse.

❧ Ingelore Mix, Gainesville, VA

Maple Syrup and Pancakes

Materials

None needed

What to do

1. Chant the following poem about pancakes with the children.
   Pancakes, pancakes
   Round and thick
   Pour on the syrup
   And eat it up quick.

More to do

(Because we live in New York state, we are able to take part in sugaring. In the spring, we tap a tree on the playground for sap. We use a drill and collect the sap in a metal bucket and then boil it down.)

Dramatic Play: Cut out cardboard circles and cover them with brown paper for pancakes. Cut out squares from yellow construction paper squares for butter, and use little pitchers for pretend syrup.

♣ Andrea Clapper, Cobleskill, NY

Birthday Cake

Materials

Two round pieces of foam
Glue
Ribbon
Birthday candles

What to do

1. Glue together two circles of foam and glue a piece of ribbon around the middle.
2. Ask the birthday child to stick the candles into the top of the foam and pretend to blow them out.

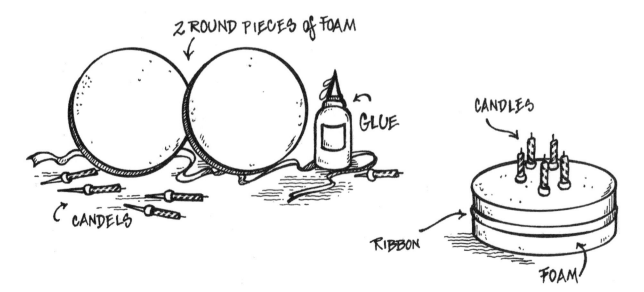

2 ROUND PIECES OF FOAM

GLUE

CANDELS

CANDLES

RIBBON

FOAM

3. As the child places the candles in the "cake," encourage the rest of the children to hold up their fingers and put down one finger at a time as the birthday child blows out the candles.

4. Say the following poem with the children:

Five birthday candles, I wish there were more.
Blow out one and then there are four.
Four birthday candles, pretty as can be.
Blow out one and then there are three.
Three birthday candles, we bought them new.
Blow out one and then there are two.
Two birthday candles, they shine like the sun.
Blow out one and then there is one.
One birthday candle—birthdays are such fun.
Blow out one and then there are none.

5. Ask the child to put on a birthday crown. Sing "Happy Birthday."

❖ Marilyn Harding, Grimes, IA

Poems for All Year Round

Materials

None needed

What to do

1. Use the following poems throughout the school year.

September

September is the month now.
Time for school to start.
We'll make lots of friends
And keep them in our heart.

October

October is the time we dress up me and you,
Put on scary costumes and then yell BOO!

November

November is for turkeys—they eat till they wobble.
Then on that special day, we say, "Gobble, gobble!"

December

Ho, ho, ho! December is here.
Santa comes with presents.
And our hearts are filled with cheer.

January

January is a cold month.
There can be lots of snow.
And if you have a sled.
Then down the hill you'll go!

February

February is a time of hearts of pink and red and white too
It's also a time of saying, "I love you!"

March

March brings St. Patrick's Day and that silly leprechaun.
When the 17th arrives you put your green on.

April

April showers bring May flowers and also Easter Eggs
Don't forget the bunny who hops upon his legs!

❖ Lisa M. Chichester, Parkersburg, PA

Ten in the Bed

Materials

Rectangle-shaped paper
Markers or wallpaper samples, scissors, and glue
Small paper cups
Teddy bear crackers or cookies

What to do

1. Teach the children the following poem:

    There were ten on the bed and the little one said, "Roll over, roll over."
    So they all rolled over and one fell out.

    Now there's nine in the bed and the little one said, "Roll over, roll over."
    So they all rolled over and one fell out.
    Now there's eight in the bed and the little one said, "Roll over, roll over."

    Continue the poem in this manner until there is one in the bed and the verse goes:

    There is one in the bed and the little one said,
    "Ah, now for a good night's sleep!"

2. Ask the children if they have a favorite blanket. Encourage them to describe it to a friend.

3. Give each child a piece of rectangle-shaped paper. Tell the children that it is shaped like a blanket, and it is called a *rectangle*. Ask the children to decorate the rectangles by coloring them with markers or tearing, cutting, and gluing wallpaper samples to them.

4. When the children are finished, give each child a cup filled with ten teddy bear crackers or cookies. (Tell them not to eat them yet.)

5. Ask the children to put the ten teddies on their "beds."

6. With the children, recite the "Roll Over" poem. In each verse, when you say, "One fell out," children eat one of their teddy bear cookies. Continue until they only have one left. Let them decide if they want to eat the last bear.

More to do

Dramatic Play: Encourage the children to act out the poem. They can lie down and pretend they are on a bed, "roll over" at the proper time, and one can pretend to fall out.

Related books

No Jumping on the Bed by Tedd Arnold
The Quilt Story by Tony Johnston

 Barbara Saul, Eureka, CA

Five Yummy Cookies

Materials

5-10 "cookies" cut out of construction paper or fabric

Pretend or real quarters, optional

What to do

1. Teach the children the words to the following rhyme and use "cookies" or quarters to act it out.

   There were five yummy cookies in the bakery shop,

   Five yummy cookies with the sprinkles on top,

   Along came _____ (child's name) with a quarter to pay

   And s/he bought one cookie and s/he took it away!

2. Continue the verses substituting four, three, two, and one.

   There were four yummy cookies in the bakery shop…

3. When you get down to no cookies left, say the following verse.

   There were no yummy cookies in the bakery shop,

   No yummy cookies with the sprinkles on top,

   Along came _____(child's name) with a quarter to pay

   And s/he bought _____(ask children what else they could buy at a bakery) and took it away!

More to do

Art: Encourage the children to cut out cookies from construction paper and decorate them with "sprinkles" (glitter).

Cooking: Bake cookies!

Dramatic Play: Place small cookie sheets in the playhouse.

Manipulatives: Make felt/flannel cookies for the felt board.

Math: Purchase plastic cookies (magnets or sewing/craft supplies) to use as counters.

Related books

The Doorbell Rang by Pat Hutchins

If You Give a Mouse a Cookie by Laura Numeroff

❖ Linda Ford, Sacramento, CA

Three Little Kittens

Materials

Mittens (one per child)
Chocolate cream pie (one piece per child)
Camera and film
Large tubs filled with soapy water
Clothespins and clothesline

What to do

1. Collect enough mittens so there is one for each child. (Gather mittens from the Lost and Found.) Hide all of the mittens. At group or circle time, recite the following verse.

   Three little kittens lost their mittens, and they began to cry,
   "Oh Mother Dear, we sadly fear, our mittens we have lost."
   "What, lost your mittens? You naughty kittens, then you shall have no pie."
   "Meow, meow, meow, we shall have no pie."

2. Ask the children to each find one mitten. When every child returns with a mitten, recite the next verse:

   The three little kittens, they found their mittens, and they began to cry,
   "Oh Mother Dear, see here, see here, our mittens we have found."
   "You found your mittens, you good little kittens, now you may have some pie."
   "Meow, meow, meow, we can have some pie."

3. For snack, give each child a piece of chocolate cream pie. Ask the children to wear the mittens as they eat their pie. (Take lots of pictures!) When snack time is over, ask the children to keep their mittens on. Recite the following verse:

   The three little kittens put on their mittens and ate up all the pie,
   "Oh Mother Dear, we sadly fear, our mittens we have soiled."
   "What! Soiled your mittens, you naughty kittens!" Then they began to sigh,
   "Meow, meow, meow," they began to sigh.

4. (Before doing this activity, fill large tubs with soapy water and place them outside.) Go outside with the children and ask them to wash their mittens in the tubs. (Hint: Use baby shampoo because of splashing.) Give the children plenty of time to play with the bubbles they create. Take more pictures!

5. When the water time is over, give each child a clothespin to hang a mitten on a low clothesline. As the mittens blow in the breeze, recite this verse:

The three little kittens washed their mittens and hung them out to dry.
"Oh Mother Dear, see here, see here! Our mittens we have washed."
"What, washed your mittens? You good little kittens, but I smell a mouse close by."
"Meow, meow, meow, we smell a mouse close by."

6. Encourage the children to say the rhyme with you.

Related book

The Mitten by Jan Brett

❖ Diane L. Shatto, Kansas City, MO

Neverending Musical Chairs

Materials

Chairs
Music of your choice

What to do

1. Begin playing the game "Musical Chairs" as usual.
2. When the music stops and the first child is left without a chair, the child will take the chair that was removed to the opposite side of the room and sit down. She is not left out—she is the first one to set up a new row of chairs.
3. Start the music again and follow the same procedure as step #2.
4. Play the game until all the chairs and children are on the opposite side of the room. Continue playing in the same manner. There is never a loser or winner!

❧ Ingelore Mix, Gainesville, VA

Puddle Jumping

Materials

Gray construction paper
Scissors
Markers
Laminate or clear contact paper
Masking tape, optional
Music of your choice

What to do

1. In advance, cut out large puddle shapes from gray construction paper. Write a letter of the alphabet on each puddle. Laminate or cover them with clear contact paper.
2. Scatter the "puddles" on the floor, taping them down if necessary. Encourage the children to jump from puddle to puddle as you play music.
3. At random intervals, stop the music and ask the children to name the letter written on the puddle on which they are standing.

4. Continue playing until the children lose interest.

More to do

Draw numbers, shapes, colors, number sets, or anything else on the puddles.

❖ Vicki Schneider, Oshkosh, WI

Special Relays

Materials

2 oranges or small foam balls
2 large bowls
2 blindfolds
2 long dowels or yardsticks
2 chairs
2 scooter boards
2 tricycles

What to do

1. Divide the children into two teams to play these special relays. Encourage the children to cheer loudly and clap for their team members. Make sure each child gets a turn.
2. Relay One: The first child picks up an orange or ball from a bowl using her elbows (no hands allowed). She runs to a second bowl, drops the orange or ball into it, and runs back to the team. The next child runs to the second bowl, picks up the object with her elbows, and then runs to the first bowl and drops it in. The third child repeats the first child's run, and so on.
3. Relay Two: Blindfold one child from each team and give each one a stick to use as a cane. Ask the two children to follow your voice to walk to a distant chair and then return to the team.
4. Relay Three: One child from each team will lie on her stomach on a scooter board and use her hands to pull herself to a distant chair, around it, and back to the team.
5. Relay Four: Use tricycles as "wheelchairs." Ask one child from each team to sit on a tricycle. She will steer it using the handlebars and rest her feet on the foot bar. A second child will rest her hands on the first child's shoulders or back and push her to a distant chair and back.
6. Reward all the children with ribbons or medals for effort.

More to do

Social Development: Discuss handicaps and how all people have feelings and dreams. Also explain that everyone has things they can do easily and things that are hard for them. People who are differently abled do many of the same things others do, only in a different way. Contact the Easter Seal Society or MS Society for educational materials. Teach the children some sign language.

Related books

Lucy's Picture by Nicola Moon
Someone Special, Just Like You by Tricia Brown
Special People, Special Ways by Arlene Maguire

❀ Sandra Gratias, Perkasie, PA

Mystery Bag

Materials

Easily recognized items, such as a feather, spoon, crayon, ball, paintbrush, block, or sock
Box
Paper bag
Blindfold, optional

What to do

1. Put easily recognized items in a box where the children can't see them.
2. Select one of the items and put it into a bag (without the children seeing).
3. Ask a child to put her hand into the bag and feel the item.
4. Encourage the child to give clues to the other children so they can guess what the item is. The child who guesses correctly picks the next item.

More to do

Get two of each item. Put one of each item into a box or bag and place the second of each item in front of the children. Pick up an item and hold it up so the children can see it. Ask a child to put her hand into the box and try to find the matching item by touch.

❀ Melissa Markham, Huddleston, VA

What's It Like?

Materials

Toys and items in the room that vary in size, shape, color, use, and so on
Bag or crate

What to do

1. Gather a collection of toys and other items from around the room that vary somewhat in size, shape, color, use, and so on and put them into a bag or crate.

2. Sit in a circle with the children. Pass the bag around and ask each child to retrieve one item from the bag.

3. Encourage the children to examine their item. Ask them to think about its color, size, shape, texture, what it is used for, and so on.

4. Begin the game by calling out a characteristic of some of the items and then a simple command (like in "Simon Says"). For example, "If it is round, pat your head!" The children should look at their item and determine whether or not to follow the command. At first, four-year-olds will have a tendency to follow all commands, regardless of whether or not it's true of their item, so you will have to remind them to wait for the next one if it does not apply to them. They'll catch on after a few trials.

5. At first, focus on visual attributes, such as color and shape. As the children begin to master the game, try some higher-level concepts. Examples include: "If it's for drawing...," "If it could fit in your pocket...," "If it can roll..," or "If you can build something with it..."

More to do

Play this game when doing various themes using theme-related items. For example, when doing a theme on the Beach or Ocean, use items such as seashells, sunscreen, sunglasses, a towel, and so on. For a theme on "Transportation," use a variety of play cars, trucks, planes, boats, and so on and use clues, such as "If it goes on land..." Once the children really learn the game, ask them to take turns giving clues to the other children.

❖ Suzanne Pearson, Winchester, VA

The Friendly Neighborhood Vet

Materials

Veterinarian tools

What to do

1. Discuss with the children the work of veterinarians. Explain that they take care of animals in zoos, circuses, farms, water parks, and hospitals.
2. Show the children some of the tools that vets use, making sure to use the correct names of the tools.
3. Play a take-away game. Show the children the veterinarian materials, cover them, and take one away (without the children seeing). Uncover the remaining materials and ask the children to guess which one is missing.

More to do

Art: Encourage the children to use paper, paint, collage materials, or clay to make a real or desired pet

Field Trips: Take the children to a zoo, pet store, or farm.

More Field Trips: Take the children to see a pet show.

Literacy: Encourage the children to dictate stories about their pets or livestock. Write down their words.

Social Studies: Invite a representative from the ASPCA to visit the class and talk about pet care.

More Social Studies: Invite a pet groomer to visit and demonstrate his or her job.

❧ Sandra Gratias, Perkasie, PA

Balloon Match

Materials

Balloons in a variety of colors
Scissors
Tissue color to match balloons

What to do

1. This activity reinforces the children's color matching and shape recognition while using their small and large muscles. The activity also lets children experience static electricity.
2. Inflate large round balloons in a variety of colors.
3. Cut out tissue paper shapes to match the colors of the balloons. (Eight of each color is a good number.) Scatter the tissue shapes around the room.
4. Ask a child to pick a balloon color. Discuss the chosen color.
5. Encourage the child to rub the balloon against her body to make static electricity.
6. The child then picks up the tissue paper shape that matches the balloon color.
7. Talk about the names of the colors as children retrieve the tissue paper balloon shapes.

Related books

Colors, Shapes, and Sizes by Michelle Warrence
Harvey Potter's Balloon Farm by Jerdine Harold

❖ Cindy Paddock, Palm Bay, FL

Circle of Shapes

Materials

Lightweight cardboard
Scissors
Safety pin

What to do

1. Cut out a 4" (10 cm) circle, square, triangle, and semi-circle from lightweight cardboard.
2. Ask the children to sit crossed legged on the floor, forming a circle.
3. Select two children of similar height. Ask them to stand in the center of the circle.
4. Ask the first child to close her eyes. Then, pin one of the shapes on the back of the second child.
5. The first child opens her eyes and moves around within the circle to try and see her opponent's back and the chosen shape.

6. The second child must move so that the first child cannot see the shape on her back. This should be done without either of the children touching.
7. The game is over when the first child has successfully seen and named the shape, or after three minutes have passed.
8. The two children sit back down in the circle. Select two more children to play.

More to do

Instead of shapes, use colors, letters, or numbers. Help the children cut out a square, circle, triangle, and semi-circle from colored paper and glue each one to a blank sheet of paper. Ask the children to name the shapes and encourage them to try to write the word under the shape.

❧ Elizabeth Bezant, Quinns Rocks, WA, Australia

Name That Shape

Materials

Cardboard or other stiff material
Scissors
Blindfold (Make a simple blindfold by tying or sewing a strip of polar fleece or other stretchy material to fit around a child's head. It will stretch to slide on or off.)

What to do

1. Cut out circles, squares, triangles, and rectangles from cardboard or other stiff material. (Puzzles or games may have these shapes.)
2. Ask several children to sit in a circle.
3. Present the shapes, one at a time, and point out the characteristics of each one. For example, a triangle has three corners; a square has four corners; a circle is round, smooth, and has no corners; and a rectangle has four corners, two long sides, and two short sides.
4. Choose one child to be "It" and put a blindfold on her.
5. Give her a shape to hold and identify.
6. Repeat the activity with each child, varying the shapes so the child cannot guess which will be next.

More to do

When children can easily identify basic shapes, add other shapes such as ovals, parallelograms, and so on. Use three-dimensional figures and teach their proper names, such as sphere, cube, prism, and pyramid. If possible, vary the size of the shapes.

❁ Mary Jo Shannon, Roanoke, VA

I Spy a Shape

Materials

None needed

What to do

1. You have probably played this game using colors or beginning sounds. Try it using shapes.
2. Demonstrate the game by saying, "I spy something that is shaped like a circle."
3. The children take turns guessing, naming all the round objects they can see until they guess the one you have in mind.
4. The child who guesses correctly chooses the next object to describe.
5. Continue playing the game until all the children have had a turn or their interest wanes.

More to do

Encourage the children to add other clues, such as color or size.

❁ Mary Jo Shannon, Roanoke, VA

Treasure Hunt

Materials

The Secret Birthday Message by Eric Carle
Construction paper
Scissors
Tape
Muffins

What to do

1. Read The Secret Birthday Message with the children.
2. Cut out various shapes from construction paper, such as triangles, circles, and squares.
3. Before the children arrive in the morning, set up a treasure hunt. Tape various shapes around the room or the school. Write little clues on each one that will eventually lead to a big "surprise." For example, on a triangular shape, write, "Go to the shape on the wall that helps us tell the time." (clock)
4. As you follow the clues, sing the following song to the tune of "The Farmer in the Dell."

   We're going on a hunt.
   We're going on a hunt.
   We're going on a treasure hunt,
   To find a big surprise.

5. End your hunt by going to the square-shaped "stove" that has a surprise batch of muffins in it.

Related books

The Berenstain Bears and Too Much Birthday by Stan and Jan Berenstain
Happy Birthday, Dear Duck by Eve Bunting
Happy Birthday, Jesse Bear! by Nancy White Carlstrom

Song

My Birthday (Tune: "This Old Man")
My birthday number one,
Watch me while I wiggle my thumb.

Chorus
With a big bop polly-wop, turn around and see,
Give a clap for you and me.

My birthday number two,
I know how to put on my shoes.

(Chorus)

My birthday number three,
Bend down low and tickle your knee.

(Chorus)

My birthday number four,
Everybody touch the floor.

(Chorus)

My birthday number five,
Let's pretend we're taking a dive.

❧ Patricia Moeser, McFarland, WI

Faces

Materials

Camera and film
4" x 7" (10 cm x 17 cm) index cards
Glue
Laminate or clear contact paper

What to do

1. Take a photo of each child. Make two copies of each child's photo.
2. Glue the photos to index cards and laminate or cover them with clear contact paper for durability.
3. Place the photos face down on a table.
4. Play like a regular memory game. The child turns over two cards at a time. If they match, the child keeps the set. If not, the child turns them back over and tries again.
5. Continue until the children have matched all the cards.

More to do

For an easier version, place one of each set face up on the table. Hold the other set in your hand. Show a child one of the cards and ask her to identify the child. Then, ask her to find the matching face on the table. For a funny version, ask the children to make funny faces when you take their photographs.

Related book

Aleksandra, Where Is Your Nose? by Christine Dubov

✤ Virginia Jean Herrod, Columbia, SC

Shoes

Materials

Camera and film
Laminate or clear contact paper
4" x 7" (10cm x 17 cm) index cards
Glue

What to do

1. Ask the children to take off their shoes and place them side-by-side.
2. Take a photograph of each child's shoes and a photograph of each child.
3. Mount the photos on index cards and cover them with clear contact paper or laminate them for durability.
4. Depending on the age level of the children, play the game two different ways.

For older fours

Turn the cards face down on a table like a regular memory game. Put photographs of the shoes on one area of the table and the photographs of the children on another. Ask a child to turn over a Shoe card and a Child card. If they match, the child keeps the set. If they do not match, the child turns them back over and tries again. Continue until the children have matched all the cards.

For younger fours

Place the Shoe cards face up on the table and hold the Child cards in your hand. Show a child one of the Child cards and ask, "Who is this?" After the child answers, ask her to find the shoes that belong to the child on the card. Offer help and encouragement until the child makes a match. Continue until the children have matched all the cards.

More to do

More Games: Play a rousing game of Shoe Scramble! Ask the children to remove their shoes and put them in a pile. Then, ask two or three children at a time to scramble into the pile and find their own shoes and put them on. (Tying is not required.) Younger children might enjoy the game more if only one child at a time scrambles for her shoes while the others cheer her on.

Math: Play Shoe Match. Ask the children to remove their shoes. Line up one shoe of each set on the floor. Put the other shoes in a pile. Each child takes a shoe from the pile and then matches it to the same shoe on the floor.

Related books

Shoes Like Miss Alice's by Angela Johnson
Shoes, Shoes, Shoes by Ann Morris
Whose Shoes? by Margaret Miller

♣ Virginia Jean Herrod, Columbia, SC

Matching Games

Materials

Juice lids
Stickers

What to do

1. Save twenty lids from juice bottles.
2. Use juice lids and stickers to make a matching game relating to the theme or unit. For example, if you are doing a unit on insects, use twenty insect stickers. Make sure you have ten pairs of insects.
3. Next, place each sticker inside of a juice lid.
4. Turn the juice lids over and encourage the children to match the lids. If the two lids match, the child keeps the pair. If not, the child turns them back over and another child tries.

More to do

Add Velcro or magnetic strips to the backs of the lids. Children can play the game individually using small Velcro boards or magnet boards.

❖ Holly Dzierzanowski, Austin, TX

Match the Mitten

Materials

Paper, in a variety of colors
Scissors
Glue
Manila file folder
Laminate or clear contact paper

What to do

1. This file folder game is good to keep out during the winter.
2. Cut out several sets of mittens with matching colors and designs from paper.
3. Glue one mitten from each set into a file folder.
4. Laminate the folders or cover them with clear contact paper.
5. Laminate the other mittens or cover them with clear contact paper.
6. On the back of each folder, make a pocket to put the matching mitten.
7. Make additional winter file folder games, such as Winter Clothing Match (match jackets, hats, ice skates, and so on) or Match the Snowman.

Related books

The Jacket I Wear in the Snow by Shirley Neitzel
The Mitten by Jan Brett

❖ Deborah R. Gallagher, Bridgeport, CT

Matching Shapes

Materials

Scraps of wallpaper
Scissors
Glue
Manila file folder
Laminate or clear contact paper

What to do

1. Cut out pairs of various shapes from scraps of wallpaper.
2. Glue one shape from each set inside a file folder.
3. Laminate the file folder or cover it with clear contact paper.
4. Make a pocket on the back of the folder to put the matching shape.
5. Laminate the other set of shapes or cover them with clear contact paper for durability.

More to do

Art: Make a shape collage. Give the children various cut-out shapes from different colors of construction paper, paper, and glue or glue sticks. Encourage them to make their own collage using the paper shapes.
Blocks: Show the children the basic shapes (circle, triangle, square, and rectangle). Ask the children to group the blocks according to their shapes.

Related books

Brown Rabbit's Shape Book by Alan Baker
Circles, Triangles, Squares by Tana Hoban
Pancakes, Pancakes by Eric Carle (pancakes are round)
The Shape of Me and Other Stuff by Dr. Seuss

Songs

"The Wheels on the Bus" (circles)
"My Hat It Has Three Corners" (triangles)

Original Songs

A Triangle (Tune: "Have You Ever Seen a Lassie?")
Have you ever seen a tri-angle?
A tri-angle, a tri-angle?

Have you ever seen a tri-angle?
It looks just like this. (make shape with fingers)
It has three sides. (hold up 3 fingers)
That look just like this. (shape with fingers)
Have you ever seen a tri-angle?
It looks just like this. (shape with fingers)

My Round Ball (Tune: "B-I-N-G-O")
I have a ball,
Its shape is round.
I like to bounce it up and down.
Bounce, bounce, bounce my ball. (3x)
I like to bounce my ball.

❖ Deborah R. Gallagher, Bridgeport, CT

Find the Animals

Materials

None needed

What to do

1. Pick three children to be the animal finders. Whisper in their ear which animal each one is to find (for example, a cow, duck, and dog). Then, give each one a location in the room where they should herd the animals.
2. Whisper in the ears of the remaining children the animal sound they are to make. Try to divide the group evenly into thirds.
3. When you give a signal, the children make their animal sounds and the animal finders move through the group and separate their animals out and herd them to the designated location.
4. Continue the game, rotating animal finders and animal sounds.
5. This is an excellent indoor activity for rainy days.

❖ Diane Weiss, Vienna, VA

Let's Do the Opposite

Materials

None needed

What to do

1. A fun way to help children learn about opposites is to play this game.
2. Tell the children that when they play the "Opposite Game," they should do the opposite of what you tell them. For example, if you say, "Run," they walk. If you tell them to sit, they should stand. Then say, "No, no, I mean stand," and they should all sit. The children who are having trouble understanding opposites will soon pick it up by watching the other children. By now, they will think the game is so funny, it is for them hard to stop laughing!
3. To end the game, say, "Stand up and make a lot of noise." This is a sure way to get the children to sit quietly.

❖ Sandra Hutchins Lucas, Cox's Creek, KY

Circle Action Games

Materials

Garden hose, 50' (15 m) long and ½" to ¾" (12 mm to 18 mm)
Wooden dowel, 2' (60 cm) long, the same diameter as the hose
Saw (adult only)
Record and record player

What to do

1. Remove the metal connectors from the hose.
2. Cut the hose into 3' (1 m) segments. Cut the dowel into 2" (5 cm) segments.
3. Force one half of a dowel piece into one end of a hose piece, making sure it fits tightly.
4. Force the other end of the dowel piece into the opposite end of the hose, forming a circle.
5. Use the circles to do the following activities:
   ◼ To teach spatial concepts: Ask the children to step inside the circle,

walk around the circle, step over the circle, stand beside the circle, hold the circle in one hand and put their other hand through the circle, put their free hand under the circle, then over the circle.

■ To teach body parts: Place the circles on the floor and ask the children to put their *hands*, then *feet, knees, elbow, fingers, toes, heels, chins*, and *noses* (be prepared for laughter!) inside the circle.

■ Rhythmic activity: Put on a record and practice hopping into and out of the circles in time to the music.

❖ Mary Jo Shannon, Roanoke, VA

Balls-in-a-Basket Scramble

Materials

Balls, about five per child (can be different sizes)
Large plastic bin or laundry basket
Flat, open playing area

What to do

1. Put all of the balls in a basket. Ask the children to sit in a group at the edge of the playing area. Explain that you are going to scatter the balls all around and at the signal, the children should try to get all the balls back into the basket as quickly as possible. The only rule is that they can only carry one ball at a time. Therefore, they must run and retrieve one ball, and then run back and toss it in the basket before going to get another one.

2. Once the children understand what to do, begin scattering the balls. Toss the balls in every direction from the basket. Tell the children not to move until you give the signal!

3. Once you have sufficiently scattered the balls, give the signal and the children will take off after the balls. Children love this game and will play it many times in a row before they start to get bored.

4. When the children understand the game well, pick two children to scatter the balls and give the signal to the other children.

5. One fun variation is for the teacher to keep throwing the balls out of the basket while the children are busy tossing them back in. The game ends when the children get all (or most) of the balls in the basket and the teacher gives up!

More to do

Instead of balls, use items related to the theme or season, such as plastic Easter eggs, pinecones, balled-up paper "snowballs," and so on. Compare and contrast all the different balls you use in the game. Which is the biggest and which is the smallest? Which ones are soft and which are hard? Which ones bounce?

✤ Suzanne Pearson, Winchester, VA

Pull the Teacher

Materials

Thick, heavy rope
Large hollow block

What to do

1. Attach a thick rope to a large hollow block. Sit on the block.
2. Ask the children to guess how many children will need to work together to move the block (with the teacher sitting on it).
3. Begin with one child, and ask additional children to assist her, one by one. Afterwards, discuss the concept of cooperation.

More to do

Brainstorm other activities where cooperation is important.

✤ Sharon Dempsey, May's Landing, NJ

Classroom Hide and Seek

Materials

Any small item (may be theme related)
Extra teacher or adult

What to do

1. Hide a small item (such as a toy dinosaur, egg, or colored block) in the classroom, making sure it is partially visible and accessible to the children. Hide it so that it will take some time for children to find it.
2. Tell the children that you have hidden an item somewhere in the classroom. Explain that you will help them find the hidden item by saying "hot" when they are close to it and "cold" when they are far away. As they get closer to the item, you will say, "Warmer" and as they move farther away, you will say, "Colder."
3. Encourage the children to look for the item as you use the "hot and cold" method.
4. When they find the item, choose one child to be the Hider and one to be Looker.
5. Send the Looker out of the classroom with another teacher or adult. Ask the Hider to hide the item.
6. Bring in the Looker and help her find the item. Encourage the remaining children and the Hider to use the "hot and cold" method.
7. Give each child a chance to be a Hider and a Looker.

More to do

Hide theme-related items. Use the "hot and cold" method to talk about hot and cold places. Instead of using the hot and cold method, try the "close" and "far" method. Use the "red" and "green" method to introduce safety. As the child move towards the item, say, "Green." As she moves away, say, "Red." Invite a police officer to come in and talk about block parents and what to do if you get lost. This activity works well as an Easter Egg Hunt and/or as a special take home game. Assign one child to be the Hider and the rest to be lookers. Instead of using the "hot and cold" method, ask the children to find the item by themselves. Whenever a child finds the item, she will leave it where it is, come back to the circle, and whisper to you where the item is hidden. Encourage them not to point. This is great for practicing spatial concepts such as *on, under, behind,* and so on.

Related books

50 Below Zero by Robert Munsch
A Difficult Day by Eugenie Fernandes
Franklin Is Lost by Paulette Bourgeois
Hiding by Dorothy Aldis
Little Bear's Trousers by Jane Hissey

Songs

"Where Is Thumbkin?"
"Found a Peanut"

❦ Mark Crouse, Port Williams, Nova Scotia, Canada

Engineer's Lantern

Materials

8" x 5" (20 cm x 12 cm) pieces of black construction paper
Scissors
Hole punch
Paper reinforcements
Yellow construction paper
Pipe cleaner
Glue stick

What to do

1. Cut a notch on each side of a piece of black construction paper, approximately ½" (1 cm) from the bottom.
2. Punch a hole on each side of the paper, approximately ½" (1 cm) from the top.
3. Put paper reinforcements around each hole.
4. Cut out a 3" (7 cm) circle from yellow construction paper. Glue it in the middle of the black "Lantern."
5. Put the ends of a pipe cleaner through the reinforced holes to form a handle. Secure the pipe cleaner ends by twisting them around the pipe cleaner.
6. Teach the children "Train Talk." Moving the lantern up and down means "Go," and moving it side to side means "Stop."
7. Similar to "Simon Says," the leader (engineer) tells the group to do a certain action. The group can only do the action if the engineer signals "Go" with the lantern. The group must stop when the engineer signals "Stop." However, if anyone misses a signal, she is not "out." This game is just for fun.

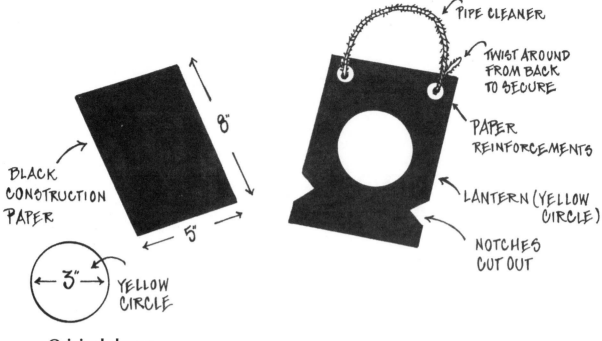

BLACK CONSTRUCTION PAPER

8"

5"

3"

YELLOW CIRCLE

PIPE CLEANER

TWIST AROUND FROM BACK TO SECURE

PAPER REINFORCEMENTS

LANTERN (YELLOW CIRCLE)

NOTCHES CUT OUT

Original rhyme

Engine in front (Point in front of you.)
Chug-a, chug-a (Bend arms at elbow and move like train wheels.)
Caboose in back (Point behind you.)
Chug-a, chug-a (Repeat wheel motion.)
Here comes the train. (Point to imaginary train.)
Chug-a, chug-a (Repeat wheel motion.)
Down the track. (Move pointing finger across imaginary horizon.)
"Wo-o-o! Wo-o-o!" (Pretend to pull whistle cord.)

Related books

Engine, Engine Number Nine by Stephanie Calmenson
The Little Engine that Could by Watty Piper

Songs

"Down by the Station"
"Little Red Caboose"

❧ Christina Chilcote, New Freedom, PA

Easy-to-Make Game Boards

Materials

Small, shaped notepad
Poster board
Glue
Laminating film or clear contact paper

What to do

1. At a teacher or school supply store, purchase a small, shaped notepad. They are usually about 3" (7 cm) in size and come in assorted designs and themes.
2. Separate the sheets and arrange them on a piece of poster board in a start-to-finish layout.
3. Label some of the spaces, such as "Move ahead 1," and so on.
4. When you have arranged the notepad pages as desired, glue them to the poster board.
5. Cover the poster board with clear contact paper or laminate it for durability.

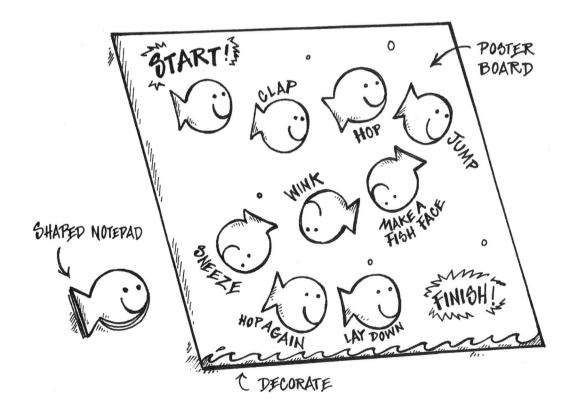

More to do

Design a game board to fit any theme or learning objective. Use standard dice and standard game pieces (or save small toys to use as game pieces). Add colored dot stickers in a random fashion and make matching cards for a customized Candyland-type game.

❧ Vicki L. Schneider, Oshkosh, WI

Yut-nol-eei

Materials

White construction paper, 12" x 12" (30 cm x 30 cm)
Scissors
4 craft sticks
Markers
Any four game pieces

What to do

1. Yut-nol-eei is a traditional game in Korea that children play on New Year's Day.

2. Cut out a diamond shape from white construction paper. Draw lines and shapes (see illustration on the next page) on it to make what is called a "yut-pan."

3. Draw an "X" on each of the four craft sticks to mark the "back" side. Leave the other side empty to make the "front" side. The four sticks are called "yut." Each "yut" stands for one of five animals (pig, dog, lamb, cow, and horse).

4. Show the children how to play with the "yut" on the "yut-pan" game board. Each child will throw the "yut" and then move her game piece forward following the arrows according to the following rules:

   ▪ One front and three back: The child will shout "Dough!" (which means pig) and move one space.

   ▪ Two fronts and two back: The child will shout "Gae!" (dog) and move two spaces.

   ▪ Three fronts and one back: The child will shout "Gur!" (lamb) and move three spaces.

   ▪ Four front: The child will shout "Yut!" (cow) and move four spaces and throw the "yut" again.

■ Four back: The child will shout "Moh!" (horse) and move five spaces and throw the "yut" again.

5. The winner is the child who gets back to the starting point first.

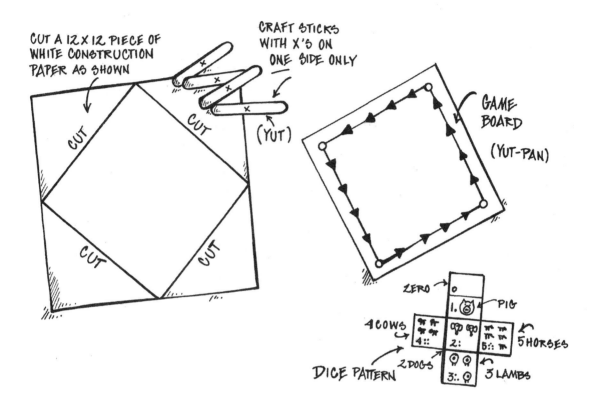

More to do

Instead of making "yut," make simple dice (see illustration). Make more game pieces to play this game in teams.

 DooHyun Shin, Lakewood, WA

Pizza

Materials

Cardboard

Scissors

Construction paper (red, gray, pink, green, and yellow)

Clear contact paper

Dice

Pizza box

What to do

1. Four children can play this game at one time.
2. Cut out four 6" (15 cm) circles from a piece of cardboard. These will be the pizza crusts.
3. Cut out four slightly smaller circles from red construction paper. These will represent the pizza sauce.
4. Cut out eight mushroom shapes from gray paper, twelve pepperoni shapes from pink paper, twelve green pepper rings from green paper, and sixteen strips of cheese from yellow paper.
5. Cover all of the shapes with clear contact paper for added strength and durability.
6. The object of the game is to complete a pizza using all of the required ingredients by rolling the appropriate number on a dice. In turn, each child will need to roll a 1 in order to begin.
7. When a child rolls a 1, give her one of the "crusts." The children will continue, in turn, to construct a pizza as follows:
   - Roll a 2, get sauce (one needed)
   - Roll a 3, get a mushroom (two needed)
   - Roll a 4, get a green pepper (three needed)
   - Roll a 5, get a pepperoni (three needed)
   - Roll a 6, get a strip of cheese (four needed)
8. The first child to complete her pizza can cheer on the others.
9. Store all the pieces in a pizza box.

❧ Barb Evensen, Ripon, WI

Feed Me

Materials

10 blank index cards
Markers
Strip of paper about 1' x 10' (30 cm x 300 cm)

What to do

1. Beforehand, draw a complete meal on one of the blank index cards. Also, write the numbers one through ten and "start" at even intervals on the strip of paper.

2. Discuss with the children what they can do to help keep their bodies healthy. For example, eat healthy foods, sleep, exercise, wash their hands before eating, clean their bodies, brush their teeth, and so on.

3. Briefly review the food groups with the children. Ask them to name some examples of foods in each group.

4. Show the children the nine blank index cards and the card with the meal picture on it. Explain the game to the children. You may want to be the "hungry person" first to demonstrate.

5. Place the number strip on the floor and put an index card face down under each number on the strip. (Mix up the cards so that the children do not know which number the meal card is under.)

6. Choose a child to be the "hungry child" and ask her to stand on "start." The other children will take turns telling the child how many steps to move. (For example, "Go forward three steps.") At each number on which the child stops, she will look at the index card to see if she has found her meal.

7. The children continue to give commands until the child finds the meal card.

8. Allow each child to take a turn being the "hungry child."

9. Depending on the children's ability, you can return the cards to their face down position to encourage them to remember which ones are blank, or collect them in your hand.

10. Review by asking the children to name the foods on the meal card and in which food group they belong.

Related book

Bread and Jam for Frances by Russell Hoban

❧ Shirley R. Salach, Northwood, NH

Big Floor Game

Materials

Shapes that relate to the theme or project
Construction paper in various colors
Scissors
Marker
Laminate or clear contact paper

What to do

1. Select a shape that relates to the theme or project. Use simple line drawings from pattern books such as frogs, cowboy hats, flowers, dinosaurs, circles, squares, and so on. Enlarge the shape.

2. Using four different colors of construction paper, trace and cut out four shapes for each color.

3. On four of the shapes, draw arrows pointing forward. On another four, draw arrows pointing backward. Write a number and dots on the shapes that have the arrows to indicate how many spaces to go backward and forward.

4. On one shape write, "Start."

5. Laminate the shapes or cover them with clear contact paper.

6. Arrange the shapes on the floor (see illustration). This game is similar to a small board game, but the markers are the children.

7. Make color cards using the same colors of construction paper as the shapes. Make at least 20 so they can be shuffled and the children will have many from which to draw.

8. The first child draws a card and proceeds to that color. If there is an arrow on it, the child will follow the arrow and count the number of spaces she needs to move. If there is no arrow on the shape, the child remains on the shape until her next turn.

9. Continue playing until all the children have had at least one turn. Then, start all over again. Place the shapes further apart or add more, depending on the size of the group.

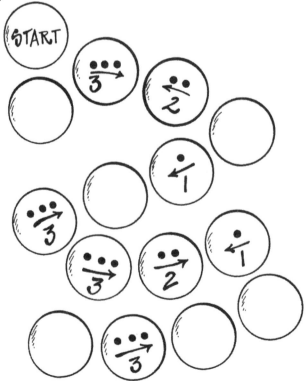

More to do

Use this activity with any theme. Instead of using arrows, try using shapes, colors, words, objects, or verbal directions (for example, "When you land on the red shape, turn around and sit down," or "jump to the next color."). Use your imagination and add your own directions to create many more floor games. Another nice feature of this activity is that the children can play it with very little guidance and can make up their own directions.

❧ Jane Hibbard, Stryker, OH

Musical ABC's

Materials

52 index cards, 4" x 6" (10 cm x 15 cm)
Permanent marker (adult only)
Envelope (large enough to hold a 4" x 6" card)
Cassette or CD player
Cassette or CD with children's music

What to do

1. Write each letter of the alphabet on index cards—one letter per card. Write the capital letters on 26 of the cards and the lower case letters on the other 26 cards.
2. Sit in a circle with the children. Stack the index cards face down. Randomly select a card and put it into an envelope. Make sure the children do not see which card you choose.
3. Play music while the children pass the envelope around the circle. When the music stops, the child with the envelope takes out the card, identifies the alphabet letter on it, and shows it to the other children.
4. Place a new letter in the envelope. Continue playing until each child has had at least one turn to open the envelope. Focus on capital or lower case letters at separate times until the children are thoroughly familiar with the alphabet.

More to do

Math: Instead of letters, write different numbers or draw different numbers of objects on the cards.

Science: When studying animals, glue pictures of different animals on index cards for identification.

Related books

Alpha Bugs by David Carter
Eating the Alphabet: Fruit & Vegetables from A to Z by Lois Ehlert

❧ Mary Rozum Anderson, Vermillion, SD

Vocabulary Toss

Materials

Two 1" (2 cm) cube blocks
Small stickers with a certain theme, such as Christmas, Halloween, insects, transportation, food, dinosaurs, and so on

What to do

1. Attach the stickers to five of the sides on both blocks, leaving one side of each block blank.
2. Play a vocabulary game with the children using the blocks. Ask a child to toss both of the blocks and name the stickers that land face up, using the term "and." For example, the child will say, "Ghost and jack-o-lantern."
3. This game is a fun activity that promotes vocabulary development. It also introduces the children to the concept of "nothing," which occurs when a block lands blank side up.

More to do

Ask the children to make up a sentence describing the pictures on the blocks. For example, "My angel is blue and the wreath is shiny." Add a third or fourth block to the game.

❧ Mary Volkman, Ottawa, IL

Alphabet Scramble

Materials

Poster board
Scissors
Markers
Large area

What to do

1. This game can get a bit boisterous so make sure you have lots of room. Also, you should limit this activity to a maximum of seven participants. Divide a larger group of children into appropriate-sized groups and either take turns or make materials for each group.
2. Cut out alphabet letters from poster board.
3. Show the children the letters. Hold up each one and say the letter together.
4. Stack the letters in your hand and throw them up in the air into a large area. (Tell the children you are going to do this beforehand and remind them to stay in their places for now). The letters will fall randomly to the floor.
5. After you give them a signal, the children scramble to the letters and pick one up. Each child will bring a letter to you and identify it. If the child gets it correct, she keeps the letter. If the child is incorrect, identify the letter for her and throw it back into the pile. The children then scramble for another letter and follow the same procedure.
6. Continue until the children have picked up all the letters. At this point, you can tally totals and pronounce a winner, but it is really not necessary. Most likely, they will want to play again, so gather the letters and throw them again.

More to do

Literacy: Make an alphabet book. On each page, paste a cutout letter and some magazine photos of items beginning with that letter.
More Literacy: Teach the children the ABCs in sign language.
Music: Sing the Alphabet Song. Sing it in many different ways, such as traditional, blues, rap, and rock and roll. Boogie on down and have some fun!

Related books

Black and White Rabbit's ABC by Alan Baker
The Handmade Alphabet by Laura Rankin
The Letters Are Lost! by Lisa Campbell Ernst
On Market Street by Arnold Lobel

♣ Virginia Jean Herrod, Columbia, SC

Piggies

Materials

Story of "The Three Little Pigs" (any traditional version)

A large area in which a small group of children can gather, preferably the upper level of a play structure. (If you don't have a play structure with levels, mark off a large area with cones, blocks, or anything handy.)

What to do

1. Read "The Three Little Pigs" to the children.

2. One day when you are outdoors, ask a small group of children (no more than eight) if they want to play a "Little Piggies" game.

3. Explain that all of the children will be piggies and you will be the wolf. Help the children choose and mark off a "house" (as noted above, the top level of play equipment is best if there is room for all the children). Tell the children this is their safe area—the wolf cannot touch them there.

4. Ask the children to gather in the "house." Pace around the house, growling and howling your best wolf howl. Bang on the sides of the house if you can and growl "Piggies!" menacingly.

5. Say, "Open up, little piggies and let me come in!" Encourage the children to respond with, "Not by the hair on our chinny chin chins." Repeat this two or three times to increase the fun. Reach into the house to grab at the children while you are saying the lines.

6. After saying the lines two or three times, shout, "Run, piggies, run!" At this signal, the children run out of the house and around the playground as you try to catch them. (Do Not Catch Any Children!) Simply chase them and growl at them and pretend you are going to catch them.

7. After a minute or two of this, shout, "Piggies, get back to your house!" Allow the children to run back to the house. Pace around the house again and repeat steps 4 to 6. Take your time before you ask them to run again to give the children a chance to rest.

8. Continue to play until the children seem tired or lose interest. Try to end the game before they grow tired of it. One good way to end the game is for the wolf have a change of heart. Beg and plead for the children to let you in because it is your birthday and you want to have a party, or flop down on a convenient quilt or blanket and invite the piggies to look at the clouds together.

More to do

While pacing around the house, improvise lines. After the children respond, "Not by the hair of my chinny chin chin" to the first request, say, "But I need piggy bellies (try to touch their stomachs) and I need piggy toes (grab at their feet). I need piggy knees (tickle their knees) and a little piggy nose (tweak a child's nose)." This will induce a round of giggles!

Related books

Pig Out by Portia Aborio
Pigs by Robert Munsch
Pigs in the Mud in the Middle of the Rud by Lynn Plourde and John Schoenherr

❧ Virginia Jean Herrod, Columbia, SC

Monster, Monster, Can You Come Out to Play?

Materials

None needed

What to do

1. For this outdoor chasing game, pick a child to be the "monster." The child will stand at the center of the play yard with the remaining children clustered nearby. The children call to the monster, "Monster, monster, can you come out to play?" The monster gives a reason why she cannot come out yet, such as "I'm busy taking a bath," "I'm reading my favorite book," or "I'm brushing my monster teeth." Encourage the monster to act out her answer, too.

2. After each answer, the group again calls, "Monster, monster, can you come out to play?" Each time, the monster gives another excuse. Finally, the monster says, "YES!" and begins chasing the children. Whoever she catches becomes the monster for the next round of the game. The game continues as long as the children are interested.

3. The first few times you play the game, you may need to be the monster to model the kinds of answers the monster can give. After a few examples, the children usually become quite creative. Stand by to give assistance to "monsters" who cannot think of an answer to give. Whisper an answer to them and act it out with them.

More to do

Art: After the children have played the monster game, encourage them to draw a picture of the monster doing something that prevents her from coming out to play. Ask the children to dictate what each of their monsters is saying and write it beneath the drawing. Mount the pictures on a bulletin board with the caption, "Monster, Monster, Can You Come Out to Play?"

Language: For each child, stack five sheets of plain paper. Place one sheet of construction paper on top and another on the bottom. Staple the papers on the left edge of the stack, forming a five-page book.

- On the cover, print "Counting Monsters."
- On page 1, print "I see 1 scary monster."
- On page 2, print "I see 2 scary monsters."
- On page 3, print "I see 3 scary monsters."
- On page 4, print "I see 4 scary monsters."
- On page 5, print "I see 5 very scary monsters."

Distribute a book to each child. Provide stamp pads and ask the children to press their thumbs or index fingers onto a stamp pad, and then onto a page of the book. Ask them to make one fingerprint on page 1, two on page 2, and so on. Encourage the children to use markers to transform each fingerprint into a monster. When all of the books are completed, read them with the children.

Snack/Cooking: Monster Toes: Give each child one section of refrigerated biscuit dough. Encourage the children to squeeze the dough into any odd, lumpy shape and put it on a baking sheet. This will be a "monster's toe." Bake as directed on the biscuit can. When the "toes" cool, serve them with spreadable fruit. The children will giggle while eating the monsters' "dirty" toes.

Related books

There's a Nightmare in My Closet by Mercer Mayer
The Very Worst Monster by Pat Hutchins

❖ Barbara R. Backer, Charleston, SC

Five-Day Treasure Hunt

Materials

Large piece of art paper
Fine-tip permanent markers
Colored pencils
Tea or coffee
Paper towel
Scissors
Various maps
Transparent tape
Special "pirate treat"

What to do

1. Design a treasure map, including different locations throughout the outside play area. On a large piece of art paper, draw a map using fine-tip permanent markers and colored pencils.

2. Be creative when labeling the map. For example, label the sand box "Little Desert," or the slide "Slippery Hill." Don't forget to decide on a hiding place for the treasure and mark it with an "X."

3. When you finish the map, give it an "aged" look. Pour some leftover tea or coffee on a paper towel and rub it over the map to make the map look old. Let it dry.

4. When the map is completely dry, ball it up, being careful not to tear it. Open it back up and re-label it. This will give the map a wrinkled and worn look. If desired, cut around the edges of the map to give it a nice shape.

5. Cut the map into five different pieces. Every day, hide one of the pieces of the map for the children to find.

Days 1 through 4

6. Tell the children that they are going on a treasure hunt and all they will need is a map. The children may wonder what a map is, so it is a good idea to show them some maps, such as road maps, fire escape plans, or even floor plans to a house. Explain to the children that you have hidden a piece of the treasure map somewhere in the center or outside. Therefore, they should keep their eyes open all day so they can find it.

7. When a child eventually finds the map, sit down with the children and talk about where they think the treasure is.

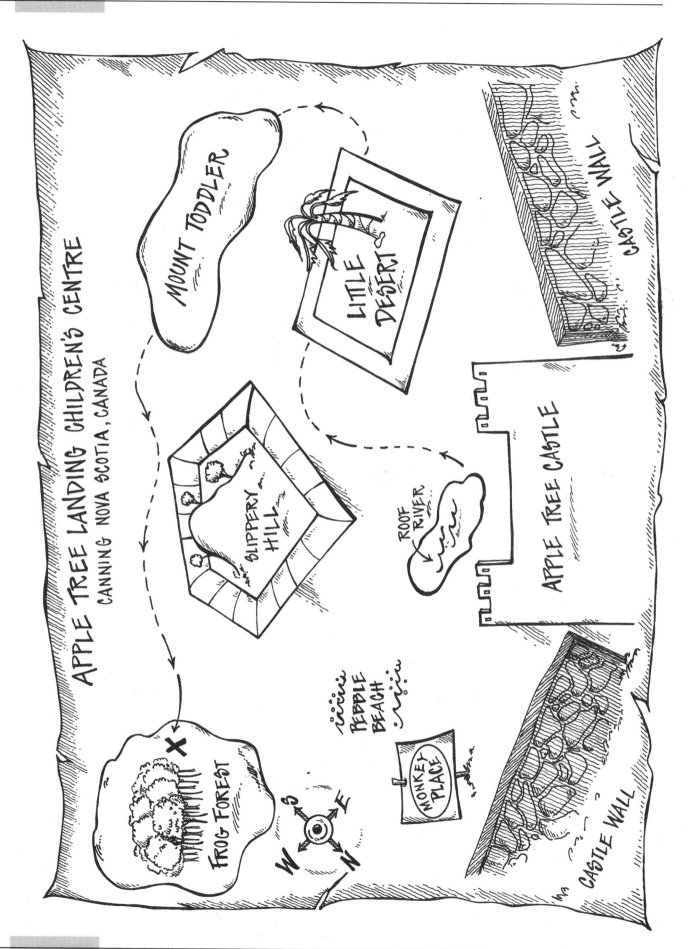

8. Post the piece of the map on the wall so parents and children can discuss the adventure as the week progresses.

9. Each day, hide another piece of the map. When the children find it, tape the map together using clear tape. Save the "X" piece for the last day.

10. On the day of the treasure hunt, hide the treasure before the children arrive. Mark the area with an "X." You might decide to put the treasure in an old tool chest and bury it in the sand box, or place the treasure in a pillowcase, tie it with a string, and hoist it into a tree. There are many different things you can use for the treasure, such as frozen ice treats buried in a small cooler, chocolate-covered coins, or even a special storybook about pirates.

11. When someone finds the last piece of map and it is taped in place, you are now ready to find the treasure. Encourage the children to make predictions and come to conclusions on their own.

More to do

Books: Fill the bookshelf with books about ships, pirates, and sunken treasures.
Dramatic Play: Put pirate costumes in the Dramatic Play Center.
Home Connection: Set up your own classroom treasure box that children can add to during the week. Encourage them to bring in special treasures from their homes.
Literacy: With the children, document your activities through photographs and observations so that you will have a permanent record of the week's activities.
Math: Children may enjoy measuring things, such as how far away things are from one another. Measure using yard or meter sticks and by pacing off areas.
Social Studies: Encourage the children to create their own maps of their homes, classroom, neighborhood, and even their daily activities.

Related books

1,2,3, to the Zoo by Eric Carle
The Berenstain Bears and the Spooky Old Tree by Stan and Jan Berenstain
Grandma and the Pirates by Phoebe Gilman
The Lost Lake by Allen Say

❖ Mark Crouse, Port Williams, Nova Scotia, Canada

What's Your Shape?

Materials

Pillows of different shapes in various colors, or placemats and scissors
Velcro
Needle and thread

What to do

1. Make shape pillows in different colors. Put a piece of thin foam in the middle. Or, cut out shapes from place mats.
2. Sew Velcro to the back of the pillows to help keep them in place on the carpet. (Wash the shapes in the washing machine when needed.)
3. At the beginning of the year, give each child his own shape and color pillow. For example, give Julia a red circle, Brian a blue square, and Beth an orange triangle. Then, everywhere you write his name, also draw his shape and color. The children will soon recognize their own name by their shape. When the children can recognize their written names, you do not need to draw their shape anymore.
4. At Circle Time or Transition times, it is fun to use pillow shapes. Ask the children to stand on their shapes and wait for directions. Examples of things you might say are "Everyone stand in front of your shape," "Put your shape on your head," "Walk around your shape," or "Everyone who has a triangle, trade with a circle." This is a fun activity that teaches children about shapes and colors. Best of all, it allows the children to stay in their own space. After the shapes are used, it is easy to just pick them up.

Related books

The Greedy Triangle by Marilyn Burns
Shapes by Jan Pienkowski
Shapes, Shapes, Shapes by Tana Hoban

Sandra Hutchins Lucas, Cox's Creek, KY

When You Finish...

Materials

Rug
Books and puzzles

What to do

1. When the children are doing a large group activity or project, it is helpful to have an area where they can go when they finish their work. Set up a small area with books and puzzles and place a rug there.
2. Children finish their work at different rates. Therefore, having an area with books and puzzles allows those who finish early the opportunity to play in an area that you can easily supervise.

More to do

Offer small manipulatives as an alternative to a puzzle. Provide small carpet rugs for children who want to work on a puzzle by themselves or to save their work to finish at a later time.

❖❖ Melissa Browning, Milwaukee, WI

My Plan for the Day

Materials

Camera and film
Red construction paper
Marker
Scissors
Glue, tape
Clear contact paper or laminate
Hole punch
Yarn
Butcher paper
Hot glue gun (adult only)
Small books or plastic game pieces

What to do

1. At the beginning of the year, take a photo of each child.

2. Trace the apple pattern (see illustration) onto red construction paper. Cut out the apple shapes.

3. Give the children their photos. Help them cut their photos to fit onto an apple.

4. Help the children glue their photos to their apple shapes.

5. Cover each apple with clear contact paper or laminate it.

6. Punch a hole into the stem of each apple. Pull a short piece of yarn through the hole and tie in a knot.

7. Draw a large tree on a piece of butcher paper and hang it near the door to the classroom.

8. Attach small plastic game pieces to the tree using a hot glue gun (adult only). Ask the children to hang their apples on the tree.

9. Every morning, call on each child individually and give him an apple.

10. Sing, "This is Steven's apple. Where will Steven play? Tell me, tell me, tell me, now what's the plan today?" (Tune: Row, Row, Row Your Boat)

11. Encourage the child to say aloud what he will do that day. For example, "I am going to play in the Block Center and make a big tower."

APPLE PATTERN

12. Finally, the child takes his apple and places it on the apple tree.

13. Continue until each child has had a turn.

14. This makes a great opening exercise each morning and gives the children experience in making a daily plan and following it.

More to do

Cut out the photos from the apple each month and glue them to a new shape, such as a pumpkin in October, a turkey in November, and so on. This makes a nice shape display for the room as well.

❧ Lisa Chichester, Parkersburg, WV

My Photo Album

Materials

Small photo albums
Camera and film

What to do

1. Children love to see photos of themselves. At the beginning of the year, get a photo album for each child. (Purchase them, make them, or ask for donations.)
2. Write the child's name on the cover.
3. As photos are taken through the year, add them to the photo albums.
4. Encourage the children to use their photo albums to tell stories, which will help them develop their language skills. Also, encourage them use their books to share what happens at school with class visitors.
5. Encourage parents to send in photos of home for comfort during stressful times. (I often see children who are feeling sad looking through their books.) To make it easier for the parents, send home a disposable camera to get "home shots." Send home a note asking parents to take five photos of their family, house, pets, and so on. Put these photos in the book. Parents are delighted to link home and school.
6. At the end of the year, each child has a great keepsake from their year in your class.

❧ Tracie O'Hara, Charlotte, NC

My Book About School

Materials

Camera and film
Photo albums

What to do

1. At the beginning of the year, photograph all the places that will be important to the children in your class. (For example, if the child's Pre-K program is located in an elementary school, there are many new and strange things for the child to learn about.)

2. Examples of what kind of photos to take include the outside of the building; where the children get on and off the bus; the playground; the principal, secretary, and custodians; the cafeteria, gym, and halls; and each center in the classroom.

3. Put the photos in a photo album and keep it on a bookshelf.

4. This book has many uses, such as explaining the various places the children will go and the people they will see, the rules for these places, and what goes on there.

5. Ask the children to make up their own story about the photos. Write the stories on paper and make a book. This book becomes a favorite, familiar way to help new children who start in the middle of the year. Often the "old guys" will get it out to give the new child "orientation!"

Related books

Little Monster at School by Mercer Mayer
Pooh's First Day of School by Kathleen Zoehfeld
Timothy Goes to School by Rosemary Wells

Song

This Is the Way We Go to School (Tune: "Here We Go 'Round the Mulberry Bush")
This is the way we go to school, go to school, go to school.
This is the way we go to school,
So early in the morning.
This is the way we walk to lunch, walk to lunch, walk to lunch
This is the way we walk to lunch,
So early in the morning.

Make up verses and motions for other school activities or let the children improvise their own verses.

❦ Tracie O'Hara, Charlotte, NC

"How Much Have I Grown?" Book

Materials

> Construction paper
> Stapler
> Marker

What to do

1. Create a "How Much Have I Grown Book?" as an end-of-the-year activity.
2. This can be as easy as stapling together two pieces of paper and writing it out with the children, or as elaborate as putting the child's picture on the cover and printing the book.
3. Suggestions of questions to include in the book are:
   - My name is: (ask the child to write her name)
   - I live with:
   - The name of my school is:
   - My favorite foods are:
   - My friends at school are:
   - At school I like to:
   - My teacher(s) name(s) is (are):
   - I am __ years old.
   - I have ____ eyes.
   - My hair is _____.
   - I am ____ inches tall.
   - I weigh _____ lbs.
   - When I go to kindergarten I will:
   - This summer I am going to:
   - Big events to remember at (school name):

Related book

Leo the Late Bloomer by Robert Kraus

❖ Caitlin E. Gioe, Tuckerton, NJ

First Day of School

Materials

Sticky label name tags
Markers
11" x 18" (27 cm x 45 cm) construction paper
Camera and film
Zipper closure plastic bags

What to do

1. First Day Name Tags: To prepare for the first day of class, I prepare sticky label name tags to put onto children's clothing to help me learn their names.

2. My Name Is… : At the beginning of the first day of class, sit in a circle and get to know each other's names by:

   ◼ Going around the circle, one child at a time, and clapping the syllables of their names. Children love to hear their names repeated. In addition, rehearsing each child's name helps you learn their names quicker, too!

   ◼ When working with an especially young group, attendance time can be more fun and interesting by singing a song about a color a child is wearing that day, for example: (tune: "Mary Is Wearing a Red Dress")

   Mary is wearing a red shirt, red shirt, red shirt.
   Mary is wearing a red shirt to school today.

3. First Day Story Ideas:

   Who's Going to Take Care of Me? by Michelle Magorian
   Will I Have a Friend? by Miriam Cohen

4. First Day Song Ideas: (keep it simple by singing just a few on the first days)

   "Where Is Thumbkin?"
   "If You're Happy and You Know it"
   "Open, Shut Them"

5. First Day "Homework" Assignment: Some children have difficulty adjusting to being away from home. Even well-adjusted children experience home sick-

ness from time to time. A good way to help bring a little bit of home into the classroom is to give the children an 11" x 18" (27 cm x 45 cm) piece of construction paper to take home and create a family picture collage with their parents. Ask the children to bring the collage back to school. Hang the collages on a wall at the children's level, so they can look at their pictures from time to time as they need.

6. Class Picture: Take a picture of the children. Put a copy of this picture along with the emergency cards into a zipper closure plastic bag. This way, if a child gets separated from the rest of the group during a class field trip, you can use the picture to show others what the missing child looks like. Also, place a few coins in the bag in case you need to make an emergency call. (Better yet, carry a portable telephone when leaving the building for field trips.)

7. Transition Warnings: Children need a signal that the current activity is about to end. I've found that giving the children two-and one-minute warnings helps. (Note: They don't have to be exact minutes). Giving them the warning helps prepare them for the upcoming change.

❖ Deborah R. Gallagher, Bridgeport, CT

General Tips

Materials

None needed

What to do

1. Physical Development

Four-year-olds need pressure-free experiences and room to move both indoors and out. At this stage of the children's development, their large muscles are more developed than their small ones. Keep projects using clay, paint, and glue simple and open-ended. Balance activities that allow the children to move about freely with quiet times. Children need to run, climb, swing, gallop, and engage in large muscle activities. Keep in mind that even though four-year-olds are energetic, they tire easily.

2. Language Development

Four-year-olds are constantly developing their receptive language; however, their rates of language acquisition and usage vary widely. Give oral directions one step at a time. Ask the children to repeat directions or tell a friend what the directions are before they act. Wait until the children follow one direction before giving another. Four-year-olds love to talk so give them plenty of opportunities to use their increasing vocabulary. Often, they would rather talk than complete an activity, and they need environments that allow them to do so.

3. Emotional Development

"Show off" is a descriptive word often used to describe a four-year-old. Give the children opportunities to express their ideas through clay, paint, music, rhythms, games, and drama. Such activities should allow the children to be able to move from one to another when their interest wanes. Four-year-olds are still at the center of their own worlds, but they are also beginning to reach out to others for friendships. They are beginning to be able to play simple games, and care providers should encourage them to take turns. Each child needs a turn and you should give each child the opportunity to be the occasional center of attention. Show affection to all children at this age. Keep in mind that outbursts of anger are easily forgotten, as children this age see life from moment to moment.

4. Social Development

Group activities are fine with children of this age, but they should be interspersed with opportunities for children to play by themselves. Often, four-year-olds engage in "parallel playing," which is when children appear to be interacting together but are actually playing by themselves close to the others in the group. Four-year-olds are eager to please, yet changeable. They can be peaceful and cooperative one minute and aggressive and fault-finding the next. Sharing and taking turns are lessons to be learned at this age, and four-year-olds understand rules and consequences. Respect for others' feelings, courtesy, and responsibility are traits that you can teach and model to four-year-olds. Reality and fantasy are both meaningful to a four-year-old; most do not always differentiate between the two. Children need guidance in identifying what is real and what is imaginary.

5. Intellectual Development

Provide four-year-olds with multi-sensory modes of learning. They have a natural curiosity about the world around them, and they need ample opportunities to explore. "Hands-on" experiences help the children explore and find information. Surround the children with an "information bath," such as books, pictures, and manipulatives that give them the opportunity to investigate. Keep in mind that four-year-olds have an attention span of ten to fifteen minutes. Therefore, activities should let the children feel success in a short amount of time. Children of this age are constantly absorbing language and information. Talking helps the children understand the meaning of words, so allow them to talk frequently. Dramatic play areas, music, construction materials, paint, water, sand, and science experiments are examples of open-ended learning centers to make available for four-year-olds.

❖ Barbara Saul, Eureka, CA

More General Tips

Materials

"Boy" clothes
Legos, puzzles, and drawing materials
Butcher paper
Markers
Tape
Photographs of the children
Artwork by the children
Books
Blank books

What to do

1. Add "boy" clothes to the dress-up area.

2. When children are resting but not sleeping, allow two children to work quietly together with Legos, puzzles, drawing materials, and so on. Match two children who do not normally play with each other. This works really well with shy children who usually play alone (match the shy child with a more outgoing child).

3. For "Child of the Week," trace a child's body onto butcher paper. Ask each child in the class to say something positive about the "child of the week." Write the comments on the body tracing. Hang it up along with photos and artwork that the child has done for everyone to see. Each week, change the "child of the week" (starting with the children who need it most). The child also might want to bring in a favorite snack and favorite book.

4. Keep plenty of books in the Book Area along with comfortable places to sit. Rotate books and add new ones every few weeks.

5. Give each child a blank book with their name in it so they can "write" or draw in it anytime. The children can use them as journals during free play or choice time. If desired, they can dictate stories to you as you write down the words.

❧ Audrey F. Kanoff, Allentown, PA

Teacher Organizational Tips and Miscellaneous Suggestions

Materials

Construction paper
Scissors
Laminate
Masking tape
Permanent markers
Zipper closure plastic bags

What to do

1. Name Tags: To prepare for the first day of class, make name tags for each child to wear on class field trips. Cut out shapes in a certain theme from construction paper and laminate them. Teddy bears are often a good four-year-old theme. Other examples are balloons, crowns, and so on. Place a piece of masking tape on the front of the name tag and write a child's name on each one. Recycle the name tags each year. (Another tip: Before laminating the name tags, put the school name, address, phone number, and teacher's name on the back.)

2. Cubby Tags: Ideas to identify each cubby include:
   - Make a large alphabet letter (use the letter of the child's first name) and write the rest of the child's name smaller (objective: letter recognition).
   - Help the children make different colored handprints and write the child's name under or through the hand print (objective: color recognition).
   - Cut out balloons from different colored construction paper and write the child's name inside the balloon (objective: color recognition).
   - Use a class theme object (for example: crown, teddy bear, clown's hat with a colored pompom on top, and so on). Another idea: ask the children to bring in a picture of themselves. Place the picture next to their name tag in their cubby.

3. Daily Craft Organizers: Plan and prepare craft items and supplies a week or two in advance. To keep everything together, make two sets of gallon size zip-

per closure plastic bags, one for each day that the class meets. On the first set, write the day of the week on each bag using a permanent marker (for example, "This Monday," "This Tuesday," and so on). On the second set, write the following words: "Next Monday," "Next Tuesday," and so on.

❖ Deborah R. Gallagher, Bridgeport, CT

Tips on Parent-Teacher Relations

Materials

None needed

What to do

1. Establish **rapport** with parents and families. Aside from the typical home visit, communicate to families all year that you value them and their role in the life and education of their child. Learn the names of siblings, pets, or other people living with the children. Without presenting yourself as being nosy, express interest in or concern about events going on in the child's home. Encourage the children to make cards or gifts for birthdays, Mother's day, Father's day, relatives who are sick, and so on.

2. Maintain **communication** throughout the year with letters, notes, phone calls, and brief exchanges whenever possible. If you even consider whether or not an incident—positive or negative—warrants a phone call, DO IT! Parents appreciate your effort in making the call ten times more than the actual information you convey.

3. Make an extra effort for a **new** family in the area or a new child to the class. Welcome them to visit the school, call you with questions, speak to previous parents, and so on.

4. Utilize parents and families as a **resource**. Ask for input or advice, invite them to join you on field trips or special events, invite them to share a talent with the class, or invite a sibling to read to the class. Most parents are happy to be a part of their child's school experience.

5. Familiarize families with your **goals** and daily schedule for the classroom early in the year so they know your priorities and are comfortable with the program.

Reasons for a Parent Conference (from the least to most challenging to conduct)

■ **Regularly Scheduled, Typical Conference:** This is a parental briefing (usually twice a year) to update them on their child's good status.

■ **Regularly Scheduled, Some Concerns:** The agenda will include some issues you or the parents feel warrant discussion.

■ **Specially Scheduled:** This is requested by you or the parent to discuss a specific problem, concern, or event.

Tips on Conducting the Parent Conference

■ Design the setting so that the parents will be as comfortable as possible. Because they are on **your** turf, most parents are much more nervous than teachers realize. If possible, consider playing quiet relaxing music in the background, and provide comfortable chairs in a private space where you don't anticipate any interruptions.

■ Begin the conference with a casual opening, such as, "Do you have any specific questions or concerns you'd like to start with?" If they have something on their minds, it will be difficult for them to listen until they have expressed their thoughts. Furthermore, you can often get an idea of what the parents view as the "agenda" for the meeting by giving them this first opening. They may simply want to hear your report so they can relax, or they may have a burning issue to raise.

■ Do not come across as the "expert" on their child—**parents** are the experts on their children. The parents know their child better than anyone, so be cautious. If appropriate, you may ask them what they do at home regarding certain issues, or if they have suggestions for you that may work better than your current methods. Many parents view the teacher as the professional expert, but you'll be much more respected if you're candid about what you know and think without attempting to come across as a highly confident leading authority on child development. Don't be ashamed to say you're not sure or you don't have an answer. You can always get more information, either by conducting some observations of their child or seeking input from other staff members. Then get back to them at a later date.

■ In addition to being candid about what you don't know, be assertive enough to be candid about what you **do** know or feel. Your wording, however, is crucial to your presentation and to parental reaction. First, be sure to include some positive aspects about a child with whom you're concerned. Think through what you need to say, practice how you say it, and imagine how you would react if **you** were the parent. Whenever possible, try to phrase things in a positive form, such as, "We've been encouraging Sue to share," or "We've been working hard on sharing" rather than, "Sue is not a very good at sharing." Strive for honesty, but do so in a professional and diplomatic manner.

■ Do not breach the confidentiality of other families. You will often be asked questions about other children and families in the classroom. Be cautious about what information you feel is appropriate to share. Word travels fast in circles of parents!

■ Provide parents with suggested resources, book lists, or articles that you think may be relevant. Again, be cautious not to communicate that they need to educate themselves, but simply that they may be interested.

■ Be sure to document the conference. Make note of issues that are raised, so that at a future date you may be able to revisit the conference notes, provide follow-up information if needed, brief new staff, and continue or update the discussion at your next conference.

■ Gather as much information as possible before conducting the conference. It's handy to consolidate all the information onto one sheet of paper, with the exception of any assessment tools or samples of artwork. Be sure to include a few specific stories, keep anecdotal notes all year in preparation for conferences, and ask all other staff for their insight before conducting the conference. Consider the advantages and disadvantages of having more than one staff member attend the conference. On one hand, you may feel more comfortable and may have more information simply because there's more than one teacher present. On the other hand, however, parents often feel **more** uncomfortable and less apt to share at an emotional level if more than one teacher conducts the conference.

■ Allow some flexibility in scheduling conferences in order to accommodate the needs of all who are interested in attending. Your time is valuable too, so inform parents ahead of time as to how long you expect conferences to last (usually about thirty minutes). Provide some type of written or verbal reminder of the time and date of the conference.

■ Encourage the parents to maintain the lines of communication, keep you informed of how they're feeling, and schedule another conference soon if they feel an issue needs to be discussed further. Express appreciation for their time and participation!

❖ Shirley R. Salach, Northwood, NH

Story Book List

Materials

Books
Crates
Paper
Plastic report cover
Hole punch

What to do

1. Many teachers have their own supply of storybooks. (I have slowly accumulated my own books for my classroom library because the school's books always seemed to be in use by another class when I needed them.) When you find great books at the local library, write down the title, author, and ISBN number and order it for your own classroom. (How many times have you needed a certain book from the library and it was checked out?)

2. Keep books in crates to make them transportable. Separate the books by subject (for example, put animal story books in one crate, seasonal and holiday books in another, and so on).

3. Compile a book list for each crate, so you won't have to look through the books to find what you want. Put this list into a plastic report cover that has three prongs. In addition, save the list on your computer and print the pages on three-hole punch paper or punch the holes after you print them (back-to-back to use less paper).

4. Suggested book lists: Animals (broken down into separate categories–pets, farm, bears, water, and so on), Community Helpers, Dinosaurs, Earth, Ecology, Nature, Space and Weather, Emotions and Feelings, Families and Homes, Food and Nutrition, Friends, Fun Stories, Holidays, Me, Safety, School, Seasons, Social Skills, Traditional Children's Stories and Fairy Tales, Transportation, and Folktales and Multicultural. Use separate pages for individual authors, such as Dr. Seuss, Eric Carle, and Berenstain Bears books.

5. Following are some examples of sample book lists:

Community Helpers – General

The Berenstain Bears on the Job by Stan and Jan Berenstain
Deadline, from News to Newspaper by Gail Gibbons
A Visit to the Sesame Street Library by Deborah Hautzig
A Visit to the Sesame Street Museum by Liza Alexander

Community Helpers – Medical

The Berenstain Bears Go to the Doctor by Stan and Jan Berenstain
The Berentain Bears Visit the Dentist by Stan and Jan Berenstain

Curious George Goes to the Hospital by Margret and H.A. Rey

Going to the Doctor by Fred Rogers

I Want to Be a Veterinarian by Michaela Muntean

Jenny's in the Hospital Seymour Reit

Just Going to the Dentist by Mercer Mayer

Robby Visits the Doctor by Martine Divison (AMA Kids)

A Visit to the Sesame Street Hospital by Deborah Hautzig

Visiting the Dentist by Althea

Community Helpers – Public Service and Safety

Buddy Bear's Bad Day by Pauline C. Peck (matches and fire)

Clifford the Firehouse Dog by Norman Bridwell

Curious George at the Fire Station by Margret & H.A. Rey

Fire Fighters to the Rescue by Jack C. Harris

No Mail for Mitchell by Catherine Siracusa

On the Beat by Barry Robinson & Martin J. Dain

The Sign Book: Stop by William Dugan

A Visit to the Sesame Street Firehouse by Dan Elliott

Food and Nutrition

The Biggest Pumpkin Ever by Steven Kroll

The Carrot Seed by Ruth Krauss

The Doorbell Rang by Pat Hutchins (counting & sharing cookies)

The Gingerbread Man retold by Eric A. Kimmel

The Hungry Thing by Jan Slepian and Ann Seidler

The Popcorn Book by Tomie dePaola

This Is the Way We Eat Our Lunch by Edith Baer

Friendship

Charlie the Caterpillar by Dom DeLuise

Chrysanthemum by Kevin Henkes

Don't Call Me Names by Joanna Cole

Ira Sleeps Over by Bernard Waber

Just My Friend and Me by Mercer Mayer

My Friend Bear by Jez Alborough

Teach Me About Friends by Joy Berry

That's What a Friend Is by P. K. Hallinan

A Tree Full of Friends by Better Homes and Garden

Two Can Share Too by Janelle Cherrington

Will I Have a Friend? by Miriam Cohen (2 copies)

❧ Deborah R. Gallagher, Bridgeport, CT

Checklists

Materials

Forms (see below)

What to do

1. Things can get hectic and crazy when preparing for the new school year. Making lists may help you remember all the things you need to do. Following are some examples of checklists to use every year.

2. The first checklist is a general list of things to do in the classroom to make sure it is ready. Include things such as taking items out of storage, bringing in certain things from home, setting up the room design, preparing bulletin boards, checking game pieces, and cleaning toys.

3. Make a second list of things to remember to do, such as preparing your attendance book, preparing the first month's calendar and parent letter, and giving necessary paperwork (for example, allergy lists and health form exam dates) to the director.

4. Make a third checklist for all the forms, paperwork, and things parents need to bring to school during the first days of class (for example, the child's emergency card, developmental history, medical form, and a shoebox with a change of clothing).

❧ Deborah R. Gallagher, Bridgeport, CT

Lead Teacher—"Administrative"

- ☐ Update parents' "Welcome" letter and duplicate
- ☐ Prepare September calendar and duplicate
- ☐ Prepare class roster in attendance book
- ☐ Work on student files and prepare checklist
- ☐ Prepare individual student sheets for Accident/Incident Book
- ☐ Write class list and post on door
- ☐ Prepare birthday certificates
- ☐ Prepare cubby tags
- ☐ Prepare name tags
- ☐ Prepare name placemats (where applicable)

- ☐ Prepare charts for room set-up and breakdown
- ☐ Prepare charts
- ☐ Regular schedule
- ☐ Visiting Day schedule
- ☐ Show & Tell schedule
- ☐ Prepare student checklist (for field trips, etc.)
- ☐ Prepare first week's crafts
- ☐ Lists for Director
  - ☐ Allergy list
  - ☐ Health form exam dates

September—Checklist

☐ Retrieve storage items from shed

Classroom

☐ Vacuum rug (last preparation day)
☐ Sweep floor (last preparation day)
☐ Personal teaching supplies (from home)
☐ Arrange room
☐ Wash windows
☐ Set up bufletin boards
  ☐ Birthday
  ☐ Helpers
  ☐ Misc.
  ☐ Hallway
☐ Decorate walls
  ☐ Welcome
  ☐ Alphabet
  ☐ Colors
  ☐ Shapes
  ☐ Reading corner

Learning Centers

☐ Housekeeping
  ☐ Clean dress-up hats
  ☐ Clean pocketbooks
  ☐ Clean misc. (i.e., cash register)
  ☐ Wash dolls
  ☐ Wash doll clothes
  ☐ Wash dress-up clothes
  ☐ Wash playdishes/pots
  ☐ Wash playfood
☐ Manipulatives
  ☐ Check games for pieces
  ☐ Check puzzles for pieces
  ☐ Check glue bottles & refill
  ☐ Check markers
  ☐ Check records & player
  ☐ Make playdough
  ☐ Refill scrap paper supply
  ☐ Wash any game pieces
☐ Toy Cabinet
  ☐ Clean toys
  ☐ Wash animals & ponies
  ☐ Wash cars & trucks
  ☐ Wash furniture, etc.
  ☐ Wash little people
  ☐ Wash blocks
☐ Art
  ☐ Check paintbrushes
  ☐ Set up paint containers
  ☐ Wash easel & cover with newspaper

Checklist

nild	Health Form	Permission Agreement	Developmental History	Emergency card	Parent Handbook Form	Shoebox	Allergies	New health form needed 1yr. from exam date

Song Cards

Materials

Card stock or tag board
Scissors
Markers or magazine pictures and glue
Words to children's songs
Laminate or clear contact paper

What to do

1. Cut card stock or tag board into 4" x 6" (10 cm x 15 cm) pieces.
2. Use one card for each song or fingerplay.
3. On one side of the card, draw a picture that represents the song (or glue a magazine photo to it). On the other side, write the words to the song.
4. Laminate the cards or cover them with clear contact paper for durability.
5. The cards will allow any adult to participate in song time, and the children can also use the cards independently for a pre-literacy activity.

More to do

For each monthly theme, use an 18" x 11" (27 cm x 45 cm) piece of tag board to make up a large song and fingerplay card related to the theme.

✤ Melissa Browning, Milwaukee, WI

Song Lists

Materials

Paper and pen, typewriter, or computer
Paper
Hole punch
Plastic report covers

What to do

1. Over the years, you have probably accumulated many songs. These include songs that your center has been doing for years, songs you have seen in pre-

school songbooks, and songs you may have written. To keep track of all the songs, put all the songs together and make your own songbook.

2. To locate songs easily, separate the songs into categories: animals, community helpers and safety, earth and ecology, me (with separate pages for me/family, me/friends, and me and health), food and nutrition, fun and silly, hello/good-bye, holidays (broken down), seasons (broken down), traditional, transition, transportation, and weather.

3. When parents ask for copies of the songs, pull the songs from the main book and make separate monthly or topical song sheets. Copy these pages and include them with the monthly calendar that you give the parents.

4. Next to each song title, write the word "traditional" or the song's author (if it's a song you wrote, include your own name).

5. Store these song lists on your computer by category, just like the story lists (see page xxx). Print them out, back-to-back, punch three holes along the side, and put them into a plastic report cover with prongs.

♣ Deborah R. Gallagher, Bridgeport, CT

Attendance Cards

Materials

Poster board
Scissors
Photo of each child
Glue
Markers
Laminate or clear contact paper
Magnetic tape

What to do

1. Cut poster board into pieces a little larger than the photos of the children. Glue a photo of each child onto a piece of poster board.
2. Write the child's name under his photo.
3. Cover the card with clear contact paper or laminate it. Place magnetic tape on the back.
4. At Circle Time, hold up one photo at a time. (This is especially helpful at the beginning of the year when children are learning each other's names.) If the

child is present, ask him to place his photo on a magnetic blackboard or other surface that is at the children's height.

5. Later in the year, cover the photo with your hand and ask the children to try to read the name, or cover the name except for the first letter and the children guess who is in the photo.

More to do

Leave photos in a basket and during choice time, the children can line them up and use the photos in other creative ways.

Song

At the beginning of the year, sing the following song using an owl puppet (Tune: "Row, Row, Row Your Boat"):

Who, who, who are you?
It would be so fine,
If you tell me what your name is.
I will tell you mine.

❧ Audrey F. Kanoff, Allentown, PA

Easy Pictures

Materials

Individual photographs of each child
Photocopier
Marker

What to do

1. Photocopy each child's photograph. (School pictures work great.)
2. Write the child's name under his photocopied picture.
3. Keep the pictures in your lesson plan book so that anytime you are gone, a substitute can easily identify the children by name.

More to do

Use the photocopies for craft projects. The child may cut out his face and glue it to a project.

❧ Jackie Wright, Enid, OK

Picture This

Materials

Camera and film
Scissors
Copy machine
Glue
Sentence strips, tag board, or paper

What to do

1. Take a close-up photo of each child's face.
2. Cut out the faces from the photos.
3. Arrange several photos on a piece of copy paper and make copies of them.
4. Cut out the pictures and glue them onto sentence strips or pieces of tag board.
5. Write the child's name next to his picture. Each child will have his own photo card.
6. Use the picture nametags in many different ways. Examples include:
   - Use them to take attendance by putting the pictures of children who are present into a box.
   - Children can use the cards to choose free play areas. Display pictures of the different play areas and ask the children to put their picture cards next to where they are going to play.
   - Put the cards on a table and encourage the children to use them to identify the other children.
   - Use the picture cards when you line up, make a circle, or sit in a particular place by placing them on the floor or countertop and asking the children to sit or stand by their photos.

More to do

Encourage the children to use their photo cards to identify anything that they make, such as dictated stories or pictures. Use the cards to make a class book. Let the children take turns bringing the book home to share with their family.
Literacy: Encourage the children to pick their cards out of a group and practice tracing their names with their fingers.
Math: Ask the children to sort the cards into categories, such as boys and girls, short hair and long hair, and so on. Encourage the children to think of their own categories.
More Math: Use the cards to make a graph on a pocket chart. For example, put

a picture of a hamburger and a picture of a hot dog in the pocket chart and ask the children to put their photos under the food that they like best.

❧ Barbara Saul, Eureka, CA

Picture Schedule Board

Materials

4″ x 4″ (10 cm x 10 cm) white construction paper
Markers or crayons
Scissors
Transparent tape
8″ x 5″ (20 cm x 12 cm) clear wrapping paper
8″ x 4″ (20 cm x 10 cm) colored construction paper
Hole punch
Pipe cleaners

What to do

1. Draw each activity picture on white construction paper.
2. Tape clear wrapping paper onto pieces of colored construction paper to make a pocket.
3. Punch four holes into the colored construction paper (two holes on the upper side and two on the lower side).
4. Tie pipe cleaners through the holes.
5. Put the activity drawings into each pocket and make a picture schedule board.

More to do

Put the activity pictures in a box or a file to organize, and change the picture schedule daily, or when needed.

❧ DooHyun Shin, Lakewood, WA

Our Day at School

Materials

Construction paper and crayons or magazines and scissors
Clear contact paper or laminate
Glue
Felt
Long rectangle of cardboard
Velcro

What to do

1. Draw or cut out pictures depicting the different activities during the day (for example, free play, book time, clean up, and snack).
2. Laminate the pictures or cover them with clear contact paper.
3. Glue felt to a long rectangle of cardboard, completely covering it.
4. Attach Velcro to the backs of the pictures and to the long rectangle of felt.
5. Hang the rectangle at the children's eye level.

More to do

Use the pictures at orientation as a visual aid for parents and children. This is very helpful for an anxious child who is missing home. As each activity is completed, pull off the picture. This is also a great visual for children to know when it's time to go home.

❖ Cindy Winther, Oxford, MI

Our Weekly Calendar

Materials

Pocket chart (available at school supply stores or catalogs)
Paper, markers, and scissors (to make symbols)
Camera and film

What to do

1. Use a pocket chart with seven pockets to help four-year-olds keep up with their week in an age appropriate way.
2. Create a "symbol" for each day. For example, a red apple for a school day, a green apple for a work day, a bus for a field trip, a pumpkin for Halloween, a house for Saturday and Sunday, and so on.
3. Take photos of the people who come into the class, such as speech therapists, volunteers, and storytellers, and post them.
4. Also, take pictures of all of the children. Post the picture of the child who is the helper and line leader on the day they will be the leader.
5. Put an arrow next to "today," so each child can easily tell what will happen that day at school. This will help them learn how to "read" a simplified calendar, teaching independence. It also eliminates having to answer, "What are we going to do today?"

❖ Tracie O'Hara, Charlotte, NC

Our Family Tree

Materials

Bulletin board (or space on a wall)
White construction paper
Brown construction paper
Scissors
Glue
Fingerpaints and paintbrushes

What to do

1. Find a space that is approximately 4' x 4' (1 m x 1 m), such as a small bulletin board or wall space, and cover it with white construction paper.
2. Cut out a tree trunk shape from brown construction paper and glue it in the middle of the white paper.
3. Explain to the children that this is going to be the classroom family tree. Whenever a parent comes into the classroom, the child will paint his parent's hands with fingerpaint (any color) and the parent will make a handprint on the tree. The children gather around the parent and the child as the child paints his parent's hand. As more parents come to the classroom, the tree begins to blossoms with many wonderful colors. This is a great way to encourage parents to volunteer or visit and become involved in their child's learning experience. The children can't wait until their parents come in to the classroom so they can paint their hands!

More to do

Add seasonal decorations to the family tree as the holidays and seasons change. At the end of the year, add the children's small handprints to the family tree. Discuss the size difference. Take a picture of the children in front of the family tree. Make a copy of the picture for each child to have as an end-of-the-year gift.

❦ Anne Lippincott, New Hartford, CT

Seasonal Birthday Chart

Materials

Bulletin board
Large piece of paper (large enough to cover the classroom bulletin board)
Brown crayon or marker
Construction paper-green, yellow, brown, and orange
Scissors
Glue

What to do

1. Cover the entire bulletin board with a large piece of paper.
2. Using a brown marker, draw four trees on the paper, each representing a season.
3. On each trunk, write one of the seasons.
4. Ask the children to cut or tear green, yellow, brown, and orange paper into small pieces and glue them to the appropriate tree.
5. Next to each tree, place the children's nametags whose birthdays falls within that season.
6. This activity helps the children learn when their birthdays are and about seasons.

🌼 Ingelore Mix, Gainesville, VA

The Birthday Bag

Materials

Birthday bag and contents (see below)

What to do

1. To create a classroom community, develop some rituals for special days, including birthdays.
2. Collect books, a banner, materials for making birthday crowns, and birthday cards and put them into a special birthday bag. This special bag only comes out on each child's birthday.
3. Make playdough birthday cakes and decorate cards for the special child. (I once overheard a child who had been in the class a while tell a new child, "We always put up the birthday flag and sing when it's your birthday.")

Related books

A Birthday Basket for Tia by Pat Mora
A Birthday for Frances by Russell Hoban
Birthday Presents by Cynthia Rylant
Carl's Birthday by Alexandra Day
Clifford's Birthday Party by Norman Bridwell
Flower Garden by Eve Bunting
Happy Birthday, Jesse Bear! by Nancy White Carlstrom
Happy Birthday, Moon by Frank Asch
Little Gorilla by Ruth Bornstein
Mary Wore Her Red Dress and Henry Wore His Green Sneakers by Merle Peek
Spot's Birthday Party by Eric Hill

❧ Tracie O'Hara, Charlotte, NC

This Is Me!

Materials

White construction paper
Crayons or markers
Stapler

What to do

1. Three times during the year (beginning, middle, and end), ask each child to draw a self-portrait using paper and crayons or markers. Save these pictures for the book.
2. Using a piece of paper for each child, draw a graph. Mark the months at the top and write various categories down the side.
3. Each month, ask each child what his favorite in each category is and record it on the paper.
4. At the end of the year, make a book about the child. Put the self-portraits in order and the graph page last.
5. Children can make a cover page and title it, "This is Me!"
6. Staple the pages together.

More to do

Take photographs of each child throughout the year, both in the room and outside as they do different things. Add a page or two of photographs to the book to show them in action and how they have grown and changed.

❧ Diane Weiss, Fairfax, VA

Mail Call

Materials

Scissors
Hanging type shoe pouches
4" x 6" (10 cm x 15 cm) index cards or calendar labels (cutouts of snow men, suns, and so on)
Markers
Clear contact paper

What to do

1. Create an area where children can store their own mail and creations. Hang shoe pouches near the sign-in or arrival/departure area of the classroom.
2. Cut an index card into four equal sections and give a calendar cutout or one piece of a cut-out index card to each child.
3. Help the children write their names on their card.
4. Cover the labeled index card or calendar piece with clear contact paper, leaving an extra amount of stickiness around the label's edges.
5. Place one label onto each of the shoe pockets.
6. Encourage the children to place their artwork, drawings, or classroom mail in their own pouches to take home every day.

More to do

If pouches are not feasible, use a cardboard shoe holder. Label it as described above.

❧ Tina R. Woehler, Oak Point, TX

Note Bracelets

Materials

Marker
Copy paper
Copy machine
Scissors
Tape or stapler

What to do

1. Using a marker, divide sheets of copy paper into sections 3" (7 cm) wide. Draw the lines down the length of the paper.
2. When sending an important message home to parents, write it on one section of the copy paper.
3. Make as many copies as you need for the children.
4. Cut the paper on the lines.
5. Right before the children leave to go home, staple or tape the note "bracelet" around their wrists.

6. If you need a reply, ask the children to tell their parents to attach the bracelet to their wrists before they leave for school in the morning.

❦ Barbara Saul, Eureka, CA

Colorful Cubbies

Materials

Colored milk crates, one for each child
Camera and film
Laminate or clear contact paper
Tape
Nametags

What to do

1. Ask each parent to bring in or buy a colored milk crate for his or her child.
2. At the beginning of the year, take a photo of each child.
3. Laminate the photo and tape it to the front of each child's crate.
4. Tape a nametag to the crate, too.
5. Place the crates in a line in the hallway just outside the classroom door or in the classroom by the door. These are the children's own "preschool lockers." They can use them to store their coats, backpacks, and so on until it's time to go home each day!

❦ Lisa M. Chichester, Parkersburg, WV

Lunch with the Teacher

Materials

Lunch

What to do

1. On a specified day of the week, invite one child to eat lunch with you at a special table, inside or out, depending on the time of year. This provides an

opportunity to get to know each other better and to share a special moment. Be sure every child has a turn.

🍀 Sharon Dempsey, Mays Landing, NJ

The Anger Corner

Materials

Pillows
Table and clay
Tape recorder and tapes of music

What to do

1. Set aside a corner of the room specifically for the children to go to when they are having trouble controlling their emotions.
2. Put big pillows on the floor. Also, put clay on a table so they can pound out their anger and a headphone system so they can dance their anger away.

🍀 Lisa Chichester, Parkersburg, WV

The Value of a Whisper

Materials

None needed

What to do

1. If a child is crying or speaking too loudly, whisper in his ear. Since he cannot cry or shout and hear a whisper at the same time, he'll often stop crying to listen.
2. Children like secrets. Whispering makes what you're saying special.
3. Whisper in a dramatic way to bring the group's attention back to you.

🍀 Elaine E. Trull, Horse Shoe, NC

Pandora and Her Box

Materials

Large box with a lid
Contact paper, optional
Paper
Pencils

What to do

1. Briefly tell the story of Pandora's box. A simplified version:

   Once there was a girl named Pandora, who was given a box. Her mother, her father, and everyone told her not to open the box. She looked at it every day, but she never opened it. One day, everyone was gone, and she was all alone with the box. She looked at it, then she held it up and shook it. Finally, she thought, "I'll just open it a little." When she slowly lifted the lid, many things came out. What do you think was in the box? It was all the troubles of the world. So if there are troubles, it is a good idea to keep them in the box and leave them there. We don't want to spread them around the room or around the world.

2. Talk about what kinds of troubles there might be in the classroom (for example, fighting, taking things that belong to others, not sharing, not listening to directions, or not cleaning up after ourselves).

3. Take out the box (if desired, cover it with contact paper beforehand). Say, "See, it is now empty. But when there are troubles in our classroom, we are going to write them on a piece of paper and put them in the box. Then we will keep them inside and not let them out."

4. Appoint a child each day to be responsible for taking care of the box and making sure that it stays closed.

5. When something happens (for example, there is not enough sharing), then talk about it, write it on a piece of paper, and put it in the box.

6. If on another day that same behavior occurs, then wonder out loud, "Who let it out of the box?" Then, put it back in. (Pull out the paper, look at it, and very deliberately put it back in.)

More to do

Make a box for good behavior. Whenever the children do something special, such as sharing, showing kindness, or behaving especially well, put a note into the box. Each Friday, count and celebrate how many good things are in the box. Pandora is a difficult name for many children. Select another name for the box, if desired. Or change the name each day by using the name of the person who is responsible for it.

❧ Lucy Fuchs, Brandon, FL

Teaching Turn Taking with Signs

Materials

Paper and markers, or computer
Tape

What to do

1. Some children have trouble taking turns at the water fountain. Create this sign to hang at eye level at the water fountain. It is a good management tool that also develops reading skills.

2. Using a computer or markers and paper, create a sign that reads: *1, 2, 3, 4, 5, Walk Away* (use large font or print).

3. As the first child in line gets a drink, the second person in line slowly reads and tracks the sign. When the reader comes to the end of the text, the first person's turn is done. The "reader" becomes the next person to get a drink while the third person in line becomes the "reader."

4. This tip allows the children to self manage taking turns in a peaceful way. It also develops number recognition and tracking skills. When children begin to push to get a drink of water, simply remind them to "count for each other."

❖ Ann Wenger, Harrisonburg, VA

Multipurpose Work Mats

Materials

Vinyl fabric
Scissors

What to do

1. Purchase vinyl fabric and cut it into individual work mats, approximately 18" x 24" (45 cm x 60 cm).
2. Stack the work mats near the manipulatives.
3. The children will use the work mats to define their space. Encourage the child to place a work mat on the floor to define his workspace before selecting the activity he want to do.
4. Ask the children to keep all of the pieces of their activity on the mat to prevent them from being stepped on or lost.
5. When the child is finished with the activity, he returns the work mat and manipulatives to their original location.

More to do

Place the mats under children eating while they are to keep juice and crumbs off the floor.

❖ Jackie Wright, Enid, OK

Carpet Square Lines

Materials

Carpet squares, one for each child (available at carpet outlets)
Small chalk slates and chalk or tiny pads and crayons, one set for each child
Small plastic bags

What to do

1. Place a stack of carpet squares in the hallway or by the classroom door.
2. Ahead of time, place a piece of chalk and small slate or tiny color pads and crayons in plastic bags.

3. During bathroom breaks when children must wait in line, ask the children to grab a mat. Give a bag to each child, too.
4. Children will be entertained while waiting in line to wash or use the bathroom.
5. When the break is over, ask the children to grab their mats and head back to the room.

❖ Lisa M. Chichester, Parkersburg, WV

Center "Flags" or Labels

Materials

Wooden clothespins, clip type
Wood glue
¼"(6 mm) dowel cut into 2' (60 cm) lengths
Rubber bands
Plaster of Paris
Water
Empty cylinder oatmeal boxes or large plastic yogurt containers
Contact paper, optional
Tag board or card stock paper
Scissors
Markers or pictures and glue

What to do

1. Glue a clothespin to the top of each dowel so that the clip part faces away from the dowel. (Use rubber bands to hold the clothespins in place while the glue sets.)
2. Mix the plaster of Paris with water, according to the directions on the side of the box.
3. Fill each oatmeal box or yogurt container with plaster.
4. While the plaster is setting, place the bottom of the dowel into the center of the plaster, making sure to push it down to the bottom of the container.
5. After the plaster has dried, remove the cardboard or plastic from the outside of the containers or decorate them with contact paper, if desired.
6. Put one of these containers in each learning center.

7. Cut tag board or card stock paper into 6" x 8" (15 cm x 20 cm) pieces. Use these pieces to identify the learning center by:

   ▪ Cutting or drawing a picture of the center, gluing it on the tag board, and labeling it. (For example, the Block Center, the Book Center, or the Art Center.)

   ▪ For group time, cut out copies of the children's photos and glue them onto the tag board.

8. Attach the labels by clipping them with the clothespins.

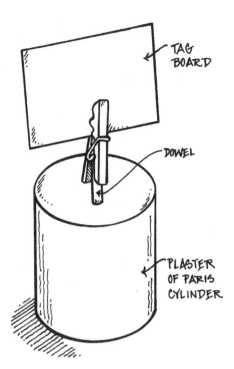

More to do

Use these labels repeatedly. One idea is to put the picture/group cards on tables or areas where you want the children to go. With the centers easily identified, the children can choose their activities. If space is limited, put a number next to the picture so the children can see how many people can go to that center. The labels help parent volunteers find the centers where help is needed. Clip different labels as needed.

❀ Barbara Saul, Eureka, CA

Free Play Pins and Butterfly Free Play Chart

Materials

Clip type clothespins, one for each child
Large paper
Permanent marker
Feathers, colored foam, and pipe cleaners
Tempera paint and brushes
Felt or colored paper
Glue
Eyes

What to do

1. Gather one clothespin for each child in the class.
2. Make up a large free play chart using the diagram (see below). Use feathers or colored foam for color, if desired.
3. Encourage the children to paint the clothespins with tempera and decorate them with colored feathers and pipe cleaners.
4. When dry, write the child's name on the clothespins with a permanent marker.
5. Glue on eyes.
6. Hang the chart with the clips near the Circle Time area. Each time the children pick free play areas, they will clip their butterfly on the butterfly play chart. This will let you see at a glance what area each child is in.

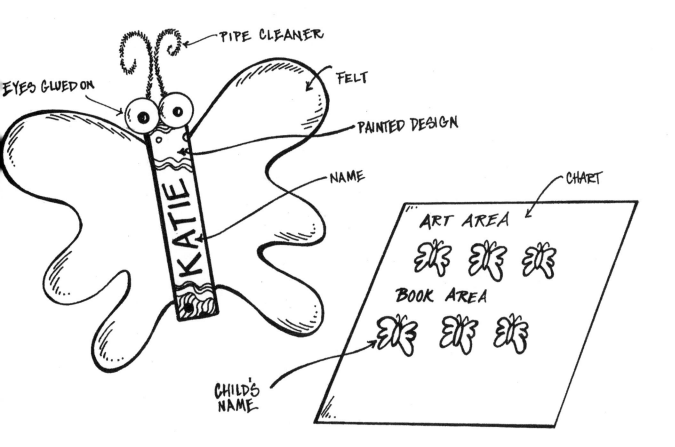

Lisa M. Chichester, Parkersburg, WV

Field Trip Clipboards

Materials

Small clipboards, one for each child
Paper
Pencils, one for each child

What to do

1. Whenever the class goes on a field trip, take along clipboards for the children to document or draw what is meaningful to them during the trip. You may want to allow a time after field trip events to let the children draw their thoughts.
2. Later, discuss what the children learned on the trip.
3. Use the children's documentation as a curriculum focus for the theme or topic. This allows for further in-depth investigations of the unit and keeps the children's interest longer. The result of the documentations may stay with the current topic or may branch off into another area of interest entirely.
4. Display the results so that the children can view them as often as necessary and allow the parents to see them, too.

❧ Tina R. Woehler, Oak Point, TX

Make Your Own Prop Boxes

Materials

Collection of tools and equipment related to prop box theme
Empty boxes with lids
Labels
Photos or posters related to theme

What to do

1. Think of several prop box themes, such as doctor/nurse, restaurant, grocery store, pet/vet, shoe store, firefighters, hair salon, and so on.
2. Begin collecting tools and equipment related to each theme at local thrift shops or weekend garage sales.

3. Place tools and equipment into empty boxes with lids. Put a label on each box identifying its contents.

4. Hang photos or posters that represent the theme in the Dramatic Play Area.

5. Set out the prop box contents and watch the children have fun!

6. Change the area as the children's interest level indicates.

More to do

Set out books related to the prop box theme in the Library Area. Invite community helpers to come and visit the class and talk about their jobs.

Resources

For more information on creating prop boxes for your program see:
Young Children, July 1993, by Sue Myhre, pages 6 – 11
Texas Child Care, Spring 1997, by Sue Myhre, pages 2 –10

✤ Sue Myhre, Bremerton, WA

Dramatic Play Centers

Materials

Cloth bags
Fabric markers

What to do

1. Use fabric markers to decorate cloth bags for various dramatic play items such as firefighters, doctors, gardening, house, and bakery.

2. Place the items into the bag in which they belong (for example, doctor items into the "doctor" bag). Hang or place the bags in a convenient location.

3. Using the bags allows you to change the items in the area on a regular basis without much fuss. In addition, you can use the bags in other areas, such as the Block Area, with only a minute's notice.

4. At the beginning of each day or week, choose a bag for the children to use and place it in the appropriate area.

More to do

Place books or pictures of people with different careers into the bags to extend the activities. Send a note home to parents asking for donations of items that they might commonly throw out (for example, old computer keyboards, empty bottles, and so on).

❧ Melissa Browning, Milwaukee, WI

Natural Beauty

Materials

A variety of items and objects made from natural materials obtained from contributions, garage sales, and thrift stores (see below)
Carpet tape
Baskets

What to do

1. Because classroom furnishings and equipment often are made of plastic, the learning environment can appear hard and cold. There are many ways to add items to soften the room's environment. Bring in fresh flowers when possible, and add live plants to the classroom. (For example, put a plant on top of a toilet tank to soften an angular bathroom.)
2. Cover tables with cotton or linen cloths, or use lengths of materials in seasonal patterns. Hang cotton or other natural fiber curtains on the windows. Add soft place mats to the Dramatic Play Area and the Snack Area.
3. Use carpet tape to join neutral-colored carpet samples, then use these rugs to soften floor areas. An Oriental-patterned rug adds a lot of visual interest and an "upscale" look to the room. Or, add a bath rug with rubber backing to the Dramatic Play Area or the Library.
4. Store small toys in straw or wicker baskets. Use baskets to store art materials.
5. Fill a few baskets with natural items that the children can explore. Select materials such as seashells, sea sponges, dried flower petals, pine cones, seed pods, fresh fruit, mixed nuts in shells, gourds, miniature pumpkins, dried flowers, or small branches. Add a magnifying glass for in-depth exploration. (Change the items regularly to help children's interest.)

More to do

Art: Provide natural materials for children to use in art. Suggestions include feathers, cotton balls, broom straw, twigs, seashells, pebbles, pressed flowers and flower petals, pressed leaves, wicker from unraveled baskets, fabric scraps, wooden clothespins, scraps of wood, wool yarn, and cotton yarn.

More Art: Designate one area as an art gallery. Collect cast-off wooden frames and refurbish them, if necessary. Before giving them to the children, pre-cut art paper to fit the various frames. Display paintings and drawings in the frames by attaching them to the backs of the frames with a few strips of masking tape. Changing the pictures from week to week is quick and easy.

Math: Provide shells, twigs, and pebbles for counting activities.

❧ Barbara F. Backer, Charleston, SC

Hand Washing with Bubble Magic

Materials

Soap
Running water

What to do

1. Many children find it difficult to wash their hands with soap. The following is a way to make it both enjoyable and magical. First, ask the children if they believe in magic. Since most of them will reply, "Yes," the steps that follow are easy.

2. Ask the children to put some soap on their hands. Tell them that the more they put on, the bigger their magic will be.

3. Then, ask the children to put enough water on their hands to make bubbles.

4. Encourage them to rub their hands together quickly. They will watch in amazement as the amount of bubbles grows larger and larger!

5. Tell them to say, "Abracadabra," and put their hands under the tap. (Usually they ask me to look away so they can do their magic.)

6. Once the bubbles have disappeared, congratulate them and tell them that it was the best magic trick ever. (Most of the children that I have done this with

have been three- or four-year olds. They can't wait to show mom or dad their "disappearing bubble trick!")

❧ Colleen Hunt, Oxford Mills, Ontario, Canada

Easy Wash-Up

Materials

Dishwashing detergent

What to do

1. Before starting an activity that requires the children to get their hands messy (such as painting), squirt two or three drops of dishwashing detergent into their hands.
2. Ask them to rub it in very well, like rubbing in hand lotion.
3. When the children are finished with their project, the detergent will be under the paint or other residue on their hands. This makes removal easy, especially when they use regular hand soap.

❧ Ann G. Glenn, Memphis, TN

No-Spill Step Stool

Materials

Small cardboard box
Newspapers
Tape
Magazine pictures
Scissors
Glue
Clear contact paper

What to do

1. With the children's help, create a step stool that is solid, will not tip over, and will last for years.
2. Find a cardboard box that is the right size and height to build a step stool to place in front of the sink or water fountain (or wherever a boost in height is needed).
3. Fill the box to the top with folded newspapers until it is packed tightly. Overfill it slightly so that when you compress the papers, there is a solid feel to the box. Tape the top of the box shut.
4. Give each child a magazine and pair of child-safe scissors. Ask the children to cut out pictures or large alphabet letters to use to cover the box. To help develop the children's oral language, encourage them to share stories of the pictures they find. Enjoy the conversation as the children explain their choices.
5. If necessary, trim and neaten the edges of the pictures.
6. Glue the pictures and large alphabet letters to all six sides of the box, forming a collage of pictures.
7. Cover the box with clear contact paper to make it waterproof and to preserve the pictures.
8. If, after several years, the pictures begin to wear, simply create a new collage on top of the existing one.

❧ Ann Wenger, Harrisonburg, VA

Frugal Fingerpainting

Materials

Fingerpaint
Large cafeteria tray
Paper

What to do

1. To save fingerpaint, ask the children to fingerpaint on a large, smooth cafeteria tray.
2. Help children make prints by placing a piece of paper onto the painted surface and pressing lightly.

3. This system has several advantages:

- No fingerpaint is wasted. Just add a little more water and a little more fingerpaint for the next child. The technique uses about half of the amount needed for the traditional method.
- Young preschoolers won't wear a hole in the center of the paper.
- You can use any shape of paper to get the prints without causing tears.
- A print dries more quickly than a traditional fingerpainting.
- Clean up is limited to the trays.

❧ Nancy M. Lotzer, Farmers Branch, TX

Handle for Sponges

Materials

Hot glue gun (adult only)
Plastic soda caps
Sponge shapes without handles

What to do

1. This is a great, inexpensive way to put handles onto paint sponges, which will allow children to handle the sponges easier.
2. Plug in a hot glue gun (adult only). Make sure it is out of the reach of any children.
3. Wash and dry the soda caps.
4. Put a generous amount of hot glue in the middle of a sponge (adult only).
5. Press a cap into the glue on the sponge (top of the cap facing down).
6. Allow the glue to dry before painting with the sponge.

❧ Darleen A. Schaible, Stroudsburg, PA

Washable Tempera

Materials

Clear dishwashing liquid
Tempera paint

What to do

1. Add 2 tablespoons (30 ml) of clear dishwashing liquid to 16 oz. (480 ml) of tempera paint.
2. Shake or stir the mixture to create tempera paint that washes out easily.

✤ Charlene Woodham Peace, Semmes, AL

Marker Organizer

Materials

Empty cereal boxes
Pen
Scissors
Plaster of Paris
Water
Ruler
Markers

What to do

1. Measure 3" (7 cm) from the bottom of a cereal box and draw a line around it.
2. Cut the sides of the box down to the lines.
3. Prepare the plaster of Paris according to the directions on the box.
4. Pour the plaster into the box, completely filling it.
5. Scrape a ruler across the top of the box to even out the plaster.
6. Allow the plaster to set (check the plaster box for an approximate time).
7. When the plaster is about half hardened, place the markers with the caps on upside down into the plaster. Stick the capped side of the marker into the plaster, making sure the marker is straight up. The bottom of the pen cap should be about even with the top of the plaster. Each box should hold

about eight markers.

8. When the plaster is dry, remove the cardboard from it.

9. Show the children how to take the markers out of the holder. The marker cap stays in the plaster. When the children are finished drawing with a color, they can put the marker back into the cap.

10. This organizer easily doubles the life of the markers, because they last longer with their caps.

More to do

Mix dry powdered tempera paint into the wet plaster for added color. Decorate the organizer with contact paper. To prevent scratching the table, glue felt to the bottoms of the organizers.

❖ Barbara Saul, Eureka, CA

Spray Starch Your Flannel Board Cutouts

Materials

Spray starch
Felt shapes and characters
Flannel board
Iron, optional

What to do

1. Place felt shapes and characters on a surface and spray a heavy coat of starch over one side of them (adults only). Allow them to dry.

2. When dry, turn the felt shapes and characters over and spray the other side with starch. Allow them to dry.

3. Iron the shapes, if desired. The shapes will be stiff and easy to place on and remove from the flannel board.

❖ Jackie Wright, Enid, OK

Picnic Snack Buckets

Materials

Ice cream tubs
Paint and brushes, stickers
Snack supplies (see below)

What to do

1. Decorate clean, empty ice cream tubs with paint and stickers.
2. Fill each tub with a colorful linen napkin, plastic utensils, regular napkin, plastic cup, and a sponge square. Place the tubs on a low shelf where they can be easily reached. Children can easily retrieve their tubs at snack time so they will have everything they need ready for snack!
3. A helper can refill the napkins and cups each morning.

❖ Lisa M. Chichester, Parkersburg, WV

Pocket Pick

Materials

Pocket jewelry organizer or shoe organizer with many pockets
Items related to the theme (see below)

What to do

1. Place items inside the pockets of a jewelry or shoe organizer. Depending on the theme, fill the pockets with letters, colors, or numbers. Or, fill each pocket with different items, such as pictures of transportation vehicles, occupations, food, and so on.
2. Ask a child to "pocket pick." The child will reach his hand into a pocket and pull out an item. Use this item to begin the game.
3. For example, if the child picks the color green, ask, "What is the color?" Name a green food, a green animal, and so on.

More to do

Use this activity to plan a daily or weekly plan.

✿ Ingelore Mix, Gainesville, VA

Quick Crowns

Materials

Sentence strips

What to do

1. The easiest way to assemble a child's crown is to use a sentence strip.
2. They are the perfect size and weight—they bend easily, they are heavy enough for painting or collage, they are long enough to go around a child's head, and they come in several colors.
3. Next time you need a crown, let a sentence strip add the "crowning" touch!

✿ Nancy M. Lotzer, Farmers Branch, TX

Balancing Acts

Materials

Colored masking tape

What to do

1. Place masking tape on the floor to create a straight line or path throughout the room.
2. Model walking on the tape, one foot after the other, with outstretched arms for added balance.
3. Remind the children to spread out for this activity.

More to do

Use spray paint to make an outdoor path on the grassy area of the playground.

❖ Charlene Woodham Peace, Semmes, AL

Imaginary Paths

Materials

Balloons
Blindfold

What to do

1. Blow up balloons and place them on the floor, creating an obstacle course.
2. Tie a blindfold on a child, hold the child's hand, then move the balloons.
3. Watch the child "high step" through this pathway with caution.

❖ Charlene Woodham Peace, Semmes, AL

Walking the Rope

Materials

Long piece of rope

What to do

1. Stretch out a long rope in a straight line on the floor.
2. Ask the children to stand behind the rope, then ask them to jump over it.
3. Tell them to put their right foot behind them. See if the children can walk while straddling the rope.
4. This is a good way to help children learn right and left, as well as listening skills. Repeat step #3, asking the children to use their other foot or one of their hands.

More to do

Leave out the rope for a while to help the children learn right and left and make patterns.

Song

"The Hokey Pokey"

♣ Sandra Hutchins Lucas, Coxs Creek, KY

Follow the Leader

Materials

Outdoors or a large gym

What to do

1. Stand at the front of a line, with the children behind you.
2. Encourage the children to follow you and do whatever movement you do.
3. Walk, run, clap, hop, take big steps or little steps, march, walk backwards, slap your thighs, put your hands on your hips, or balance on the edge of something. Then start all over again!

More to do

This is a good transition activity to move children from one activity to the next.

❧ Sue Myhre, Bremerton, WA

Grocery Bag Balls

Materials

Paper grocery bags, one per child
Newspapers or scrap paper
Masking tape
Scissors

What to do

1. Give each child a paper grocery bag. Ask the children to stuff their bags with newspapers to make a ball.
2. Tape together the open side of the bag, then crush and wad it together to form a smaller ball. Wrap long strips of masking tape around it. This creates a lightweight ball that can be used inside or outside.
3. Demonstrate to the children all the ways they can move their ball. For example, they can kick, throw, or bat it.

More to do

Use lunch bags to make small balls.

❧ Patricia T. Cawthorne, Lynchburg, VA

Pass the Beach Ball

Materials

Beach ball

What to do

1. Ask the children to stand in a circle.
2. Then, ask the children to turn to their right, forming a circle line.
3. Give the ball to one child in the circle line.
4. Ask the child to use two hands to pass the beach ball to the person behind her. She can pass the ball by holding it over her head, between her legs, or the child can twist and turn.
5. The children must work together, take turns, and use bilateral movement.
6. When each child has had a couple of turns passing the ball, change the direction.

More to do

Break the children into smaller groups. Add more than one beach ball to the group. Try the same task with other objects, such as beanbags, small balls, or shoes. Play music to go with the activity. Ask the child to verbalize how she will pass the ball to the child behind her. To extend the activity, encourage the children to lie on their stomachs and pass the ball. The children can sit and roll the ball to each other, too.

❖ Sandra Nagel, White Lake, MI

Snowball Fun

Materials

Newspaper
Trash basket

What to do

Snowball rolling

1. Ask the children to scrunch sheets of newspaper with their hands and fingers.

Encourage them to scrunch the paper into balls as small as they can get them.

2. Then, invite the children to throw their balls into a trash basket. (You may want to limit how close to the basket they can get.)

3. Tossing the snowball into the target helps improve eye-hand coordination. To promote balance, encourage the children to stay on their knees during the activity.

Snowman Making

1. Encourage the child to get on her hands and knees, tuck her head in tight, and make herself into a snowball.

Related books

Annie's Gifts by Angela Shelf Medearis
Funny Walks by Judy Hindley
Wave Goodbye by Rob Reid

❧ Sandra Nagel, White Lake, MI

Beanbags

Materials

Beanbags, one for each child*
Clear area of floor, blacktop, or grass

What to do

1. Give each child a beanbag. Encourage the children to explore the bags.

2. Play the "Can You?" game with the children in the following way:
   - ■ Can you put your beanbag on top of yourself?
   - ■ Can you put your beanbag underneath yourself?
   - ■ Can you put your beanbag in your right hand?
   - ■ Can you put your beanbag on your right shoulder?

3. Continue in this manner, with the children following oral directions. Be sure to let them use their creativity to complete their tasks.

More to do

Divide the children into pairs and give each pair a beanbag. Ask the partners to stand about 5' (1.5 m) apart and take turns throwing the beanbag to each other. Using an empty box or laundry basket as a target, ask the children to stand about

4' (1 m) away from it and try to throw their beanbags into it. Challenge the children to walk with the beanbag on their head, their hands, or their shoulders.

■ Parents and/or volunteers can make the beanbags. Send a note home asking for help. Cut out two squares of fabric, sew three sides, fill it about ¾ full with small beans or rice, and sew the open side closed.

❖ Barbara Saul, Eureka, CA

Beanbag Toss

Materials

Construction paper in assorted colors
Tape
Beanbags, one for each child

What to do

1. Tape sheets of construction paper randomly to the floor.
2. Make a tape line a short distance from the construction paper.
3. Assemble the children and distribute the beanbags.
4. Invite the children to toss the beanbags on top of the construction paper and name the color on which the beanbag lands.

More to do

As children develop skills, do the same activity with shapes, letters, and numbers.

❖ Margie Kranyik, Hyde Park, MA

It's in the Bag

Materials

Beanbags, one for each child

What to do

1. Assemble the children and distribute the beanbags.
2. Encourage the children to squeeze and toss the bags from one hand to another.
3. Provide the following instructions to the children:
   - Place the beanbag on the floor.
   - Pick up the beanbag with your hands and hold it high.
   - Place it back on the floor.
   - Pick up the beanbag with another part of your body. (Cue the child if needed: elbows, feet, one hand and one foot, and so on.)
   - Balance the beanbag on your head. (Review the meaning of "balance," if necessary.)
   - Balance it on another part of your body (hand, foot, shoulder).
   - Show other ways to balance the beanbag.

More to do

Try each segment of the activity with a partner, finding ways to pick up and balance the beanbag together.

❖ Margery Kranyik, Hyde Park, MA

Container Catch

Materials

Empty gallon milk, juice, or punch container
Scissors
String or rope
Plastic ball with holes in it (found in sports sections of stores)

What to do

1. Cut off the bottom of a container below the handle.
2. Tie a piece of string or rope to a ball. Tie the other end of the string to the handle of the container.
3. Encourage the children to hold the handle and swing the ball, trying to "capture" it in the container.
4. The length of the string or rope varies the degree of difficulty.

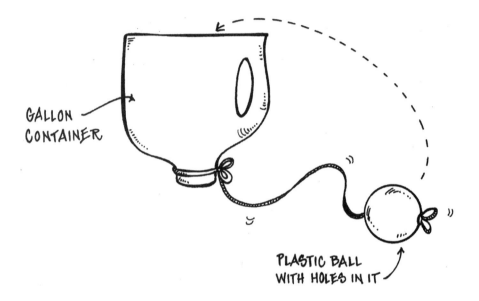

GALLON
CONTAINER

PLASTIC BALL
WITH HOLES IN IT

■ For the greatest success, the whole body must maintain a slow, rocking back-and-forth motion.

❧ Debbie Hugli, Downey, CA

The Puppet Says

Materials

Favorite puppet, bought or handmade

What to do

1. Use a favorite puppet as a vehicle for giving children instructions for body awareness or spatial relationships.
2. Provide commands such as, "Bo-Bo the Monkey says, 'Touch your toes.' Bo-

Bo says, 'Reach up high, bend down low, spin around, touch your back, stand on one foot.'"

3. This game differs from Simon Says in that there are no trick commands and nobody makes a mistake and loses the game.

More to do

Invite a child to use the puppet and give commands to the rest of the children. Use this time to observe who has trouble following directions.

❖ Margie Kranyik, Hyde Park, MA

Terrific Tunnels

Materials

Large appliance boxes
Duct tape

What to do

1. Cut open both ends of a few large appliance boxes. Leave the flaps attached, if possible.
2. Place the boxes on their sides, end to end.
3. Form a tunnel by putting the flaps of one box inside the flaps of another and securely taping them together.
4. After the children have explored the tunnel for a while, add another box or two to make the tunnel longer.
5. For more adventure, cut a hole into one side of the tunnel and tape another box or tunnel at a right angle to the first tunnel.

More to do

Art: Give the children plain paper and ask them to draw a picture of something that might be in a tunnel. Give each child a piece of black construction paper that is at least 4" (10 cm) wider than the plain paper. Help the children staple together the two papers along one long edge, then arch the black paper above the plain paper and staple together the two remaining long edges. This forms a black tunnel over the picture on the plain paper. The children will enjoy peering into each other's tunnels to see what is inside.
Blocks: Add oatmeal boxes, salt boxes, or any other boxes with both ends

removed to the Block Area. Children can use these boxes to make tunnels for toy cars, trucks, and trains.

Song

With the children, sing the following song while they are crawling in the tunnel (Tune: "Ten Little Indians").

Crawling, crawling, we are crawling.
We are crawling in our tunnel.
Crawling, crawling, we are crawling.
Crawling to the end.

❦ Barbara F. Backer, Charleston, SC

Left and Right

Materials

Watercolor markers, 1 green and 1 red

What to do

1. On each child's right hand, print a large capital "R" in red.
2. On each child's left hand, print a large capital "L" in green.
3. Play the "Left and Right" game. Ask the children to look at their hands and do the following:
   ◼ Raise your right hand
   ◼ Raise your left hand
   ◼ Kick your right foot out
   ◼ Pull your left ear
4. Continue in this manner.

More to do

Art: Paint the children's right hand red and make a handprint. Paint their left hand green and make a handprint. When the handprints are dry, label them "left" and "right."

More Art: For an outside activity, ask the children to take off their shoes and socks. Paint the bottoms of their feet and help them stand on a piece of paper to make footprints. Wash and dry their feet. When the footprints are dry, label them "left" and "right."

Music and Movement: Do the "Hokey-Pokey" and use the letters to help the children figure out which arm, leg, and so on to put into the circle.

Related book

My Hands by Aliki

❖ Barbara Saul, Eureka, CA

Mouse Paint Dancing

Materials

Mouse Paint by Ellen Stoll Walsh
Red, blue, and yellow construction paper, approximately 8" x 6"
  (20 cm x 15 cm)
Laminate or clear contact paper
Lively music, if desired

What to do

1. Read *Mouse Paint* by Ellen Stoll Walsh to the children.
2. Laminate the pieces of red, blue, and yellow construction paper.
3. Distribute two different color sheets to each child.
4. Demonstrate how to mix colors by putting one foot on each sheet and doing "The Twist." The laminate makes this easy and fun.
5. Play some lively music, if desired

More to do

Art: For a hands-on activity, finger paint with red, yellow, and blue paint.

❖ Marybeth Hurd, Flower Mound, TX

Five Little Speckled Frogs

Materials

Balance beam

What to do

1. Choose five children to be the five little speckled frogs sitting on a speckled "log" (the balance beam).
2. As you sing the song, touch each frog on the head when it is time for them to jump into the "pool." Specify that the children must leap like frogs leap as they leave the log.

   Five little speckled frogs
   Sitting on a speckled log
   Eating some most delicious bugs. (yum yum).
   One jumped into the pool, where it was nice and cool.
   Now there are four green speckled frogs. (glub, glub).

3. Continue the song until the last frog has leaped from the "log."

More to do

Have leap frog races. Use the frog song on the Hap Palmer "Pretend" album. Instruct the children to leap like a frog to the appointed finish line. Specify that they must leap like a frog or they will have to start over again.

❧ Penni Smith, Riverside, CA

Preschool Olympics

Materials

Jump rope
Ball
Hula hoop
Balance beam or masking tape
Whistle
Red, white, and blue ribbons or chocolate coins
Large blocks or crate

What to do

1. Ask the children to sit in a large circle. Give each child a turn to "compete" in each of the "events."
2. Swing a jump rope back and forth and ask the children to jump over it.
3. Encourage each child to bounce a ball. Ask the child to count how many bounces the ball makes.
4. Ask the children to jump from one hula hoop to another.
5. Encourage the children to walk across a balance beam (or a line of tape on the floor).
6. Use the whistle to signify when to begin. Encourage the other children to cheer and chant the child's name.
7. When all the children have had a turn, award the "medals" (chocolate coins) or ribbons.
8. Ask each child to stand on a large block or crate to receive his medal.

❖ Teresa J. Nos, Baltimore, MD

Fitness Fair Time

Materials

Colored tape
Tennis racquets and balls
Jump rope
Paper and pen

What to do

1. Discuss with the children why it is important to stay fit, such as for health reasons and to feel good.
2. Explain to the children that they will be participating in a fitness fair in their class.
3. Ahead of time, set up the fitness fair this way:
   - ■ Place a line of colored tape on the floor so the children can practice balancing while walking forward and backward on the line.
   - ■ Provide tennis racquets and balls so the children can practice bouncing the ball off the racquet (explain eye-hand coordination).
   - ■ Give the children jump ropes and see how many times the children can jump using both feet without stopping; introduce Chinese jump

rope (explain how lots of sports utilize jumping skills).

■ Practice running in a three-legged race.

■ Set up an obstacle course where the children must run jump, kick, balance, jump rope, bounce a ball, and so on.

4. After the children have completed the course, give each child a certificate.

❖ Lisa M. Chichester, Parkersburg, WV

Rhyming Objects

Materials

Assorted objects in rhyming pairs, such as a toy spoon and cardboard moon, a
toy car and star, a rock and a sock, a man and a fan, a bell and shell, and
so on
Pictures, glue, and cardboard squares, optional
Box or basket

What to do

1. This activity teaches children about words that rhyme and helps develop their
auditory discrimination. Change the objects frequently to maintain interest.
2. Collect objects from games, party favors, and so on. Or, glue pictures onto
cardboard squares for hard-to-find words (for example, a moon or tree).
3. Place the objects into a box or basket. Make sure the child knows the names
of all the objects. (Remember, some objects may have more than one name,
such as hen and chicken).
4. Encourage the child to arrange the objects in pairs.

More to do

Think of another rhyming word for each pair.
Math: Count the individual objects. Discuss the meaning of the word "pair" and
count the pairs.

❧ Mary Jo Shannon, Roanoke, VA

The Talking Stone and the Listening Pebbles

Materials

A clean, medium-sized stone
Many pebbles

What to do

1. Ask for a volunteer to tell a story. Select a child and hand the stone to him. Give a pebble to each of the other children to hold.
2. The child holding the stone is the storyteller. The children holding the pebbles are listeners.

More to do

This activity also works well during Story Time.

Related book

Tell Me a Mitzi by Lore Segal

♣ Ingelore Mix, Gainesville, VA

Paper Bag Stories

Materials

Pictures or comic strips
Small paper bags

What to do

1. Place a picture or part of a comic strip into paper bags.
2. Give each child a bag. Ask each child to make up a story about her picture.
3. As the children become more skilled at story telling, encourage them to put their stories together to make one story.

More to do

Add more pictures to the story bags and ask each child to put together a story with their pictures. Write their stories on a piece of paper. Put each story into a book for each child, or make a group storybook.

Introduce story time like this:
I have a story to tell.
I have a story to tell.
I'll look in my bag and find out what story I am going to tell.
(Make up your own tune or clap each time you say a word.)

♣ Jane Hibbard, Stryker, OH

Language

Materials

None needed

What to do

1. Make up a story with the children. Begin with a sentence, such as "I have a cat, and..."
2. Ask a child to add a sentence to your sentence. (Ahead of time, give examples of things the children might add, such as where it lives, what size it is, its name, its favorite food, things it plays with, whether it has brothers and sisters, and so on.)
3. Ask the next child to add another sentence, and so on.
4. Afterwards, retell the story. What can you tell me about this cat? (For example, it is red, it is soft, it says, "Meow.")
5. Tell the children, "I will tell you the story again. If I say something wrong say, "Stop," and correct me so it is right." Then say, "I have a cat. It is blue." The children will say, "Stop. It is red."

More to do

Art: Encourage the children to draw a picture of the cat or the story.

❧ Marilyn Harding, Grimes, IA

Stories from Home

Materials

Blank tapes

What to do

1. Send home blank tapes and invite parents and grandparents to record a favorite story. They can record stories from their own childhood or about the child, or they can read books or poetry, and so on.
2. Place the tapes in the Listening Center so children can have wonderful language experiences and strengthen the home/school bond.

More to do

Incorporate this activity into Grandparents' Day (September).

Related book

Nana Upstairs and Nana Downstairs by Tomie DePaola

Charlene Woodham Peace, Semmes, AL

Tape Recorder Fun

Materials

Tape recorder and tape

What to do

1. During circle time, ask the children to come up, one at a time, and say something into the tape recorder.
2. When everyone has had a turn, play the recording for the children and encourage them to guess who is talking.

More to do

Encourage the children to tell a story and tape record it. Encourage the children to sing their favorite songs together as they tape it. Tape record different everyday sounds and ask the children to identify the sounds.

Sue Myhre, Bremerton, WA

Puppet Story

Materials

Paper
Scissors
Paint or crayons
Cardboard
Glue
Sticks or dowels
Tape

What to do

1. Cut out oval shapes from paper.
2. Encourage the children to paint or color pictures on the oval paper shapes (for example, animals, people, creatures from outer space, flowers, and so on).
3. Cut out the figures from the paper and glue them on a piece of cardboard.
4. Tape the cardboard figures to a stick or dowel.
5. Encourage the children to act out a story using the puppets.

More to do

Use stories that are familiar to the children, such as "The Three Little Pigs" or "The Three Bears."

❧ Sandy L. Scott, Vancouver, WA

Catalog Puppets

Materials

Catalogs (children's clothing catalogs or American doll catalogs are good choices)
Glue
Poster board
Craft sticks
Tape
Basket or box

What to do

1. Cut out full body pictures of children, dolls, animals, and so on from catalogs.
2. Glue the pictures to poster board.
3. Tape sticks to the backs of the pictures to make puppets.
4. Place the puppets in a basket or box and put it out during free choice time. Encourage the children to make up plays, using tables or chairs as a stage (or build a stage with blocks). This is a wonderful language activity.

More to do

Art: Place catalogs in the art area so the children can make their own puppets to add to the basket or take home.

❧ Audrey F. Kandoff, Allentown, PA

Possible/Impossible

Materials

None needed

What to do

1. Many four-year-olds have difficulty distinguishing between events that are absurd and those that are conceivable. This activity helps to clear up the confusion.

2. Discuss the meaning of the words "possible" and "impossible." When you feel that the children understand the definitions, present a series of statements and ask the children to respond with either "possible" or "impossible." Some examples are:

   ▪ Elephants can fly.
   ▪ A bear sleeps in a bed.
   ▪ Children ride bicycles.
   ▪ Cats drink milk.
   ▪ A gingerbread man can talk.
   ▪ Zebras can drive cars.

More to do

Discuss the possible/impossible statements at story time. Ask the children if they think the things that happen in the story are possible or impossible. Encourage the children to use examples from the story to support their decisions.

Related books

The Carrot Seed by Ruth Kraus
The Doorbell Rang by Pat Hutchins
Frog and Toad Are Friends by Arnold Lobel
Pete's Chicken by Harriet Ziefert

Poem

April Fool
Little bears have three feet
Little birds have four feet
Little cows have two feet
Girls and boys have more
Do you believe this story? Do you believe this song? I can tell it once a year,
When April comes along.
April Fool!

❖ Iris Rothstein, New Hyde Park, NY

A "Mazing" Language Activity

Materials

Things to make a maze, such as chairs, table, tunnel, blocks, steps, or whatever is handy

4 to 5 of the same item, such as cutout circles, beanbags, balls, or blocks

What to do

1. Set up a maze as space allows.
2. Place the circles, beanbags, blocks, or whatever items you choose along the path *on, behind, under, over, or in* the maze items.
3. Ask a child to go through the maze and ask him to stop when he sees the item. Ask him to then describe where it is, such as *under* the block, *on* the chair, *beside* the block, and so on. This is great practice for learning positional words or as a language activity for developing sentences.
4. After describing where it is, the child may pick up the item and go to the next one.
5. After the child has collected all of the items, ask the children to turn their backs while you or a child put the items in other places (or the same places depending on the level of the children involved).

More to do

Use this activity for number recognition, letters, shapes, and so on. Place these items in the maze and ask children to identify them when they find them. Do the activity outside if the weather permits.

❧ Linda Yuska, Buckingham, IA

Pete and Repeat!

Materials

Any favorite story, such as *The Very Hungry Caterpillar* by Eric Carle
Art materials, such as pencils, markers, construction paper, tissue paper,
paper plates, crepe paper streamers, crayons, and glue

What to do

1. Read a favorite story to the children (for example, *The Very Hungry Caterpillar*).
2. Encourage the children to re-tell story by acting it out.
3. Help the children design and make costumes for the story, such as the different fruits and foods, the caterpillar, the cocoon, and of course, the beautiful butterfly.
4. Encourage the children to practice the story again and perform for another group of children. (Children can tell the story in their own words, or you can read the story for them.)

More to do

Music and Movement: Encourage the children to make up dances or movements to music that is light and airy (like a butterfly!).
Writing Center: Ask the children to dictate the story to you as you write it down. Encourage them to illustrate it.

❖ Sheryl A. Smith, Jonesborough, TN

Crazy Colors

Materials

Markers and paper or magazines and scissors
Glue
Construction paper (red, blue, white, green, brown, black, orange,
   yellow, and purple)
Chart paper

What to do

1. Before starting this activity, draw or cut out pictures of a red strawberry, blue sky, white dove (or any other white bird), green toad, brown bear, black horse, orange juice, yellow dandelion, and purple Jell-O.
2. Glue each picture to its corresponding colored construction paper. If drawing or finding pictures is not an option, just use sheet of red, blue, white, green, brown, black, orange, yellow, and purple construction paper.
3. Write the poem "Crazy Colors" on a piece of chart paper. For each color word, write the word using the appropriate corresponding marker.
4. Read the poem to the children.
5. Repeat the poem, and as you say the words, encourage the children to clap in a pat-a-cake rhythm (they use both hands to pat their thighs, clap their hands together, then pat hands with a partner). A rhythm children can do without partners is to pat their thighs twice, clap once, and repeat the actions with each line.

   Crazy Colors by Jeannie Gunderson
   Colors, colors, colors
   Crazy colors carry
   Red-umtious strawberry
   Blue sky above
   Whitetail dove
   Travel down the road
   Green hoppy toad
   Brown bear dances
   Black Beauty prances
   Sing about rain
   Orange juice stain
   Dandelion yellow
   Jiggly, purple Jell-O
   Colorlitious, colors
   Colors, colors, colors.

6. Give the children the pictures or colored construction paper. Ask the children to hold up their picture when they hear their color word. Exchange pictures until all the children have had a chance to hold up a color word picture or piece of colored construction paper. The children who do not have a color word picture can do the pat-pat-clap rhythm until it is their turn.

❧ Jeannie Gunderson, Casper, WY

Follow the Flashlight

Materials

Flashlight with fresh batteries
Darkened room

What to do

1. Ask the children to lie on the floor, on their backs, all facing the same direction.
2. Close the curtains and turn off the lights to make the room as dark as possible.
3. Lie down with the children on the floor. Use the beam of the flashlight to "write" letters, shapes, or numbers on the wall or ceiling.
4. Ask the children to name the letters, numbers, and so on that they see.

❖ Vicki L. Schneider, Oshkosh, WI

Alphabet Matching Bags

Materials

Sandpaper
Scissors
Paper bags

What to do

1. Cut out every letter from sandpaper.
2. Encourage the children to decorate each paper bag with a different sandpaper letter.
3. The child feels the sandpaper and then finds an object that starts with the letter to put in the bag.

❖ Lisa M. Chichester, Parkersburg, WV

Alphabet Letter Books

Materials

Sandpaper squares
Scissors
Construction paper
White paper
Glue
Hole punch
Yarn
Magazines
Markers

What to do

1. Cut out a large letter from sandpaper for each child.
2. Cut out larger versions of the same letters from construction paper and a few sheets of white paper.
3. Help the children glue the sandpaper letter to a large, corresponding construction paper letter.
4. Put the construction paper letter on top of a few sheets of white paper that have been cut into the same letter shape. Punch a hole through the pages and tie yarn through it to make a book.
5. Encourage the children to look through magazines and cut out pictures that start with that letter. Then, they can glue the pictures into their books.
6. Children can also draw pictures that start with that letter.
7. Encourage the children to touch the sandpaper letter of each book. They can trace it with a finger and feel the way each letter is shaped.

Lisa Chichester, Parkersburg, WV

It Feels Like _____?

Materials

Sandpaper
Scissors
Blindfold

What to do

1. Cut out letters and numbers from sandpaper.
2. Discuss with the children how people can touch things, without seeing them, to find out what they are.
3. Show the children the letters and numbers. Encourage them to feel them and see if they can tell the difference.
4. Blindfold a child and place the letters and numbers in front of him. Ask the child to feel them and try to guess which ones are letters and which are numbers.
5. Put out the game so the children can play it by themselves or with a friend.

More to do

Do this activity using shapes.

Related book

26 Letters and 99 Cents by Tana Hoban

❖ Sandra Hutchins Lucas, Cox's Creek, KY

Skipping Alphabet Game

Materials

Index cards
Marker
Safety pins or hole punch and string
Music on tape, piano, or drum

What to do

1. Make upper and lowercase alphabet cards. For example, write "A" on one card and "a" on another, "M" and "m," and so on. The number of cards you use depends upon the ability of the group. Use safety pins to attach the cards to the children or punch holes into them and tie string through them so children can wear them around their necks.
2. Do this activity with a small number of children (6-10). Pin an alphabet card onto each child.
3. Play music as the children skip around the room. When you stop the music,

each child looks for his letter match. When the children find their "match," start the music again. The children with matching letters will skip together.

4. At the end of the song, children can either trade letters to play a new game or give their letters to other children who have been watching and clapping to the music.

More to do

This activity lends itself to many variations. Play a matching game using colors and color words, numbers and number words, or letters and pictures of things that start with the letter (for example, the letter "c" and a picture of a cat). The variations are endless, and the children get physical activity too! Another variation is to change the action from skipping to hopping, marching, and so on.

Related books

26 Letters and 99 Cents by Tana Hoban
Chica Chica Boom Boom by Bill Martin Jr. and John Archambault
Curious George's ABCs by H.A. Rey

❧ Iris Rothstein, New Hyde Park, NY

Letter and Word Hunt

Materials

Paper and pencil
Poster board or chart paper
Crayons or markers
3" x 5" (7 cm x 12 cm) index cards
Glue

What to do

1. Explain to the children that we use letters and words every day to give us information. Tell them that they will be going on a letter and word hunt outside the classroom. They will look for examples of letters and words that tell us things we need to know.

2. Some examples are: restrooms labeled *Men, Women, Boys, Girls*; water faucets with H(ot) and C(old); *Enter* and *Exit* signs; school signs such as Office, Cafeteria, and the name of the school; traffic signs such as *Stop* or *Yield*;

street name signs; and billboards. Using a pencil and paper, list all the environmental letters and words that you find outside the classroom.

3. When you get back to the classroom, transfer these letters and words to the poster board or chart paper. Leave plenty of room beside and between each letter and word.

4. Ask the children to illustrate one of these letters or words on an index card. Glue the card beside the letter or word on the chart. For example, beside the words "Stop sign," glue the card with the drawing of a stop sign.

More to do

Explain the letter and word hunt to the children's families. Send two index cards home with each child. Ask the families to go on a letter or word hunt together around their home and neighborhood. What letters and words did they find? Make a chart labeled "Words Around Our Homes" and add the words and card illustrations.

❖ Nancy Dentler, Mobile, AL

Rainbow of Words

Materials

White tag board or butcher paper
Scissors
Markers

What to do

1. Cut out a large rainbow shape from a piece of tag board or butcher paper.
2. Outline six bands on the rainbow using the appropriate color marker.
3. Show the children the rainbow at group time and ask them to name some things that are red. Write their ideas in red ink on the red outlined band.
4. Tell them to look for things that are orange when they get home so they can share their ideas tomorrow.
5. Continue each day until the rainbow is complete and ready for you to display.
(See illustration on the next page.)

More to do

Art: Pour water into an ice cube tray. Add a few drops of food coloring to the water to make all the colors of the rainbow.

More Art: Give the children rainbow shaped paper to paint.

Music: Sing rainbow songs and color songs and ask a child to stand next to the Rainbow of Words and point to the colors when they are mentioned.

Related books

A Rainbow of My Own by Don Freeman
Little Blue and Little Yellow by Leo Lionni
The Rainbow Goblins by Ul De Rico

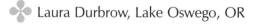 Laura Durbrow, Lake Oswego, OR

What's in a Name?

Materials

Pocket chart
Photo of each child
Index cards
Marker

What to do

1. Place photos of the children in the pocket chart ahead of time.
2. Write each child's name on an index card.
3. Give each child his own name card. Encourage the children to come up, one at a time, and place their name card beside their photo.
4. Repeat this activity daily and begin to call attention to the letters in their names, such as similarities and differences, first and last letters, and so on.
5. When the children are ready, move to the next step. Hand out the name cards randomly. Ask each child to read the name on his card and place it next to its matching photo.
6. Later in the year, replace the photos with another set of name cards. Encourage the children to match the name cards with matching name cards instead of photos.

More to do

Use this activity as a center time choice. One or two children can match name cards to photos, or cards to cards. Turn this activity into a memory match game by placing the cards in the pocket chart blank side up. The children will try to make matches by finding name pairs.

Ruth Cohenson, Pleasantville, NJ

Word Book: Clothes That I Wear

Materials

Construction paper
Scissors
Stapler
Glue
Old magazines or catalogs

What to do

1. Place the materials in the Art Center.
2. Fold the construction paper in half, then cut along the fold line. Make sure you have enough paper to make books for each child in the class.
3. Make a cover for each of the books titled "(Child's name) Word Book: Clothes That I Wear." Staple the pages together.
4. During Circle Time, talk about clothes. Ask the children what they put on in the morning when they get ready for school. For example, ask, "What do you wear if the weather is cold? What do you wear if it rains? What do you wear when you play? What do you wear when you go to bed at night?" Make a list of everything they say.
5. Take the children to the Art Center. Give each child a word book and explain that they are going to look through magazines and catalogs to find pictures of the clothes they talked about during Circle Time.
6. Encourage the children to cut out the pictures and paste them into their word books.
7. When each child has finished, go through his book and write the word for each picture at the bottom of the page. As you do this, connect the picture with the word by saying, "This is a picture of a sock and this is how you spell sock."
8. The children can take their books home and share them with their parents.

More to do

This idea can be extended with themes or concepts. A few examples are:
■ Use shapes or numbers instead of clothes.
■ Ask the children to find different colored objects and paste them in a word book. Write the color at the bottom of the page. For example, they can look

for a red apple, blue bird or ball, an orange, a purple grape, a brown bear or dog, a black cat, a yellow star, a green tree, and a white snowman.

■ Make a "parts of the body" word book. Ask the children to cut out pictures of eyes, ears, noses, and mouths from old magazines and paste them into the books. Write the word at the bottom of the page.

The list is endless on ways to use a word book. This project helps the children learn how words connect to the pictures, which will help them learn to read eventually.

❦ Sherri Lawrence, Louisville, KY

Message Chalk Board

Materials

Small chalk boards
Tempera paint and brushes
Decorations, such as pompoms and rickrack
Glue
Permanent marker
String
Chalk

What to do

1. Purchase a small chalkboard for each child.
2. Encourage the children to decorate the borders of their chalkboards using tempera paints, pompoms, rickrack, and so on.
3. Write each child's name on his board with a permanent marker.
4. Tie a piece of string around a piece of chalk and attach it to the chalkboard. The children can hang their boards on their cubbies and use them to write reminders or messages.

❦ Lisa M. Chichester, Parkersburg, WV

Literacy Area

Materials

Alphabet poster
Stapler
White paper
Children's photographs
Glue
Paper, pens, markers, pencils
Junk mail, old date books, maps, and so on

What to do

1. Display a poster of the alphabet in upper and lowercase letters.
2. Make a journal for each child by stapling a few pieces of paper together.
3. Glue each child's photo on the inside cover of his journal.
4. Provide children with pencils, markers, stamps, junk mail, and so on. Encourage them to write or draw in their journals. (For some children, this is a good way to let their parents leave while they are busy writing and drawing in their journal.)

More to do

Write the daily snack menu on a blackboard and read it aloud at group time.
Blocks: Put paper, pencils, and masking tape in hanging baskets in the Block Center. Encourage the children to make signs, draw designs, or tell who built the structure. Use adding machine tape rolls to make maps, signs, take messages, or as note paper.
Dramatic Play: Make paper and pencils available to take orders, write up bills, and so on. Hang a tablet of paper and a pencil on a string so children can write messages.

❖ Andrea M. Clapper, Cobleskill, NY

Salt Boxes

Materials

3 or 4 shallow boxes (ask a camera shop for empty photo-paper boxes)
3 or 4 large boxes of salt

What to do

1. Fill each shallow box about ¾ full of salt.
2. Help the children wash their hands before and after this activity. Working with small groups, give each child a salt box.
3. Encourage the children to use their fingers to draw and write in the salt. To erase the drawings, the children can shake the salt box. Supervise this activity closely to make sure that the children don't eat the salt and to clean up spills.
4. When done, put the lids on the boxes and keep them indefinitely.

More to do

Instead of salt, fill the boxes with sand. Encourage the children to draw or write with their fingers in a sandbox.

Field Trips: Take the children on a field trip to a beach. Encourage them to use their hands or a stick to write and draw in the sand.

❧ Barbara Saul, Eureka, CA

Creating a Writing Center

Materials

Several containers
Markers, crayons, writing and coloring pencils, and colored chalk
Stationary, various types of writing tablets and paper, old mail
Sentence strips
Laminate or clear contact paper

What to do

1. Designate and label an area of the classroom as a Writing Center.
2. Store writing utensils and paper in large containers. Label the containers using pictures and words so that the children can store the items by themselves.
3. Write popular words or phrases on sentence strips. Laminate or cover them

with clear contact paper for durability. Mount the words or phrases near or on a desk or table or place them in a storage container.

4. Encourage the children to write and create letters using the papers and writing utensils. Encourage the children to visit this center as often as desired.

5. Display the children's creations or let them take them home each day. For parent conferences and to document children's writing progress, save creations from time to time.

More to do

Create word cards related to the current theme by drawing a picture and writing the word next to it. Make name cards for each child in the classroom. If you have a photograph of each child, add the child's name and laminate or cover it with clear contact paper.

❧ Tina Woehler, Oak Point, TX

Book Making

Materials

Paper
Stapler
Markers, crayons, colored pencils, and rubber stamps

What to do

1. Fold paper into small books and staple them on one side. (Only a few pieces of paper are needed per book.)
2. Place the pre-made books in the Writing Area along with rubber stamps, markers, crayons, and colored pencils.
3. Encourage the children to draw pictures in their "books." Be available to write the words on each page as dictated by the children.

More to do

Put the completed books in the Library Area and read them to the children.

❧ Susan Myhre, Bremerton, WA

I Can Read That!

Materials

Actual logo and product labels from well known foods, toys, and fast food chains
Glue
Index cards
Laminate or clear contact paper
Marker or pen
Pocket chart

What to do

1. Glue product labels onto index cards and laminate them or cover them with clear contact paper.
2. Make black and white copies of the labels and make a second set of cards. Laminate them or cover them with clear contact paper.
3. Make a third set of cards by simply writing the words from each logo or label on an index card. Laminate them as well.
4. Introduce the activity at Circle Time, using the pocket chart. Begin with the first two sets of cards. Place the original logo cards in the pocket chart.
5. Give each child a card from the second set. Ask the children to come up, one at a time, and find the match to their logo.
6. "Read" the logos, and talk about the letters as you go through the cards. Encourage the children to play the game in pairs during center time.
7. Introduce the third set of cards (with no graphics to help them find matches) with those children who are ready for the next level of print awareness.

More to do

Make a duplicate game to send home with the children, one at a time, to play at home with their families. Parents love to feel connected to what goes on in their child's classroom, and children love to "show off" what they can "read" on their own!

❖ Ruth Cohenson, Pleasantville, NJ

Beginning Sounds

Materials

Any object for which you want to stress the beginning sound. (Add other objects that have the same beginning sound as well as a few that have very different beginning sounds.)
Bag or other container

What to do

1. Place the chosen objects in a bag or other container.
2. Show an object chosen for its selected beginning sound (such as a ball). Demonstrate the beginning "b" sound and encourage the children to practice saying "b…b" as a part of "ball."
3. One at a time, remove objects from the bag and name them, stressing their beginning sounds. Classify the objects according to whether or not they have the same beginning "b" sound as "ball."

More to do

Place the objects in a learning center and encourage the children to classify them according to the selected beginning sound. Encourage the children to find other objects in the room that begin with the same sound.

❧ Barbara L. Lindsay, Mason City, IA

Names of Colors

Materials

Colorful objects or pictures of colorful items (for example, various types of trees; flowers; fruits and vegetables; rocks; and common household items, such as toothpaste, shampoo, and soap)

What to do

1. Talk about colors. Hold up an item that is yellow, for example, a banana. What color is this? Yellow. Now look at another yellow item, for example, a dandelion. What color is this? Are they the same color? Not exactly, but a banana is yellow and so is the dandelion.

2. Repeat this process with a large number of items.

3. This activity will help children begin to distinguish colors. For example, the leaves of trees are green, but they are not all the same shade of green. Magnolia leaves are dark green (called "magnolia green"). Apple tree leaves in the spring are light green and can be called "spring apple leaf green." Other examples are "rock gray" and "dirty snow gray," or "fresh snow white" and "milk white."

4. Look at the names of the colors in a box of crayons. Some are simple names, such as green, blue, and so on. Others are mixed, such as red-orange, while others have fanciful names.

5. Compare the names of colors with each other and with those in the crayon boxes.

More to do

Ask the children to bring in items in a particular color. For example, one day it might be red and another day blue, and so on. Then, compare different colors of red, blue, and so on.

Science: Combine this lesson with a science and nature lesson about colors in nature. Discuss with the children the colors in nature that change with the times and the seasons. For example, the leaves in spring and in fall, the sky on different days, the clouds, and the sun.

❖ Lucy Fuchs, Brandon, FL

My Child the Author

Materials

Lined printing paper

Pictures from greeting cards, old discarded books, advertisements, magazine ads, and so on that show actions or amusing or touching pictures

Pencil and crayons

What to do

1. Spend several days discussing what an author is. Explore the way stories are arranged with a beginning, middle, and end. All stories have characters and a problem that must be solved.

2. Fold several sheets of lined paper in half to create booklets.

3. Ask each child to select a picture and dictate a story about it. Encourage them to select names for their characters. Ask open-ended questions to help the child organize his thoughts.

4. When writing down the child's dictation, leave the front page blank to make a title page.

5. Glue the picture at the top of the title page. Below the picture, print the title selected by the child. Below the title, write "by (child's name)." Encourage the child to trace his name with a crayon.

6. At Circle Time, read each child's story to the rest of the children.

More to do

Provide assorted felt board pieces from different stories. Encourage the children to use them to make up their own stories.

Dramatic Play: Provide puppets, hats, and felt clothes and encourage the children to create characters and plots.

Field Trips: Take a class trip to the local library.

Related books

The Colors (Mouse book) by Monique Felix
The House (Mouse book) by Monique Felix
The Wind (Mouse book) by Monique Felix

❧ Sandra Gratias, Perkasie, PA

Visiting Teddy Bear Girl and Boy

Materials

Two wooden or stuffed bears
Gift bag that has a picture of a bear on it
Bear-shaped cookie cutter
Spiral notebook
Bear stickers
Corduroy by Don Freeman
Bear pen or pencil

What to do

1. Make two wooden bears, one to look like a boy and the other to look like a girl. Or, buy inexpensive stuffed bears and glue on bows, and so on.
2. Purchase a gift bag with a picture of a bear on it. Place a bear-shaped cookie cutter, a spiral notebook that has a picture of a bear or put bear stickers on it, the book *Corduroy*, and a bear pen or pencil inside the bag.
3. Copy this note:

Dear Mom and Dad,

My name is Visiting Teddy. I am here to spend the weekend with your child. Please have lots of fun with me but make sure you use the journal in the bag to write down everything we do together this weekend so your child can share this with the class on Monday! Oh, and don't forget to use the cookie cutter to make some cinnamon bear toast!

❖ Lisa M. Chichester, Parkersburg, WV

Star of the Week

Materials

Stuffed animal
Book
Baby blanket
Blank journal
Canvas bag or backpack

What to do

1. Make a "Star of the Week" bag. Put a stuffed animal, a book, a baby blanket, and a blank journal into a canvas bag or backpack.
2. Introduce the Star of the Week bag to the children and explain that everyone will have a turn to bring the stuffed animal home with them. Explain that the bear has a blanket, a favorite book, and a diary. Not only do the children need to take care of the bear, but they also they need to have their parents help write down the animal's adventure for the week that the animal is with them.
3. Create a spot to hang the Star of the Week information each week. If desired, ask the Star of the Week to bring in a photo from home. Questions to ask the Star of the Week:

- What is your favorite color? _____
- Who are your friends?_____
- What is your favorite thing to do at school?_____
- What is your favorite food?_____
- What don't you like?_____
- What is your favorite book?_____

4. Make a certificate that says:

_____ is our star of the week

This entitles _____ to have our mascot spend the week with him/her. Please read our mascot his/her favorite story and make sure you write in his/her diary and tell us of your adventures.

5. Write a letter to the parents informing them of the importance of the home-to-school connection with literacy.

❖ Caitlin E. Gioe, Tuckerton, NJ

Color Sorting

Materials

Tape or glue
6 or more envelopes
Large piece of cardboard, at least 16" x 24" (40 cm x 60 cm)
Construction paper, at least six different colors
Scissors
Laminate or clear contact paper

What to do

1. Tape or glue six or more envelopes to a large piece of cardboard.
2. Cut out squares from six or more colors of construction paper. Cut the squares small enough to fit into the envelopes. Also, make enough so that the child will have plenty to sort.
3. Laminate the squares or cover them with clear contact paper for durability.
4. Encourage the children to sort the construction paper squares and put them in the different envelopes.

ENVELOPES ATTACHED TO CARDBOARD

FALL COLORS
BURGUNDY
BROWN
YELLOW
RED
ORANGE

More to do

Begin by asking the children to sort three colors. When the children master this, add more colors. Change the colors. Begin with primary colors, then fall colors, holiday colors, and pastel colors. For a more complicated activity, choose a wide range of graduated hues for the children to sort. Expand the activity by playing other color games, painting with colors, mixing colors, and eventually naming the colors. Use the envelope board to sort other objects such as shapes, animals, and so on. Children also enjoy making their own games. Supply stickers and paper and encourage them to create their own games.

❖ Jane Hibbard, Stryker, OH

Color Sorting Game

Materials

Scissors
Construction paper or colored contact paper, same colors as plastic lids
Empty icing containers, one for each chosen color
Glue or tape
Various colored plastic jug lids
Storage container

What to do

1. Cut sheets of colored construction paper or contact paper to fit around an icing container.
2. Glue or tape the pieces of paper around the outside of each icing container.
3. Put the icing containers and plastic lids inside a large storage container (for example, a plastic basket or solid open container).
4. Encourage the children to sort the lids and put them into the icing container of the same color.

More to do

Use small objects instead of plastic lids to sort by color.

Related books

All the Colors of the Earth by Sheila Hamanaka

Brown Bear, Brown Bear, What Do You See? by Bill Martin, Jr.

Colors (A First Discovery Book) by Gallimard Jeunesse and Pascale de Bourgoing

Do You Know Colors? by J.P. Miller and Katherine Howard

Green Eggs and Ham by Dr. Seuss

Harvey Potter's Balloon Farm by Jerdine Nolen and Mark Buehner

Let's Paint a Rainbow by Eric Carle

Mouse Paint by Ellen Stoll Walsh

Planting a Rainbow by Lois Ehlert

White Rabbit's Color Book by Alan Baker

Songs

"I'm a Little Red Train"

"I'm a Little White Duck"

"Lavender's Blue"

"Little Green Frog"

✿ Deborah R. Gallagher, Bridgeport, CT

All Sorts of Seashells

Materials

Variety of shells

Sand table, optional

Graph sheet

Pen or marker

Poster to match shells

What to do

1. Set out a variety of shells on a table (or a sand table, if desired). Try to have at least five different kinds of shells.

2. Ask the children to choose five shells to classify.

3. Encourage the children to classify their shells by matching them to the pictures on the shell poster.

4. Design a graph to include the type, shape, and color of the shells as well as anything else you feel is important, such as whether the shell is rough or

smooth. This encourages the children to really research their shells and, hopefully, to realize that the shells are really different from each other!

5. Children can record their answers by drawing pictures. Or, you can ask questions and make tally marks (for example, "How many of your shells are rough? How many are smooth?" and so on).

More to do

Ask the children to seriate the shells from smallest to largest. Also tally shells in a group. Tally shells with the same shape, size, roughness, smoothness, and so on.
Art: Make jewelry, such as a bracelet or necklace, using small shells and beads. Decorate a picture frame with shells. Make an animal with shells—be creative!
Language: Encourage the children to make up a story about a favorite shell. Then they can illustrate the story.

❧ Sheryl A. Smith, Jonesborough, TN

"Finger Lids" Patterning and Sorting

Materials

Lids from dried out markers
Plastic storage tub

What to do

1. Collect lids from markers that have dried out. Store them in a plastic tub. (The children in my class discovered that the lids fit on their fingertips and named them "finger lids!")

2. During a period of initial exploration, encourage the children to place the lids in random order on all ten of their fingers.

3. As the children's fine motor skills develop, encourage them to sort the lids by putting one color on one hand and a different color on the other hand. Encourage the children to explain their sorting, which helps to develop their oral language.

4. As the children's math skills develop, encourage patterning activities using the

"finger lids." Begin by using simple "ABAB" patterns (red, blue, red, blue). Later, encourage more complex patterns (for example, red, blue, blue, red, blue, blue).

5. With early patterning experiences, begin the pattern and ask the children to continue it. Later, ask the children to make up their own pattern. To confirm what the child understands, ask questions such as, "What color would come next?"

More to do

Ask parents to donate other kinds of plastic lids for sorting and patterning activities. Create patterns using blocks and beads.

Dramatic Play: Add finger puppets to the Dramatic Play Area to continue fine motor exploration during storytelling.

Related book

Piggies by Audrey Wood

❧ Anne Wenger, Harrisonburg, VA

Pattern Cards Galore

Materials

Markers or pictures of different items, scissors, and glue
Poster board
Laminate or clear contact paper
Paper and markers

What to do

1. Use pictures of several items from the classroom to create a pattern/sequence card.
2. Choose toys, thematic items, colored items, poker chips, tangrams, circular shaped dry cereal, or counting bears and create a color or pattern for the children to follow.
3. Use actual pictures from catalogs or draw pictures on a piece of poster board. Glue them to the poster board.
4. Laminate or cover the poster board with clear contact paper for durability.
5. Encourage the child to follow and complete the pattern.

6. For a more challenging activity, complete a line and then partially complete the next one. Make the sequence of items as complicated or simple as necessary.

7. Leave out paper and markers for the children to make their own pattern charts to share with the other children.

More to do

Go on a scavenger hunt following a sequence. Create a surprise for the children to find after they have found certain objects or followed a series of events. If the children are finding certain objects, give the clues in a pattern. For example, ask the children to find an empty ice cream carton, an empty bowl, a spoon, another empty carton, a bowl, a spoon, and then a full carton of ice cream in the freezer. Read the clues or draw them on a map for the children to follow. The object could be to find items related to the surprise. Make this as repetitive as necessary until the children are able to predict what will come next.

❖ Tina R. Woehler, Oak Point, TX

Shape Collages

Materials

My Very First Book of Shapes by Chuck Murphy
Shapes, Shapes, Shapes by Tana Hoban
Large pictures of a circle, square, rectangle, triangle, and diamond
Brightly colored construction paper
Scissors
Black construction paper
Paste or glue

What to do

1. Read one or more of the shape books (see above) to the children.
2. Point to a picture of a circle. Ask the children to describe to a partner what it looks like. Encourage the children to get up and explore the room and point to something that is a circle. Ask them to take turns telling the rest of the children what they have found.
3. Follow this procedure with the other shapes.
4. Cut out a variety of shapes from brightly colored construction paper. Place a

variety of shapes on each table.

5. Give each child a piece of black construction paper. Encourage the children to make different designs on their on their construction paper using the shapes.

6. When they have found a design that they want to keep, ask them to glue the shapes to the paper.

More to do

Put stencils of the shapes at a table with pencils and paper for the children to experiment.

Art: Show the students a fine art print of a Mondrian painting and talk about the shapes that the artist uses.

More Art: Leave out the leftover shapes, paper, and glue for the children to explore during free play.

Field Trips: Go on a "shape walk" around the neighborhood looking for the different shapes.

Gross Motor: Encourage the children to make shapes with their bodies. For example, say to them, "Make your body into a circle," or "With a partner, make your bodies into a square."

Manipulatives: Put out magnetic shapes and a magnet board or felt shapes and a felt board for the children to use for construction.

❖ Barbara Saul, Eureka, CA

Shape-O-Saurus

Materials

Construction paper
Scissors
Glue
Crayons or markers

What to do

1. Cut out shapes, such as triangles, squares, rectangles, octagons, and so on from construction paper.

2. Give each child a large piece of construction paper. Encourage the children to use the cutout shapes to create their own dinosaurs.

3. Help the children glue the "Shape-o-saurus" onto the paper.

4. Encourage the children to draw a background using crayons or markers.

More to do

Show the children pictures of various dinosaurs to give them an idea of how to create their own dinosaur. Be sure to include the flying and swimming dinosaurs.

Related books

The Dinosaur Alphabet Book by Jerry Pallotta
The Dinosaur Who Lived in My Backyard by B.G. Hennessy
Giant Dinosaurs by Erna Rowe
If Dinosaurs Came to Town by Dom Mansell
Patrick's Dinosaurs by Carol Carrick
Tyrannosaurus Was a Beast by Jack Prelutsky
We're Back! A Dinosaur's Story by Hudson Talbott

❧ Kaethe Lewandowski, Centreville, VA

Number Day

Materials

Toys, pictures, and objects in the child's environment

What to do

1. Pick a number for the day, such as "three." Try and incorporate that number in all the day's activities. Following are some examples:

   ■ Set three places at each table.
   ■ Move in groups of three.
   ■ Serve three crackers for snack.
   ■ Give the children three crayons to draw a picture.
   ■ Take three steps forward and three steps backward.
   ■ Do matching in sets of three.
   ■ Sort in three's.

More to do

Do a different number day periodically.

❧ Sandy L. Scott, Vancouver, WA

Edible Counting

Materials

Bite-size snacks
Cup, optional

What to do

1. Give each child a pile or cup of bite-size snacks.
2. Call out numbers and encourage the children to count out their snack and put it into piles.
3. Give simple instructions such as, "Eat the pile that has *less*."
4. As you proceed with this activity, reinforce concepts such as, "Ten is *more* than five."
5. Continue giving instructions until everyone has finished their snack.

More to do

Extend this activity to the Manipulative Center and encourage the children to work together, comparing quantities.

Related books

Each Orange Had 8 Slices by Paul Giganti, Jr.
Feast for 10 by Cathryn Falwell

♣ Wanda K. Pelton, Lafayette, IN

Counting Apples

Materials

Camera and film
Bag of apples
Glue
Poster board
Marker
Clear contact paper or laminate
Hole punch
Yarn or metal rings

What to do

1. Take a series of pictures of children holding apples.
2. Start with one child holding one apple. Take the next picture of two children, each holding an apple, and so on.
3. Glue the pictures onto sheets of poster board.
4. Help the children write the number under each corresponding picture.
5. Cover the pictures with clear contact paper or laminate them for durability.
6. Punch three holes along the left side of each page.
7. Tie yarn through the holes or use metal rings to attach the pages together to make a book. Place it on a bookshelf in the Library Area. This book is sure to be a popular choice!

More to do

Sort and count the apples.

Home Connection: Encourage the children to take turns bringing the book home to share with their families.

❧ Cindy Winther, Oxford, MS

Math Snacks

Materials

Oak tag cards with assorted amounts of dots on them and a matching set with corresponding numbers on them
Napkins and cups
Small snacks (teddy grahams, pretzel sticks, fish or animal crackers, oyster crackers, cheese nips, and so on)
Plates
Slips of paper

What to do

1. Place a numeral card at each place at the table. Give each child a card with dots. Ask the children to count the dots and then find the correct number at the table. This will be the child's seat for snack.
2. Encourage the cup and napkin helpers to count the number of children at the table and use one-to-one correspondence to decide how many cups or napkins are needed.

3. Serve several different snacks of the same shape and ask the children to identify how they are similar.

4. Serve snacks of different shapes and identify them. Encourage the children to match them.

5. Use pretzel sticks to make shapes on a plate or napkin.

6. Encourage the children to count how many pieces they have for snack. Ask them to eat some and count how many are left.

7. If you serve seconds, see if the children can add up the first and the second helpings to find the total number of pieces they ate.

8. Write numbers on slips of paper. Place a plate of small snacks on each table and put a paper with a number on the plate. Ask the children to count out that many pieces of the snack and put them onto their plate or napkin. Check the amount before the children eat.

❖ Sandra Gratias, Perkasie, PA

Counting with Anything

Materials

Items to sort, such as rocks, shells, dog biscuits, large marbles, large beads, or buttons
Cups or bowls
Poster board
Laminate or clear contact paper

What to do

1. Choose many different colors and sizes of one type of item for the children to sort. As an example, this activity will use buttons. Gather lots of different sizes and colors of buttons, including two-hole and four-hole buttons.

2. Use small cups or bowls to sort the buttons (or other item).

3. Encourage the children to sort by color, size, and two-hole or four-hole type. If the buttons have different shapes, sort them by shape too.

4. Ask the children to count each time they sort something different.

5. Make a graph—by color, size, and so on. Use tally marks to count, or draw circles to represent the buttons.

6. Make special work mats for the children to do their counting on. Cut out a large circle from poster board and laminate it or cover it with clear contact

paper. (For example, I use a picture of a puppy when the children are sorting dog biscuits. The children LOVE this! The flavored snack bones are good to use because they come in different colors.)

7. Ask any kind of question that requires math thinking.

More to do

Graph the math problems. Encourage the children to use individual graphs, and then make a giant class graph. Encourage the children to come up with their own "counters" and ideas. Ask them to bring in something from home (cotton balls, Q-tips, band-aids, safety pins, and so on).

❧ Sheryl A. Smith, Jonesborough, TN

Random Counting

Materials

Shallow box (such as a cardboard box top)
Hardware cloth (a wire screen with large openings, available at hardware stores)
Scissors
Duct tape
Marbles

What to do

1. Counting is the basis of all math. After children learn to count by rote, they should have many opportunities to count objects. This group activity provides four-year-olds an opportunity to practice random counting.

2. Make a random counting tray by cutting hardware cloth to fit inside a shallow box. Be sure to tape the edges of the hardware cloth so it won't injure inquisitive little fingers!

3. Toss a few marbles into the box. They will stay where they land on the hardware cloth.

4. Ask one child to count the marbles.

5. To check the child's math, ask her to count out loud as she picks up the marble, one at a time, to return them to the container.

6. Repeat the process with a different number of marbles and another child until everyone has had a turn.

More to do

At each turn, ask, "Were there more marbles or fewer marbles this time?" Encourage the children to count other things, such as all the yellow (or red, blue, green, and so on) objects in the classroom, or all the children in the Block Area or other areas of the classroom. Ask the children to count the cups on the snack table, or all the pencils, crayons, and other objects.

❖ Mary Jo Shannon, Roanoke, VA

Frozen Numerals

Materials

Cookie cutters in 0 to 9 number shapes
Tray
Water
Freezer or freezing outside temperature
55 ice cubes
Water table
10 containers

What to do

1. Pour water into the number cookie cutters. Put them into a freezer or outside if the temperature is below 32° F. Discuss with the children the changes that take place when water freezes.
2. Allow the frozen numerals to sit at room temperature for 15 to 20 minutes. Observe what happens.
3. As the ice begins to melt, carefully remove them from the cookie cutters, being careful not to break the ice.
4. Display the frozen numerals along with 55 ice cubes in a water table.
5. Provide ten containers for sorting the ice cubes into sets of one to ten.
6. Encourage the children to use the water table as a math center and watch the hands-on learning fun.

More to do

Art: Before freezing a tray of ice cubes, insert Popsicle sticks into each cube. After they have frozen, remove the ice cubes from the tray. The children can hold the ice cubes by the Popsicle stick handle and "ice paint" sprinkles of dry tempera on a piece of paper by moving the ice cubes through them to make designs.

❦ Jackie Wright, Enid, OK

Number Book

Materials

9″ x 12″ (22 cm x 30 cm) colored construction paper, one per child
9″ x 12″ (22 cm x 30 cm) white or manila construction paper, two per child
Hole punch
Yarn
One sheet of paper per child
Markers or crayons
Scissors
Glue
Stickers

What to do

1. Fold the three sheets of construction paper in half into a 9″ x 6″ (22 cm x 15 cm) booklet, with the colored sheet on the outside.
2. Punch two or three holes along the folded edge of the pages. Tie yarn through the holes to bind the book together.
3. Fold a piece of 9″ x 12″ (22 cm x 30 cm) paper in half. On one side, make a title page labeled "My Number Book" (leave space for the child's name). Divide the other half of the paper into ten sections with outlines of the numerals 1 – 10. Make a copy for each child.
4. Help the child cut the title page half of the sheet and glue it to the front of her book. Encourage the child to add her name underneath the title.
5. This project will continue for ten weeks, with a featured number of the week from one to ten.
6. At home each week, the child will cut out a picture from a magazine or sale circular depicting the number of objects for that week and bring it in.
7. When the children bring in their pictures, ask them to glue them into their books. The children will also (with help if necessary) write the number beside the picture. Use the inside front cover for number one and the inside back cover for number ten so there will be a page for each number.

8. When the child completes a page, give her a sticker to add to the outside cover of the book. (This also acts as a tracking device for you.)

Related books

Little Rabbit's First Number Book by Alan Baker
Ten Black Dots by Donald Crews

❦ Sandra Gratias, Perkasie, PA

Counting Spiders and the Bugs

Materials

Blank index cards
Markers or crayons
Pictures, stickers, or drawings of a spider, beetle, firefly, bumblebee, rubber or plastic bug, ant, cake, moths, cup and saucer, and violets
Glue
Popsicle sticks
Miss Spider's Tea Party by David Kirk
The Big Bug Book by Margery Facklam, optional
White or light colored construction paper
Laminate or clear contact paper, optional
Bulletin board border, plain colored or with a bug design
Tape or stapler
Hole punch
Pipe cleaners

What to do

1. Ahead of time, count out enough blank index cards so that each child will have one. Number the cards 1-12 and repeat until all the cards have a number on them.

2. On the cards with the number 1, put a picture or sticker of a spider. On the cards with the number 2, a beetle; number 3, a firefly; number 4, a bumblebee; number 5, a fake bug; number 6, an ant; number 7, a butterfly; number 8, a cake; number 9, a moth; number 10, a cup of tea; number 11, a couple different bugs; and number 12, violets. Instead of putting the pictures on the

index cards, cut the cards into shapes (bug, cake, butterfly, and so on) and color them, if desired.

3. Glue each card to a Popsicle stick.

4. Gather the children into a circle. Read *Miss Spider's Tea Party* by David Kirk out loud. Ask the children to listen for number words.

5. Give one of the number cards to each child. Go around the circle and ask the children to say the number on their card. Explain to them that you are going to read the story again and when they hear the number on their card, they are to hold the card up in the air. They can put the card down when they hear the next number.

6. At this point, you might want to share the pictures of the bugs from *The Big Bug Book* by Margery Facklam. Then give the children white or light colored construction paper and markers and encourage them to draw any kind of bugs they want. (If desired, laminate or cover the pictures with clear contact paper and use them as place mats for an extension activity.)

7. While the children are busy creating bugs, ask an adult helper to assist you in measuring bulletin board strips to the size of each child's head so it will fit like a crown.

8. Tape or staple together the ends. Next, punch two holes about 3" (7 cm) apart.

9. When the children are finished with their bug place mats, give each of them two pipe cleaners. Ask them to thread one pipe cleaner through each of the holes in the crown. Bend the end far enough so that it does not poke the child's head. Put a little curl or bend in the top of the pipe cleaner to make antennae.

More to do

Show the children an African violet plant so they can see what real violets look like.

Snack: At snack time, serve tea and cakes or cookies (like Miss Spider).

Related books

Counting Caterpillars and Other Math Poems by Betsy Franco
The Very Busy Spider by Eric Carle

Jeannie Gunderson, Casper, WY

Peanut Butter Tasting Graph

Materials

Large piece of paper
Marker
Different brands of peanut butter
Tape
Small wooden spoons
Markers in enough colors for each different brand of peanut butter

What to do

1. Make a graph on a large piece of paper, listing each brand of peanut butter. Hang it on the wall.
2. Encourage the children to look at all the brands of peanut butter and taste each one using small wooden spoons.
3. Ask them to list descriptive words for the tastes of each type of peanut butter, such as smooth, crunchy, sweet, salty, and so on. List these characteristics on the chart.
4. Encourage the children to use colored markers to graph the differing tastes of each brand of peanut butter.

Note: As with any food activity, be aware of all food allergies.

♣ Lisa M. Chichester, Parkersburg, WV

How Many People Are in Your Family?

Materials

Paper
Scissors
Large poster board
Marker
Glue

What to do

One way to do the activity

1. Cut out people shapes from paper.
2. Write the title "How Many People Are in Your Family?" across the top of a piece of poster board and set up vertical columns.
3. Glue two people cutouts in the first column, three in the second column, four in the next, and so on. Write the corresponding number in the column, too.
4. Go around the circle and ask each child how many people are in her family. Write the child's name (or attach a piece of paper with the child's name on it) in the appropriate column. (See illustration on next page.)
5. When you finish, compare the columns. Identify which column has the most people and which has the least.

Another way to do the activity

1. Set up horizontal rows on poster board, one for each child in the class.
2. Go around the circle and ask each child how many people are in her family. Attach the appropriate number of people cutouts in each child's row.
3. When you finish, compare the rows. Identify which child has the most people in her family and which child has the least.

Related books

The Berenstain Bears Are a Family by Stan and Jan Berenstain
This Is My Family by Gina and Mercer Mayer

❖ Deborah R. Gallagher, Bridgeport, CT

LARGE POSTER BOARD

HOW MANY PEOPLE ARE IN YOUR FAMILY?

ANNE

NICK
RYAN

KEVIN

LAURA

BRIANA

PEOPLE
CUT OUTS

How Long Is a Dinosaur?

Materials

100' (30 m) measuring tape
Pictures and measurements of different types of dinosaurs
Chalk or masking tape
Paper and marker

What to do

1. Read about dinosaurs, including how big dinosaurs were.
2. Ask the children to decide which dinosaur they would like to measure.
3. Help the children measure the length of a dinosaur using the measuring tape.
4. Compare the measurement to measurements of other dinosaurs, buildings, or people.
5. Make a graph to show which things or dinosaurs were the longest and shortest.

More to do

Investigate what the dinosaurs ate, make comparisons, and make a chart. Draw and measure life-sized dinosaur footprints. Also graph these to see the similarities and differences.

Snack: Serve dinosaur cookies for snack, along with a fruit salad on a lettuce leaf to resemble an herbivore's diet.

Related books

An Alphabet of Dinosaurs by Peter Dodson
Danny and the Dinosaur by Syd Hoff
Dinofours book series by Steve Metzger
If Dinosaurs Come to Town by Dom Mansell
The Magic School Bus in the Time of the Dinosaurs by Joanna Cole
New Questions and Answers About Dinosaurs by Seymour Simon
A Picture Book of Dinosaurs by Claire Nemes

❖ Tina R. Woehler, Oak Point, TX

Good Morning Greeting

Materials

None needed

What to do

1. First thing in the morning, sit in a circle and sing the following to the tune of "Where Is Thumbkin?"
   "Where is (child's name)? Where is (child's name)?"
2. The child whose name is called stands and sings, "Here I am. Here I am."
3. Then the group sings, "How are you today, Sir (or Ma'am)? How are you today, Sir (or Ma'am)?"
4. The child sings, "Very well, I thank you. Very well, I thank you."
5. Then the group replies, "Have a happy day. Have a happy day."
6. The child sits back down in the group. Repeat the song until each child has had a turn.

More to do

Ask each child to hold up a large card with his name on it when you call his name. This will help each child recognize the names of all the children.

♣ Ann G. Glenn, Memphis, TN

Hello Song

Materials

None needed

What to do

1. The group sits in a circle and sings the "Hello Song."
   The Hello Song (Tune: "Skip to My Lou")
   Hello everybody, yes indeed.
   Hello everybody, yes indeed.
   Hello everybody, yes indeed.
   Sing, children sing.

2. Encourage the children to tap out the beat of the music on their legs.

3. Substitute a child's name for "everybody" and change the last line of the song to "How are you?" For example, "Hello to Billy, how are you?" The child can state something simple such as, "Good" or "Fine," or a more complex feeling such as, "I am happy."

4. Change the song throughout the year, if desired. For example, "What's your favorite color?" "What do you like to do?" Encourage the children to choose their first activities of the day. "What are you going to do?"

❖ Sandra Nagel, White Lake, MI

Hello in Different Languages

Materials

None needed

What to do

1. Teach the children the following verse:
   Hello, everybody,
   Hello, everybody,
   Hello, hello, hello.

2. Then substitute the following for hello:
   Guten Tag (Gooten Tock) (German)
   Jambo (Johm-bo) (African)
   Hola (Oh-lah) (Spanish)
   Neeha (Chinese)
   Bonjour (Bon-joor) (French)
   Salaam (Sah-lamn) (Arabic)
   Shalom (Shah-loam) (Hebrew)
   G'day (Australian)

More to do

Ask the children to hold up a flag of the country for which they are saying "hello."

❖ Kaethe Lewandowski, Centreville, VA

Good Morning to You

Materials

None needed

What to do

1. It is important for children to learn good manners and poise when greeting adults. Recognize this need and give the children regular practice to develop their confidence.
2. Ask the children to stand in a circle around the edge of a rug.
3. Move around the circle. Look one child in the eye, smile, extend your right hand, and say, "Good morning, John."
4. The child grasps your hand with his right hand and replies, "Good morning, Mrs. Shannon." If possible, demonstrate the greeting with an aide before you begin so the children understand their roles.
5. When the greeting is over, the child sits down. Move to the next child and repeat the greeting.

Note: This will move quickly if two adults participate. The children will become more at ease in social situations when they know the proper way to shake hands and greet one another. Occasionally ask the children to take the adult roles.

More to do

Discuss greeting customs in other cultures. Learn to say, "Good morning" in other languages.

❧ Mary Jo Shannon, Roanoke, VA

What's New?

Materials

None needed

What to do

1. After singing a good morning song with the children, address each child individually by saying good morning to him and asking, "How are you?"

Encourage the child to respond appropriately by answering, "Good morning" and "fine," "sleepy," and so on. Often, four-year-olds need practice in answering adults politely in simple conversation.

2. Then ask the child, "What's new with you today?" Four-year-olds are usually full of stories and information that they really want to share on whatever topic is relevant to them at the moment! This open-ended question will usually spark a response, even with the shyest child. Allow each child to finish his thoughts, if possible, or help the child finish by saying, "Thank you for telling us about that. Now it is someone else's turn to share."

3. Continue until everyone has had a turn to share what's new with him. Remember to stress the importance of listening respectfully to others while they are sharing.

More to do

Art: Encourage the children to draw a picture of "what's new" with them.
Games: Encourage the children to listen to one another while they are talking. Later in the day, ask, "Who can tell me what's new with Sarah?"
Transitions: Use "What's New?" during down times, such as waiting for lunch to be served or on a bus ride to a field trip.

❖ Suzanne Pearson, Winchester, VA

Morning Greeting

Materials

Various types of colored paper or index cards
Markers or stickers

What to do

1. Make simple cards listing the day's activities.
2. On paper or index cards, draw pictures or attach stickers of things related to that day's activities, such as a fire engine if you're taking a field trip to a fire station, or a dog if one is coming to visit. These pictures will help the children see what will happen that day.
3. If these pictures are posted where parents can see them, the pictures will also help parents know what to discuss with the child at home.

TODAY!
MAKE SNOWMAN WITH SNOW
DO RHYTHM STICKS
READ "BIGGEST SNOWMAN"
DRAW SNOWMAN

❖ Marilyn Harding, Grimes, IA

Sign in, Everyone

Materials

Large paper or bulletin board paper
Scissors
Marker
Yarn

What to do

1. Cut large paper into 24" x 24" (60 cm x 60 cm) sections. Write each child's name on the piece of paper along the left margin.
2. Draw columns on the paper, giving the children a place to sign in and out each day.
3. Label the days so that the children may begin to recognize the composition of a week.
4. Place the paper near the location where the parents sign in each day.
5. Tie a piece of yarn onto a marker and hang it near the sign-in sheet.

Poem

Good Morning Everybody

Good morning everybody, yes indeed,
Yes indeed, yes indeed;
Good morning everybody, yes indeed
I'm glad you came!

Sing or chant "hello" by singing the children's names in place of "everybody."

Marta is here, yes indeed,
Yes indeed, yes indeed.
Marta is here, yes indeed,
I'm so glad you came!

Tina R. Woehler, Oak Point, TX

Balloon Dance

Materials

Balloon for each child
Music
Large open space

What to do

1. Give each child a balloon.
2. Play music and encourage the children to try to keep their balloons from touching the ground using their heads, hands, knees, and feet.

More to do

Play balloon volleyball.

❖ Sandy L. Scott, Vancouver, WA

Scarf Dancing

Materials

Plastic shower curtain rings
Old nylon scarves and/or large ribbons, cut into 3' (1 m) lengths
Hot glue gun, optional (adults only)
Music

What to do

1. Attach scarves or ribbons to shower curtain rings using a hot glue gun (adult only) or by tying knots securely. (Use one ribbon or scarf per ring.)
2. Turn on the music and dance! This is a great activity to do outside.

More to do

Purchase some old flowing skirts at a second-hand store. Children like the feeling of twirling in such skirts!

Related books

Barn Dance by John Archambault
Color Dance by Ann Jonas

Songs

Music for Little People has some very good collections of music:
"A Child's Celebration of Rock and Roll"
"A Child's Celebration of Dance Music"
Putumayo's "World Playground" is also very good.

❧ Linda Ford, Sacramento, CA

Streamers

Materials

Dowel rods, 24" (60 cm) in length
Sandpaper
Tulle
Scissors
Pencil cap erasers

What to do

1. Lightly sand the cut ends of the dowel rods.
2. Cut tulle into 6" x 24" (15 cm x 60 cm) strips.
3. Twist one end of a piece of tulle and fold it over the tip of the dowel.
4. Attach the tulle to the dowel with a pencil cap eraser.
5. Play music and model moving the streamer with the flow of the music.
Note: These streamers are safe and inexpensive.

More to do

Use a variety of styles and tempos.

Related book

Color Dance by Ann Jonas

❧ Charlene Woodham Peace, Semmes, AL

Marching Musical

Materials

Musical instruments, or blocks, cans, or sticks

What to do

1. Give each child a musical instrument. If musical instruments are not available, use blocks, cans, or even sticks.
2. Encourage the children to march around the room playing their instruments. Remind the children to listen because you will be giving them instructions.
3. While the children are marching, give them various instructions. For example, ask them to march with their instruments behind their backs, over their heads, to the side, behind their legs, behind their backs, in front of them, and so on. Ask them to play their instruments as quietly as they can or as loud as they can, or to march without playing or play without marching.

❧ Sandra Hutchins Lucas, Cox's Creek, KY

Dance Shakers

Materials

Tall potato chip canisters, one per child
Medium-sized pebbles, gravel, dry macaroni, rice, Styrofoam packing pieces, buttons, and beads
Construction paper, 9" x 10" (22 cm x 25 cm)
Glue or tape
Colored paper streamers in 12" (30 cm) lengths
Markers

What to do

1. Give each child a clean, empty tall potato chip canister. Encourage the children to experiment with the sound made by putting different objects in the can and shaking it.
2. Help the children wrap construction paper around the cans and glue or tape it along the overlapping edge.

3. Ask the children to put their selection of items into the can.

4. Place two streamers over the top of each can and cap it.

5. Encourage the children to decorate the sides of their cans with markers.

6. Use the shakers to dance and play along with varieties of music.

More to do

Encourage the children to make sounds with different parts of their body. Learn about musical instruments and how their sounds are made.

Field Trips: Visit a high school band rehearsal.

Science: Play Sound Matching Cans: Collect ten matching plastic containers or film canisters. Create matching pairs by putting each of the following items into two containers: rice, jingle bells, wooden beads, bottle caps, and Styrofoam pieces. Spread a thin line of glue on the inside edges of the lids and seal the containers. Encourage a child to shake a container and listen to the sound, then find the matching container. Put colors or stickers on the bottom of the canisters so the children can self-correct.

Related books

The Maestro Plays by Bill Martin, Jr.
Polar Bear, Polar Bear, What Do You Hear? by Bill Martin, Jr.
Shake My Sillies Out by Raffi

❖ Sandra Gratias, Perkasie, PA

Drum Drum Drumming

Materials

Large, wooden hollow blocks or the largest regular blocks you can find
Large area, preferably outdoors
Drumsticks, rhythm sticks, or wooden spoons

What to do

1. Set up the blocks so they stand on one end.

2. Begin to drum on one block. Encourage the children to join in.

3. Continue to drum as more children join the group. Encourage the children to drum using their own pattern and style.

4. Drum a certain rhythm, then pause. See if the children attempt to imitate your pattern. Continue this for a few minutes.
5. Encourage the children to drum a pattern for you to repeat.
6. Continue until interest wanes or the children fall down in a fit of giggles!

More to do

Chant with your drumbeat. As you are drumming, chant a single vowel sound over several notes. The children will most likely echo you. Continue chanting more complicated sounds. Wait for the children to respond. Make your own drums to keep. Use old coffee cans, oatmeal containers, or any other large container with a plastic lid. Decorate them as desired and drum away!

Related books

Boom Baby Boom Boom by Margaret Mahy
Max Found Two Sticks by Brian Pinkney

Virginia Jean Herrod, Columbia, SC

Making a Banjo

Materials

Cardboard
Scissors
Stapler
Small paper plates
Tape or glue
Craft sticks
Paper fasteners, four for each child
Rubber bands, two per child

What to do

1. Cut cardboard into the shape of a banjo neck.
2. Staple a cardboard neck to a paper plate.
3. Tape or glue a craft stick to the back of the neck and plate to stabilize it.
4. Put two paper fasteners at the top and two at the base of the craft stick.
5. Stretch two rubber bands from the neck to the plate to make the strings of a "Banjo."

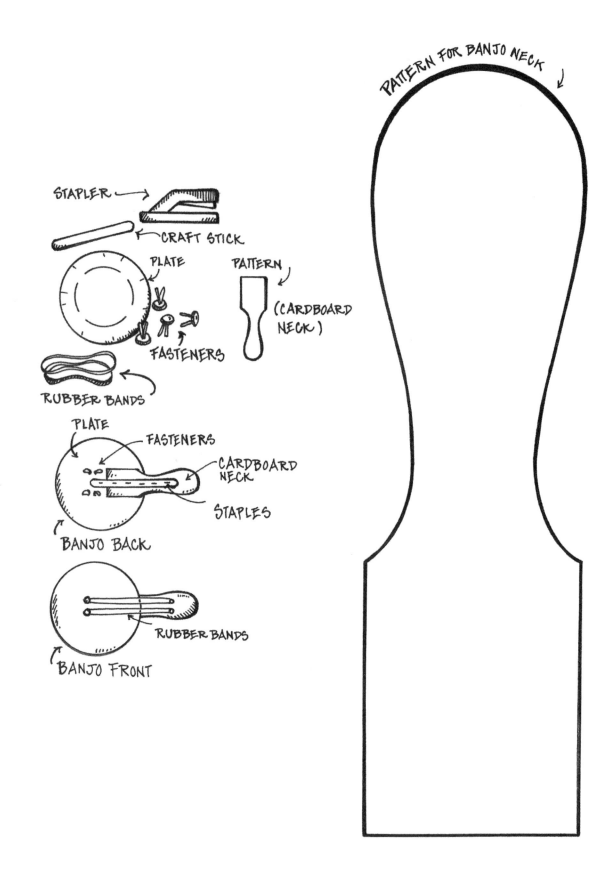

STAPLER

CRAFT STICK

PLATE

PATTERN

(CARDBOARD NECK)

FASTENERS

RUBBER BANDS

PLATE

FASTENERS

CARDBOARD NECK

STAPLES

BANJO BACK

RUBBER BANDS

BANJO FRONT

PATTERN FOR BANJO NECK

More to do

Show the children real string instruments, especially a Banjo. Listen to a recording of string music.

Related books

Big Band Sound by Harriet Diller
Bouncy Mouse by Barbara DeRubertis
The Happy Hedgehog Band by Martin Waddel

❖ Sandra Nagel, White Lake, MI

Kazoo Fun

Materials

Hole punch
Empty toilet paper tube
Wax paper
Rubber band

What to do

1. Using a hole punch, punch a hole into the toilet paper tube, about ¾" (2 cm) from the end.
2. Cover the end of the tube near the hole with wax paper. Put a rubber band over the wax paper to secure it. (Take care not to cover the hole you punched.)
3. Hum into the open end of the tube. If the opening is too large for the child, show her how to cup her hand over the end to make the opening smaller.
4. Practice, practice, practice!
5. Encourage the children to try and make different sounds. For example, they can make busy bee sounds ("bzzzzz"), foghorns ("Baa-ahhh"), bird sounds ("caw, caw, caw"), and engine sounds ("brroommm, brroommm"). Making these sounds help the children, lower and raise their voices, pause, and repeat sounds.

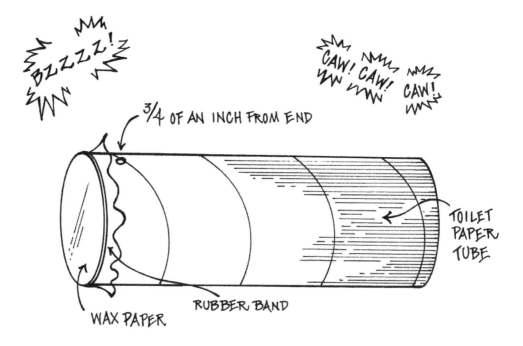

BZZZZ!

CAW! CAW! CAW!

¾ OF AN INCH FROM END

TOILET PAPER TUBE

RUBBER BAND

WAX PAPER

More to do

Have real kazoos available, one for each child. (Write the children's names on their kazoos with a permanent marker and store them in individual paper cups to keep them from touching each other.) Have a variety of kazoos available for the children to see and touch. You can make kazoos from paper, plastic, metal, and even using a comb and wax paper. Encourage the children to explore making sounds in water, by covering and uncovering the top hole and end of the kazoo. The kazoo works well with jazz and blues music.

Note: To play a kazoo, hum, sing, or make noises—don't blow—into the wider end. The kazoo reportedly began in the 1840s by an African American named Alabama Vest. Inspired by the African mirliton (a ceremonial instrument used to disguise the voice), he took the idea to a clock master, Thaddeus Von Clegg, who crafted the first kazoo.

Related books

Big Band Sound by Harriet Diller
The Happy Hedgehog Band by Martin Waddel

Songs

"Peanut Butter Sandwich" by Raffi (This song has kazoo music on it.)
"Twinkle, Twinkle Little Star," "Row, Row, Row Your Boat," "Mary Had a Little Lamb," and other familiar rhymes work well.

Sandra Nagel, White Lake, MI

Do You Hear What I Hear?

Materials

No materials needed, just listening ears

What to do

1. Talk to the children about noises. Explain that sometimes there are quiet noises, and sometimes there are noises that everyone hears.
2. Go on a quiet walk with the children and ask them to listen to the sounds. Walk through the school, listening for any noise. Walk outside and see if you hear any noises.
3. Go back inside, still being as quiet as possible, and encourage the children to take turns describing one of they noises they heard while walking through the school and one of the noises they heard outside. Ask them which was the loudest and which was the quietest.
4. The next time you say you're going on a quiet walk, the children are sure to listen for every noise.

More to do

Encourage the children to draw pictures of the things they heard on their walk. They can also make a "Noise" book by cutting out pictures from old magazines of things that make noise. This will give the children new things to listen for on your next quiet walk.

Related books

The Listening Walk by Paul Showers
My Five Senses by Aliki

Sandra Hutchins Lucas, Cox's Creek, KY

Catching Colored Rainbows

Materials

White construction paper
Large child-size paintbrush
Glue
Colored popcorn kernels (uncooked)

What to do

1. Give each child a piece of white construction paper and a paintbrush.
2. Encourage the children to dip their paintbrushes into glue and "paint" a rainbow shape on the paper.
3. Go outside.
4. Ask the children to stand in a circle and hold up their paper.
5. Along with other adults, toss colored popcorn into the air and encourage the children to catch it with their papers. When the children have caught all the popcorn, go back inside to see the colored rainbows!

Note: The birds and squirrels will be happy to "clean up" the remaining popcorn.

❧ Gloria C. Jones, Great Mills, MD

Water Paints

Materials

Large paintbrushes
Roller brushes with paint trays
Clean, empty paint cans
Painter's caps
Water

What to do

1. Take the above materials outdoors and encourage the children to paint the fence, tables, buildings, sidewalk, and so on.

Related book

The Painter by Peter Catalanotto

❖ Ann Gudowski, Johnstown, PA

Safety Town

Materials

Small riding toy (from home)
White spray paint (adult only)
Grassy area
Poster board
Paint and brushes
Paint sticks
Tape

What to do

1. Ask each child to bring in a small riding toy to use during Safety Town week. (Send a note home to parents requesting this.)
2. Create "roads" using white spray paint on the grass (adult only).
3. Make a variety of traffic signs on poster board.
4. Tape paint sticks to the signs for handles.
5. Encourage the children to have fun "driving" around town!

More to do

Art: Paint large boxes to create buildings to place around the "town."
Literacy: Help the children paint traffic signs and write the words ("stop," "yield," and so on).

❖ Cindy Winther, Oxford, MI

Signs and More Signs

Materials

Index cards or file folders cut into strips
Markers
Hole punch
Pipe cleaners/chenille stems

What to do

1. Bring the above materials along when the children go outdoors to play.
2. Help the children add to their imaginative play by making signs for the play yard. Children may want to label an area (for example, "Cinderella's Castle!" or "Danger! Alligator Pond"). Others might want to make signs to regulate tricycle traffic, such as "STOP" or "YIELD."
3. Show the children how to punch holes into the signs and put pipe cleaners through the holes. Use the pipe cleaners to attach the signs to a fence or to playground equipment.

More to do

Blocks: Help the children make small signs to add to their block play. Tape the signs to cardboard tubes or small blocks.

❖ Barbara F. Backer, Charleston, SC

Outside Fun from the Inside

Materials

Dramatic play items related to the current theme
Plastic storage container with lid

What to do

1. Gather several thematic items that are conducive for outside use. For exam-

ple, for a firefighter theme, use cut-up hoses, fire helmets, raincoats, boots, pails, and so on.

2. Store the items in a watertight plastic container.

3. The items in the box are exclusively for outdoor use. If duplicate items are not available, then assign two children to be the outside helpers. They will be responsible for collecting the items and placing them in the box before outside time begins, carrying it outside, and returning it indoors.

4. Even though the children may use the same items indoors, using them outdoors allows for an entirely different aspect of play and also gives the children more space in which to play.

5. If desired, keep this box outdoors for easier use and less transition challenges.

♣ Tina R. Woehler, Oak Point, TX

Flying Fish

Materials

Easel size newsprint, 2 pieces per child

Scissors

Stapler

Markers

12" (30 cm) pipe cleaner, one per child

Yarn

What to do

1. Cut out a fish shape from each sheet of newsprint, as large as the paper allows. Leave a tab by the mouth of the fish (to insert a pipe cleaner later).

2. Staple together the two fish along the edges. Leave the tail and mouth tab open.

3. Encourage the children to decorate the fish on both sides and add a face.

4. Bend a pipe cleaner into a circle and twist together the ends. Open the tab end of the fish's mouth and insert the wire circle. Fold the tabs over the pipe cleaner and staple securely.

5. Tie a 6" (15 cm) piece of yarn to the two exposed sides of the pipe cleaner.

6. Tie a 24" to 36" (60 cm x 90 cm) piece of yarn to the center of the shorter piece of yarn.

7. Bring the fish kites outside. Encourage the children to hold the long yarn over their heads and run! The fish will twist and flap behind the runner.

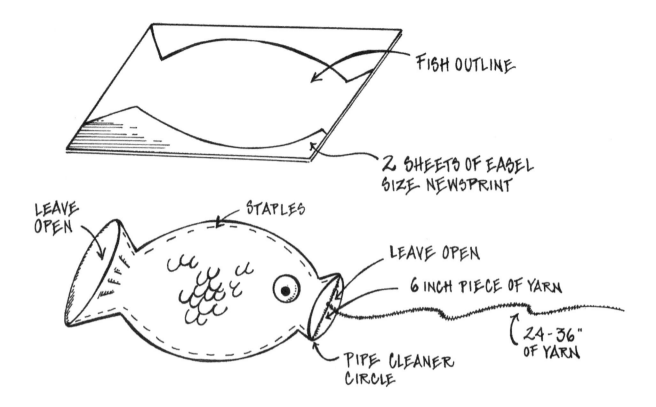

FISH OUTLINE

2 SHEETS OF EASEL SIZE NEWSPRINT

LEAVE OPEN

STAPLES

LEAVE OPEN

6 INCH PIECE OF YARN

24-36" OF YARN

PIPE CLEANER CIRCLE

More to do

Look at pictures of fish in books or nature magazines. Notice the scales, colors, and patterns. Observe live fish in classroom fish tanks. Visit an aquarium or pet store. Learn about the Japanese holiday for flying kites. Do some wind and air experiments.

Related book

The Magic Kite by Kira Daniel

❖ Sandra Gratias, Perkasie, PA

Jump Rope Shapes

Materials

Book about shapes
Blacktop or grass
Individual jump ropes, one for each child
Pen
Whiteboard
Eraser

What to do

1. Read a book about shapes to the children.
2. Go outside and ask the children to find an area they can spread out in.
3. Give each child a jump rope.
4. Demonstrate how to make a circle on the ground with a jump rope.
5. Draw a shape on the whiteboard and encourage the children to make that shape on the ground with their jump ropes.

More to do

Gross Motor: Ask the children to lay their jump ropes on the ground. Using an audible signal (such as a bell or tambourine), invite them to jump over their ropes whenever they hear the sound.

More Gross Motor: Put the children into pairs and give each pair one jump rope. One partner will wiggle the jump rope while the other tries to jump over it. Ask the children to switch roles.

Literacy: Use jump ropes to make letters and numbers.

✿ Barbara Saul, Eureka, CA

PVC Pipe Car Wash

Materials

1 ½" (4 cm) PVC pipe in the following sizes:
twelve 2' (60 cm) pieces
six 64" (160 cm) pieces

three 48″ (120 cm) pieces

one 4″ (10 cm) piece

twelve couplings

seven tees

six 90° elbow pieces

Caps

Drill

Duct tape

4 pompoms

Shower curtain

Scissors

Hose with running water

PVC cleaner

PVC glue

What to do

1. This is a wonderful outdoor summer activity. The children will enjoy running and riding their bikes through the car wash.
2. Lay out all the PVC pipe materials.
3. Attach one coupling to each end of each piece of 2′ (60 cm) pipes.
4. Use one tee to connect two of the 2′ (60 cm) pipes. Repeat this step for the remaining 2′ pipes. Lay all six pieces flat.
5. Insert one 64″ (160 cm) pipe into each remaining hole on each of the tees, as assembled in step 4.
6. Attach a 90° elbow to the top of each 64″ piece of pipe.
7. Insert one of the 48″ (120 cm) pipes between two of the 90° elbows. Then, insert one of the two remaining 48″ pipes between two other 90° elbows. Each structure should stand upright. Put them aside.
8. Drill ⅛″ (3 mm) holes along the side of the remaining 48″ pipe. With the holes facing down, insert one cap. Insert the 48″ pipe into the elbow on the 64″ pipe from step 5. On the opposite end, attach a tee.
9. On one end of the 4″ (10 cm) pipe, attach the cap. On the opposite end, insert the elbow that extends from the 64″ pipe as completed in step 5.
10. Attach the cap end of the 4″ pipe to the tee from step 7. Make sure the tee is facing upward.
11. Using one of the structures from step 6, tape pompoms on the inside of each 64″ pipe.
12. On the second structure from step 6, tape the top of a shower curtain along the 48″ pipe. (The shower curtain should be hanging.) Next, cut the shower curtain into 3″ to 4″ (7 cm x 10 cm) vertical strips.
13. When in use, insert a hose into the tee on top of the final structure. Turn on

the water and a sprinkle effect occurs.

Maintenance suggestion: To help keep the PVC pipes secure, brush the structures with PVC cleaner followed by PVC glue. Allow it to dry.

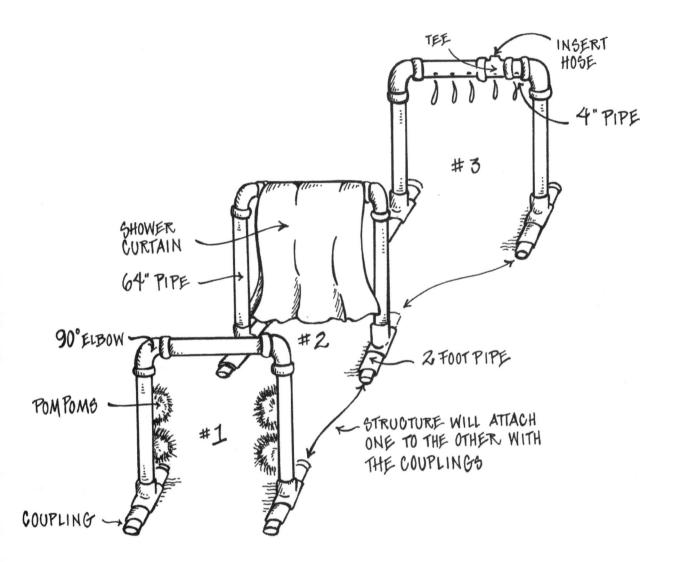

More to do

Make a soapy mixture and encourage children to wash different items in the classroom. Make bubbles to use with a variety of bubble wands.

Field Trips: Take the children to a car wash so they can see how the brushes operate and how cars get cleaned.

Helen Doran, St. Louis, MO

Goodnight, Sweet Children

Materials

None needed

What to do

1. As the children are settling down for nap, sing the following version of "Goodnight Sweetheart" to them.
2. Wait until all children are settled on their mats and you have said individual goodnights. (Substitute whatever phrase you use—I actually say "good night.")
3. Sing the following verse to the children:

    Goodnight sweet children
    Well, it's time to go to sleep.
    Goodnight sweet children
    Well it's time to go to sleep.
    I hate to tell you, but I really must say
    You must take a nap today.

4. Repeat the verse as many times as you wish. Substitute individual names for the "Sweet Children" part, as time and circumstances permit.

Related books

Goodnight Moon by Margaret Wise Brown
Just Go to Bed by Mercer Mayer
Time to Sleep by Denise Fleming
Winnie the Pooh's A to Zzzz by Don Ferguson

❦ Virginia Jean Herrod, Columbia, SC

Naptime DJ

Materials

Various instrumental or lullaby cassettes or CDs
Books on tape
CD or tape player

What to do

1. To help the children get settled for naptime, designate a different child each day to choose a quiet story and a musical story.
2. Ask the child to insert the tape into the tape player and begin the story tape.
3. When the story tape is over, insert the musical tape. (It is a good idea for you to insert the music tape, because the child is settling down for naptime.)

More to do

Designate a particular child to be the "Naptime DJ" for the next day. Then, the child can pick music from her home to bring the next day. This will vary the sounds and keep the children more quiet and interested.

Related books

Goodnight Moon by Margaret Wise Brown
Just a Nap by Mercer Mayer
The Napping House by Audrey Wood

Tina R. Woehler, Oak Point, TX

Hints for Quiet Time

Materials

None needed

What to do

1. Quiet time is a fact of life in most childcare centers—it is required by government in most states and provinces. Try the following ideas:

What's in a Name?

Quiet Time verses Nap Time. We all know how hard it is to get children to go to sleep at night so refer to Nap Time as Quiet Time. Or, the children may come up with their own name.

From Both Sides

Parents are a key resource in any children's program. Explain to them the program policy in regards to Quiet Time. Children in child care programs expend lots of energy, and it is important that their bodies have a chance to rest. Many programs run a full twelve hours, and tired children are a real safety factor. It is always great to have parents on your side!

Home Away from Home

Many children love to have a familiar friend at Quiet Time. Also, a special blanket and stuffed toy are always comforting.

Ready to Grow

Don't expect miracles to occur overnight. Starting out, it is important that children feel like part of the program. Encourage them to help label the mats and to choose a spot in the room where they wish to rest. In many programs, new children start in September, so this tends to be a very difficult time for children. Take small steps for your first Quiet Time—it might only be ten minutes.

Setting the Mood for Success

When placing mats or cots throughout the room, leave enough space between them so that the children can get up safely without falling on top of another child. Be consistent and have the children rest in the same area each day. Play soft music in the background. (Classical, lullaby, and relaxation music are all great choices.) Darkening the room slightly helps enhance the environment. However, don't darken the room too much because some children are frightened by the dark. Use a few nightlights. Group children according to sleep patterns. Use a good transition activity before Quiet Time. For example, having a storybook bag helps prepare the children to rest (see below).

What's So Special?

Establish a storybook bag that is accessible only at Quiet Time. Choose a variety of books, such as children's favorites, picture books, and theme-related books. Encourage the children to bring books from home to add to the bag, too. (Don't forget to change books on a regular basis.) Read a few stories with the children before putting the books away. This is also a great chance to do some one-on-one reading with the children.

"My Child Doesn't Rest"

Each child is unique. Some parents say that their children will not rest. Some of the children will rest, while others won't. It is important to realize this and make adaptations within your program for the spirited child.

2. Give the children a chance to sleep. Remember, though, that it is not so important that every child actually goes to sleep; it is important that they are quiet while others are resting. Many children enjoy having their backs rubbed while they are resting.

3. Dramatized story tapes and CDs are a wonderful addition to any Quiet Time. Many children make sounds or have habits associated with settling down for sleep. For example, some children may like to mumble to themselves before they actually fall asleep. If it is not disturbing anyone, don't worry. As children get up, encourage them to participate in special quiet activities, such as playing with clay, painting, and solving puzzles.

Related books

Chitty Chitty Bang Bang by Ian Fleming
The House at Pooh Corner by A.A. Milne
Peter Pan by J.M. Barrie
Winnie the Pooh by A. A. Milne

Tapes and CDs
"Journey to Giant Land—Tall Tales About Giants" narrated by Jim Weiss
"Alligator Pie and Other Poems" performed by the author Dennis Lee Caedmon
"The Wizard of Oz" by Record Guild of America
"The Adventures of Peter Pan" by Record Guild of America

♣ Mark Crouse, Port William, Nova Scotia, Canada

At the Sand/Water Table

Materials

(See below)

What to do

1. These are suggestions to use throughout the year for the sand and water table.
2. The object of the sand/water table is to encourage experimentation with different textures and substances. The following are some creative things to fill the sand/water table with besides water or sand: smelly salt (add peppermint or vanilla oil to salt), packing chips, balls, leaves, jingle bells, or plastic Easter eggs.
3. Another fun thing to do is to add food color dye to the water each month to match the color you are studying or to match the season, such as red for Christmas and green for St. Patrick's Day.

❧ Lisa M. Chichester, Parkersburg, WV

Sensory Table Ideas (Sand and Water)

Materials

Sensory table or empty tubs
Different sensory items (see below)

What to do

1. Change the sand/water table many times to offer children as many interesting experiences as possible. Some of the different things to use in the sand/water table include:
   Birdseed
   Bubbles
   Clean white sand
   Corks

Cornmeal
Cornstarch and water
Ice or snow
Sand/water

More to do

Encourage the children to help decide what toys and accessories to use. Ask the children to help empty the contents in the table, put them away, and add new sensory materials to it.

❦ Sue Myhre, Bremerton, WA

Water Play

Materials

Towels, one for under the tub and one for drying hands
Sand/water table or large tub
Various items (see below)

What to do

1. Add any the following combination of items to the sand/water table or a large tub.
   ▪ Egg beaters, bottles (plain and squirt), whisk, turkey baster, foam balls, and sieve.
   ▪ Boats (The children can use several items to make their own boats, such as egg cups or foam.)
   ▪ Measuring equipment, such as plastic measuring cups and spoons
   ▪ Dolls, doll clothes, and mild detergent (so the children can wash them)

More to do

Fill the tub with snow instead of water and give the children gloves, plastic cups to make shapes for igloos, small shovels to dig and build, and cardboard cut into different ridge patterns to make designs in the snow.

❦ Marilyn Harding, Grimes, IA

Water Play With a Baster

Materials

Water
Two containers (or more)
Plastic baster

What to do

1. Pour water into one of the containers.
2. Demonstrate how to squeeze the bulb on the baster to take up water. Then, show the children how to release the bulb. The water remains in the tube.
3. Show the children how to transfer water to the other container by squeezing the bulb.
4. Encourage the children to practice the same procedure. The children can move the water from one container to the other indefinitely.

More to do

Add food coloring to the water. Use several containers of colored water and encourage the children to observe what happens when two colors are blended. Use eyedroppers and small containers.

Art: Make drip paintings using eyedroppers and colored water on coffee filters.

Language: Build vocabulary with words such as *squeeze, bubble, drip, pour*, or even *spill*.

Science: Explain how the baster works. Squeezing the air out of it creates a vacuum and picks up the water.

❖ Mary Jo Shannon, Roanoke, VA

Kitchen Utensils in Water

Materials

Smocks
Water table full of water
Cooking utensils (measuring cups, measuring spoons, strainer, funnel, and so on)

What to do

1. Let two children play at a time.
2. Help each child put on a smock.
3. Make a rule that the cooking utensils are to stay *in* the water.
4. Remove the metal utensils from the water before closing the table to prevent rusting.
5. Use language like such as:
   You are using a _____.
   A _____ is used to _____.
   What do you think a chef would use this utensil for?
   What could you do with this cooking utensil?
   Have you used a _____ before?
   You are moving the _____.

❧ Cristy Bawol, Utica, MI

Can You Find It?

Materials

Sand table and sand
Small objects such as plastic numbers, wooden shapes, and so on

What to do

1. Hide small objects in the sand.
2. Ask the children to take turns digging in the sand.
3. Ask them if they can find a circle, and encourage them to hunt for it. Tell the children to feel around in the sand, and pull out the item that feels like a circle. (You can also use plastic numbers or ABC's.)

4. Children can play by themselves or with a friend.

More to do

After the children take turns finding their shapes, encourage them to go around the room and find more shapes like the one they found.

Art: Ask the children to take their objects to the Art Center and trace around them, or make a rubbing.

❖ Sandra Hutchins Lucas, Cox's Creek, KY

Floating Fish

Materials

Water
Plastic, reusable fish-shaped ice cube trays
Freezer
Water table
Small plastic tongs

What to do

1. In advance, freeze fish-shaped ice cubes.
2. If possible, place the water table outside and fill it about ¾ full.
3. Place the frozen fish ice cubes in the water.
4. As the fish are floating, encourage the children to use the plastic tongs to catch the fish.

More to do

Snack: Make goldfish Jell-O. Follow the directions on the back of the box. Pour the liquid Jell-O into a flat aluminum tray. Place the tray in a refrigerator until the liquid becomes solid. When the Jell-O is firm, use a fish cookie cutter to cut out goldfish. Serve and eat!

Related books

Fish Is Fish by Leo Lionni
One Fish, Two Fish, Red Fish, Blue Fish by Dr. Seuss
The Rainbow Fish by Marcus Pfister
Rainbow Fish and the Big Blue Whale by Marcus Pfister

Rainbow Fish to the Rescue by Marcus Pfister
Swimmy by Leo Lionni

✤ Quazonia J. Quarles, Newark, DE

Color Sand

Materials

Water
Four 1 cup (240 ml) measuring cups
Food coloring
Eyedroppers
Large area of sand, either outdoors or in the sensory table

What to do

1. Pour ½ to ⅔ cup (120 to 160 ml) water into each of the four measuring cups.
2. Add a different color of food coloring to each cup. (Add enough to make very bright colors.)
3. Put an eyedropper into each cup.
4. Place the cups in a circle in the middle of the sand area.
5. Encourage the children to use the eyedroppers to create color pictures in the sand. Encourage them to explore with color and designs. Be supportive and give lots of praise for their artistic efforts. They will soon discover on their own that when they mix together two colors, a third is created. Comment on this and encourage them to experiment more.
6. Take a picture of the children's artwork before they mix everything together to create multicolored sand.

More to do

Use purchased or handmade stencils to create intricate designs, such as a sunburst or rainbows. Put the colored water into spray bottles and encourage the children to spray large areas of the sand play area to create a large picture. Collect the separate colors or the multicolored sand and put it into shaker jars (old spice or glitter shakers work well). The children can then create sand pictures by "drawing" with glue and shaking the colored sand on it.

Related books

A Beasty Story by Steven Kellogg and Bill Martin, Jr.
Blue Hat Green Hat by Sandra Boyton
Brown Bear, Brown Bear, What Do You See? by Eric Carle
Chuck Murphy's Color Surprises: A Pop-Up Book by Chuck Murphy
A Color of His Own by Leo Lionni
The Crayon Box that Talked by Shane Derolf and Michael Letzig
Little Blue and Little Yellow by Leo Lionni
Mouse Paint by Ellen Stoll Walsh
My Many Colored Days by Dr. Seuss

❧ Virginia Jean Herrod, Columbia, SC

Find the Fossils

Materials

Chicken bones, washed and cleaned
Sandbox or dishpans filled with sand
A book about dinosaurs
Dishpan filled with water
Towels

What to do

1. Before the children arrive, bury chicken bones in the sand.
2. Read a book about dinosaurs to the children.
3. Explain to the children that fossils are bones that have turned into rock. Tell the children that the reason we know what dinosaurs looked like is because people called archeologists found fossilized bones and pieced them together to make dinosaur skeletons.
4. Explain to the children that they are going to be like archeologists and dig in the sand to find bones.
5. Encourage the children to dig for the bones.
6. After the children find the bones, help them wash the bones in a dishpan of water and dry them using towels.
7. Encourage the children to compare and contrast their bones with the bones found by other children. They can experiment to see if they can fit any together.

8. When the activity is done, ask the children what kind of an animal they think the bones came from.

More to do

Art: Ask the children to draw and color pictures of the bones and the animals that the bones come from. The children may tape their bones to the drawings, if desired.

Language: Encourage the children to dictate stories about their experience or about what kind of animal the bones came from.

Literacy: Put the drawings and stories on a bulletin board or bind them together to make a book. Encourage the children to take turns bringing the book home to read with their parents.

Related books

The Dinosaur Alphabet Book by Jerry Pallotta
My Visit to the Dinosaurs by Aliki

❧ Barbara Saul, Eureka, CA

Erupting Volcano

Materials

Sand bucket
Sand and sand table
Empty 20 ounce (600 ml) soda bottle
Water
Large baking pan
2 measuring cups
1 tablespoon (15 g) flour
1 tablespoon (15 g) baking soda
Spoon
Funnel
Red food coloring
1 cup (240 ml) white vinegar

What to do

1. Place a sand bucket into the sand/water table. Put an empty soda bottle upside down in the center of sand bucket.
2. Mix sand and water to make wet sand. Pack the wet sand around the soda bottle in the bucket.
3. Turn over the sand bucket inside a baking pan and remove the bucket. (This will be the volcano.)
4. In one of the measuring cups, mix together the 1 tablespoon (15 g) flour and 1 tablespoon (15 g) baking soda.
5. Pour the mixture through a funnel into the soda bottle.
6. Add 15 to 20 drops of red food coloring to the bottle.
7. Pour about one half of the vinegar into the bottle.
8. This will cause the mixture to foam, like a volcano eruption! When the foaming stops, pour in the rest of the vinegar.

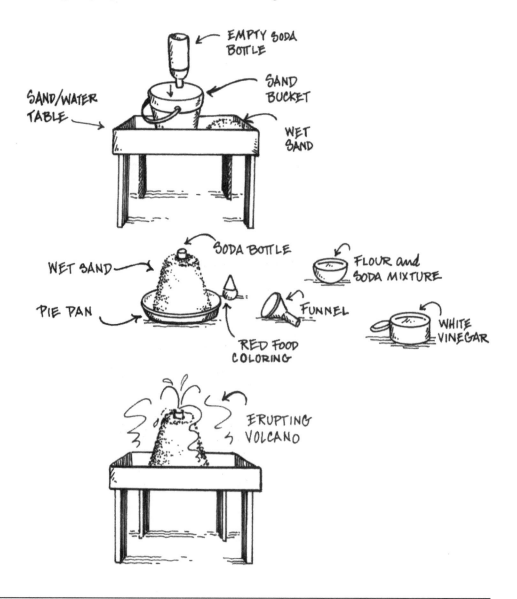

Related books

I Can Read about Earthquakes and Volcanoes by Deborah Merrians
Volcanoes by Seymour Simon
Volcanoes! Mountains of Fire by Eric Arnold

❦ Angie Miller, Hilliard, OH

Science Talk

Materials

(See below)

What to do

1. When planning for science exploration, keep in mind actions that children directly perform. Examples are actions that produce (1) movement of objects and (2) changes in objects.

Movement of objects

Pushing
Pulling
Rolling
Sledding
Dropping
Patting
Bouncing
Balancing
Spinning
Swinging
Blowing
Kicking
Throwing
Jumping

Changes in objects

Putting objects in water or oil
Cooling objects in refrigerator or freezer
Heating objects in an oven or microwave

2. When planning science activities, encourage language and vocabulary development along with cause and effect relationships. Soon the children will begin using science talk during other exploration experiences.

Related books

Alistair's Time Machine by Marilyn Sadler
Fritz and the Mess Fairy by Rosemary Wells
June 29, 1999 by David Wiesner

❖ Sandra Nagel, White Lake, MI

Five Senses in the Garden

Materials

Flower garden, vegetable garden, or orchard
Construction paper, optional
Tape, optional

What to do

1. Discuss with the children the five senses.
2. Take small groups of children to a garden.
3. Ask the children to stand very still and look carefully at the garden. After about a minute, encourage them to describe what they see using color words and descriptive vocabulary.
4. Ask the children to be very quiet and listen. After about a minute, ask them what they hear.
5. Invite the children to touch the leaves, flowers, and fruit and describe the various textures, such as smooth, rough, prickly, fuzzy, or sticky.
6. Encourage the children to smell the flowers and plants and describe which ones are sweet, sour, or funny smelling.
7. Ask the children to pick a fruit or vegetable, supervising closely. After the children wash and taste their food, ask them to describe the taste (for example, sweet, sour, crunchy, soft, or squishy).

More to do

Art: Ask the children to pick one leaf, flower, or vegetable. Back in the classroom, the children can tape it to a piece of construction paper that is labeled "smell," "touch," or "taste." Invite them to draw a picture of what they saw and heard in the garden.

Related book

A Gardener's Alphabet by Mary Azarian

❖ Barbara Saul, Eureka, CA

Can You Tell What You Smell?

Materials

Empty, clean frozen juice cans with non-transparent covers
Scissors or poking instrument (adult only)
Items with various discernible odors, such as cotton soaked in perfume,
    an orange peel, an onion, popcorn, and so on
Marker

What to do

1. Poke small holes into the lids of juice cans (adult only).
2. Place one item into each container and cover it with a perforated lid. Label the bottom of the can with a picture and the name of the item so the children can check their guess.
3. Encourage the children to take turns choosing a can, smelling the item through the lid, and guessing what is inside.

More to do

Ask the children to guess what they are having for lunch before they enter the lunchroom. Can you tell by the smell?

Related book

My Five Senses by Margaret Miller

❖ Iris Rothstein, New Hyde Park, NJ

Matching Sounds

Materials

An equal number of small, opaque plastic jars (film containers work well)
Objects to put into the jars, such as sand, jingle bells, small stones or sticks,
and paper clips

What to do

1. Put matching objects into two jars. Start with just a few items and increase the number as the children get more proficient.
2. Encourage the child to shake one container and listen to the sound. Then, the child can try to find the matching sound by shaking the remaining containers. The child can continue until she has matched all of the pairs.
3. Make this activity self-checking by putting matching symbols under each matching pair. For example, put a triangle shape under the two containers that contain sand.

More to do

Books: Extend the activity by reading stories such as *The Noisy Book* by Margaret Wise Brown.

Literacy: This activity teaches children to listen carefully and distinguish sounds, which will be helpful when they learn the sounds that letters of the alphabet make.

Rest or Nap Time: At rest time, ask the children to close their eyes and listen very closely to all of the sounds they hear. Make a list of what they hear, such as a car horn, an airplane, water dripping, a person walking, and so on.

❖ Iris Rothstein, New Hyde Park, NJ

Body Parts Identification Puzzle

Materials

Leftover wallpaper
Marker
White paper
Scissors
Glue

What to do

1. Trace an outline of a body on a piece of wallpaper and a large sheet of white paper.
2. Cut out both body outlines.
3. Cut the wallpaper body outline into six to twelve pieces at the natural joints (wrists, shoulders, neck, waist, hips, knees, ankles, and so on).
4. Mix up the pieces. Ask a child to reassemble the wallpaper parts onto the white paper body outline. As the child reassembles the pieces, ask her to identify the correct names of the body parts. (See the illustration on the next page.)
5. Encourage the child to glue the pieces to the outline.

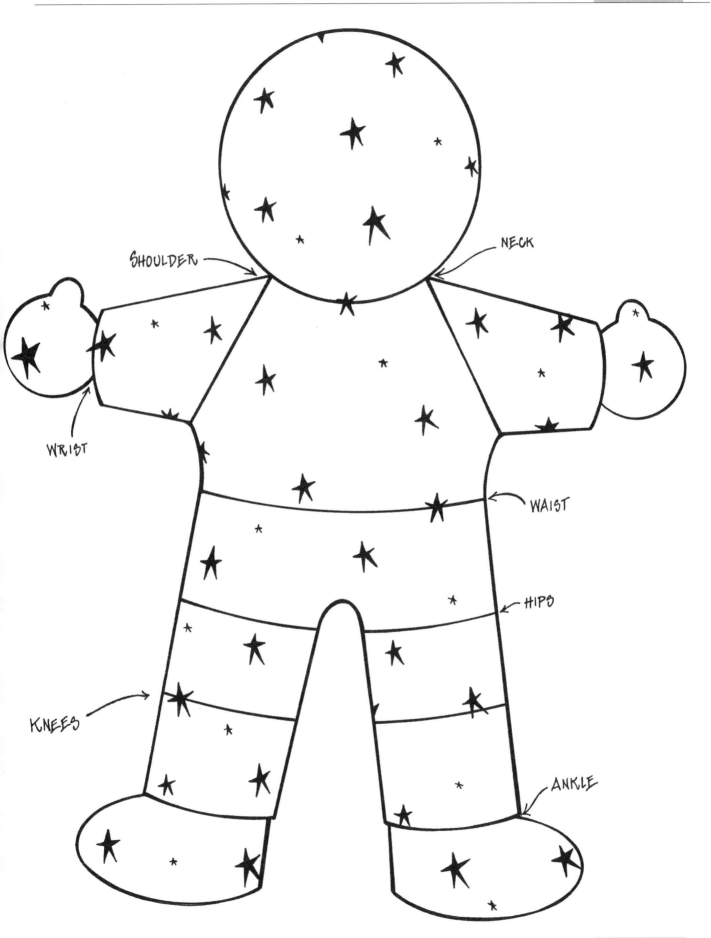

Related books

Clap Your Hands by Lorinda B. Cauley
From Head to Toe by Eric Carle
Here Are My Hands by Bill Martin, Jr.
Two Eyes, a Nose, and a Mouth by Roberta G. Intrater

❖ Linda J. Becker, Rochester, MN

Your Heart

Materials

Pictures, diagrams, or models of the human heart

What to do

1. Discuss the heart with the children and show them pictures of it.
2. Ask the children to make a fist and place it in the center of their chests. Explain to the children that this is about the size and location of their hearts.
3. Encourage the children to tightly clench and unclench their fists, explaining that this is similar to how their heart works to pump blood.
4. Recite the following poem with the children:

   Your Heart
   Your heart pumps your blood to your fingers and your toes
   All through your body, even to your nose!

More to do

Provide stethoscopes for the children to listen to their hearts.
Field Trips: Take a trip to the school nurse's office or a local doctor's office.

Related books

The Heart and Circulatory System (The Human Body) by Carol Ballard
The Heart: The Kids' Question and Answer Book by J. Willis Hurst
The Heart: Our Circulatory System by Seymour Simon

❖ Linda Ford, Sacramento, CA

All About Corn

Materials

Corn on the cob, one for each child
Garbage bag
Pots
Hot plate or stove (adult only)
Butter
Plastic knife
Salt
Paper plates and napkins

What to do

1. Show the children how to shuck corn, preferably outside because it will be a messy process. Provide a garbage bag for the children to put the discarded corn silk.

2. While the children shuck their corn, point out the different parts of the corn. Husks are the outer coverings of the corn. (You may want to save the husks and dry them to use for a future art project.) Corn silk is the thread that is pulled away from the corn. They are sticky and sometimes hard to pull off. Kernels are the corn itself, and the cob is the hard core under the kernels. Explain to the children that they won't see the cob until after they eat the corn.

3. Next, help the children wash their ears of corn and put them into a pot of water.

4. Place the pot on a hot plate or stove and cook the corn in boiling water until it is tender (adult only).

5. While the corn is cooking, ask the children where corn comes from and what it needs to grow. Discuss the different ways to buy corn (cans, frozen, fresh, and for popping).

6. When the corn is ready, allow it to cool and put butter and salt on it. Enjoy!

More to do

Take a field trip to a local farm to see corn growing in the field.

❖ Constance Heagerty, Westborough, MA

Apples

Materials

Red, green, and yellow apples
Chart paper
Markers
Knife
Zipper closure plastic bag

What to do

1. Look at the apples with the children and ask them to predict which ones they think will taste the best. Chart their responses on a bar graph labeled "Predictions."
2. Cut the apples into pieces and encourage the children to taste each kind. Chart the children's preferences and label the graph "Preferences."
3. Compare the two charts.
4. Next, talk to the children about oxidation. What is the purpose of the skin on the apples? Brainstorm possible answers.
5. Explain that when an apple is peeled, it turns brown, gets mushy, and so on. This happens when oxygen mixes with a peeled apple. However, this doesn't happen when the apple is unpeeled.
6. Set up an experiment by placing an unpeeled apple, half of an apple, and another half of an apple in a plastic bag on a table. Note the results. Try this experiment with different kinds of apples to see if there are any differences.

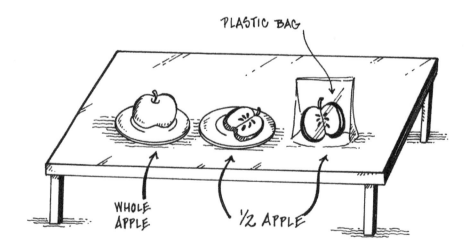

Ivy Sher, Sherman Oaks, CA

Creative Cress

Materials

Sponges
Scissors, optional
Water
Three packages of garden cress or peppercress seeds
Waterproof containers (flat, shallow, rectangular are best, such as dishpans)

What to do

1. If desired, cut sponges into geometric shapes, letters, and so on. Then, thoroughly rinse the sponges several times with fresh water.
2. Line a waterproof container with the sponges.
3. Encourage the children to sprinkle small amounts of cress seed lightly on sponges.
4. Place the container in an area where there is some sunlight. Keep the sponges moist with water.
5. The cress is ready to eat when it has grown about 1½" (4 cm) and has grown its third pair of leaves.

More to do

Art: Experiment using different shades of green paint.
More Art: Cut out pictures from seed catalogs or magazines. Make collages of vegetable pictures.
Outdoors: Grow radishes or other quick growing vegetables.
Snack: Serve a variety of green veggies for snack, such as watercress, broccoli, green beans, snap peas, and green peppers.

Related books

Eating the Alphabet: Fruits, and Vegetables from A to Z by Lois Ehlert
Growing Colors by Bruce McMillan
Oliver's Vegetables by Vivian French

Jill E. Putnam, Wellfleet, MA

Making Butter

Materials

½ pint whipping cream
Clean baby food jar (or small jelly jars with tight lids)
Bowls
Salt
Yellow food coloring, optional
Crackers
Plastic knife
Chart paper and markers, optional

What to do

1. Pour whipping cream into a baby food jar, filling it ⅓ to ½ full.
2. Screw on the lid of the jar, making sure it is secured tightly.
3. Encourage the children to take turns shaking the jar. They can jump, dance, and shake to keep the jar moving. Two children can sit on a carpeted area and roll the jar back and forth to one another. Within ten to fifteen minutes, the whipping cream will separate.
4. Pour off the thin liquid into a bowl and encourage the children to taste it.
5. The remaining thick substance is the butter.
6. Put half of the butter into a bowl and mix in a pinch of salt. Encourage the children to do a taste test to see if they prefer the salted or unsalted butter. If desired, graph the results on a piece of chart paper.
7. Add yellow food coloring to a portion of the butter and have a new taste test. Again, if desired, chart the results.

More to do

Discuss where milk comes from. Make a web diagram showing how we get from the cow to the butter in our stores.
Dramatic Play: Pretend to make butter using a bucket and a stick for a churn.

Related books

Pioneer Sisters by Laura Ingalls Wilder
Summertime in the Big Woods by Laura Ingalls Wilder

Songs

Shake It (Tune: "The Grand Old Duke of York")

Shake it, shake it, shake it.
Shake it all around.
And if you do not shake it,
Then we will have to frown.

Shake a Jar of Butter (Tune: "Pick a Bale of Cotton")

Jump down turn around,
Shake a jar of butter.
Jump down turn around,
Shake the milk away.

❖ Sandra Nagel, White Lake, MI

Life Cycle of Peanut Butter

Materials

Peanuts in shells
Sand in a sandbox
Shovels
Bowls
Measuring cups
Blender
Oil
Salt
Blunt knife
Crackers
Construction paper
Markers

What to do

1. Before the children arrive, bury peanuts in the sandbox.
2. Explain to the children that peanuts grow underneath the ground and that farmers must dig up the roots to get the peanuts out.
3. Give the children shovels and encourage them to dig up the peanuts in the sandbox. Ask them to count how many peanuts they dug up.

4. Ask the children to crack the peanuts and separate the peanut from the shells into two different bowls. (Save the shells for a future art project.)

5. After the children have shelled all the peanuts, measure how many cups of peanuts there are.

6. Make peanut butter. Put peanuts into a blender, add a little oil and salt. Turn on the blender and grind the peanuts (adult only). Grind the peanuts until they are the desired texture—crunchy or smooth.

7. Measure the peanut butter and compare it to the peanut measurements. Is there more peanut butter than peanuts or less?

8. Spread the peanut butter on crackers and encourage the children to taste it. Remember to check for any food allergies.

9. Encourage the children to write or dictate a story about how to make peanut butter.

10. Use the peanut shells for an art project, if desired.

More to do

More Science: Talk about other foods that are grown underground, such as potatoes, carrots, and so on.

Music: Sing the "Peanut Butter and Jelly" song while you are making the peanut butter.

❧ Holly Dzierzanowski, Austin, TX

Food Pyramid

Materials

10 boxes, all the same size
Bulletin board paper, in a variety of colors
Tape
White paper
Markers or crayons
Scissors
Glue

What to do

1. Discuss nutrition and the food pyramid.
2. Wrap the boxes with various colors of paper to represent the food groups. For example, use brown for the bread and cereal group.
3. Give the children white paper and markers or crayons and ask them to draw pictures of food.
4. Help the children cut out the pictures.
5. Encourage the children to glue the pictures on the boxes.
6. Help children build a food pyramid using the boxes.

Related books

Banana Moon by Janet Marshall
Food Crafts by Chris Deshpande
Rabbit Food by Susanna Gretz

❧ Elizabeth Thomas, Hobart, IN

Name That Herb

Materials

A variety of herb plants, such as oregano, mint, and lemon balm

What to do

1. Encourage the children to gently rub the leaves of each plant. Encourage them to name to each plant. They will probably identify the mint as "gum," the oregano as "pizza," and the lemon balm as "lemon."
2. Transplant the plants into a corner of the playground. These plants require minimal care and will grow in almost any sunny location. They grow back year after year and the more you pick, the more they grow!

More to do

Use fresh or dried herbs. Children especially enjoy making "mint tea" by adding mint leaves to iced tea. Have a tea party and serve the "homemade" iced tea.

❧ Sharon Dempsey, Mays Landing, NJ

See How They Grow!

Materials

Bean seeds
Container of water
Plastic zipper closure bag
Paper towel
Permanent marker
Cardboard
Tape

What to do

1. Soak the bean seeds overnight in water.
2. Give each child a plastic sandwich bag with a damp paper towel in it. Help the children print their names on top of their bag.
3. Ask each child to place a bean seed inside the bag, in front of the paper towel, so the seed can be observed clearly.
4. Seal the bags.
5. Tape the bags onto a large piece of cardboard and place it near a window.
6. Each day, encourage the children to observe what is happening to the seeds.

More to do

Make three "bean bags" as above. Cover one of the bags so it does not get light, do not water the second one, and water and keep the third one in sunlight. Make weekly comparisons of the three bags.

Related books

The Carrot Seed by Ruth Krauss
From Seed to Plant by Gail Gibbons
Green Beans by Elizabeth Thomas
Growing Vegetable Soup by Lois Ehlert
How a Seed Grows by Helene J. Jordan
Jasper's Beanstalk by Nick Butterworth
Something Is Growing by Walter Lyon Krudop
The Tiny Seed by Eric Carle

Song

See How They Grow (Tune: "Three Blind Mice")

See how they grow.
See how they grow.
They grow very tall.
They grow very tall.
Roots, leaves, and stems.
Roots, leaves, and stems.
See how they grow.
See how they grow.

❧ Sandra Nagel, White Lake, MI

Seed Match

Materials

5-10 different seed packets with seeds
Glue
10-20 3" x 5" (7 cm x 12 cm) note cards
Various colored markers

What to do

1. Glue several seeds from one seed packet onto a blank note card. Label the name of the seed directly underneath the seeds.
2. Make a matching card by gluing the empty seed packet onto another blank note card. Label this card, too, making sure to use the same color marker as the matching seed card.
3. Repeat this with five to ten different types of seeds. When finished, mix up all the cards. Encourage the children to identify the seeds by matching the cards. The color-coded label will help the children, if needed.

❧ Laura Gremett, Sunnyvale CA

Fall Bracelet

Materials

Masking tape

What to do

1. Wrap a piece of tape around each child's wrist, sticky side out.
2. Take a fall walk and encourage the children to find small leaves, weeds, and so on to decorate their bracelet.

❦ Cindy Winther, Oxford, MI

Propagate a Geranium

Materials

Geranium plant
Scissors
Container of water
Potting soil
Flowerpot

What to do

1. Discuss the three ways plants grow: from cuttings, bulbs, or seeds.
2. With the children, make a cutting from a geranium plant.
3. Place the cutting in a container of water for a few weeks to let roots form.
4. Pour potting soil into a flowerpot and transplant the cutting.
5. Enjoy a new plant in the classroom. Encourage the children to help care for the plant.

More to do

Art: Make tempera flower pictures using little fingers to make the blooms.

Song

"Flower Garden" from *Piggyback Songs* by Jean Warren

❦ Jackie Wright, Enid, OK

Grassy Haired Friend

Materials

Newspaper, if needed
8-ounce paper or foam cups
Markers
Planting soil
Easy growing grass seed
Water
Watering can or small pitcher
Craft sticks or tongue depressors

What to do

1. This is a good outdoor activity. If you do the activity indoors, cover the work area with newspaper.
2. Give each child a paper or foam cup. Help the children draw a face on their cups using markers. Write the child's name on the back of her cup.
3. Put an extra cup next to the soil and ask the children to use it to scoop soil into their cups. Fill it to about ½" (1 cm) from the top of the cup.
4. Show the children how to sprinkle grass seed onto the soil. Encourage the children to cover the seeds lightly by sprinkling some soil on top of them.
5. Pour water from a watering can to dampen the soil.
6. Ask the children to name their cup characters.
7. Give each child a craft stick. Help each child write the name of her cup character on one side of the craft stick and draw line markers in centimeters or inches on the other side.
8. Check the progress of the seeds daily.

More to do

More Science: Make experimental cups of grass using different soils, grass seeds, light, and watering. Explore and discuss the possible effects of these variables.
Math: The children can use scissors to cut the "hair" of their characters. Ask the children to chart the growth of their grass.

Related books

Hats Off to Hair by Virginia Kroll
How Emily Blair Got Her Fabulous Hair by Susan Garrison Beroza
Hubert's Hair Raising Adventure by Bill Peet
In the Tall, Tall Grass by Denise Fleming

❖ Sandra Nagel, White Lake, MI

Buggy Grass

Materials

Plastic bugs
Magnifiers

What to do

1. Hide plastic bugs outside in the grass, on tree branches, and so on.
2. Give the children magnifiers and encourage them to find the bugs.

More to do

Sand and Water Table: Hide the plastic bugs in a sensory table among plastic green grass. Encourage the children to find the bugs.
Snack: Eat foods that insects eat, such as vegetables (lettuce, radishes, celery, carrot), peanut butter, fruit (apples, watermelon, oranges, and so on), raisins, fruit juice, honey, and crackers.

Related books

Bugs by Nancy Winslow Parker and Joan Richards Wright
The Grouchy Ladybug Board Book by Eric Carle
Have You Seen Bugs? by Joanne Oppenheim
Icky Bug Alphabet Book by Jerry Pallotta
Icky Bug Counting Book by Jerry Pallotta
In the Tall, Tall Grass by Denise Fleming
The Very Hungry Caterpillar by Eric Carle
The Very Lonely Firefly by Eric Carle
The Very Quiet Cricket by Eric Carle

Songs

"Ants Go Marching"
"Baby Bumblebee"

🍀 Quazonia J. Quarles, Newark, DE

Under Rocks and Rotting Logs

Materials

In a Nutshell by Joseph Anthony or *A Log's Life* by Wendy Pfeffer
Forest or wooded area

What to do

1. Read *A Log's Life* or *In a Nutshell* to the children.
2. Discuss with the children:
   What creatures live in a tree?
   Why do trees fall?
   What happens to the tree dwellers when a tree falls?
   What creatures move into logs?
   How long does it take for a fallen tree to become dirt?
   How does this help make another tree?
3. Take the children for a walk in a wooded area and look for a fallen tree.
4. When you find a fallen tree, encourage the children to scoop some of the decaying log into their hands.
5. Ask the children to look at it, smell it, and feel it. How is it like dirt?
6. Encourage the children to pick up rocks and sticks to find small creatures under them. Discuss why these creatures live under rocks and rotting logs.

More to do

More Science: Ask the children to bring in insects in plastic jars to observe. Be sure to return them to their original habitats.
Art: Encourage the children to draw pictures of their walk.
More Art: Draw a giant log on mural sized paper. Ask the children to draw creatures that live under rocks and rotting logs. Children may finish the mural scene

by drawing trees, porcupines, and so on.

More Art: Make three-dimensional creatures using clay. For example, make a spider by shaping a ball of clay like a spider's body. Add a tiny head. Cut eight pieces of rubber bands for legs and press four into each side of the body. Attach a long piece of a rubber band to the top of the spider. Paint the spider. Bounce the spider up and down with the piece of rubber, and sing "The Eensy-Weensy Spider" as the spiders bounce. Another example is to make a porcupine using clay and toothpicks. Snakes and salamanders are also easy to make with clay.

Circle Time: Discuss what creatures the children saw on their walk.

Movement: Ask each child to pretend to be a tree standing in a forest. Encourage the children to shake as a storm blows in and fall to the ground as the storm knocks down the tree.

Outdoors: Grow a tree. Bring some of the tree dirt back to the classroom or buy a bag of rich soil. Gather some acorns and plant them in the dirt. Watch a tree sprout and plant it outside.

❈ Wendy Pfeffer, Pennigton, NJ

Watching Ants

Materials

Ants and anthills
Magnifying glasses

What to do

1. Take the children outside and ask them to look for anthills. Beforehand, discuss the importance of approaching an anthill carefully to avoid stepping on it or disturbing it.
2. Encourage the children to lie on the grass or squat to look at the ants. Ask the child to watch the activity with and without a magnifying glass.
3. When you get back to the classroom, discuss the children's observations.

More to do

Chart the children's observations. Outside, section off an area using string and make a sign that reads, "No Walking. Ant Construction Zone."

Art: Encourage the children to draw pictures of ants and anthills and label the parts.

Language: Ask the children to create ant stories.

Related books

The 512 Ants on Sullivan Street by Carol A. Losi
The Ant and the Elephant by Bill Peet
How Many Ants? by Larry Dane Brimmer
One Hundred Hungry Ants by Elinor J. Pinczes
Sarah's Story by Bill Harley
Step by Step by Diane Wolkstein
Want a Ride? (Road to Reading) by Bill Gordh

Song

"The Ants Go Marching One by One..."

❧ Sandra Nagel, White Lake, MI

Wormy Science

Materials

Book about worms
Wet paper towels
Earthworms, one per child
Magnifying glasses
Flashlight

What to do

1. Read a book about worms to the children, then have a discussion about worms.
2. Give each child a wet paper towel and place a live worm on it.
3. Encourage the children to observe the worms for a few minutes, using magnifying glasses.
4. Shine a flashlight on the worm's head and observe what happens. Then, shine the light on the end of the worm and see what happens.
5. Talk about where worms live, what they eat, and why they are good for the soil.
6. Show the children how to return the worms to the soil, by putting them in a garden or a lawn area.

❧ Lisa M. Chichester, Parkersburg, PA

I Spy Frogs

Materials

Frog patterns
Pen or marker
Brown, green and tan construction paper
Scissors
Clear contact paper or laminate

What to do

1. Explain to the children that frogs can change the color of their skin to match the woods around them to prevent their enemies from seeing them (camouflage).

2. In advance, use the frog pattern to trace frogs onto brown, green, and tan paper. Make enough so that each child will have five frogs.

3. Cut out the frogs and laminate them or cover them with clear contact paper.

4. Go outside and hide the frogs in a wooded area, among trees, picnic tables, leaves, and grass.

5. Bring the children outside and encourage them to find the frogs.

6. After each child has found five frogs, help her count them.

Related books

Frogs by Susan Canizares and Daniel Morton
Jump, Frog, Jump! by Robert Kalan

 Quazonia J. Quarles, Newark, DE

Who Is at the Pond?

Materials

Camera and film
Blue bulletin board paper
Masking tape
Pictures of pond life from magazines
Construction paper in a variety of colors
Scissors
Glue

What to do

1. Take the children on a field trip to a pond. Be sure to have plenty of chaperones.
2. Take lots of pictures of the animals, plants, and insects at the pond.
3. After returning from the trip to the pond, have a discussion with the children about what they saw.
4. After the discussion, tape blue bulletin board paper to a wall and hang pictures from nature magazines around the room.
5. Give the children construction paper, scissors, and glue and encourage them to draw cattails, lily pads, frogs, logs, trees, grass, ducks, fish, snakes, snails, crayfish, beavers, turtles, and dragonflies.
6. Glue or tape the pond features to the blue bulletin board paper.

More to do

Games: Play "What Belongs and What Doesn't?" Using felt, cut out things that can be found at a pond, such as ducks, pond, logs, grass, lily pads, and so on. Then, cut out felt pieces that do not belong, such as cats, bears, and so on. Place all of the felt pieces on a flannel board and ask the children to name the items that belong at a pond.

Sand and Water Table: Place pond animals, such as rubber frogs and ducks, and plastic flowers in the water table.

Related books

Around the Pond: Who's Been Here? by Lindsay Barrett George
In the Small, Small Pond by Denise Fleming

❖ Quazonia Quarles, Newark, DE

Swimmin' Tadpoles

Materials

Wooden ramp
Waxed paper
Masking tape
Two baby food jars
Water
Yellow and blue food coloring
Several eyedroppers

What to do

1. Borrow a large wooden ramp from the Block Area.
2. Cover the top of the ramp with a piece of waxed paper and secure it with masking tape.
3. Pour water into two baby food jars. Add yellow food coloring to one jar and blue food coloring to the other.
4. Provide several eyedroppers. Encourage the children to squeeze out yellow and blue drops of water down the ramp.
5. As the droplets of water merge, they not only become green, they also look like baby tadpoles swimming down the ramp.

More to do

Collect tadpoles from a nearby pond. Place them in the science discovery area, along with magnifying glasses. Encourage the children to observe and chart the many changes that take place with the tadpoles.

Related books

Frog and Toad Are Friends by Arnold Lobel
Frog's Eggs by Alex Ramsay and Paul Humphrey
Jump, Frog, Jump! by Robert Kalan

❖ Patricia Moeser, McFarland, WI

What Comes from Trees

Materials

Chart paper
Marker
Mighty Tree by Dick Gackenbach

What to do

1. Ask the children to name as many things that come from trees as they can. List their suggestions on a piece of chart paper.
2. Read *Mighty Tree* to the children.
3. After reading the story, add to the list, if necessary.

More to do

Art: Ask the children to draw illustrations to accompany the list.

Songs

"The Tree in the Wood"
"The Green Grass Grows All Around"

❖ Jackie Wright, Enid, OK

Making a Sun Design

Materials

Dark-colored construction paper
White paper
Marker
Scissors
Tape

What to do

1. Talk about the power and heat of the sun with the children. Ask them what they think would happen if they left colored paper in the sun for a week.
2. Draw an outline of the sun on a piece of white paper. Make enough copies to give one to each child.

3. Give each child a piece of dark colored paper and a picture of a sun outline. Ask the children to cut out the outline of the sun and tape it onto their piece of construction paper.

4. Hang the papers in a sunny window for a week, with the sun outline facing the window.

5. In a week, take down the papers and remove the sun outlines.

6. Talk about what happened to the colored construction paper and why.

More to do

Math: Hang the pictures in different windows to see if different amounts of light will affect the experiment. Use shape cutouts instead of the sun outline to help reinforce shapes to the children.

Related book

The Magic School Bus: Lost in the Solar System by Joanna Cole

❖ Suzanne Maxymuk, Cherry Hill, NJ

Rainbow Weather Vane

Materials

Styrofoam cups
Blunt pencils
Clay
Plastic straws
Pins
Index cards
Scissors
Glue
Paint and brushes
Streamers

What to do

1. Give each child a Styrofoam cup.

2. Show the children how to punch a hole into the cup using a pencil.

3. Ask the children to place clay inside their cups. Make sure they put in enough clay to hold it in windy weather.

4. Help the children poke a pin through a drinking straw and into the eraser of the pencil (which should now be sticking out of the cup).

5. Show the children how to cut out triangles from index cards and glue them to each end of the straw.

6. Encourage the children to paint the cups with rainbow paints.

7. Help the children attach different colored streamers to the bottom of their cups for decoration.

8. Place the cups in the wind and watch which way the vane goes!

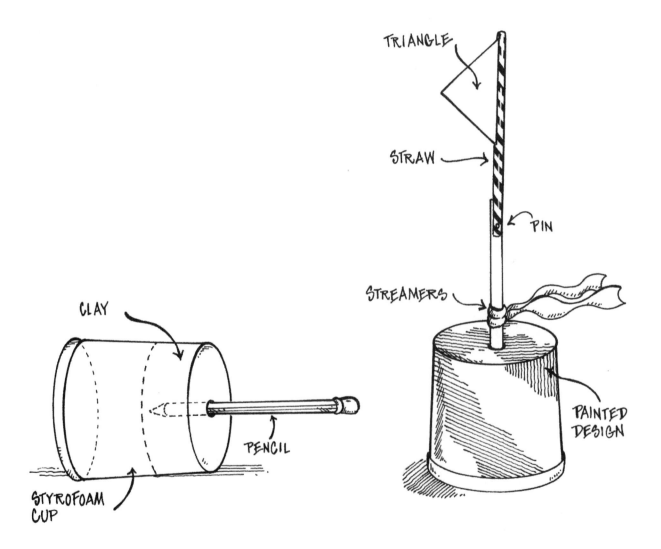

 Lisa M. Chichester, Parkersburg, WV

The Weather Bear

Materials

Different types of clothing for all types of weather, such as a bathing suit, sun suit,
shorts, T-shirts, overalls, sweater, jacket, hats, shoes, and so on
Basket
Stuffed bear, approximately the size of a three-month-old baby

What to do

1. This activity helps the children associate external conditions to body comfort
and protection. It also teaches matching and coordinating, and it helps develop fine motor skills such as buttoning, snapping, and zippering.
2. Collect various types of clothing and store them in a basket.
3. Every day, designate a different child to be the weather person.
4. Ask the child to check the weather by looking or going outside.
5. Encourage the child to dress the Weather Bear in the appropriate clothing for
that day's weather. The child will present it to the class with the weather
report.

More to do

To extend this activity, ask the child to undress the Weather Bear from the
previous day. Encourage discussion about the differences (or lack of change) in
the weather from day to day. This helps children develop an understanding of
time concepts and changes.

❧ Terri L. Pentz, Melbourne Beach, FL

Fossils

Materials

Fossils Tell of Long Ago by Aliki
Items to press into the dough
Playdough
2 cups (500 g) sand
1 cup (125 g) cornstarch
2 tablespoons (30 g) alum
Bowl
Mixing spoon
Hot water
Electric skillet (adult only)
Airtight container
Paper and pen

What to do

1. Read Fossils Tell of Long Ago by Aliki to the children.
2. Ask the children to collect items from the classroom, home, and playground.
3. Encourage the children to explore making fossils by pressing their items into playdough.
4. Make fossil mix: Mix sand, cornstarch, and alum in a bowl. Add hot water and stir vigorously. Set the electric skillet to medium heat and add the contents of the bowl (adult only). Cook until thick and let it cool. (Makes four ½ cup portions.) Store in an airtight container.
5. Ask each child to choose an item with which to make a fossil.
6. Give each child playdough and ½ cup of the fossil mix. Encourage the children to press their items into the fossil mix and remove.
7. Write each child's name on a piece of paper, place the fossil mix on the paper, and place it in the sun to dry.
8. Encourage the children to share their fossils with their friends.

More to do

Pass the fossils around at Circle Time. Encourage the children to try to guess what could have made the fossil.

Related book

Eyewitness Handbooks: Fossils by Walker and Ward

❖ Ann Gudowski, Johnstown, PA

Magnifying Glass

Materials

Bowl or basket

Magnifying glass

Objects to observe, such as a blade of grass, flower, shell, and so on

What to do

1. Place various objects in a bowl or basket.
2. Invite the children to take turns looking at the objects using the magnifying glass.

More to do

Encourage the children to roam the room with the magnifying glass, observing patterns and objects.

❖ Mary Jo Shannon, Roanoke, VA

Science Trays

Materials

Several small trays

Eyedroppers

Specimen trays

Plastic tubes

Small containers

Sponges and paper towels

Water

Food coloring

What to do

1. Place the trays side by side on a table.
2. On each tray, place one eyedropper, one specimen tray, one plastic tube, and several small plastic containers. Place sponges (to clean up spills) and paper towels (to dry hands) on the table, too.
3. Fill the small containers with water and food coloring.
4. Encourage the children to sit down and explore, transfer water, measure, collect, estimate, and so on.

Song

I'm a Little Scientist (Tune: "Mary Had a Little Lamb")
I'm a little scientist, scientist, scientist.
I'm a little scientist, look at me explore!

❖ Sue Myhre, Bremerton, WA

Color Cube

Materials

Construction paper (see colors below)
Glue
Square gift box
Clear contact paper

What to do

1. Glue a square of yellow, brown, orange, red, green, and white construction paper onto each side of a square gift box.
2. Cover it with clear contact paper for durability.
3. Take a fall walk and ask each child to take a turn rolling this Color Cube on the ground (like a die).
4. Encourage the children to look for something in nature that is the same color they rolled.

More to do

Circle Time: Use the Color Cube for a circle time color game.

❖ Cindy Winther, Oxford, MI

Color Tubes

Materials

> Baking powder cans with plastic lids (or a cardboard tube)
> Scissors
> Colored cellophane
> Rubber bands
> Self-adhesive plastic
> Plastic tape

What to do

1. This activity lets children look at the world through rose-colored (or other colored) glasses.
2. Cut off the ends of the cans. Make sure no rough edges remain.
3. Cover one end of the can with colored cellophane, holding it in place with a rubber band.
4. Trim the cellophane.
5. Cover the can with self-adhesive plastic
6. Carefully cut out the inside of the plastic lid, leaving a ¼" (6 mm) rim.
7. Place the lid on the can, over the cellophane. Seal it with plastic tape.
8. Encourage the children to look through the tube to view objects and observe the change in color.

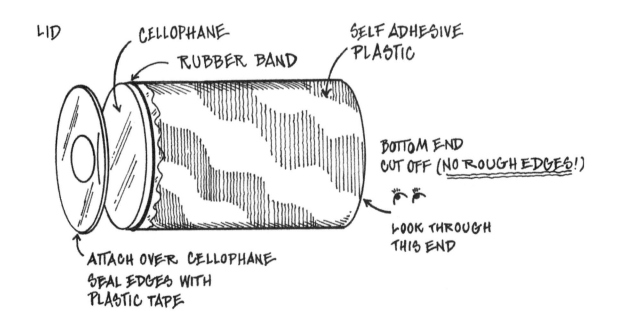

LID CELLOPHANE SELF ADHESIVE PLASTIC
RUBBER BAND

BOTTOM END CUT OFF (NO ROUGH EDGES!)

LOOK THROUGH THIS END

ATTACH OVER CELLOPHANE SEAL EDGES WITH PLASTIC TAPE

More to do

Insert a flashlight in the end of the tube and observe the beam on the ceiling. Move the beam across the ceiling, in different movement patterns. This is a good eye tracking exercise. Use two tubes with two flashlights. See what happens when the beams meet.

Language: Practice reinforcing color names.

❖ Mary Jo Shannon, Roanoke, VA

Magnet Activity

Materials

Sectional plastic plate
Permanent marker
Metal objects, such as a paper clip, nail, washer, and so on
Non-metal objects, such as a crayon, Popsicle stick, plastic top, and so on
Horseshoe magnet

What to do

1. On one section of the plastic plate, write "Yes" using a black permanent marker.
2. On another section of the plate, write "No."
3. Put all of the metal and non-metal objects into the third section of the plate.
4. Tell the children what the words say, and ask them to point out "Yes" and "No" until you are certain they understand. Explain to the children that they should put the metal objects into the "Yes" section and the non-metal objects into the "No" section.
5. Place a metal object on the table. Pick it up with the magnet and say, "Yes." Place it into the "Yes" section of the place.
6. Repeat with a non-metal object. Say, "No," and place it into the "No" section.
7. Invite the children to take turns testing the objects.

More to do

Ask the children if they can tell why the magnet attracts some objects and not others. Name other objects, and ask the children if they think the magnet would attract them. Add a penny to the objects. Why doesn't the magnet pick up the penny? Explain that a penny is made of copper, while the other objects are made of iron. Magnets only attract iron. Collect a number of metal objects and encourage the children to test them to see if they contain iron.

❖ Mary Jo Shannon, Roanoke, VA

Big and Little Shadows

Materials

A sunny day
Blacktop or concrete area
Chalk

What to do

1. Talk to the children about shadows and how they are made by light shining behind a person or an object.
2. Take the children outside on a sunny day and ask them to stand so that they can look at their shadows.
3. Encourage the children to make their shadows as big or as small as they can (and short, tall, wide, and so on). Continue this game. Ask the children to stand near a partner and make shadows together.
4. Give the children time to explore the different shapes that their shadows make.
5. Using chalk, ask the children to trace around each other's shadows.
6. Later in the day, take the children back outside and ask them to find their shadow outlines. Encourage them to compare their outlines with their shadows now. Ask them why they might be different (the sun has moved to a different position in the sky).

More to do

More Science: Take the children outside on a cloudy or overcast day and ask them where they think their shadows went.

Gross Motor: Set up a projector in the classroom and encourage the children to experiment making shadows on a blank wall.

❖ Barbara Saul, Eureka, CA

Follow the Bouncing Beams

Materials

Flashlight
Small mirrors
Periscope

What to do

1. Shine a flashlight on a mirror. Tilt the mirror so the light bounces onto the ceiling, wall, or floor.
2. Wiggle and tilt the mirror to move the light.
3. Shine the light from one mirror to another and onto the ceiling or wall.
4. Explain to the children that light bounces off most objects that it hits and into our eyes. That is how we see.
5. Experiment using a periscope. Shine the flashlight into the top of the periscope and see it shine through the bottom.
6. Encourage the children to look through the periscope and observe how it works.

More to do

Shine the light on other objects (shiny and dull). Do all objects reflect the same way?

❧ Sandra Gratias, Perkasie, PA

The Eensy Weensy Spider

Materials

Glass of water, one for each child
Straws

What to do

1. Give each child a glass of water and a straw.
2. Ask the children to place their straws into the water, covering the top of it with their index fingers.

3. Show the children how to raise the straw just above the glass and lift their fingers from the straws so that the water rolls out into the glass.
4. Encourage the children to practice this while singing "The Eensy-Weensy Spider."

   The eensy weensy spider went up the waterspout. (Lift straw with finger covering the top.)

   Down came the rain and washed the spider out. (Remove finger from the straw.)

   Out came the sun and dried out all the rain,

   And the eensy-weensy spider went up the spout again.

5. Ask the children why they think the water stays in the straw when their fingers cover the tops. Explain how their fingers keep the air out and create suction. When they lift their fingers from the straws, the air flows in and releases the water.

♣ Dotti Enderle, Richmond, TX

Ice Painting

Materials

Sunny day
Ice cubes

What to do

1. On a sunny day, take the children outside and give each one an ice cube.
2. Encourage the children to use their ice cubes to draw a picture on the cement.
3. Ask the children if they think they will finish their picture before it begins to disappear. Ask them whether the ice painting disappears faster in a sunny spot or a shady spot.

More to do

Sand and Water Table: Put ice cubes in the sensory table.
Snack: Have juice Popsicles for snack.

♣ Sandy L. Scott, Vancouver, WA

Slip, Slide Ice

Materials

Items to use as ramps, such as lids to large tubs, step stools,
   pieces of wood or plastic, and so on
Items to prop the ramps at various angles, such as large blocks
Ice cubes

What to do

1. Place items to use as ramps and things to prop the ramps at different angles on the floor.
2. Give a child an ice cube. Encourage the child to experiment sliding the ice cube on items with different surfaces and ramps at varying degrees to explore how the angle and surface affects how it slides.

More to do

Do this activity inside or outside. Encourage the children to make predictions, have races with ice cubes, and summarize their observations. Add different variables, such as different sizes of ice cubes, shapes, and so on. Encourage the children to come up with their own ideas.

❖ Sandra Nagel, White Lake, MI

Snow and Ice

Materials

Snow
A Snowy Day by Ezra Jack Keats
Buckets or plastic bags
Icicles
Water table
Sand shovels
Mittens
Clean white cups
Ice cubes

What to do

1. On a day that there is snow on the ground, read *A Snowy Day* to the children. (If you live in an area where it doesn't snow, make "snow" for this activity using a snow cone machine.)
2. Give the children buckets or plastic bags and take them outside for a discovery walk. Ask them to collect snow and ice in their buckets or bags. Ask them to look at all the different tracks in the snow (animal, human, tire, and so on) and any icicles that may be hanging.
3. When you return to the classroom, put the collected snow and ice into the water table along with shovels.
4. Provide mittens for the children to wear while exploring the snow and ice.
5. Do melting experiments. Ask the children to predict what will happen to the ice and snow in the water table. Put snow into a clean white cup. Ask the children to look in the cup after the snow melts. Where did the dirt come from? Put one ice cube under a light and one away from the light. Which one melts faster?

More to do

Art: Give the children white playdough and items for making tracks, such as plastic vehicles and animals.

More Art: Encourage the children to create snowflake prints using snowflake sponges, paint, and paper.

Literacy: Make and display a list of new words that the children learned (melt, tracks, icicle, and so on).

Related books

Caps, Hats, Socks and Mittens: A Book About the Four Seasons by Louise Borden
The First Snowfall by Anne and Harlow Rockwell
The Mitten by Jan Brett
White Snow, Bright Snow by Alvin Tresselt

❖ Ann Gudowski, Johnstown, PA

Wave Bottles

Materials

Clear plastic bottles with lids
Water
Funnels
Food coloring, optional
Oils (vegetable, baby, canola, mineral)
Various small items to put in the bottles, such as beads, marbles,
    ribbons, and glitter
Cloth
Duct tape

What to do

1. Give each child a clear plastic bottle and lid. Help the children use funnels to fill their bottles half full with water.
2. If desired, the children can color their water by adding a drop of food coloring. However, if they add too much food coloring, it becomes difficult to see the items placed inside. If the water appears too dark, pour out some water and dilute it with clear water.
3. Ask each child to choose a type of oil to add. Each type of oil adds a different effect to the flow and is a different color.
4. Put various small items into the bottle.
5. Place the lid on the bottle (making sure it is very tight). Wipe the lid and bottle with a cloth to remove excess oil, and tape the top to secure it.

More to do

Ask the children to bring in items from home to place into the bottles. Encourage the children to compare and contrast the different bottle creations.

Related books

My Life with the Wave by Catherine Cowan
The Old Woman and the Wave by Shelley Jackson

Sandra Nagel, White Lake, MI

Volcano Action

Materials

Small plastic bottle
Tub
Spoon
Baking soda
Vinegar
Small pitcher
Paper towels

What to do

1. Place a small plastic bottle into the tub. (The tub will catch the run off.)
2. Help the child pour two spoonfuls of baking soda into the bottle.
3. Pour a small amount of vinegar into a small pitcher to control the amount of vinegar used. The pitcher is also easier for the child to use.
4. Ask a child to pour the vinegar into the bottle.
5. As the vinegar touches the baking soda, a chemical reaction takes place and a foaming volcano erupts.
6. Each time the child repeats the eruption, she should add an additional two spoonfuls of baking soda. The children can repeat this several times before they must pour out the liquid mixture and begin again.
7. Children are amazed at the chemical reaction. Have lots of baking soda and vinegar on hand. The children become excited when the chemical reaction takes place and want lots of turns.

More to do

Outdoor Play: Do this activity outside in the sand box. Children can build up sand mountains around the bottle, then complete the process to make the volcano erupt.

Related book

Volcanoes by F.M. Branley

❖ Sandra Nagel, White Lake, MI

Colorful Recycled Paper

Materials

Newspapers
Mixing bowl
Water
Egg beater
Measuring cups and spoons
2 tablespoons (20 g) cornstarch
Food coloring
Screen (to fit into flat pan)
Flat pan

What to do

1. Ask each child to tear a page of newspaper into tiny bits. Place the bits into a mixing bowl and cover them with water.
2. Allow the paper to soak for an hour.
3. Help the children use an egg beater to beat the paper until it forms a pulp.
4. Mix in cornstarch, one cup (240 ml) water, and food coloring.
5. Place a screen in the bottom of a flat pan.
6. Pour the pulpy mixture into the pan and let it sit for three minutes.
7. Remove the screen (covered with the mix) and put it on newspaper to dry.
8. Place more newspaper over the top of the screen and press down hard.
9. Remove the top newspaper and let the pulp dry overnight.
10. When it is dry, peel the paper from the screen.
11. Help the children write a note on this recycled stationery!

❧ Lisa M. Chichester, Parkersburg, WV

Stepping Stones

Materials

Masks
9 cups of fiber-reinforced ready-mixed concrete
2 cups (480 ml) water
Small tub or bucket

Stick or large, old spoon

Wax paper

Scissors

12″ (30 cm) round, plastic plant drain tray with straight vertical sides

Latex gloves

Objects to press into concrete (see below)

Paper towels, if necessary

Damp cloth

What to do

1. Help the children (and yourself) put on masks because of the concrete dust.

2. Using a stick or old spoon, mix the concrete with 1 ¾ (420 ml) cups of water in a tub or bucket. Add all the water at once and stir well to moisten all of the dry powder. If more water is needed, add one teaspoon (5 ml) at a time until the mixture has the consistency of thick brownie batter. (Less wet is better.)

Note: The concrete is easier to use if you measure it out and place it in freezer bags prior to involving the children.

3. Cut out a 12″ (30 cm) circle from wax paper. Place it into the bottom of the plant drain tray (this will be the mold).

4. Pour the mixture into the mold. Use your hands, a spoon, putty knife, or stick to press the mixture down into the mold. (If you use your hands, put on latex gloves.) Jiggle the mold from side to side to level the surface.

5. Clean the tools immediately with water—spray from a garden hose works great. DO NOT RINSE THE RESIDUE DOWN THE SINK.

6. Help the children make a handprint or footprint in the concrete. For added interest, add stones, marbles, or tiles. Or make shapes using cookie cutters or draw letters with the point of a rattail comb or stick. Some suggestions for adding items are:

   ■ Push in objects half way so they will stay in place and will not fall out.

   ■ As soon as your craft stick makes a dry, clean mark, you are ready to begin.

   ■ Push the writing tool into the mixture—do not drag it.

7. If the stone seems very wet, soak up some of the water by placing a paper towel on the top of the concrete. Depending on the dampness of the mixture, you will have ten to forty minutes to complete the stone.

8. Put the stone in a place where it does not have to be removed for twenty-four hours. If you move it before it dries, some of the letters, shapes, and prints may disappear. It could also crack.

9. Once the stone is firm, cover it with a damp cloth for a few days to make it stronger. Wait at least two days before trying to remove the mold. Then, wait at least two weeks for it to cure before putting any pressure on the stone or putting it outside.

Note: A sixty-pound bag of concrete makes seven to eight stones.

More to do

This activity is great when the children are learning about dinosaurs or fossils. The children are making their own fossil prints. It provides an example of how dust and dirt-like material can become a solid, like the fossils.

❖ Sandra Nagel, White Lake, MI

Space Station

Materials

Two refrigerator boxes
Utility knife (adult only)
Black tempera paint
Paintbrushes
Small pebbles, rocks, or gravel
Silver spray paint (adult only)
Tape
Scissors
Black mesh netting
Glow-in-the dark stars and planets
Beanbag chair or soft furniture
Small (child-sized) table and chair
Small magnifiers, penlights, and containers of ground sand
Books about space exploration
Construction paper and crayons

What to do

1. Using a utility knife, cut along a seam on each of the refrigerator boxes so that they lay flat (adult only).
2. Cut out two or three small windows and one child-sized door in the sides of the boxes.

3. Encourage the children to paint both sides of the boxes completely black. Allow the boxes to dry.

4. While the boxes are drying, paint the pebbles, rocks, or gravel with silver spray paint to create moon rocks and meteorites (adult only).

5. Tape together the boxes to form one large enclosure. Ask the children to hold the boxes in place while you tape them.

6. Stand up the large enclosure, squaring it up so it stands nicely. This is the base for the space station. If the box is unsteady, tie each corner of the box to chairs (poke small holes in the box, thread strong packing twine through them, and tie it to the backs of the chairs).

7. Tape black mesh securely to the top of the box and to the door and window cutouts. This allows the inside of the enclosure to appear dark to the children while still allowing for supervision from above and through the windows.

8. Ask the children to apply glow-in-the-dark stars and planets to a wall inside the space station.

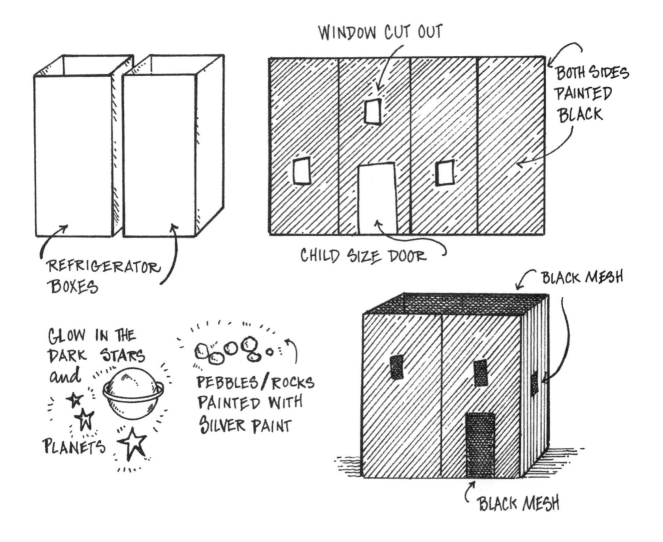

REFRIGERATOR BOXES

WINDOW CUT OUT

BOTH SIDES PAINTED BLACK

CHILD SIZE DOOR

GLOW IN THE DARK STARS and PLANETS

PEBBLES/ROCKS PAINTED WITH SILVER PAINT

BLACK MESH

BLACK MESH

9. Place a beanbag chair (or other soft furniture) and a small table and chair inside the space station. Place magnifiers, penlights, moon rocks, and containers of finely ground sand (moon dust) on the table for exploration. Also be sure to include some good books on space exploration.

10. Encourage the children to visit the space station. They can use the magnifiers to explore the rocks, sand, and the stars on the wall. They can lounge on the beanbag chair and use the penlights to read books about outer space. Provide construction paper and crayons so the children can draw pictures of the solar system and space aliens. Add special pens or markers that will show up on black paper. They make great outer space pictures.

More to do

Art: Make constellations. Ask the children to draw a picture of the solar system. Then, encourage them to place star stickers at certain points to make a constellation.
More Art: Create aliens from clay. Make up stories about where the aliens live.
More Art: Make planets by covering balloons with paper maché. Paint, decorate, and enjoy!
Music and Movement: Dance to outer space music.

Related books

Moon Man by Tomi Ungerer
Owl Moon by Jane Yolen

❖ Virginia Jean Herrod, Columbia, SC

Clay Critters

Materials

Posters, pictures, or plastic replicas of real bugs
Artist clay (the type that air dries) or Sculpey clay (can be baked
in a regular oven)
Stick-on wiggly eyes
Chenille stems
Various craft items, such as beads and small buttons
Glue

What to do

1. This is a good activity to do when the children are learning about bugs.
2. Show the children posters, pictures, or plastic replicas of real bugs (such as beetles, grasshoppers, flies, ladybugs, caterpillars, and millipedes).
3. Have a discussion about the bugs.
4. Encourage the children to examine the bugs closely and notice the construction of each body type. Ask questions such as, "How many legs does this bug have?" and "Does this bug have wings?" Encourage the children to touch the replica bugs and play with them.
5. Give each child a medium-size ball of clay to create a bug.
6. Encourage the children to add wiggly eyes, chenille stems (for antennae), and other craft items to create their bugs. Encourage them to use their imagination! If they have questions about a bug, such as how many legs it has, remind them to think about the bugs they handled. Or, they can look at the bugs again.
7. Allow the clay to air dry for a few days until it is completely hard. (If you use Sculpey clay, bake according to the directions.)

More to do

Art: Draw or paint bugs. Make bug collages. Create bugs out of everything you can find!

Math: When talking about the body type of each bug, make a graph with "Bug Bodies" as the heading. Divide the chart into four columns: "How many eyes?" "How many legs?" "How many wings?" and "Does it fly?" Make five or six rows. Ask the children to name some bugs and help them print the name of one bug at the beginning of each row. Fill in the rows as needed for each bug.

Music and Movement: March to music like bugs. Slither, hop, crawl, and fly! Sing "The Ants Went Marching" and march around the room together.

Related books

Bees (First Discovery Book) by Gallimard Jeunesse and Raoul Sautai
Peck Slither and Slide by Suse MacDonald
The World of Ants by Melvin Berger

❖ Virginia Jean Herrod, Columbia, SC

Interesting Insects

Materials

Playdough (see recipe)
Scissors
Pipe cleaners

What to do

1. Make playdough ahead of time.
   2 cups (250 g) flour
   1 cup (250 g) salt
   2 cups (480 ml) water
   2 tablespoons (30 ml) vegetable oil
   2 teaspoons (20 g) cream of tartar
   Food coloring
   Mix the ingredients in a saucepan. Stir over medium heat until it forms a ball. Let it cool and knead it. If the playdough is too crumbly after it cools, add more oil and knead some more.
2. Cut pipe cleaners into 2" to 3" (5 cm to 7 cm) sections.
3. Encourage the children to make insects using playdough and pipe cleaners. The only requirement is that their insect should have body parts. Insects have three body parts—a head, thorax, and an abdomen. They also have six legs and two antennae.

More to do

Look at insect pictures. Encourage the children to count the body parts and try to identify the head, thorax, and abdomen. Count the legs, too. Find an anthill and watch the ants.

Related books

The Best Book of Bugs by Claire Llewellyn
How to Hide a Butterfly by Ruth Heller
The Very Hungry Caterpillar by Eric Carle

Jill Putnam, Wellfleet, MA

Here's Looking at You, Spiders

Materials

Live spider
Small fish tank, fish bowl, or see-through jar
Mesh or nylon netting
Rubber band or piece of string
Small pieces of shrubbery and grass
Damp cloth or sponge
Spray water bottle
Flies or mealworms
Spiders by Lillian Bason
White construction paper
Crayons
Paint shirts
Watercolor paints
Lined paper
Pencils

What to do

1. This is a fun activity to do around Halloween. However, the timing of this activity depends on when you can catch a spider!
2. Capture a spider and put it into a see-though jar, fish tank, or fish bowl.
3. Cover the top of the jar with nylon netting or a fine mesh lid and secure it with a rubber band or string. To make the spider's home "cozy," put in a small piece of shrubbery, a handful of grass, and a small damp cloth or sponge. Periodically spray the cloth with water to keep it damp (but not wet).
4. Every couple of days, feed the spider one or two flies or mealworms.
5. With the children, share pictures and facts from *Spiders* by Lillian Bason.
6. Bring out the jar with the spider and encourage the children to observe it. Discuss some of the facts you read about in *Spiders*.
7. After the children have watched the spider for a while, discuss some of their observations.
8. Give the children white construction paper and crayons. Ask them to draw a picture of the spider engaged in one of the activities they observed.
9. When they finish drawing, help them put on their paint shirts.

10. Put out watercolor paints and encourage the children to paint over their crayon pictures to create a watercolor wash effect.

11. Ask the children to describe their observations of the spider (a sentence or two) and write it for them on lined paper.

12. When the pictures are dry, help the children glue the descriptions to the back of the pictures.

More to do

Literacy: Read the following poem with the children.

About Spiders by Jeannie Gunderson

Let me tell you about the spiders
Creeping all around.
Quiet little spiders
Spin webs without a sound.
Brown, gray, and black spiders
On plants can be found.
Busy trap-door spiders
Dig holes in the ground.
Watch for water spiders
In ponds and streams not drowned.
Look for the spiders
Around you they abound!

Music: This is a great time to sing *The Itsy-Bitsy Spider* with hand movements.

The Itsy-Bitsy Spider

The itsy-bitsy spider went up the waterspout
Down came the rain and washed the spider out
Out came the sun and dried the spider off
So, the itsy-bitsy spider went up the spout again.

Related books

Outside and Inside Spiders by Sandra Markle
Spiders by Lillian Bason
The Very Busy Spider by Eric Carle

Jeannie Gunderson, Casper, WY

Life Cycle of a Monarch Butterfly

Materials

Large sheets of tissue paper

What to do

1. Give each child a sheet of tissue paper. Explain to them that they are going to act out the life cycle of a butterfly.
2. Explain to the children that butterflies begin their life as an egg on the underside of a leaf. Ask the children to cover themselves with their tissue paper so they are hidden like an egg.
3. Ask the children if they know what comes out of the egg (caterpillars). Ask them if they know what caterpillars do and how they act. They will probably guess that caterpillars eat and crawl around, so encourage them to pretend to eat their paper as they crawl around on the floor.
4. Explain to the children that caterpillars spin a chrysalis. Encourage them to wrap their paper tightly around themselves to make their own chrysalis.
5. Tell the children that after two weeks, a butterfly emerges. At first, their wings are wet and weak but as they dry, the butterfly flies around and drinks nectar. The children can act like their paper is wet and weak, but as their "wings" dry, they can fly around the room.
6. Now the butterflies are monarchs. When it starts getting colder, the monarchs must migrate to someplace warmer. Tell the children that monarchs fly twelve miles per hour, so encourage them to fly faster using their "wings."
7. Explain to the children what happens when spring comes again (they lay their eggs and the cycle starts all over again).
8. The children will want to do this activity over and over again. The children are learning the activity the first time they do the activity. Therefore, repeat it at least one more time. By the second time, they will know about the life cycle of a monarch butterfly and will be able to act it out.

More to do

With the children, find real live caterpillars in various stages of a butterfly. Bring them back to the classroom and make a butterfly house. Keep the butterflies in it and encourage the children to observe them for a few hours before releasing them.

Art: Place pipe cleaners, pompoms, glue, paint, and squiggle eyes into egg cartons and encourage the children to make caterpillars.

Related books

The Magic School Bus and the Butterfly Bog Beast by Joanna Cole
The Monarch Butterfly by Gail Gibbons
The Very Hungry Caterpillar by Eric Carle

Holly Dzieranowski, Austin, TX

Seven Little Butterflies

Materials

Books and pictures about butterflies
Butterfly kit, optional
Scissors
4" x 6" (10 cm x 15 cm) tissue paper in assorted colors
Newspaper
Markers
Ballpoint pen
Pipe cleaners, two per child
Chart paper

What to do

1. With the children, explore facts about butterflies. Read the children stories about butterflies and show them pictures and exhibits of butterflies. If possible, order a kit of live caterpillars to watch the whole process.
2. Precut tissue paper rectangles into thick "dogbone" shapes (these will be butterfly wings). Keeping the center of the bone thick provides a more gathered look for the wings.
3. Cover the work surface with newspaper. Give each a sheet of wing-shaped tissue paper to decorate. Caution the children to color the wings gently so the tissue paper will not tear. (It is best to avoid completely filling in the wing area with the marker.)
4. Help each child write her name on her wings using a ballpoint pen (gently). Allow the wings to dry.

5. Give each child two pipe cleaners. Help the children fold one of the pipe cleaners in half.

6. Slide the tissue butterfly through the folded pipe cleaner and gather gently. Twist the doubled pipe cleaner together about 1" to 2" (2 cm to 5 cm) from the fold to secure the wings. Extend the remaining ends and curl the tips for antennae. Adjust the gathers in the wings.

7. Slip the second pipe cleaner through the body of the butterfly, being careful not to tear the wings. Then, carefully bend the pipe cleaner to encircle the child's wrist. The butterfly is now on top of the wrist.

8. Copy the following fingerplay onto chart paper. Practice reading the rhyme with the children until they are familiar with it. (Make a copy for the children to take home with their tissue butterflies at the end of the activity.)

Seven Little Butterflies

The first little butterfly flutters in the sun.
How many butterflies? Only one.
The second little butterfly is
*   landing on my shoe!*
Now let's count them: one
*   and two.*
Here is the third one, floating by the tree.
Let's count them all: one, two, three.
The fourth little butterfly adds one more
And again we count: one, two, three, four.
The fifth little butterfly goes so high!
We see one, two, three, four, five.
The sixth one knows some flying tricks!
One, two, three, four, five, and six.
The seventh one isn't too far from heaven.
One, two, three, four, five, six, seven.

TISSUE TAPER (WITH "DOGBON SHAPE)

PIPE CLEANER FOLDED IN ½

TISSUE PAPER

TWISTED PIPE CLEANER

SECOND PIPE CLEANER (SLIPPED THROUGH THE BOTTOM)

9. Choose seven children at a time to dramatize the rhyme. Encourage the children to "fly" from one location to another as the rest of the children recite the poem. Practice first indoors and then move outside. Make sure every child gets a turn.

More to do

Learn about the life stages—from caterpillar to butterfly.

Art: Demonstrate symmetry by making blob paintings. Drop "blobs" of tempera paint onto paper, fold it together, press with the fingertips, and then open it to reveal a symmetrical design.

Literacy: Make word cards for the rhymes: sun, one; shoes, two; tree, three; tricks, six; seven, heaven. With word cards, let the children match the cards to the words on the chart.

More Literacy: Discuss the ordinal words from the poem: first, second, third, and so on.

Related books

The Very Hungry Caterpillar by Eric Carle
Where Does the Butterfly Go When It Rains? by May Garelick

❧ Susan O. Hill, Lakeland, FL

Birds and Nests

Materials

Scissors
Pictures of birds and their nests from old workbooks or science books
Glue
Felt
Flannel board

What to do

1. Cut out pictures of birds and their particular type of nest from old workbooks or science books.
2. Glue felt to the back of the pictures.
3. Display the nests on a flannel board and discuss their differences.
4. Show the children one bird at a time and ask them to name the bird and identify which nest the bird built as its home.
5. Place the bird next to the correct nest on the flannel board. Continue until the children have identified all of the birds and their nests.
6. Leave out the activity and encourage the children to play with it on their own free choice time.

More to do

Bring in a real bird's nest for the children to observe.

Snack: Make bird nests using melted butterscotch bits, chow mein noodles, and chopped peanuts. Fill them with jelly beans.

Related book

Birds (Now I Know) by Susan Kuchalla

Song

"Blue Bird" from *Wee Sing and Play* by Pamela Conn Beall

❧ Jackie Wright, Enid, OK

Animal Matching

Materials

4" x 6" (10 cm x 15 cm) cards
Glue
Pictures of different animals (one picture of an animal baby
    and another of its mother)
Big Red Barn by Margaret Wise Brown

What to do

1. Prior to the activity, glue pictures of baby animals and mother animals on 4" x 6" (10 cm x 15 cm) cards. Make an even number of cards. (For each set, glue a picture of a baby animal on one card and its mother on another card.)
2. Introduce this activity by reading *Big Red Barn* to the children.
3. Show the children the cards of the animal babies and mothers and discuss them.
4. Randomly distribute a card to each child, face down. Make sure that one child gets an animal baby and another gets its mother. If there are an uneven number of children, give yourself or another adult one of the cards.
5. Encourage the children to try and find the person who has the matching card to their card. When they have found their partner, ask them to indicate this by sitting down.

6. When all the children are seated, the pairs of children can each have a turn to show and identify the animal and baby on their cards.

More to do

More Science: Share information with the children about each animal, such as where it lives, what it eats, and other interesting facts.

Art: Encourage the children to paint a picture of their favorite animal mother and baby.

Related books

Snuggle Wuggle by Jonathan London
Where Is My Baby? by Harriet Ziefert

❖ Mary Rozum Anderson, Vermillion, SD

Tree Homes

Materials

Glue
Pictures of animals who make their homes in a tree: bird (nest), spider (web), bee (hive), squirrel (hole), caterpillar (cocoon), insect (under the bark), and so on
Oak tag
Clear contact paper or laminate
Felt
Flannel board

What to do

1. Glue animal pictures onto pieces of oak tag.
2. Laminate the pictures or cover them with clear contact paper for durability.
3. Glue felt to the back of the pictures.
4. Discuss with the children all the animals that make their homes in trees. As you discuss each animal, place its picture on the flannel board.

More to do

Games: Play a classroom game called "Squirrels in a Tree." Separate the children into groups of three. Ask two children in each group to join hands to form a "tree" around the third child, who is the "squirrel." Ask a couple of other children (not in a group) to be squirrels, too. When an adult gives the signal, the squirrels change trees. The extra squirrels try to find trees too!)

Related book

Mighty Tree by Dick Gackenbach

❧ Jacki Wright, Enid, OK

Marsupial Soup

Materials

Pictures of a kangaroo, wombat, koala, and possum
Large manila envelope

What to do

1. Place the animal pictures into a manila envelope and sit with it in your lap. (The envelope becomes your pouch.)
2. Explain to the children that marsupials are animals with a pouch and that most of them are found in Australia.
3. Reach into the envelope and pull out a picture. Explain each animal to the children.
4. Ask the children to imitate the animal (such as hopping for a kangaroo, digging like a wombat, climbing like a possum or koala).
   Kangaroo facts: A kangaroo lives for the first six months inside its mother's pouch. A baby kangaroo is called a joey.
   Wombat facts: Wombats are furry little creatures that like to dig underground. They are nocturnal, which means they sleep during the day.
   Possum facts: An Australian possum looks different from an American possum. They have fuzzy tails and large ears. The American possum hangs upside down by a skinny tail.
   Koala Facts: Koalas love to climb. They eat only eucalyptus leaves. Many people call them koala bears, but they are not bears at all.

More to do

Find out about more Australian animals, such as the platypus, emu, and kookaburra. Encourage the children to imitate these fun animals, too!

Related books

Katy No-Pocket by Emmy Payne
Koala Lou by Mem Fox
Possum Magic by Mem Fox

❖ Dotti Enderle, Richmond, TX

Oviparous Animals

Materials

Miniature, plastic oviparous animals (alligators, crocodiles, ducks, birds, chicks, snakes, and dinosaurs)
Large plastic eggs

What to do

1. Prior to the activity, place miniature plastic animals into plastic eggs.
2. Explain to the children that oviparous animals are animals that hatch from eggs.
3. Describe one of the animals that is hidden in one of the eggs. Give the children clues such as, "I am an animal that flies," "I have feathers," and so on. Ask the children to guess the animal in the egg.

More to do

Games: Have an Oviparous Egg Hunt. Place gummy snakes, alligators, and fish into plastic eggs and hide them on the playground. Encourage the children to hunt for the eggs.
Sand and Water: Place miniature plastic animals in the plastic eggs and hide them in the sand. Encourage the children to hunt for them.

❖ Quazonia J. Quarles, Newark, DE

Useful Tails

Materials

Pictures of a possum, horse, lizard, rattlesnake, peacock, fish, bird, and beaver

What to do

1. Display the animal pictures so the children can see them.
2. Say the following sentences. Ask the children to guess the animal by the usefulness of its tail.

    I use my tail for hanging upside down. (possum)

    I use my tail as a fly swatter. (horse)

    When my tail breaks off, I grow a new one. (lizard)

    I shake my noisy tail when I am about to strike. (rattlesnake)

    My tail opens like a beautiful fan. (peacock)

    I use my tail as a propeller. I cannot swim without it. (fish)

    I can't fly without my tail. (bird)

    I use my powerful tail for building. (beaver)

More to do

Ask the children if they can name other animals that have tails. Ask them how these animals' tails might be useful.

Games: Cut out the tails of each of the animals. Encourage the children to pin the tails on the pictures (like "Pin the Tail on the Donkey").

❖ Dotti Enderle, Richmond, TX

Dino Dig

Materials

Plastic or rubber dinosaurs or bones

Sand

Wide-tip, medium-sized paintbrushes

Plastic sand shovels

Small plastic buckets

Clipboards

Paper

Pencil or pens

What to do

1. Beforehand, hide plastic or rubber dinosaurs or bones in the sand.
2. Give each child a paintbrush, shovel, and bucket.
3. Encourage the children to uncover the items in the sand. The children can place their archeological finds in the bucket after they dig them up and brush them off.
4. Give each child a clipboard with a piece of paper. Encourage the children to draw a picture or write about what they found.
5. Replace the items in the sand and encourage another child to be a "paleontologist."

More to do

Make fossils of the dinosaurs or bones using plaster of Paris or clay. Place the fossils in the sand after they have hardened. Encourage the children to uncover them and guess what they might have found.

Games: Musical Dinosaur Step Game: Play this game just like musical chairs. The only difference is that instead of using chairs, the children will follow cutout dinosaur footprint tracks. Ask the "winner" to name what kind of dinosaur she would like to be and why.

Related books

An Alphabet of Dinosaurs by Peter Dodson
The Magic School Bus: In the Time of the Dinosaurs by Joanna Cole
New Questions and Answers About Dinosaurs by Seymour Simon

❧ Tina R. Woehler, Oak Point, TX

Names-O-Saurus

Materials

Nametags
Paper
Markers

What to do

1. Help the children create their own "dino" names by adding "O-Saurus" or "A-Top" to their names. For example, "Billy" becomes "Billy-A-Top" and "Betty" becomes "Betty-O-Saurus."
2. Print each child's dino name on a nametag and on a sheet of paper.
3. Encourage the children to illustrate themselves as dinosaurs.
4. Ask each child to share with the rest of the children how her dinosaur moves, what it eats, how it protects itself, and its characteristics.

More to do

The activity can be a part of a museum display. Help the children make footprints and handprints using plaster as part of their dinosaur display.

Related books

Andy: That's My Name by Tomie dePaola
Christopher Changes His Name by Itah Sadu
Chrysanthemum by Kevin Henkes
Digging Up Dinosaurs by Aliki
Magic School Bus: In the Time of the Dinosaurs by Joanne Cole
Naming the Cat by Laurence Pringle

❧ Sandra Nagel, White Lake, MI

Life-Sized Whale

Materials

Books and photos of whales
100′ (30 m) measuring tape
Large butcher paper
Pencil
Scissors
Markers, paint, or crayons
Hole punch and paper hole reinforcer
Fishing line or yarn and large paper clips

What to do

1. During a whale or sea life unit, make a life-sized whale to display in the classroom or in the hallway.
2. Read books about whales to the children and show them photographs of real whales.
3. Ask the children to decide collaboratively which whale they would like to create.
4. Measure how long the actual whale would be using a tape measure. (If the children choose an extremely large whale, it might be better to construct it outdoors.)
5. Roll out enough butcher paper to equal the length of the whale.
6. Draw the whale onto the paper. Be sure to include an eye, mouth, blowhole, fins, and other specific markings. Cut it out.
7. Encourage the children to color or paint the whale the actual color it would be in the wild.
8. Carefully punch out holes along the top edges of the whale. Place hole reinforcers on both sides of the holes to provide sturdiness for hanging.
9. Tie fishing line or yarn through the holes. Secure paper clips to the other ends of the line to mount it from ceiling tiles. (Or, use punch pins to attach it to a wall.)
10. Help the children carry the whale to where you will display it.

More to do

Field Trips: Visit a local marine park, aquarium, or museum to find out additional whale facts and/or actually see a whale. Take plenty of photos for the children to reference later.

Math: Make a graph comparing the lengths of several different types of whales.

Outdoors: Have a whale spout splash day. Ask the children to dress in wet play clothing and bring in squirt toys or bottles from home. Or, purchase enough squirt toys for several children to use at one time. Explain to the children that it is air that makes the water squirt out of the bottle. Then explain that when a whale exhales, it doesn't squirt water out of its blowhole. Instead, it is the water on the whale's body and the warmth of the whale's breath that makes the spray.

Related books

Baby Beluga by Raffi
Humpback Goes North by Darice Bailer
Humphrey the Lost Whale by Wendy Tokuda
Orca Song by Michael C. Armour
Whales by Laura Bour

Whales, Dolphins & Porpoises by Mark Cowadine

The Whales' Song by Dyan Sheldon

❧ Tina R. Woehler, Oak Point, TX.

Baking Day Fun

Materials

Plain aprons (from a dollar store)
Fabric paints
Sponges

What to do

1. To add to the fun of cooking with young children, give each child a plain apron to decorate and personalize.
2. Set out fabric paint in a variety of colors and sponges. Encourage the children to stamp designs onto their aprons.
3. Help the children make handprints and write their names on their aprons to personalize them.
4. Encourage the children to wear their aprons every time they bake!

More to do

Home Connection: The aprons make a nice end-of-the-year keepsake for the children. Invite parents to come in and be a guest "chef." Make a guest chef apron to keep in the classroom for parents to wear. (We also give each guest "chef" a golden spoon magnet as a thank you.)

❦ Cindy Winther, Oxford, MI

Chef Linguinio

Materials

Glue
Large moveable eyes
Yarn
Glove-like oven mitt (preferably in a neutral color)
Scissors
White felt
Old, scrap bandana

What to do

1. Help the children glue moveable eyes and yarn on the mitt to make a face and hair.
2. Cut out a chef hat from white felt and glue it onto the puppet's head.
3. Using an old, scrap bandana, cut out clothes and glue them onto the mitt.
4. Each day before snack or lunch, bring "Chef Linguini" out to talk about what the children will be eating. Also use the puppet to give nutrition information, such as which vitamin is in the food the children are eating and what it does for their bodies.

❦ Lisa Chichester, Parkersburg, WV

Creating a Recipe

Materials

Cookbooks
Recipe "form"
Pen

What to do

1. Display a variety of cookbooks.
2. Encourage the children to suggest ingredients and create their own recipes. Write down all their suggestions on a recipe card.
3. Ask the children to determine the directions for preparation.

 Cristy Bawol, Utica, MI

Read and Eat

Materials

Books and recipes (see below)

What to do

1. Read a book to the children that relates to the current unit and prepare a snack to go along with it. Suggestions include:
   - *Moon Cake* by Frank Asch: Serve angel food cake, whipped topping, and sprinkles (for snow!).
   - *Strega Nona* by Tomie de Paola: When learning about the letter "N," use this book to emphasize the sound of the letter—"N" for noodles. Boil noodles in a great big pot (adult only). Add butter and Parmesan cheese.
   - Halloween Activity: Make "Booberry Muffins."
   - Summer Activities: Make s'mores and pretend to be camping (sleeping bags and all!).
   - Fall activities: Make applesauce. Use an apple peeler and help the children peel the apples.
   - *Stone Soup* (various authors): Ask each child to bring in an item from home to make soup.

■ *Piggie Pie* by Margie Palatini: Wrap little hot dogs in refrigerated rolls.
■ *The Giant Jam Sandwich* by John Vernon Lord: Make jam sandwiches, using cookie cutters to make fun shapes.

❖ Sheryl A. Smith, Jonesborough, TN

Coffee Filters for Serving Snack

Materials

Large, bowl-shaped coffee filters, one per child

What to do

1. When serving the children their snack, give each child his own coffee filter filled with his portion for the day. (This works especially nice for popcorn, trail mix, chips, or anything else that tends to fall off a napkin.)
2. Encourage the children to throw away their cups, napkins, and coffee filters when finished.

More to do

Art: Fold the coffee filters and dip them into food coloring.

❖ Jackie Wright, Enid, OK

Self-Service Snack

Materials

Various food items (see below)
Recipe rebus card
Marker
Bowl
Measuring scoop
Several small, plastic 1-quart (1 L) pitchers

Plastic or blunt knives
4-ounce (60 ml) plastic tumblers
Napkins
Spoons or forks

What to do

1. Set up an area in the room to be the Snack Center. Encourage the children to spend as much time in the Snack Center as desired.
2. Plan a snack that the children can prepare easily. Some ideas might be peanut butter and crackers, cold cereal, jelly and toast, cinnamon toast, or anything else the children would enjoy and be able to prepare for themselves.
3. Draw and label a recipe rebus for the children to follow and hang it near the Snack Center.
4. If the children are going to be making toast, use an automatic toaster, if possible. Supervise closely to prevent any injuries. Or, to simplify the snack, prepare the toast before presenting it to the children.
5. Pour dry goods into a bowl using a measuring scoop or place them on a plate for easy accessibility and even distribution.
6. Pour liquids into the pitchers.
7. Give each child a plastic or blunt knife for the spreadable items.
8. Encourage the children to prepare the snack at the snack table.
9. Ask helpers to distribute tumblers, napkins, and spoons or forks. Eat and enjoy!

More to do

Plan and prepare lunch as a group project. Ask each child to be responsible for a particular step of the meal preparation or table arrangements. Some ideas include vegetable soup, sandwiches, pizza, and desserts. Encourage the children to plan a snack. Ask them to prepare a recipe rebus and gather all the items needed for the snack.

Related books

Growing Vegetable Soup by Lois Ehlert
Mouse Mess by Linnea Riley

🍀 Tina R. Woehler, Oak Point, TX

Cooking Trip

Materials

Candy or canning factory

What to do

1. Contact a candy or canning factory in your area.
2. Take the children to the factory and enjoy the sights, sounds, smells, and activity. (My class went to a candy factory and saw chocolate being melted and mixed in huge kettles being stirred by large spoons. We smelled bottles of flavoring and guessed what was in them. We saw workers boxing up the candies and saw that everyone used hairnets, aprons, and rubber gloves for sanitary reasons. Best of all, we got to sample the candy!)

❦ Marilyn Harding, Grimes, IA

A Rainbow of Foods!

Materials

Variety of different-colored foods and drinks (see below)

What to do

1. In conjunction with a unit on colors, ask the children to help prepare and cook foods to go with the corresponding color of the day or week.
2. Some examples include:
    - RED – fruit punch, strawberry smoothies (strawberries, milk, vanilla ice cream)
    - ORANGE – fresh-squeezed orange juice, carrot slices, orange sherbet
    - YELLOW – banana milk shakes (bananas, milk, vanilla ice cream), lemonade
    - GREEN – lime Jell-O, pistachio pudding (from a mix), green eggs (mix green food coloring into a bit of milk and use it to scramble the eggs)
    - BLUE – blueberry muffins (from a mix), sugar cookies with blue icing (white icing and food coloring)
    - PURPLE – toast with grape jelly, grape Popsicles

More to do

Serve the Rainbow of Foods for snack or have a Rainbow Picnic on a special day. To involve families, send a note home suggesting that parents and children brainstorm color food ideas to bring in and share with the class.

Art: Make playdough to go along with the corresponding color of the day or week. A simple recipe is: 1 cup (125 g) white flour, ½ cup (125 g) salt, 1 cup (240 ml) water, 1 tablespoon (15 g) cream of tartar, 2 tablespoons (30 ml) oil, and food coloring. Mix together all the ingredients and cook over medium heat, stirring constantly until it forms a ball. Remove the mixture from the heat and let it cool.

Related book

Green Eggs and Ham by Dr. Seuss

❖ Suzanne Pearson, Winchester, VA

Blender Drinks

Materials

Fruit
Knife (adult only)
Cutting board
Blender
4 ounces (112 g) yogurt
½ cup (120 ml) milk
2 ice cubes
1 teaspoon (7 g) sugar
Pitchers
Cups
Marker

What to do

1. Cut the fruit into pieces on a cutting board.
2. Ask the children to place the ingredients into a blender. Use ½ cup (80 g) fruit for each batch.
3. As the children blend their smoothies, supervise them closely.

4. Pour the blender drink into a pitcher. Then, pour the drink into cups marked with each child's name.

❧ Cristy Bawol, Utica, MI

Little Miss Muffet's Curds and Whey

Materials

Container of plain yogurt (not nonfat)
Strainer to fit over bowl
Bowl
Refrigerator
Glass container
Knife
Crackers

What to do

1. This activity uses foods to integrate nursery rhymes into the curriculum.
2. Familiarize the children with "Little Miss Muffet" by reciting it often to them.
   Little Miss Muffet sat on a tuffet, eating her curds and whey.
   Along came a spider and sat down beside her
   And frightened Miss Muffet away.
3. When the children are familiar with the nursery rhyme, ask them what Little Miss Muffet was eating. Explain to the children what curds and whey are.
4. Demonstrate how to make a simple cheese. (The curd is the cheese and the whey is the liquid).
5. Help the children empty a container of yogurt into a strainer over a bowl.
6. Let the yogurt drain for two days in the refrigerator until it has a soft, solid consistency.
7. Pour the liquid (whey) into a glass container and show it to the children.
8. Spread the cheese on crackers and eat!
9. Try some other flavors. For example, lemon yogurt tastes great on ginger snaps.

❧ Janice Bodenstedt, Jackson, MI

Banana Dipping

Materials

Bananas, one per child
Granola, coconut, or wheat germ
Paper plates
Spoons

What to do

1. Ask the children to peel their bananas.
2. Spoon a bit of granola, coconut, or wheat germ onto one or more paper plates.
3. Encourage the children to dip their bananas into the granola, coconut, or wheat germ. If desired, the children can try all of the different items.

More to do

Ask the children to suggest other foods to use as dips. Cut up the banana and roll it in the different items. Eat the banana slices with a toothpick.

❖ Sandra Nagel, White Lake, MI

Apple Butter in a Crock Pot

Materials

3 pounds (1.5 kg) medium-sized cooking apples
Vegetable peeler (adult only)
Knife (adult only)
Cutting board
1 cup (240 ml) water
2 teaspoons (10 g) cinnamon
Crock-pot
3 ¾ cup (940 g) sugar
1 teaspoon (7 g) ground cloves
Baby food jars and lids

What to do

1. Peel, core, and slice the apples into chunks (adult only).
2. Put the apples, water, and cinnamon into a crock-pot to make applesauce. Cover and cook for eight to ten hours. (Savor the aroma!)
3. The next day, mix the applesauce, sugar, and cloves in the crock-pot.
4. Turn the crock-pot on high heat and stir hourly for eight hours or until night-time.
5. In the evening, turn the crock-pot to low heat and let it cook all night. The apple butter will be ready in the morning.
6. Fill small baby food jars with apple butter. Let the butter cool, and then refrigerate.

More to do

Make a fabric cover for the jar lid. Cut a piece of fabric into a circle. After screwing on the lid of the jar, place the fabric circle on top. Tie a ribbon around the lid to gather the fabric. This makes a wonderful gift for the children to share with their families.

Related books

An Apple a Day by Melvin Berger
Rain Makes Applesauce by Julian Scheer

♣ Jackie Wright, Enid, OK

Homemade Applesauce

Materials

Apples
Newspaper
Folder labels
Marker
Baby food jars, one for each child
Apple stickers
Vegetable peeler
Knife (adult only)
Blender

What to do

1. Discuss with the children the different kinds of apples and ask them to bring in their favorite type of apple from home.
2. Help the children spread newspaper over the table on which they will be working.
3. Give the children folder labels and help them write their names on them.
4. Give each child a jar. Encourage him to put his folder label on it and decorate it with apple-shaped stickers.
5. Peel, core, and slice the apples into pieces (adult only).
6. Help the children follow a handwritten recipe for blender applesauce.
7. Pour a small amount of applesauce into each child's jar to take home.

✤ Lisa Chichester, Parkersburg, WV

Rainbow Fruit

Materials

Strawberries, blueberries, green grapes, and pieces of cantaloupe, banana, and orange
Toothpicks
Paper plates

What to do

1. Help the children wash their hands.
2. Ask the children to put three to five pieces of fruit on each toothpick.
3. Encourage the children to arrange their fruit on paper plates to look like a rainbow.
4. Eat the rainbows!

More to do

Art: Make a rainbow using paint and paper or colored construction paper and glue.

Related book

The Very Hungry Caterpillar by Eric Carle

✤ Sandy L. Scott, Vancouver, WA

Banana and Peanut Butter

Materials

Plastic knives
Bananas
Peanut butter
Round crackers

What to do

1. Ask the children to help peel and slice the bananas.
2. Encourage the children to spread peanut butter onto crackers and place a banana slice on top.
3. Eat the treats!

More to do

Encourage the children to suggest other foods to use as spreads and to place on top (for example, cream cheese and a cucumber slice).

Related books

In the Night Kitchen by Maurice Sendak
What's Cooking, Jenny Archer? by Ellen Conford

❧ Sandra Nagel, White Lake, MI

Celery Race Cars

Materials

Peanut butter
2" (5 cm) pieces of celery
Plastic knife
¼" (6 mm) slices of carrots

What to do

1. Help the children wash their hands.
2. Encourage the children to spread peanut butter into their celery "cars."

3. The children can put peanut butter on the carrot slices and attach them to the celery to create "wheels."

More to do

Blocks: Add toy cars to the Block Center.

❖ Sandy L. Scott, Vancouver, WA

Lettuce Roll-Up

Materials

Plastic knife
Peanut butter
Lettuce leaves
Celery and/or carrot sticks

What to do

1. Help the children spread peanut butter on a lettuce leaf.
2. Encourage the children to place a celery or carrot stick in the middle of the leaf and peanut butter.
3. Show the children how to roll up the lettuce around the celery or carrot stick to make a roll-up.

More to do

Encourage the children to come up with their own ideas for roll-up sandwiches. Ask the children to decide if they prefer celery or carrots. Take a vote and make a chart of the results. Use cream cheese instead of peanut butter.

Related books

In the Night Kitchen by Maurice Sendak
What's Cooking, Jenny Archer by Ellen Conford

❖ Sandra Nagel, White Lake, MI

Dinosaur Eggs-actly

Materials

Easter egg dying kits
Cups
Spoons
Hard-boiled eggs, several per child
Towels and diaper wipes
Empty egg carton
Pencil or permanent marker
Magnifier
Sand table, optional

What to do

1. Mix the Easter egg dye according to the package directions in each cup.
2. Give each child several hard-boiled eggs.
3. Encourage the children to dye their "dinosaur eggs." Demonstrate how to use multiple colors per egg for a tie-dye look. (Make sure to let the egg dry for a few seconds before dipping it into the next color choice.)
4. Keep towels and diaper wipes handy for easy wipe ups.
5. Place the eggs in an egg carton to dry. Refrigerate until ready to use.
6. Help the children write their names on their eggs for easy identification.
7. Encourage the children to examine their eggs using a magnifier. Or, they can hide them in the sand table to be "discovered."

More to do

Games: Make a matching game using the eggs. Show the children pictures of what real dinosaur eggs may have looked like. Then, encourage them to draw a picture of the exact dinosaur and place it beside the egg. Be sure to label the egg and picture with the correct dinosaur names.
Math: Make a chart showing which kind of dinosaur eggs the children created. Compare the results.

Related books

Bones, Bones, Dinosaur Bones by Byron Barton
Digging Up Dinosaurs by Aliki
Dinosaur Babies by Kathleen Weider Zoehfeld
Dinosaur Days by Joyce Milton

 Tina R. Woehler, Oak Point, TX

Bread and Honey

Materials

Bread and Honey by Frank Asch
Bread
Honey
Blunt knife

What to do

1. Read *Bread and Honey* to the children.
2. Serve a snack of bread and honey sandwiches.

More to do

Discuss where honey comes from. Bring in a real honeycomb for the children to examine.

Song or poem

"Here Is a Beehive" fingerplay
"Baby Bumblebee"

❧ Jackie Wright, Enid, OK

Pumpkin Face Sandwiches

Materials

Paper plates
Bread, one slice per child
3" (9 cm) diameter circle cookie cutters or jar lids
Plastic spoons and knives
Orange-colored cheese spread (at room temperature)
Sliced olives
Pimentos

What to do

1. Give each child a paper plate and a slice of bread.
2. Show the children how to use a cookie cutter or jar lid to cut out a circle from the bread. (Save the leftover pieces of bread for additional snacks or toast them to make croutons.)
3. Encourage the children to scoop a spoonful of cheese spread and spread it on the bread using a plastic knife.
4. Make pumpkin faces using sliced olives for eyes and a nose and pimento for a mouth.
5. Eat the pumpkins!

Related books

Apples and Pumpkins by Anne Rockwell
The Biggest Pumpkin Ever by Steven Kroll
It's Pumpkin Time by Zoe Hall

Poem

Teach the children the following poem:

Five little pumpkins sitting on the gate,
The first one says, "Oh my, it's getting late!"
The second one says, "There are witches in the air."
The third one says, "But we don't care."
The fourth one says, "Let's run and run and run."
The fifth one says, "I'm ready for some fun."
"Ooo-wee!" said the owl
And out went the light,
And five little pumpkins rolled out of sight.

Barbara Saul, Eureka, CA

Stained Glass Toast

Materials

Milk, ¼ cup (60 ml) for each color
Bowls and spoons
Food coloring
Sliced bread
Pastry brushes
Toaster (adult only)
Butter and plastic knife

What to do

1. Pour ¼ cup (60 ml) of milk into each bowl. Ask the children to mix food coloring into the cups of milk. (Use primary colors.)
2. Give each child a piece of bread.
3. Encourage the children to "paint" their bread with the colored milk using clean pastry brushes. Note what happens when the colors mix together on the bread.
4. Put the bread into the toaster (adult only). For prettier colors, adjust the toaster on the light side.
5. Spread the toast with butter. Eat and enjoy!

Related books

Color Dance by Ann Jonas
Mouse Paint by Ellen Stoll Walsh

❖ Phyllis Esch, Export, PA

Pretzel Kabobs

Materials

Small, thin pretzel sticks
Hot dog slices, apple slices, cheese pieces, and grapes

What to do

1. Help the children place pieces of food on a pretzel stick.
2. Eat the kabobs.

More to do

Encourage the children to discuss and make up their own ideas for kabobs.

Math: The children can practice patterns by putting the foods on the pretzel sticks in a certain order. For example, apple, cheese, apple, cheese, and so on.

Related book

Walter the Baker by Eric Carle

✤ Sandra Nagel, White Lake, MI

Assembly Line Pizza

Materials

Mozzarella cheese
Cheese grater
Bowls
Paper plates
Spoons
English muffins, one for each child
Pizza or spaghetti sauce
Cookie sheets
Oven

What to do

1. Ask children to take turns grating cheese into a bowl.
2. Organize an assembly line of five workers:
    Worker 1 puts a muffin half on a plate.
    Worker 2 spoons sauce on the muffin.
    Worker 3 adds cheese.
    Worker 4 puts the finished pizza on a cookie sheet.
    Worker 5 returns the empty plate to worker 1.
3. After this group makes ten pizza halves, assemble another team of workers to make the next batch of pizzas.
4. Place the cookie sheet into the oven and bake the pizzas at 350° for ten minutes (adult only).
5. Eat the pizzas for lunch or snack.

More to do

Field Trips: List all the parts of a car. Explain to the children that many people work together to assemble a car. Discuss how it takes the work of many people to grow, process, package, deliver, and sell our food and other goods. Visit a local factory or construction site to see people working as a team on a project.

More Field Trips: Visit a farm, packing plant, grocery, or restaurant.

Home Connection: Ask a parent to come in and talk about his or her assembly or construction work.

Related books

Curious George and the Pizza by Margaret Rey
Let's Find Out About Ice Cream by Mary Ebeltoft Reid
The Milk Makers by Gail Gibbons
Stone Soup, any version

❖ Sandra Gratias, Perkasie, PA

Pizza Faces

Materials

English muffin, ½ per child
Paper plates
Tomato or pizza sauce and spoons
Shredded cheese
Pepperoni or hot dog slices, green pepper slices, and olive slices
Cookie sheet
Oven

What to do

1. Give each child ½ of an English muffin on a paper plate.
2. Help the children place three spoonfuls of sauce onto their English muffins.
3. Encourage the children to sprinkle cheese on top of the sauce.
4. The children can choose different items to make a face on their pizzas.
5. Place the pizza faces on a cookie sheet and bake at 350° until the cheese melts (adult only).
6. Eat and enjoy the pizza!

More to do

Encourage the children to suggest other items to put on the pizza. Read a monster story to the children, then make pizzas and call them Pizza Monsters. To keep track of the pizzas, line the cookie sheet with foil and use a permanent marker to print the child's name next to his pizza.

Related book

Pizza Party by Grace Maccaroni

Song

"I'm a Pizza" by Raffi

♣ Sandra Nagel, White Lake, MI

Vegetable People

Materials

Toothpicks
Variety of vegetable chunks such as carrots, celery,
green peppers, mushrooms, and so on

What to do

1. Encourage the children to create their own "people" using vegetable chunks and toothpicks.

Related book

The Very Hungry Caterpillar by Eric Carle

♣ Sandy Scott, Vancouver, WA

Stone Soup

Materials

Stone Soup, any version
Cutting boards
Knives (both table and sharp)
Large pot and ladle
Clean river stone
Can opener
Stove
Serving bowls
Spoons
Crackers

What to do

1. Read Stone Soup to the children.
2. Send a note home to parents describing the activity and requesting that they send in a specific ingredient.
3. Use the following recipe to make the soup. (Alter the recipe to suit the tastes of the children, if desired.)
   1 clean river stone
   2 potatoes
   2 celery sticks
   2 cans of chicken
   2 to 4 cups (480 to 960 ml) water
   2 carrots
   1 small onion
   2 cans of chicken broth
   1 small box of macaroni (pre-cooked)
   Salt and pepper to taste
4. Help the children wash the vegetables.
5. Help the children cut the vegetables into bite-size pieces and then add them to the big pot. Cut the potatoes lengthwise so the children can cut them easily into smaller pieces. Supervise this step closely.
6. Put the river stone into the pot. Encourage the children to add the chicken broth, chicken, and water. (Do not add the macaroni until the soup is ready to serve).
7. Bring the soup to a boil, then simmer for about 30-40 minutes (adult only).
8. Remove the pot from the heat (adult only) and add the macaroni. Let it cool slightly.

9. Pour the soup into bowls and serve it with crackers.

10. While eating, talk about who brought in which ingredient and how important it was to make the soup complete. Discuss the changes in the consistency of the vegetables after cooking. Ask how the soup might have been different. What part did the stone play?

❧ Terri L. Pentz, Melbourne Beach, FL

Vegetable Soup

Materials

Growing Vegetable Soup by Lois Ehlert
Large can of chicken broth
Can opener
Crock-pot
Assorted fresh vegetables (such as carrots, celery, green beans, peas, zucchini)
Vegetable peeler
Small paring knife and cutting board
Ladle
Small pasta
Small bowls and spoons

What to do

1. Read *Growing Vegetable Soup* to the children. Discuss the vegetables mentioned in the story.

2. Help the children wash their hands.

3. Open the can of chicken broth and pour it into the crock-pot.

4. Help the children wash the vegetables and cut them into small pieces, peeling if necessary. Supervise this step closely.

5. Talk about each vegetable as it is added to the soup, noting its texture and color. Stir and heat the soup until the vegetables are tender (approximately three hours depending on the size of the vegetables).

6. Add the pasta ten to fifteen minutes before serving.

7. Let the soup cool before eating. As the children eat their soup, discuss what happened to the vegetables.

More to do

Field Trips: Visit a local vegetable garden to can observe vegetables growing.
More Field Trips: Go to a supermarket to purchase the items needed for the soup.
Math: Add shaped pasta to the soup, such as hearts for Valentine's Day or Christmas trees at Christmas. Make a list and count the number of different kinds of vegetables added to the soup.

Song

I'm a Little Soup Pot (Tune: "I'm a Little Teapot")
I'm a little soup pot, short and wide.
Here is my handle, here is my lid.
When the heat is turned up, I bubble away,
Cooking vegetables
Tender today.

❖ Mary Rozum Anderson, Vermillion, SD

Quesadillas

Materials

Sharp knife (adult only)
Cutting boards
Avocados
Rebus recipe cards
Spoons and forks
Tomatoes (that can be easily cut with a plastic knife)
Plastic knives
Small green onions
Herbs (cilantro or parsley)
Bowls
Variety of grated cheeses (Monterey Jack, mild cheddar, and so on),
   mild salsa, and sour cream
Corn tortillas
Electric skillet (adult only)
Oil
Spatula
Paper plates and napkins

What to do

1. This is a great activity if the children are learning about Mexico. With the children, make quesadillas for snack. When making the snack, make sure to keep the electric skillet and sharp knife out of the reach of children.

2. Help the children wash their hands.

3. To make guacamole filling, cut into the middle of the avocados, cutting completely around the pits (adult only). Twist and pull them apart. Remove the pits and place them on the table for the children to explore. Provide the children with a rebus recipe card with the following steps:
   1. Scoop out the soft green center with a spoon and place it into a bowl.
   2. Mash with a fork.

4. To make tomato salsa filling, core the tomatoes and place them on the cutting board. Provide the children with a rebus recipe card with the following steps:
   1. Chop two tomatoes with a plastic knife and place them into a bowl.
   2. Chop one green onion and add it to the tomatoes.
   3. Chop cilantro or parsley.
   4. Add one spoonful of cilantro or parsley to onions and tomatoes.
   5. Stir.

5. Place each type of cheese (for filling), salsa, and sour cream (for topping) into separate bowls. Add serving spoons to the bowls.

6. Encourage the children to create their own quesadillas by spooning fillings onto a corn tortilla and putting a second tortilla on top.

7. Heat oil in the electric skillet and cook the tortillas (adult only).

8. Remove the quesadillas with a spatula and place them onto paper plates.

9. Encourage the children to top their quesadillas with salsa and sour cream.

10. Eat and enjoy!

More to do

Science: Place one avocado seed in a pan of shallow water and another in a cup of dirt. Observe any signs of growth.

Social Studies: Show the children authentic Mexican clothing, instruments, music, and books.

Related book

The Tortilla Factory or *La Tortilleria* by Gary Paulsen

✤ Ann Gudowski, Johnstown, PA

Easy Rollers

Materials

1 ¼ cups (140 g) crushed graham crackers
¼ cup (60 g) sugar
½ teaspoon (2 g) cinnamon
½ teaspoon (2 g) nutmeg
½ cup (160 g) peanut butter
Mixing bowl and spoon
⅓ cup (80 ml) light corn syrup
Powdered sugar and wax paper
Cookie sheet and refrigerator

What to do

1. Combine crushed graham crackers, sugar, cinnamon, and nutmeg in a bowl.
2. Stir in peanut butter and corn syrup. Mix well.
3. Help the children wash their hands.
4. Show the children how to form the mixture into ½" (1 cm) balls.
5. Pour powdered sugar onto wax paper and encourage the children to roll the balls in it as desired.
6. Place the balls on a cookie sheet and allow them to chill in the refrigerator. (Makes two dozen.)

✤ Sandy L. Scott, Vancouver, WA

Moon Rocks

Materials

1 cup (30 g) crushed cornflakes
½ cup (160 g) peanut butter
2 tablespoons (60 g) honey
Mixing bowl and spoon
Paper plate
Cookie sheet
Refrigerator
Tang, optional

What to do

1. This is a fun snack for the children to make and eat while learning about planets, astronauts, or the phases of the moon.
2. Mix together ½ cup (15 g) cornflakes with peanut butter and honey in a bowl.
3. Pour the remaining cornflakes onto a paper plate.
4. Help the children wash their hands.
5. Encourage the children to shape the mixture into small, round balls and roll them in the cornflakes.
6. Place the balls on a cookie sheet and refrigerate for one hour.
7. Serve with Tang, if desired.

More to do

Discuss real moon rocks. Discuss Apollo 11 and the lunar samples that the astronauts gathered and brought back to Earth.

❧ Dottie Enderle, Richmond, TX

Peanut Butter Ball Monsters

Materials

Small bowls
Measuring cups
Peanut butter
Honey
Granulated sugar
Spoons
Refrigerator
Flour
Wax paper
Mini gumdrops, mini M&M's, and shoestring licorice
Plate

What to do

1. Give each child a small plastic bowl and help him measure and mix one cup (320 g) peanut butter, one cup (360 g) honey, and one cup (250 g) sugar.
2. After the children have mixed the ingredients, place the bowls in the refrigerator for about an hour.
3. After the goop has cooled, help the children wash their hands. Put flour on the children's hands and encourage them to form balls the size of a spoonful and drop them onto wax paper.
4. Encourage the children to add mini M&M eyes, mini gumdrop noses, and licorice antennae to the "monster" heads.
5. Put the monsters on a plate and refrigerate until ready to eat.

❦ Lisa Chichester, Parkersburg, WV

Peanut Butter Playdough

Materials

1 cup (320 g) peanut butter
1 cup (360 g) honey
1 cup (125 g) powdered milk
1 cup (90 g) oatmeal
Measuring cups
Large bowl
Large spoon

What to do

1. Help the children measure and mix peanut butter, honey, powdered milk, and oatmeal in a bowl.
2. Ask each child to get a spoonful of dough to mix, roll, manipulate, and eat.

More to do

Roll the dough in coconut or powdered sugar to make "snowballs."

❖ Sandra Nagel, White Lake, MI

Snowman Straw

Materials

Straws
Marshmallows
M&M's
Licorice, optional
Hot chocolate
Cups

What to do

1. Give each child one straw, three marshmallows, and five M&M's.
2. Help the children stick the marshmallows onto the straw close to the top.
3. Encourage the children to decorate the snowmen with M&M's (two for the eyes and three for the buttons).

4. If desired, tie a piece of licorice between the first and second marshmallow to make a scarf.
5. Stick the snowman into a cup of hot chocolate and slurp away!
6. The children can eat the snowman as desired.

❧ Lisa Chichester, Parkersburg, WV

Marshmallow Snowmen

Materials

Marshmallows, 3 for each child
Toothpicks
Miniature peanut butter cups
Red shoestring licorice
Small tubes of black gel icing

What to do

1. Help each child stick marshmallows on a toothpick to resemble a snowman. Leave some room at the top of the toothpick above the snowman's head.
2. Ask each child to attach a peanut butter cup (wide side down) to the top of the toothpick to resemble a hat.
3. Help the children tie a piece of licorice around their snowman's neck to make a scarf.
4. Encourage the children to use the black gel icing to make eyes, mouth, and buttons on the snowmen.
5. Eat and enjoy!

❧ Lisa Chichester, Parkersburg, WV

Marshmallow Rabbits

Materials

Marshmallows, two for each child
Pink mini marshmallows, four for each child
Black icing in a tube
Scissors
Pink stick gum, two pieces for each child

What to do

1. Help each child stick two marshmallows on a toothpick as shown.
2. Stick mini marshmallows on as shown: one for the tail, two for the cheeks, and one for the nose.
3. Encourage the children to use black icing to make eyes and whiskers.
4. Help the children cut the gum sticks into ear shapes and stick them into the marshmallow bunny's head.

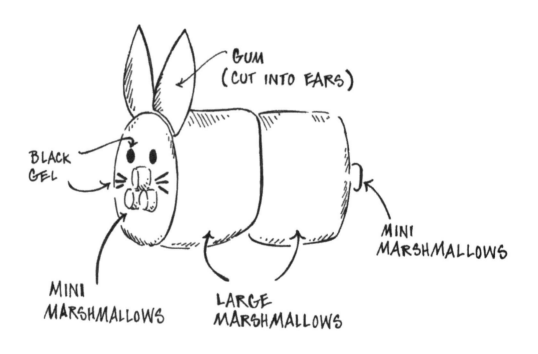

Lisa Chichester, Parkersburg, WV

U.S. Flags

Materials

Pound cake, one slice for each child
Whipped topping
Plastic knife
Strawberry slices
Blueberries

What to do

1. Help the children wash their hands.
2. Give each child a slice of pound cake. Encourage the children to spread whipped topping on the cake.
3. Help the children add blueberries ("stars") and sliced strawberries ("stripes") to resemble the U.S. flag.
4. Eat and enjoy.

More to do

Talk about the U.S. flag, what it represents, and how many stars and stripes are on it.

Sandy L. Scott, Vancouver, WA

Cooking for Easter

Materials

Tubes of refrigerated biscuits
Knife (adult only)
Food coloring
Water
Small bowls
Paintbrushes
Cookie sheet
Oven (adult only)
Green colored coconut

What to do

1. Give two, uncooked biscuits to each child. Cut one of the biscuits in half (adult only).
2. Attach the halved biscuit to the whole biscuit to form ears.
3. Mix food coloring with water in bowls.
4. Encourage the children to use paintbrushes to paint a face on their biscuit bunny.
5. Place the bunnies on a cookie sheet and bake according to the directions on the biscuit tube (adult only).
6. Allow the bunnies to cool and serve with green coconut. Enjoy!

✤ Marilyn Harding, Grimes, IA

Caterpillar Cupcakes

Materials

Unfrosted cupcakes, one for each child
White frosting
Bowls
Green and red food coloring
Spoon
Plastic knife
Assorted small candies

What to do

1. Beforehand, prepare cupcakes and bake them in paper liners (or use prepared cupcakes).
2. Divide the frosting into two bowls.
3. Add green food coloring to one bowl and red food coloring to the other.
4. Frost one cupcake with red frosting. Spread green frosting on all of the other cupcakes.
5. Place the cupcakes in an S-shaped formation with the red cupcake as the head.
6. Encourage the children to decorate the caterpillar using assorted candies. They can add eyes, legs, and other "caterpillar" features.
7. Eat the "caterpillar!"

Related books

The Caterpillow Fight by Sam McBratney
The Very Hungry Caterpillar by Eric Carle

❖ Charlene Woodham Peace, Semmes, AL

Dirt Cake

Materials

Pudding
Bowl
Refrigerator
Whipped topping
Small marshmallows
Gummy worms
Chocolate sandwich cookies
Small silk flower bouquet
Flowerpot (new)
Spade (new)
Paper plates and spoons

What to do

1. Mix pudding in a bowl according to the directions on the box. Place it in the refrigerator to chill and set.
2. Layer pudding, whipped topping, marshmallows, and gummy worms in the flowerpot.
3. Crush the chocolate cookies and place the crumbs on the surface of the flowerpot.
4. Place flowers in the center of the pot.
5. Refrigerate until ready to serve.
6. Serve with a spade.

Related book

Counting Wildflowers by Bruce McMillan

❖ Charlene Woodham Peace, Semmes, AL

Traffic Lights

Materials

Graham crackers
Plastic knives
Peanut butter
Red, yellow, and green M&M's

What to do

1. This is a great snack to make when discussing traffic safety.
2. Split graham crackers in half.
3. Encourage the children to spread peanut butter on the graham crackers with a plastic knife.
4. Ask the children to put a red M&M on top, a yellow M&M in the middle, and a green M&M on the bottom.
5. Enjoy a yummy traffic light treat.

❧ Lisa Chichester, Parkersburg, WV

Cool Pool Slushy

Materials

Clear plastic cups
Black marker
Assorted gummy fish
Berry blue juice
No-spill plastic pitcher
Freezer
Plastic spoons

What to do

1. Give each child a cup and help him write his name on it.
2. Ask the children to place three gummy fish into their cups.
3. Help the children pour juice into their cups.

4. Place the cups in the freezer for approximately four hours or until frozen.

5. Give the children a spoon and their cup.

6. Enjoy a cool treat!

❧ Quazonia J. Quarles, Newark, DE

Trail Mix

Materials

Rebus recipe cards
Measuring cups
Trail mix ingredients (see recipe below)
Large bowl
Mixing spoon
Zipper closure plastic bags

What to do

1. Make a rebus recipe card with the following recipe:

In a large bowl, add the following ingredients:

    1 cup (125 g) crushed walnuts
    1 cup (125 g) almonds
    1 cup (160 g) raisins
    1 cup (160 g) golden raisins
    1 cup pretzel nubs
    1 cup (160 g) dried cranberries
    1 cup (125 g) sunflower seeds
    1 cup (30 g) mini marshmallows

2. Mix the ingredients together with a spoon.

3. Put a cup of trail mix into each zipper closure bag. Make a bag for each child.

4. Take the bags and go on a nature walk. Eat along the way or stop at a nice location to rest and eat.

More to do

On the return trip, use the empty bags to gather nature items to explore in the Science Center or use for a creative art project.

Related book

I Took a Walk by Henry Cole

♣ Ann Gudowski, Johnstown, PA

Creepy Bats

Materials

3 packages grape flavor gelatin
1 package orange flavor gelatin
Large bowl and mixing spoon
2 ½ cups (600 ml) boiling water (adult only)
13" x 9" (32 cm x 22 cm) pan
Refrigerator
Bat-shaped cookie cutter

What to do

1. Empty the gelatin packets into a large bowl.
2. Pour boiling water (adult only) into the bowl. Stir for three minutes or until the gelatin is completely dissolved. (Do not add cold water.)
3. Help the children pour the gelatin into a 13" x 9" (32 cm x 22 cm) pan.
4. Refrigerate for at least 3 hours or until firm.
5. Remove the pan from the refrigerator and dip the bottom of the pan in warm water for about 15 seconds.
6. Cut the gelatin into bat shapes using a bat-shaped cookie cutter. Make sure to cut all the way through the gelatin.
7. Remove the bats from pan. Eat and enjoy!

More to do

Cut out bats from construction paper. Hang them from the classroom ceiling.

Related book

Stellaluna by Janell Cannon

❖ Jackie Wright, Enid, OK

Yummy Pond

Materials

Blue gelatin
Boiling water (adult only)
Mixing spoon
Bowl

Pan

Swedish fish

Refrigerator

Gummy frogs

Blunt knife

What to do

1. Help the children wash their hands.
2. Pour boiling water into a bowl of powdered blue gelatin according to the directions on the box (adult only).
3. Pour the liquid gelatin into a pan and add Swedish fish.
4. Chill the gelatin in the refrigerator for about three hours or until firm.
5. Remove the gelatin from the refrigerator and place gummy frogs on top.
6. Cut out squares and serve to the children.

More to do

Obtain a frog hatchery kit. Place magnifiers near the aquarium so the children can observe the eggs up close. Encourage the children to draw what they see daily.

Related book

Pond Year by Kathryn Lasky

❖ Quazonia J. Quarles, Newark, DE

Gator Swamp Cups

Materials

Blue gelatin

Pitcher with no-spill lid

Small disposable dessert cups

Black marker

Cookie sheet

Refrigerator

Plastic spoons

Chocolate pudding (prepared beforehand)

Medium-size plastic bowl

Tablespoon

Gummy alligators

What to do

1. Help the children wash their hands.
2. Prepare the gelatin by following the directions on the back of the box.
3. Pour the liquid gelatin into a pitcher with a no-spill lid.
4. Give each child a dessert cup. Help the children write their names on their cups.
5. Using a marker, mark each cup to the half point and help the children fill their cups half full with gelatin.
6. Place the dessert cups on a cookie sheet and put it in the refrigerator.
7. When the gelatin is ready to serve, give the children their dessert cups and plastic spoons.
8. Place pudding (prepared beforehand) in a plastic bowl.
9. Show the children how to use a tablespoon to spoon pudding on top of the gelatin.
10. Encourage the children to add a gator on top of the pudding.

More to do

Field Trips: Go to the zoo and visit the alligators. Compare the differences between alligators and crocodiles.

Related books

All About Alligators by Jim Arnosky
Alligator Shoes by Arthur Dorros
Alligators All Around by Maurice Sendak
The Lady with the Alligator Purse by Nadine Bernard Westcott
There's an Alligator Under My Bed by Mercer Mayer

❧ Quazonia J. Quarles, Newark, DE

Jellyfish

Materials

12 ounces (360 ml) 100% juice concentrate
Measuring cup
3 envelopes of unflavored gelatin
Water
Saucepan
Hot plate or stove

Mixing spoon

Spray oil

Small bowls

Masking tape and markers

Ladle

Refrigerator

String licorice, 2 pieces for each child

Scissors

What to do

1. Pour half of the juice concentrate (6 oz.) into a measuring cup.
2. Add 3 envelopes of unflavored gelatin to the juice.
3. Pour 1 ½ cups (360 ml) water into a saucepan and boil it on a hot plate or stove (adult only). Add it to the gelatin and juice.
4. Stir the mixture until the gelatin dissolves.
5. Add the rest of the juice concentrate and 1 ½ cup (360 ml) cold water.
6. Spray small bowls with spray oil and give one to each child. Put a piece of masking tape on each bowl and help the children write their names on it.
7. Encourage the children to ladle the gelatin mixture into their bowls.
8. Place the bowls in the refrigerator.
9. While the gelatin is chilling, help the children cut their licorice pieces into thirds.
10. When the gelatin is firm (but not too firm), remove the bowls from the refrigerator and give them to the children.
11. Encourage the children to stick their licorice pieces into the gelatin, making sure half of each piece is sticking out.
12. Put the gelatin into refrigerator to finish firming.
13. Take the gelatin out of the bowls. Turn them upside down so the licorice is hanging down. Jellyfish!

More to do

Make Balloon Jellyfish. Put flour into a balloon. Tie the end and squeeze it gently to watch it move.

❦ Darleen A. Schaible, Stroudsburg, PA

No-Bake Chocolate Cookies

Materials

2 cups (500 g) sugar

½ cup (120 ml) milk

½ cup (250 g) margarine

3 ½ tablespoons (35 g) cocoa

Mixing spoon

Medium saucepan

Hot plate or stove

½ cup (160 g) peanut butter

4 cups (500 g) granola

1 cup (125 g) chopped walnuts

1 teaspoon (5 ml) vanilla

Teaspoon

Wax paper

What to do

1. Help the children mix together sugar, milk, margarine, and cocoa in a saucepan.
2. Put the saucepan on a hot plate or stove and bring it to a boil for one minute (adult only).
3. Quickly stir in the peanut butter until it is melted.
4. Add granola, walnuts, and vanilla and mix well.
5. Drop the dough by teaspoonfuls onto wax paper.
6. Allow the cookies to cool before eating. (Makes about four dozen.)

❖ Sandy L. Scott, Vancouver, WA

Fluffy Bunny Cookies

Materials

Wax paper

Vanilla wafer cookies

Plastic knives and spoons

Tub of vanilla frosting

Fruit roll-ups
Mini chocolate chips
Thin black licorice

What to do

1. Help the children wash their hands.
2. Give each child a square of wax paper to use as a work surface.
3. Give each child a vanilla wafer, a spoon, and a knife.
4. Pass around the tub of frosting and ask the children to scoop a spoonful onto their wafer and spread it with their knife.
5. Give each child ½ of a fruit roll-up. Encourage them to use their plastic knives to cut out bunny ears. (If cutting is too difficult, they can tear the roll-up.) Ask the children to place the ears where they think a bunny's ears would be.
6. Encourage each child to count out three chocolate chips and use them for the bunny's eyes and nose.
7. Give each child a licorice stick. Help the children cut off pieces of it to use for whiskers.
8. Nibble away on your bunny snacks!

❧ Constance Heagerty, Westborough, MA

Cooking with Shapes

Materials

Word Bird's Shapes by Jane Belk Moncure
Cookie cutters in the following shapes: rectangle, square, circle, and triangle
Sugar cookie dough
Clean, flat surface
Rolling pin
Cookie sheet
Oven

What to do

1. Read *Word Bird's Shapes* to the children. Discuss the different shapes shown in the book.
2. Hold up each of the cookie cutters and ask the children to identify the different shapes.
3. Place the sugar cookie dough on a clean, flat surface and roll it out.

4. Encourage the children to use the different shaped cookie cutters to cut out different shapes.

5. Place the cookie shapes on a cookie sheet and put it in the oven (adult only). Bake the cookies as directed on the package or recipe.

6. Allow the cookies to cool. As the children eat the cookies for snack, discuss the shapes that they made.

More to do

Art: Dip cookie cutters into tempera paint and make print shapes on a piece of paper.

Math: Discuss the different shapes found in nature. Take the children on a walk and identify the different shapes they see. For example, round bushes, triangle shaped trees, square hedges, and any other shapes the children discover.

Related books

Shapes, Shapes, Shapes by Tana Hoban
Spot Looks at Shapes by Eric Hill
Word Bird's Shapes: Word Bird Library by Jane Belk Moncure

❖ Mary Rozum Anderson, Vermillion, SD

Paintbrush Decorating Cookies

Materials

Clean, flat surface
Sugar cookie dough
Rolling pin
Circular cookie cutter
Cookie sheet
4 egg yolks
4 small bowls or butter dishes
Food coloring
1 teaspoon (5 ml) water
New, clean paintbrushes
Oven

What to do

1. Place the cookie dough on a clean, flat surface and roll it out.
2. Help the children cut out cookies using a circular cookie cutter. Place them on a cookie sheet.
3. Put one egg yolk into each of the four bowls. Add ¼ teaspoon (1 ml) water and food coloring to each bowl.
4. Paint the cookies with the egg mixture. (If the egg mixture becomes thick, add a few drops of water.) Use a different paintbrush for each color.
5. Place the cookie sheet into the oven (adult only). Bake the cookies according to the recipe.

More to do

This is a great activity for unit themes or special occasions. Use homemade or store-bought dough and various cookie cutter shapes.

Related book

Case of the Missing Cookies by Denise Lewis Patrick

Song

"Who Took the Cookie From the Cookie Jar?"

Sandra Nagel, White Lake, MI

Colorful Cookie Caterpillar

Materials

½ cup (125 g) margarine
½ cup (75 g) powdered sugar
¾ teaspoon (4 ml) vanilla
1 cup (125 g) flour
8 bowls
Food coloring
Fork
Cookie sheet
Oven

What to do

1. Make butter cookies using this simple recipe:
   Combine ½ cup margarine (softened), ½ cup powdered sugar, ¾ teaspoon vanilla, and 1 cup flour. If it is very soft, refrigerate for one hour.

2. Divide the dough into eight equal parts. Place each part into a separate bowl and give one to each child.

3. Encourage the children to choose a food color and add two drops to one of the eight parts of dough. Mix it with a fork.

4. Ask the children to divide their portion into four pieces and roll each piece into a ball.

5. Encourage the children to place each ball in a "caterpillar" row on an ungreased cookie sheet. Slightly flatten each ball. The children may make an individual caterpillar or contribute their balls to make a multi-colored group caterpillar.

6. Put the cookie sheet in the oven and bake at 350° for ten minutes (adult only).

7. Allow the cookies to set for two to three minutes after removing them from the oven.

🍀 Eileen Bayer, Tempe, AZ

Oatmeal Refrigerator Cookies

Materials

Mixing bowl
Hand or electric mixer
1 cup (250 g) shortening
1 cup (170 g) brown sugar
1 cup (250 g) white sugar
3 beaten eggs
1 teaspoon (5 ml) vanilla
1 ½ cup (190 g) flour
Sifter
1 teaspoon (7 g) salt
1 teaspoon (5 g) baking soda
1 teaspoon (5 g) cinnamon
3 cups (270 g) quick cooking oatmeal
1 cup (160 g) raisins
¾ cup (70 g) coconut
Wax paper
Refrigerator
Blunt knife
Cookie sheet
Oven

What to do

1. Cream shortening, brown sugar, and white sugar in a large mixing bowl until it is light and fluffy.
2. Mix in the vanilla and eggs.
3. Sift flour with salt, baking soda, and cinnamon. Add it to the mixture.
4. Mix in oatmeal, raisins, and coconut.
5. Form the dough into two long rolls and place them on a piece of wax paper.
6. Place the dough in the refrigerator and let it chill overnight.
7. The next day, cut the dough into ¼" (1 mm) thick slices and place them on a cookie sheet.
8. Place the cookie sheet in the oven and bake at 350° for 10 minutes (adult only).

Related book

If You Give a Mouse a Cookie by Laura Joffe Numeroff

Jackie Wright, Enid, OK

Opposites Muffins

Materials

Large bowl
Long handled spoon
1 egg
⅓ cup (170 g) sugar
1 ¼ cups (300 ml) milk
⅓ cup (80 ml) oil
1 cup (125 g) flour
4 teaspoons (60 g) baking powder
1 cup (125 g) wheat germ
Muffin tin and muffin cup papers
Oven
Sink or tub of water, dishwashing soap, and dishcloth

What to do

1. Beat together the egg, sugar, milk, and oil in a large bowl.
2. Mix in flour and baking powder. Stir in the wheat germ.
3. Line a muffin pan with muffin papers and fill each muffin cup ⅔ full.
4. Put the muffin pan in the oven and bake at 425° for 20 minutes (adult only). (Recipe makes twelve muffins.)
5. Follow the recipe and encourage the children to take turns measuring, pouring, and mixing. Encourage the children to feel and examine the ingredients as they work.
6. While making the muffins, talk about opposites such as wet/dry, smooth/rough, empty/full, fast/slow (mixing), raw/cooked, hot/cold, in/out (egg), big/little (cups and spoons).
7. While muffins bake, wash all the tools. Again, talk about opposites (for example, wet/dry and clean/dirty).

More to do

Art: Assemble a collection of big and little pairs of matching objects, such as measuring cups, blocks, pencils, jar lids, gift boxes, and so on. Give each child a piece of 12" x 18" (30 cm x 45 cm) paper and a piece of 9" x 11" (22 cm x 27 cm) paper. Encourage the children to dip the objects into shallow pans of paint and make prints of the big object on the big paper and the matching small object on the small paper.

Movement: Encourage the children to clap the opposite of loud, jump the opposite of high, walk the opposite of slow, and so on.

Related books

Opposites by Monique Felix
Paddington's Opposites by Michael Bond
Tops and Bottoms by Janet Stevens
Winnie the Pooh's Opposites by A.A. Milne

❧ Sandra Gratias, Perkasie, PA

Pancakes!

Materials

Real wheat stalks (from a farm or farmer's market) or
    homemade cardboard wheat stalks
Flowerpot
Plush toy chicken
Four eggs
Plush toy or homemade cardboard cow
Container of whipping cream
Jelly or jam
Pancakes! Pancakes! by Eric Carle
Safety scissors
Bag of flour
Small containers with tight fitting lids
Mixing bowl and spoon
Electric griddle with "cool touch" sides (adult only)
Masking tape, optional
Nonstick skillet
Ladle

Spatula
Paper plates and forks

What to do

1. Without the children, "plant" the wheat stalks in a flowerpot and put it on the playground. Place the plush toy chicken in a protected area of the playground and put four eggs under it. In yet another part of the playground, place the plush toy or cardboard cow and put a container of whipping cream under it. In the classroom, hide a jar of jam in a low cupboard.

2. Read *Pancakes! Pancakes! to the children.*

3. Ask the children if they like pancakes. Tell the children that they will be making pancakes and ask them if they can remember the ingredients.

4. Begin reading the story again. When you get to the part where Jack has to cut the wheat, take the children (and the book) out to the playground and ask them to search for wheat. When a child finds the flowerpot, use safety scissors to "harvest" the wheat. Give it to one child to carry.

5. Continue reading the story. When you get to the part where Jack gives the wheat to the man at the mill, ask the child who is carrying the wheat to give it to an adult helper who is inside the classroom. This person can promise to "thresh the wheat" and have a bag of flour ready when they get back.

6. Continue to read the story. Ask the children to search for the chicken and carefully gather the eggs she has "laid."

7. Continue to read the story. Ask the children to search for the cow. Pretend to be amazed that the milk is already in a carton ready for you to take.

8. Head back to the classroom as you continue to read the story. By now, the helper will be done "threshing the wheat" and will have a nice bag of flour ready when the children enter.

9. At the part of the story where Jack goes to the cellar to get the jam, encourage the children to search in the low cupboards until someone discovers the jam.

10. Pour the whipping cream into small containers with tight lids. Give them to two or three children and show them how to shake the container to make butter.

11. Assemble the tools, naming each item as you set it on the table.

12. Follow the recipe in the book as closely as you can. Mix together the ingredients in a bowl. Make sure each child has a chance to stir, mix, or add ingredients.

13. Heat the electric griddle (adult only). Make sure the children stay away from it. If desired, put a line of masking tape on the floor to mark a "no walking" zone.

Note: In the book, Jack's mother put butter on the hot skillet; however, you should NOT do this as it will splatter when the pancake mixture is added and could possibly burn a child. Instead, put the butter on the table so the children may put it on their pancakes when they eat.

14. Help each child put a ladle full of pancake mixture onto the hot skillet. Ask the children to stand behind the masking tape line until the pancake is done. Flip the pancake using a spatula. Talk about the pancake as it cooks. Make observations about how the heat causes the pancake to change.

15. When the pancake is done, help the child put it on a paper plate.

16. Help the children put jam or butter on their pancakes. Eat and enjoy.

Note: If you do not have the prep time or resources to do the make-believe scenes, just buy the various ingredients and do the activity. Keep them nearby and when you review the story, put the ingredients on a table as they are mentioned.

More to do

Field Trips: Go on a field trip to a local farm. Some zoos have working farms as part of their permanent displays. Call your local zoo to find out.

❖ Virginia Jean Herrod, Columbia, SC

Edible Castles

Materials

Small candy, such as gum drops, M&M's, peppermints, and so on
Candy sprinkles
Cake decorations
Licorice
Fruit snacks
Plastic bowls
Spoons
Small cups
White icing
Plastic butter knives
Styrofoam plates
Marker
Cupcakes, one for each child
Ice cream cones
Plastic wrap

What to do

1. Put candy, sprinkles, cake decorations, licorice, and fruit snacks into separate bowls on one table. Put spoons into each bowl.
2. Put icing into cups and place three or four cups at each table. Put two knives next to each cup.
3. Ask the children to sit at the tables. This is a good time to go over safety rules about knives. In addition, set some ground rules. For example, ask the children to take only a few of each item—they can always come back for more after everyone else is done.
4. Give each child a Styrofoam plate. Help the children write their names on the bottom of their plates.
5. Give each child a cupcake and an ice cream cone. Explain that they are going to decorate their plates, cones, and cupcakes with the goodies.
6. Ask three or four children to select the candy and fruit snacks that they want. Give the children cups to put their goodies in as they come up to the table.
7. Encourage the children to make castles with their goodies.
8. Wrap the castles in plastic wrap so the children can bring them home.

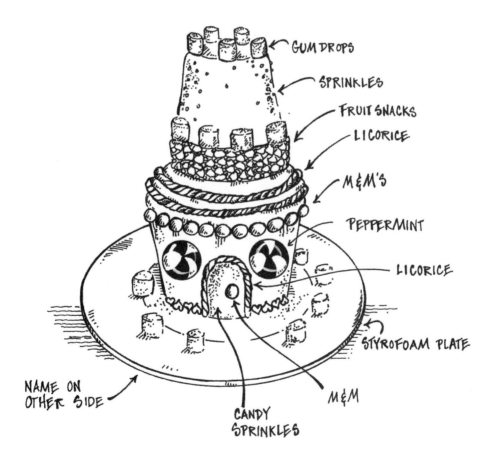

GUM DROPS
SPRINKLES
FRUIT SNACKS
LICORICE
M&M'S
PEPPERMINT
LICORICE
STYROFOAM PLATE
NAME ON OTHER SIDE
CANDY SPRINKLES
M&M

More to do

Art: Make crowns and act like kings and queens.

Math: Make a chart of who used gumdrops, M&M's, peppermints, and so on.

Music and Movement: Dance to medieval music.

❖ Darleen A. Schaible, Stroudsburg, PA

"I Can" Quilt

Materials

Magazines or advertisements
Scissors
Construction paper
Glue
Crayons or markers
Butcher paper

What to do

1. Beforehand, cut out pictures from magazines or advertisements that represent things the children can do. For example, cut out a picture of a bedspread to represent the child's being able to make her bed. Other examples are pictures of bicycles, jump ropes, and so on.

2. Encourage the children to choose pictures that represent some of the things they are able to do.

3. Help the children glue their pictures on construction paper to make a collage. Or, they can draw their own pictures using crayons or markers.

4. When the children are finished, ask them to dictate why they chose their pictures as you write their words on the paper.

5. Arrange and glue the children's pictures on a large sheet of butcher paper to make a paper quilt. If desired, cut the construction paper into squares for easy quilt assembly. Or, simply arrange the paper rectangles on the butcher paper. (Some children may turn their paper, so the papers might not all be same size.) When arranging odd-shaped papers, let some of the butcher paper show through.

More to do

Work on building the children's self-esteem. Acknowledge what the children are able to do by themselves. And remember to never compare the abilities of the children.

Related book

All By Myself by Aliki

Phyllis Esch, Export, PA

Be a Help-O-Saurus

Materials

Chart paper with "Help-O-Saurus" printed at the top
Markers

What to do

1. Explain to the children that they are going to look for people ("dinosaurs") that are helpful to others. Tell them that they will call a helpful person a "Help-O-Saurus."
2. Demonstrate this idea by pointing out when someone is being helpful to another. By the end of the week, children will be able to find people being a Help-O-Saurus.
3. Use a chart to write down the names of the helpers, who they helped, and how they were a Help-O-Saurus.

More to do

The children can state when they have been helpful to someone or someone has helped them. Make paper dinosaurs and tell the children to bring one to an adult whenever someone helps them. This way, an adult can record the event immediately before it is forgotten. Review the helpful events at the end of the day. Send home the dinosaur helper paper with the Help-O-Saurus.

Related books

If the Dinosaurs Came Back by Bernard Most
Magic School Bus in the Time of the Dinosaurs by Joanne Cole

❖ Sandra Nagel, White Lake, MI

My Turn Next!

Materials

Index cards
Markers

What to do

1. Sharing is hard for everyone, but we do expect four-year-olds to share as part of their social development.
2. On an index card, write "My Turn Next."
3. Explain to the children that if they are waiting for a desired toy or activity, they can hold the card. Then, when the child who is using the toy or playing in the center is done, the child with the card gets the next turn. She can give the card to another child. For example, three children can play at the water table. But if a fourth child really wants to join, you can restate the rule that only three can play, but offer her the "My Turn Next" card.
4. Depending on the situation and child, you can wait for the natural time to trade, or set a bell.

Related books

One of Each by Maryann Hoberman
Pumpkin Soup by Helen Cooper
The Rainbow Fish by Marcus Pfister
We Share Everything by Robert Munsch

Song

"The More We Get Together"

❖ Traci O'Hara, Charlotte, NC

Happy/Sad Puppets

Materials

Paper plates
Stapler
Markers
Collage materials and glue

What to do

1. Staple two paper plates together, leaving enough space for a child's hand to slip between the two plates.
2. On one side of the plate, children can draw or use collage materials to make a happy face. On the other side, they can draw a sad face (or any emotion).

3. On the plate or on a separate piece of paper, help the children write what makes them happy, sad, angry, excited, and so on.

4. The child can flip her hand around as she talks about the different emotions.

Related book

Glad Monster, Sad Monster by Ed Emberley

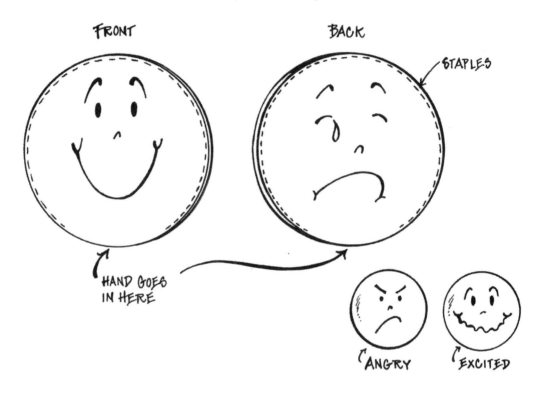

FRONT   BACK

STAPLES

HAND GOES IN HERE

ANGRY   EXCITED

❦ Audrey F. Kanoff, Allentown, PA

Puppet Play

Materials

Puppets

What to do

1. To create a positive atmosphere in the classroom, help the children learn good responses to negative situations.

2. Using puppets, act out situations where one of the puppets "gets into trouble."

For example:

Puppet 1: She took my car.

Teacher: How can we settle this?

Puppet 2, 3, 4: (They offer suggestions.)

or

Puppet 1: He pushed me.

Teacher: What happened and how could we have acted differently?

Puppets 2, 3, 4: (They offer suggestions.)

Teacher Tip: Speak positively and praise children when they are doing things correctly instead of calling attention to what they are doing incorrectly. Use a soft voice so they need to listen to hear you.

❧ Marilyn Harding, Grimes, IA

Sharing Friendship

Materials

The Friendship Tree by Kathy Caple
Scissors
Chart paper
Marker

What to do

1. Read *The Friendship Tree* by Kathy Caple with the children. The book has four chapters, so you might want to read a chapter a day.
2. After reading the book, discuss the many ways we can show we care for others. Talk about simple things such as letting others have a turn, sharing art supplies, including others in our play, reading with a friend, caring for pets and plants, cleaning up after ourselves, and helping others clean up. Encourage them to talk about people they care about, too.
3. Cut out a large heart shape from chart paper.
4. On the heart, write down the children's suggestions for ways to show caring.

More to do

Art: Provide a variety of art materials. Pair the children and encourage each child in the pair to make something for the other. Ask each child to show her item at group time and present it to the other child in her pair.

Snack: A Shared Snack: Provide tablespoons, quart-size plastic bags, and bowls of small snack items such as raisins, different cereals, and sunflower seeds. Ask two children to take turns putting a spoonful of each item into one bag. Then, ask them to close the bag and take turns shaking it to mix the ingredients. Give both children a small paper cup and ask them to pour half of the mix into each cup. Now they can sit together and enjoy eating their "shared snack."

Related book

George and Martha by James Marshall

❖ Barbara F. Backer, Charleston, SC

Teacup Invite

Materials

Teacup shapes (see pattern)
Construction paper
Scissors
Glue stick
Pouch piece
Marker

What to do

1. Cut out teacup shapes from construction paper using the teacup pattern. Make two teacups for each child.
2. Give each child two teacup shapes and help her glue together the handles of the two shapes.
3. Help the child glue the pouch piece onto the back of the front

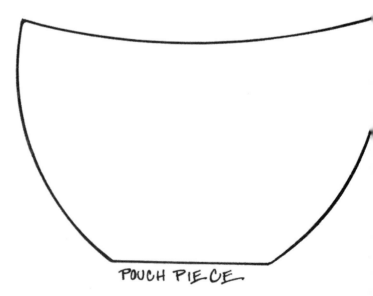

POUCH PIECE

teacup so that the pouch is on the inside of the cup. Be sure to only glue the side and bottom edges of the pouch.

4. With the children, decide what to write on the front and inside of the invitations. Print the words, and when appropriate, the child can print her name.

More to do

Host a parent-child tea party or a tea for bus drivers. Invite family members, friends, or grandparents.

Related books

The Doll's Tea Party by M.C. Leeka
I'm a Little Tea Pot by Iza Trapani
Miss Spider's Tea Party by David Kirk
Tea for Two by Kari James

❧ Sandra Nagel, White Lake, MI

Tea Party

Materials

Tablecloth
"Fancy" cups and saucers
Centerpiece, optional
Mild tea (mint or chamomile)
Teapot

What to do

1. Work with a small group of children. Assign or ask children to choose roles beforehand. Some children will be the hosts/hostesses and the others will be guests.
2. Encourage the hosts/hostesses to arrange the table using a tablecloth, "fancy" cups and saucers, and a centerpiece (if possible). These children will serve the guests.
3. Help the hosts/hostesses make tea in a teapot.
4. Tell the children that they are required to use their best manners. For example, they must say, "please," "thank you," and "no thank you."
5. After cleanup, they can change roles. Hosts/hostesses can become guests, and guests can become hosts/hostesses.

More to do

Encourage the children to use good manners at snack time as well.

Related books

Mrs. Giggleberry Is Coming for Tea by Donna Guthrie
What Do You Say, Dear? by Sesyle Joslin

❖ Sharon Dempsey, May's Landing, NJ

Puzzle Pads

Materials

One puzzle for every two children
Paper
Markers
Scissors

What to do

1. Have a discussion with the children about cooperation. Ask them to tell you what it means.
2. Divide the children into pairs.
3. Give each pair a puzzle and an area on the floor to work.
4. Encourage the children to work together. Remind them about cooperating, sharing, and problem solving.
5. To extend the activity, give the pairs paper, markers, and scissors and ask them to create their own puzzles!
6. Encourage the pairs of children to take turns showing and telling the rest of the children about their project or puzzle.

Patricia Cawthorne, Lynchburg, VA

Signs of Cooperation

Materials

Liquid starch
Water
Paint cups
Several 1" (2 cm) flat-tip paintbrushes
Tissue paper in a variety of colors
Permanent black marker
Large sheets of paper (as large as space allows, approximately 2' x 2' (60 cm x 60 cm))
Scissors
Tape

What to do

1. Pour liquid starch and water into the paint cups (three parts starch to one part water).

2. Place the cups, paintbrushes, and tissue paper on a table or floor.

3. Explain to the children that they need a sign to mark their classroom door. Help them develop inviting words to put outside their door, such as "welcome" or "come on in."

4. Using a black marker, write the words in huge block letters on the large paper. Write only one letter on each sheet.

5. Demonstrate the technique using one of the letters.

6. Show them how to paint inside the lines with starch. Then, place a torn piece of tissue paper on the starch and paint over it with more starch. This gives the letter a look of decoupage.

7. Divide the children into small groups. Give one letter to each group to work on together.

8. Allow the letters to dry. Draw over the outlines with the black marker, if necessary.

9. Cut out the letters.

10. Ask the children for help as you tape the inviting sign outside the classroom.

LARGE SHEETS OF PAPER

BLOCK LETTERING

TORN TISSUE PAPER

FLAT TIP BRUSH

PAINT CUP WITH LIQUID STARCH

CUT OUT LETTER (WITH TISSUE PAPER AND BLACK OUTLINE)

More to do

Encourage the small groups of children to decide what color to make their letter.

Related book

I Like Being Me: Poems for Children, About Feeling Special, Appreciating Others, and Getting Along by Judy Lalli

❖ Ann Gudowski, Johnstown, PA

Family Night Program: Theme "Me"

Materials

Cardboard, cut to postcard size
Markers or colored pens
Stamps
Large paper plates
Yarn or string
Crepe paper
Glue
Paper from roll
Paper dolls
Names of children on stickers
Lamp
White paper
Pencil
Scissors
Black construction paper
Sugar cookie ingredients

What to do

1. Make postcards with the children. Ask each child to draw a picture of herself and sign her name. Write the children's addresses on their postcards and put stamps on them. With the children, bring the postcards to a post office and

mail them. Then, take a tour of the post office.

2. Encourage the children to make pictures of themselves by decorating paper plates using yarn, crepe paper, and markers.

3. Cover a table with paper from a large paper roll. Encourage the children to draw on the paper using crayons and markers. Sing songs about "Me" and "Family."

4. Help the children make nametags using paper dolls. Encourage them to use markers to draw clothes and faces. When they are finished, place stickers with the child's name on the doll. Hang the tags around everyone's neck using yarn or string.

5. Draw a portrait of each child. Attach a piece of white paper to a wall. Ask the child to sit in front of the paper, so you can see her profile. Position a lamp so that the shadow of her profile is on the paper. Trace the child's profile using a pencil. Help the child cut out her profile from the paper and glue it to a piece of black construction paper. Ask her to sign her name.

6. Make "people cookies" using a simple sugar cookie recipe. Help the children decorate the cookies to look like people using frosting, candy, and dried fruit.

7. To finish the "Me" theme, make yearbooks. Write on the covers, "From the top of my head to the tip of my toes, I am special!"

CARDBOARD CUT TO POSTCARD SIZE

CHILD'S PICTURE

CHILD'S NAME

NAME, ADDRESS and STAMP ON OTHER SIDE

❀ Marilyn Harding, Grimes, IA

Marvelous Me

Materials

Tie-dye strings (strings with tie dye solution on them—find them at craft stores)
T-shirts with a pocket, one for each child
Fabric paint pen in any color

What to do

1. Send a questionnaire home with each child asking the parents to help their child describe five or six things she can do at home. For example, "I can ride my two wheeler, I can help set the table, I can give my dog a bath," and so on. Ask them to decide both things the child does to help and things the child enjoys doing.
2. Give each child a piece of tie-dye string and a T-shirt. Show them how to bunch up the T-shirt and wrap the string around it.
3. Follow the directions on the tie-dye string package to create a tie-dye pattern. Help children with the actual tying part, but encourage them to make the designs on their own. Allow the shirts to dry completely.
4. Using a fabric paint pen, write "Marvelous Me" on the edge of the T-shirt pocket. For a splashier design, write "Marvelous Me" diagonally across the front of the shirt.
5. On the back of the shirt, write in large type, "I can..." Underneath that, in smaller print, list three of the things the children can do from their list. (To protect the front of the shirt from the pen bleeding through, place a grocery bag inside the shirt before writing on it.)
6. Encourage the children to wear their shirts with pride!

Note: Remember never to print the child's name on any visible place on the shirt.

More to do

Find things around the classroom that the children are able to do. Notice what the children are able to accomplish on their own. Make a big deal about small things. For example, "Wow, Clark, you sure can put your shoes on fast!"
When the children respond to a request with "I can't...", encourage them to say "I can try..." instead. Stay with them as they attempt to accomplish the task. Offer lots of praise and encouragement. Be ready to step in and help out if needed.

Literacy: Make a class book. Ask the children to illustrate a page on which you can print their "I can..." items from their list.

Related book

Little Miss Star by Roger Hargreaves

Song

I Can Try! (Tune: "This Old Man")
I can try!
I can try!
If I'm not sure I can do it, I can try.
I can try to tie my shoe.
You never know what I can do!
(Substitute anything the child is trying to accomplish for the italicized part.)

❖ Virginia Jean Herrod, Columbia, SC

Have Fun in Korea

Materials

Map (mark the United States and Korea with a marker)
Pictures and other items about Korea (chopsticks, bowl, etc.)
Books about Korean folktales (see below)
Chalk

What to do

1. Before the children arrive, decorate the room with a map, a flag of Korea, pictures and traditional objects from Korea, and books of Korean folktales.
2. Talk about the location of the United States with the children by showing them the map. Explain to the children that if they traveled for a long time, they would arrive in a country called Korea. Show them Korea on the map.
3. Explain to the children that just like we have our songs and play, Korean children also have their own songs and play.
4. Count with the children in Korean.
    1 – il
    2 – yee
    3 – sam
    4 – sa
    5 – oh
    6 – yuk

7 – chil

8 – pal

9 – gu

10 – ship

5. Draw a Korean-style hopscotch board and an American-style hopscotch board.

Related books

The Green Frogs: Korean Folktale by Yumi Heo

Magic Spring: Korean Folktale by Nami Rhee

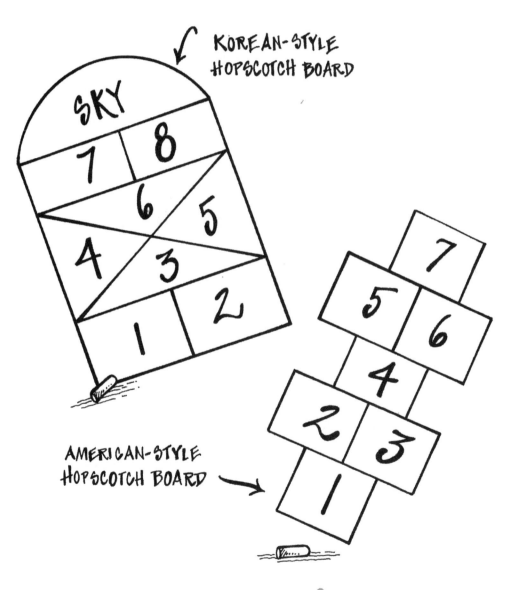

KOREAN-STYLE HOPSCOTCH BOARD

AMERICAN-STYLE HOPSCOTCH BOARD

✿ DooHyun Shin, Lakewood, WA

Quiet Mouse Hall Poem

Materials

None needed

What to do

1. Recite the following poem when the children need to move from one place in the building to another.

   I can walk, I won't talk, when I go down the hall.

   I'm as quiet as a mouse who's only inches tall.

   His whiskers twitch, his eyes they glow, and his tail is long.

   He pitter patters down the hall and always sings this song. (repeat)

❖ Lisa Chichester, Parkersburg, WV

Transition Time

Materials

None needed

What to do

1. When going to group time with the children, recite the following chant:

   Watch my hands, because they just might change.

2. Pat different parts of your body and vary the pattern.

❖ Sandy L. Scott, Vancouver, WA

Musical Instruments Game

Materials

None needed

What to do

1. Sing the following song while you and the children are moving from one place in the building to another. Encourage the children to pretend they are playing a flute as they sing.

   This is the way we play the flute, play the flute, play the flute.
   This is the way we play the flute all the way to (wherever you are
   *   going).*

2. Change the instruments as you go along. To keep the children interested, encourage them to name other instruments and pretend to play them.

❖ Holly Dzierzanowski, Austin, TX

Easy Transitions

Materials

None needed

What to do

1. When transitioning from one activity to the next, try one of the following ideas. The big advantage of these ideas is that they keep the children listening!

   ■ Give directions such as, "If your shoes have Velcro on them, you may get your coat on." Follow with other types of footwear classifications, such as laces, buckles, and slip-ons. Use this transition with other articles of clothing too. For example, "If you have buttons (or zippers, letters, stripes, and so on) on your shirt..."

   ■ Suggest a category, such as favorite breakfast cereal, and ask each child in turn to name his favorite. After they do so, they may move to the next activity. Tell them you'll ask the quietest one first!

   ■ Tell the children that you are going to describe them one at a time.

When the child thinks he knows that you are talking about him, he may line up at the door. Start with a broad description, and then get more specific. For example, "I'm thinking of a girl...she has blond hair...she has a baby brother..."

■ Ask each child to move to the next activity in a different way, such as waddling like a duck or hopping like a frog.

❖ Vicki L. Schneider, Oshkosh, WI

Hat Transitions

Materials

A variety of hats that are appropriate for different activies, such as a chef hat for cooking, baseball cap for gym, marching band hat for music, special hat for story time, and beret for art time
Hat rack

What to do

1. Store the various hats on a hat rack.
2. Children will identify the next activity by which hat you select.
3. Young children identify with symbols. When you put on the appropriate hat before the next activity, the children will know what to expect next or what area or center to go to.

More to do

Challenge the children to guess the occupation of the person wearing a particular hat.

Related books

Hats, Hats, Hats by Ann Morris
Martin's Hats by Joan Blos

❖ Janice Bodenstedt, Jackson, MI

Transition: Moving to a New Location

Materials

None needed

What to do

1. Suggest ways for the children to move to a new location, such as:
   - Pretend you are rabbits and quietly hop to the door.
   - Pretend you are a train moving in a straight line.
   - Pretend you are mice that no one can see or hear.
   - Walk slowly and softly like a kitten.
   - Flitter and float like a butterfly.

❦ Sandy L. Scott, Vancouver, WA

Transitions

Materials

None needed

What to do

1. This activity provides opportunities for children to practice motor skills as they transition from one activity to another.
2. When moving from a floor activity to a table, encourage the children to crab walk, hop, walk backwards, tiptoe, or any other fun way.

More to do

Think of movements that relate to the theme you are working on, such as:
- crab walk—underwater theme
- bunny hop/frog jumps—pet theme
- jumping from one shape to the next—shape theme
- elephant walk/bear walk—zoo theme
- rolling—ball games

Song

Incorporate any songs that go with the theme, or make up a song. For example, sing the following song to the tune of "The Mulberry Bush."

This is the way we hop like a frog,
Hop like a frog, hop like a frog.
This is the way we hop like a frog,
When we go to the table.

❦ Sandra Suffoleto Ryan, Buffalo, NY

Pattern Transitions

Materials

None needed

What to do

1. Give the children a pattern to follow.
2. Change the pattern each time you move the group from one place to another, or ask a child to make up the pattern.
3. For example, clap your hands two times above your head, then clap your hands two times on your shoulder. Stop and start again. Repeat this until you get to your destination.
4. On the way back, change the pattern. (At the beginning of the year, I start with a four-count pattern, but by May we are up to a seven-count pattern.)

❦ Holly Dzierzanowski, Austin, TX

Silly Mixed-Up Feet

Materials

None needed

What to do

1. Ask the children to sit in a circle and put their feet in the middle.
2. Ask them to mix up their feet by jumbling their feet and legs on top of each other.
3. Close your eyes and grab one foot at a time. Try to guess whose foot it is.
4. When you guess the correct child, he can go to the next activity.

More to do

Ask the children to put one of their shoes in a pile. Then, ask one child at a time to pick a shoe and find whom it belongs to. This is a good matching one-to-one correspondence activity, and it also helps children practice putting on and taking off their shoes (especially tying).

Related book

The Foot Book by Dr. Seuss

 Caitlin E. Gioe, Tuckerton, NJ

Statues

Materials

None needed

What to do

1. Getting children's attention at a transition time can be difficult. Try turning it into a game.
2. Talk about statues. Do they move? Do they talk?
3. Encourage the children to practice being statues.
4. Tell them the "secret signal" (for example, ring a bell, clap loudly, or blink the lights).

5. Explain that when they hear or see the signal, they should freeze like a statue. Then, when they hear or see the signal again, they can move again.
6. While they are "frozen" as statues, give them instructions for the next activity.
7. Signal again and the children will proceed to the next activity.

More to do

Art: Make statues out of playdough or clay.
Outside play: Play freeze tag.

❧ Suzanne Maxymuk, Cherry Hill, NJ

How Many Can You Name?

Materials

Chart paper (adding machine tape is fun!)
Pen or marker

What to do

1. Anytime you have a few minutes to fill, suggest a topic (such as animals, foods, things that are green, and so on) and challenge the children to name as many things as possible that fit the category.
2. Be prepared to write quickly!
3. Occasionally, stop and encourage the children to count the number of items on the list. You'll be surprised at how many items the children can come up with when everyone thinks together!

More to do

Using the same concept, make pages of words that begin with each letter of the alphabet. Add new words when they arise and review the pages occasionally.

❧ Vicki L. Schneider, Oshkosh, WI

Transition Toys

Materials

Plastic boxes
Transition toys, such as play cell phones, cush balls, Slinkies, finger puppets, hand-held water games, mini Etch-a-Sketches, and mini binoculars

What to do

1. Fill several plastic boxes with small toys.
2. To build anticipation, take out these particular toys only when gathering for group.
3. As the children come to the rug, they can choose toys from the box. The toys will help them relax and transition from noisier, more active play.
4. Give the children about five minutes to use the transition toys, then put them back in the box.
5. Children will want to hurry and finish cleanup so they will have lots of time to play. Sometimes a child may dawdle and miss his turn, which may provide him with an incentive to move faster tomorrow.

❧ Tracie O'Hara, Charlotte, NC

Small Choice Activity Board

Materials

Photographs of activities or wipe-off markers
Laminated piece of heavy cardboard, approximately 24″ x 24″ (60 cm x 60 cm)
Children's nameplates with Velcro on back

What to do

1. Place photographs of activities or draw pictures of activities on a piece of laminated cardboard. Use this choice board to transition children to small group activities after a gathering time.
2. Provide each child with his own nameplate that has Velcro on the back.

3. Encourage the children to choose their desired activity by placing their name-plates under the picture of the activity. (You can do this earlier in the day too.)

4. Call the children's names to let them know when to go to their chosen activity.

Note: This board is also ideally suited for activities led by teachers with a small group of children or activities that are self-directed. Possible ideas for activities can include music, movement, literacy, small group games, manipulatives, science or nature discovery, large motor skills, art, and fine motor materials.

More to do

You can use the choices of activities daily for a week or longer. This allows the children to try different activities and repeat their favorites.

❀ Nancy Schwider, Carol Stream, IL

Have a Seat!

Materials

None needed

What to do

1. Use this activity when children need to settle down and be seated. Make sure the children know where they should sit before you begin.
2. Chant the following:
   Have a seat young children, have a seat.
   It would be so nice if you would have a seat.
   Won't you please sit down instead of walking around?
   Have a seat young children. Won't you please have a seat?
3. Continue the chant as the children begin to seat themselves. Smile at each child as they sit down. When some of the children have sat down, change the chant to offer praise and encourage others to follow suit.
   You have a seat, dear Johnny, you have a seat.
   It's so nice you decided to have a seat.
   I'm glad you sat down instead of walking around.
   You have a seat, dear Johnny. I'm so glad you have a seat.
4. When all the children are seated, insert "Dear Children" in place of a child's name in the chant above and chant one last time.

❦ Virginia Jean Herrod, Columbia, SC

Transitioning Rap

Materials

None needed

What to do

1. Teach the children the words to the following rap:
   Shane, Shane, is his name,
   Going home is his game,
   This is his front,

This is his back,
Give us a bow,
And we'll give you a clap.

2. Replace "Shane" with each child's name.
3. Ask each child in turn to come forward, place both hands on the front of his body, then both hands on the back of his body. Then, while everyone claps, encourage him to bow by placing one hand in front and one hand in back and bowing at the waist.

More to do

Hold up a card with the child's name on it for name recognition. Change words to fit the area they are transitioning to—lunch, playground, buses, gym, and so on.

❧ Kaethe Lewandowski, Centerville, VA

Transition Tunes

Materials

Favorite children's tunes

What to do

1. Using a favorite tune, make up words for the desired activity. For example, for naptime, sing the following to the tune of "The Farmer in the Dell."
   It's time to take your nap,
   It's time to take your nap,
   Get your blanket, lie down on your mat,
   It's time to take your nap.
2. For lunch time, sing the following to the tune of "If You're Happy and You Know It."
   If you're hungry and you know it, let's get ready.
   If you're hungry and you know it, let's get ready.
   If you're hungry and you know it wash your hands and go sit down. If you're hungry and you know it, let's get ready.

❧ Phyllis Esch, Export, PA

Ten in the Class

Materials

Voices of the teacher and children

What to do

1. When it is time for the children to line up for an activity (such as outside time, lunch, or field trips), ask all the children to sit quietly on the floor. Designate a spot for them to line up when it is their turn.
2. Sing "Ten in the Class" as a fun way for the children to hear each other's names and participate in a gross motor activity before lining up.
3. Sing a verse of the song for each child in the class when it is his time to line up. Decrease the number in the song to correspond to the number of children and change the gross motor activity for each child.
4. Sing the song to the tune of "Ten in the Bed."

    There were ten in the class
    And the teacher said,
    "(insert child's name) stand up,
    and (insert gross motor activity) (repeat two more times).
    Line up, line up."

5. For example, when it is Avery's turn to line up and there are only five children left on the floor, ask him to jump before he lines up. Sing, "There were five in the class and the teacher said, 'Avery, stand up, and jump, and jump, and jump, and jump. Line up, line up.'"
6. After the child completes the gross motor activity that was indicated in his verse, he can line up at the designated spot.

More to do

Alter the song for other transitional activities. For example, change the line up verse to say wash up when it is time for the children to wash their hands for lunch.

❧ Kacie Farmer, Evansville, IN

Clean-Up Engine

Materials

Train whistle

What to do

1. Blow a train whistle and warn the children that the clean-up engine will be arriving at the station in five minutes.
2. After five minutes have passed, blow the whistle again and say, "All aboard!"
3. Begin chugging around the room and invite the children to be cars on your train.
4. Stop at a center and ask the group to clean up that area so that the train can go to the next stop.
5. Continue making stops around the room until the whole room is clean.
6. If the centers are too small for the whole group to clean up, ask the engineer to select volunteers or assign children to different centers as the train chugs around the room.

More to do

Assign a different child each day to be the engineer. Provide him with an engineer hat to wear for the day or at clean-up time. It is the engineer's job to lead the train around the room and ensure that the centers are cleaned satisfactorily.

Related book

Freight Train by Donald Crews

✤ Ann Gudowski, Johntown, PA

Shocka Laka Shaka

Materials

An enthusiastic group of children
A few moments of time

What to do

1. This is a good activity to use when there is not enough time to start an extended activity, but you still need to fill a few minutes or when the group transitions from one activity to another (such as from group time to lunch).

2. Ask the children to sit in a large circle. They need to be able to tap their knees, so they can fold their legs or stretch them out.

3. Begin a tap-and-clap rhythm. Tap your knees, then clap your hands. Repeat.

4. As you are tapping and clapping, begin to chant. Chant one line at a time, and the children repeat it after you.

5. Chant:
   Shocka Laka Shaka
   Shocka Laka Shee
   Shocka Laka Shooka
   Shocka Laka Wee
   Shocka Laka Shaka
   Shocka Laka Shat
   Shocka Laka Shooka
   Shocka Laka Wat

6. Now, change the rhythm to meet a transitional need, such as:
   Shocka Laka Shaka
   Shocka Laka Shee
   Shocka Laka Shooka
   Shocka Laka Wee
   Shocka Laka Shaka
   Shocka Laka "Shaitlyn"
   Shocka Laka Shooka
   Go wash your hands, "Caitlyn"

7. Continue rhyming the last word in the sixth line with the child's name in the eighth line along with a command until you have called everyone.

More to do

You can also use the rhythm as a unique and fun way to communicate needed information to the children, such as:

Shocka Laka Shaka
Shocka Laka Shee
Shocka Laka Shooka
Shocka Laka Wee
Shocka Laka Shaka
Shocka Laka Shisten
Hey there, children
I need you to listen.

Shocka Laka Shaka
Shocka Laka Shup
When you play in centers
You need to clean up.
Shocka Laka Shaka
Shocka Laka Wean
So, whoever was in blocks
Please go back and clean.

❖ Virginia Jean Herrod, Columbia, SC

My Favorite January Activities

Name of the Activity   **Page Number**

_____   _____

_____   _____

_____   _____

_____   _____

_____   _____

_____   _____

_____   _____

_____   _____

_____   _____

_____   _____

_____   _____

_____   _____

_____   _____

_____   _____

My Favorite February Activities

Name of the Activity	Page Number
_____	_____
_____	_____
_____	_____
_____	_____
_____	_____
_____	_____
_____	_____
_____	_____
_____	_____
_____	_____
_____	_____
_____	_____
_____	_____

My Favorite March Activities

Name of the Activity   **Page Number**

My Favorite April Activities

Name of the Activity	Page Number

My Favorite May Activities

Name of the Activity	Page Number
_____	_____
_____	_____
_____	_____
_____	_____
_____	_____
_____	_____
_____	_____
_____	_____
_____	_____
_____	_____
_____	_____
_____	_____
_____	_____
_____	_____
_____	_____

My Favorite June Activities

Name of the Activity   **Page Number**

_____   _____

_____   _____

_____   _____

_____   _____

_____   _____

_____   _____

_____   _____

_____   _____

_____   _____

_____   _____

_____   _____

_____   _____

_____   _____

_____   _____

My Favorite July Activities

Name of the Activity	Page Number
_____	_____
_____	_____
_____	_____
_____	_____
_____	_____
_____	_____
_____	_____
_____	_____
_____	_____
_____	_____
_____	_____
_____	_____
_____	_____
_____	_____
_____	_____

My Favorite August Activities

Name of the Activity   **Page Number**

_____   _____

_____   _____

_____   _____

_____   _____

_____   _____

_____   _____

_____   _____

_____   _____

_____   _____

_____   _____

_____   _____

_____   _____

_____   _____

_____   _____

My Favorite September Activities

Name of the Activity   **Page Number**

_____   _____

_____   _____

_____   _____

_____   _____

_____   _____

_____   _____

_____   _____

_____   _____

_____   _____

_____   _____

_____   _____

_____   _____

_____   _____

My Favorite October Activities

Name of the Activity	Page Number
_____	_____
_____	_____
_____	_____
_____	_____
_____	_____
_____	_____
_____	_____
_____	_____
_____	_____
_____	_____
_____	_____
_____	_____
_____	_____
_____	_____
_____	_____

My Favorite November Activities

Name of the Activity   Page Number

_____   _____

_____   _____

_____   _____

_____   _____

_____   _____

_____   _____

_____   _____

_____   _____

_____   _____

_____   _____

_____   _____

_____   _____

_____   _____

_____   _____

My Favorite December Activities

Name of the Activity   **Page Number**

_____   _____

_____   _____

_____   _____

_____   _____

_____   _____

_____   _____

_____   _____

_____   _____

_____   _____

_____   _____

_____   _____

_____   _____

_____   _____

_____   _____

_____   _____

_____   _____

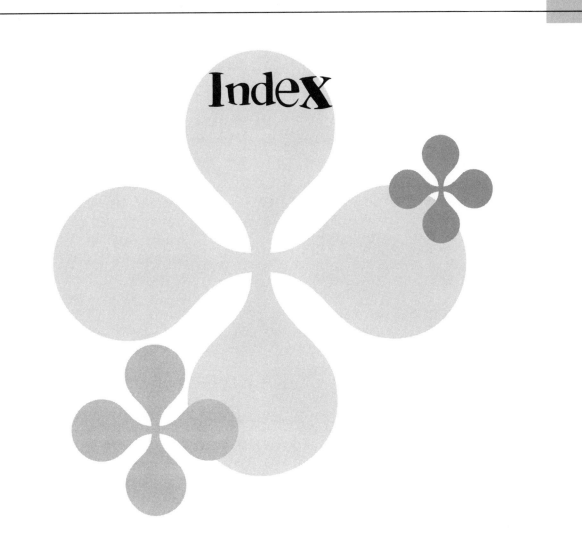

Index

INDEX

Book Index

Activity Index